The Addiction Concept

THE ADDICTION CONCEPT

Working Hypothesis
or Self-Fulfilling Prophesy?

Glenn D. Walters

Federal Correctional Institution—Schuylkill

Allyn & Bacon

Boston • London • Toronto • Sydney • Tokyo • Singapore

The assertions and opinions contained herein are the private views of the author and should not be construed as official or as reflecting the views of the Federal Bureau of Prisons or the United States Department of Justice.

Editor-in-Chief, Social Sciences and Education: Sean W. Wakely
Series Editorial Assistant: Susan Hutchinson
Manufacturing Buyer: Suzanne Lareau
Editorial-Production Service: Omegatype Typography, Inc.
Electronic Composition: Omegatype Typography, Inc.

Library of Congress Cataloging-in-Publication Data

Walters, Glenn D.
    The addiction concept : working hypothesis or self-fulfilling prophesy? / Glenn D. Walters.
       p.   cm.
    Includes bibliographical references and index.
    ISBN 0-205-28642-9
    1. Substance abuse.   2. Compulsive behavior.   3. Lifestyles.
I. Title.
RC564.W365   1999
616.86—dc21   98-23863
                                    CIP

Printed in the United States of America

10 9 8 7 6 5 4 3 2   02 01 00 99

I would like to dedicate this book to my wife, Patti,
whose love and support
have served as a source of inspiration
for me in the writing of this book.

CONTENTS

PREFACE

This is not the first book to critically evaluate the addiction-as-disease model of substance misuse. More than a quarter century ago, Thomas Szasz (1971) laid siege to the addiction monolith, calling it a myth perpetuated for political and economic gain. Since that time a number of other authors have voiced their dissatisfaction with the addiction-as-disease model of drug-seeking behavior. Stanton Peele (1989) is perhaps the most vocal critic of the addiction-as-disease model, but is not alone in finding fault with a perspective that conceives of substance misuse as a progressive, irreversible disease. He is joined in his renunciation of the addiction-as-disease model by Fingarette (1988), Truan (1993), and Wilbanks (1989). Given the number and eloquence of prior critiques, one might well wonder whether another commentary on the addiction-as-disease model is really necessary. However, there are at least four reasons why the reader will find this book unique among the many that have been written on this subject.

One unique aspect of this book is that whereas previous works have examined the logical and empirical limitations of the addiction-as-disease model, the present volume surveys the overall concept of addiction. This book, like many before it, addresses the issue of substance misuse, but unlike the majority of previous works, also considers pathological gambling, sexual preoccupation, eating disorders, and compulsive buying. Second, this book, unlike some of the earlier critiques, subjects the addiction concept to a comprehensive analysis in an effort to determine whether this concept conforms to the parameters of a testable hypothesis and is capable of furthering our understanding of various forms of "addictive" involvement. A third unique feature of this book is that it proposes an alternative to the addiction concept with implications for further theoretical development, intervention, and prevention. Finally, this book, despite finding fault with the addiction concept, attempts to incorporate key elements of the addiction model into the body of an alternative formulation.

Before the addiction concept can be properly evaluated, it must be defined. Using the DSM–IV (American Psychiatric Association [APA], 1994) criteria for substance dependence as a general guideline, a definition of addiction is presented in Chapter 1. The second chapter of this book introduces the reader to an alternative view of addictive behavior known as the lifestyle paradigm. Next, various models of addiction, as well as arguments against the addiction concept, are entertained. The manner in which the lifestyle alternative handles these criticisms and limitations is the subject of the next chapter, followed by a discussion on change and how this process can be facilitated. The principal goal of this book is to determine whether the addiction concept is capable of furthering our understanding of addictive behavior. The data and arguments reviewed in the pages that follow suggest that it is not. Whether the lifestyle paradigm will fare any better in the face of rigorous experimentation remains to be seen, but the fact that it is more open to empirical scrutiny and critical discussion suggests that it warrants further consideration.

ACKNOWLEDGMENTS

I thank the following reviewers of the manuscript for their helpful comments: Emil Chiauzzi, Innovative Training Systems, Newton, MA; Henry R. Lesieur, Institute for Problem Gambling, Pawtucket, RI; Stanton Peele, Private Practitioner, Morristown, NJ; Jean J. Rossi, Behavioral Consultants, Inc., Des Plaines, IL; and John J. Shannon, Seton Hall University.

The Addiction Concept

1

ADDICTION DEFINED

The addiction concept may well be the Frankenstein monster of modern American life. Originally created to explain physical dependence on alcohol and other abusable substances, it has recently been applied to an ever-growing number of nondrug activities and behaviors. The rate at which these behaviors, commonly referred to as "activity addictions," have been assimilated into the addiction concept has been truly phenomenal. Over the course of just a few decades the addiction concept has evolved into a popular explanation for problem gambling, eating disorders, shopping sprees, frantic exercise, habitual television watching, and sexual preoccupation. Of the many factors responsible for this trend, three deserve special mention.

First, the concept of addiction makes good intuitive sense to someone who feels compelled to engage in a repetitive pattern of behavior. Second, the addiction concept may relieve a person of responsibility for the negative consequences of his or her behavior, a theme highly congruent with the American zeitgeist of externalizing blame for the negative consequences of one's actions. Finally, the addiction concept simplifies life by supplying people with intuitively appealing, responsibility-easing solutions to the problems of everyday living, while simultaneously furnishing them with pat answers to complex questions. In support of this last point, research indicates that many people are drawn to oversimplified models of the world (Mednick, 1989).

Despite the attention the addiction concept has received, it does not appear to have shed much light on the nature of behavior so classified. With this in mind, I set out to investigate this issue, the fruits of which are contained in the pages that follow. My purpose in writing this book was to ascertain whether the addiction concept is capable of advancing our understanding of addictive comportment, and if not, to provide the reader with a workable alternative viewpoint. Before this can be accomplished, however, we must first understand what is meant by the term *addiction* and something about the history of this concept.

The term *addiction* appears to have worked its way into the standing vocabularies of most Americans. This is a time–culture phenomenon in which theories of human behavior have become increasingly more vested in factors over which the individual has little or no control. Genetics and environmental contingencies have come to replace volition and choice in the minds of many people. This shift in perspective may, in fact, be a consequence of the perfunctory nature of modern life whereby information, rather than being acquired through interpersonal contact, is accessed immediately and impersonally over a radio wire, television cable, or the internet. Despite its influence, the information explosion has not changed the fact that sociocultural teachings still mold individual belief systems. As such, these teachings, and the belief systems to which they give rise, may help explain the derivation and popularity of concepts like addiction.

This book will explore addiction as a construct capable of influencing the belief systems of both individual citizens and entire cultures. Phrases such as "addictive behavior," "conduct viewed to be addictive," and "actions considered addictive" will be used to describe behavior that has traditionally been labeled addictive. It should be kept in mind, however, that these are descriptive terms only and are in no way meant to convey a belief in a unified addictive syndrome. In subsequent sections of this chapter a succinct history of the addiction concept will be presented, followed by a review of definitional issues and an overview of how this book is organized.

A BRIEF HISTORY OF ADDICTION

The history of addiction in this country begins, but does not end, with alcohol. Although colonial Americans consumed more beverage alcohol per person than the average, modern-day American, there were many fewer problems associated with its usage (Peele, 1989). This has been attributed to the fact that alcohol was well integrated into the fabric of colonial American society, and that while the use of this substance was tolerated, if not encouraged, its misuse was not. By the end of the eighteenth century, however, problem drinking had become a national disgrace, presumably because informal social control networks were breaking down under the weight of the Industrial Revolution (Clark, 1976). Urbanization accompanied industrialization as a significant portion of the population pulled up its roots and relocated to urban centers. This, in turn, freed many young adults from the informal social controls that had structured life for their agrarian ancestors.

It was shortly after the advent of the American Industrial Revolution that the temperance movement gained momentum and alcohol earned a reputation as an inherently dangerous substance, giving rise to the term "demon rum." Another group with a view on alcohol, the Washingtonians, also rose to prominence during this period. A brotherhood of reformed drinkers, the Washingtonians preached about the evils of alcohol. They are often seen as the forerunners of Alcoholics Anonymous (AA), but unlike AA which adheres to a host-centered view of alcohol abuse as a disease, the Washingtonians attributed alcohol abuse to the intoxicating effects of the agent (alcohol). The temperance movement, which began during the first half of the nineteenth century, reached its peak by the end of the century. The movement achieved its goal of a "dry nation" when Congress passed the Eighteenth Amendment to the U.S. Constitution in 1919, prohibiting the sale, transportation, manufacture, and importation of alcohol.

Although there was an unmistakable rise in the amount of alcohol consumed after the repeal of Prohibition in 1933, it is uncertain whether there was a corresponding increase in the rate of problem drinking. There was a change, nevertheless, in how alcohol and addiction were conceived. Prior to this time, the misuse of alcohol was attributed to the inebriating properties of alcohol or a lack of willpower on the part of the host. Encouraged by the growing popularity of AA, American society rediscovered the disease model initially invented by Dr. Benjamin Rush in the late eighteenth century.

According to the disease model of alcohol abuse behavior, a certain portion of the population is biologically predisposed to alcoholism. Some versions of the disease model accept a literal translation of the disease concept, equating problem drinking with an allergy to alcohol, while other versions treat the concept of disease as a metaphor. The American Medical Association initially rejected the disease model, but is now one of its most ardent supporters. It has been alleged that the medical profession embraced the disease concept after it came to realize the financial and political influence that could be gained from labelling such behavior a disease (Peele, 1989).

The disease model of addiction was given some degree of scientific credence with the publication of E. M. Jellinek's *The Disease Concept of Alcoholism* in 1960. However, whereas Jellinek proposed disease processes for only two of the five categories of alcoholism he identified, his system has since been corrupted. Some argue that this corruption was motivated by financial interests (e.g., Peele, 1989), so that now nearly everyone who abuses alcohol is viewed as "diseased," unless, of course, they display a behavioral outcome (e.g., natural recovery or controlled drinking) inconsistent with the underlying tenets of the disease model.

Alcohol is not the only drug for which a disease-based self-help group has been devised; persons who abuse substances other than alcohol have available to them Narcotics Anonymous (NA), Cocaine Anonymous (CA), and Marijuana Anonymous (MA). Edward Levinstein, a German physician, was perhaps the first professional to study the "addictive" properties of morphine. Dependence and tolerance were two behaviors he observed regularly in his patients and, interestingly enough, are the two behaviors that serve as the foundation for modern-day definitions of substance dependence (APA, 1994).

Throughout the nineteenth century people were using opium-based medical remedies with few ill effects. At one time, marijuana and cocaine were freely available, the latter being viewed as a "miracle drug" that worked its way into the original formula for Coca Cola (Rathus & Nevid, 1991). This all ended, however, with passage of the Harrison Act in 1914, which made it illegal for physicians to maintain patients on narcotic drugs. Although this act was held to be in the best interests of the populace, it was probably motivated more by politics and racism than by concerns for public welfare. The classification of marijuana as a narcotic, for instance, had more to do with expanding the power base of the Federal Bureau of Narcotics than with the perceived medical dangers of cannabis (Brecher, 1972). Moreover, opiate-based drugs were never viewed as particularly dangerous until large numbers of Chinese immigrants began settling in this country in the mid to late 1800s. Szasz (1971) reports that in spite of opium habits, these immigrants were a hard working, law-abiding people. However, animosity towards opium grew after the Chinese arrived—a racial hatred borne out of economic competition.

A major development in the evolution of the addiction concept occurred just prior to the turn of the century when Norman Kerr, president of the Society for the Study of Inebriety, proposed a model in which the abuse of alcohol, opium, and morphine were connected by a common disease process. Since that time self-help groups have helped bridge the gap between the so-called addictions by extending the addiction concept to such varied behaviors as gambling, overeating, and sex. Gamblers Anonymous (GA) was founded in 1957, with Overeaters Anonymous (OA), Sex Addicts Anonymous (SAA), and Sexaholics Anonymous (SA) following in short succession. The discovery of endorphins in the 1970s (Cooper, Bloom, & Roth, 1987) opened the door to a possible biochemical link between the drug-based "addictions" and such "activity" or "process" "addictions" as pathological gambling and sexual preoccupation. However, medicalization of behavioral deviance, and the political advantages this affords certain groups, may have been an even more powerful motive for expansion of the addiction concept (Rosecrance, 1985).

More and more, behaviors that had previously been viewed as behavioral disorders or bad habits were being labeled as addictions. It was not long before there was an addictive theory of domestic violence, job commitment, compulsive exercise, excessive buying, and religious fanaticism. Relationship "addictions" also began to proliferate during the period following the discovery of endorphins, as exemplified by the co-dependency and adult children of alcoholics movements. What had begun as a preliminary attempt to understand the driven quality of alcohol and other drug abuse, had become a national epidemic of attributing various bad habits, poor choices, and rewarding behaviors to addiction.

A CRITERION DEFINITION OF ADDICTION

Researchers investigating the addiction concept have long been criticized for failing to provide an unambiguous definition of addiction. After reviewing the addiction literature, one might be inclined to conclude that there are as many definitions of addiction as there are investigators conducting research in the area. Although this is somewhat of an exaggeration, there are distinct problems with how addiction has been defined in the past. Carnes (1992), for instance, characterizes the "sexual addict" as someone who "substitutes a sick relationship to an event or process for a healthy relationship with others... (and whose) secret lives become more real than their personal lives" (p. 4). Although colorful, this definition provides us with few, if any, concrete behaviors upon which to base an operational definition of addiction. Nakken (1988) offers a similarly nebulous definition, calling addiction a progressive illness that undergoes continual development and exists as an attempt by the host to control uncontrollable processes and cycles.

Gamblers Anonymous (1989), like its progenitor, AA, holds that "compulsive gambling is an illness, progressive in its nature, which can never be cured, but can be arrested" (p. 8). Definitions such as these frustrate research and interfere with the development of a common dialogue between investigators. Operationality of terms, as students of research methodology well know, is a necessary prerequisite for the development of a meaningful program of research. With the goal of constructing an operational definition of addiction clearly in mind, the present discussion turns to the psychiatric nomenclature on alcohol and other drug abuse.

General criteria for alcoholism and drug dependency were constructed for the first edition of the *Diagnostic and Statistical Manual of Mental Disorders* (DSM–I: APA, 1952). However, these diagnoses were subsumed under the more general category of sociopathic personality disturbance. Alcoholism and drug dependency became independent diagnoses in DSM–II (APA, 1968), but the diagnostic criteria were no more specific than those found in DSM–I. Under this system, alcohol dependence, a subcategory of alcoholism, was characterized by withdrawal symptomatology or heavy drinking for three consecutive months, whereas a diagnosis of drug dependence was recorded in the presence of withdrawal symptomatology, habitual use, or an expressed need for the drug. These definitions are of limited value for research and are only slightly more specific than those proposed by Carnes (1992) and Nakken (1988). Some clarity was achieved, however, with the publication of DSM–III (APA, 1980).

Under the heading of Substance Use Disorders, DSM–III divided the various substances—alcohol, cannabis, barbiturates, opioids, cocaine, amphetamine, phencyclidine—into subcategories of abuse and dependence: the former indicating a pattern of pathological use, impairment in social or occupational functioning, and duration of at least three months; and the latter requiring the presence of either tolerance or withdrawal symptomatology. DSM–IV (APA, 1994) refined these criteria further and added diagnoses for substance induced disorders (e.g., intoxication, psychosis, sexual dysfunction) to those that already existed for substance use (abuse, dependence).

The DSM–IV criteria for substance dependence, more precise than the criteria for DSM–III, will guide our efforts to construct an operational definition of addiction. Diagnosing a substance dependence disorder under DSM–IV requires the presence of a maladaptive pattern of substance use, resulting in distress or clinically significant impairment, and involving at least three of the following symptoms (all of which must occur within the same twelve month period):

- tolerance
- withdrawal
- use of the substance longer than intended
- unsuccessful attempts to control or reduce consumption
- spending excessive amounts of time using or procuring the substance
- reduced involvement in important social, occupational, or recreational activities
- continued use despite the presence of recurrent physical or psychological problems (APA, 1994)

The DSM–IV criteria for pathological gambling were modeled after the criteria for substance dependence and restrict diagnoses of pathological gambling to persons satisfying five or more of the following 10 criteria:

- preoccupation with gambling
- increased wagering in order to achieve the desired effect
- repeated unsuccessful attempts to reduce or stop gambling
- restlessness or irritability when attempting to reduce or stop gambling
- gambling as a way of escaping problems and reducing dysphoric mood
- gambling in an effort to recoup one's losses

- lying to family members or to one's therapist about gambling
- involvement in illegal activities to support gambling
- endangering or losing a significant relationship, job, or career or educational opportunity because of gambling
- relying on others to provide money to relieve financial hardship caused by gambling (APA, 1994)

Although not included in DSM–IV, similar criteria are available for sexual addiction. Goodman (1993) has proposed a DSM-like diagnosis of sexual addiction based on the following major criteria:

1. recurrent failure to resist the impulse to engage in sexual behavior
2. increased tension immediately before initiation of the behavior
3. pleasure or relief while enacting the behavior
4. persistence of symptomatology for at least one month, and at least five of the following additional conditions:

   - preoccupation with sexual behavior
   - engaging in the behavior longer than intended
   - repeated unsuccessful attempts to control or stop the behavior
   - spending excessive amounts of time engaged in the behavior
   - performing the behavior to the exclusion of important social, domestic, academic, and occupational obligations
   - abandonment or reduced involvement in important social, occupational, or recreational activities as a consequence of involvement in the behavior
   - execution of the behavior despite the presence of recurrent social, financial, physical, or psychological problems
   - the need for increased intensity or frequency of the behavior in order to achieve the desired effect (Goodman, 1993)

Lesieur and Blume (1993) offer an addiction-based definition of eating disorders, which while not as specific as the DSM–IV criteria for drug dependence and pathological gambling or Goodman's (1993) criteria for sexual addiction, are helpful in understanding the addiction concept as applied to anorexia and bulimia. The symptoms Lesieur and Blume propose as possible indicators of eating disorder-related addiction include progression, preoccupation, loss of control, negative family consequences, negative occupational consequences, and escape from negative affect.

The DSM–IV criteria for substance dependence and pathological gambling and Goodman's (1993) criteria for sexual addiction are matched for content and listed in Table 1–1. Similarity in criteria is readily apparent even from casual inspection and can be traced to the fact that the pathological

TABLE 1-1 A Comparison of Diagnostic Criteria for Substance Dependence, Pathological Gambling, and Sexual Addiction

DSM–IV* Substance Dependence	DSM–IV* Pathological Gambling	Goodman (1993) Sexual Addiction
Tolerance	Need to increase amount of money gambled in order to achieve the desired effect	Tolerance
Withdrawal	Restlessness or irritability when gambling is reduced or terminated	Restlessness or irritability when unable to engage in the desired sexual behavior
Taking substance in larger amounts than was intended		Engaging in the sexual behavior for a longer period than originally intended
Persistent desire or unsuccessful efforts to reduce or control use	Repeated unsuccessful attempts to reduce or terminate gambling	Repeated efforts to reduce, control, or cease sexual behavior
Significant amounts of time spent procuring and using the substance	Preoccupation with gambling	Frequent preoccupation with the sexual behavior
Social, occupational, and recreational activities reduced or abandoned because of substance use	Has jeopardized or lost a significant relationship, job, or occupational or educational opportunity because of gambling	Social, occupational, or recreational activities sacrificed or reduced because of involvement in sexual behavior

Recurrent physical or psychological problems because of substance use	Commits illegal acts as a way of financing gambling activities	Continuation of sexual behavior despite persistent social, financial, physical, or psychological problems created by the behavior
	Gambles in order to escape problems or relieve feelings of guilt, anxiety, frustration, and depression	
	After losing money gambling will return the next day as a way of getting even	
	Lies to others to conceal the extent of gambling involvement	
	Relies on others to provide money to relieve financial burden of gambling	
		Significant time spent engaging in the sexual behavior or recovering from its effects
		Sexual behavior interferes with fulfillment of occupational, academic, domestic, or social obligations

*Adapted from: American Psychiatric Association. (1994). *Diagnostic and Statistical Manual of Mental Disorders: Fourth Edition (DSM-IV)*. Washington, DC: Author.

9

gambling and sexual addiction criteria were modeled after the substance dependence criteria. Thus, while such similarity cannot be considered proof of validity, it does show the potential applicability of the addiction concept to gambling and sexual behavior. Consideration of the criteria for these three disorders, as well as the Lesieur and Blume criteria for eating disorders, implies the presence of at least four distinct symptom clusters.

One cluster denotes progression, as characterized by tolerance, withdrawal, and a temporal increase in the severity of symptomatology. A second cluster centers around the issue of preoccupation. Spending significant amounts of time engaged in the "addictive" activity or in behaviors that support this activity would be indicative of this cluster. Several criteria also appear to cluster around perceived loss of control. Here, the individual engages in the behavior longer than anticipated or is unsuccessful in reducing or terminating his or her involvement in the activity. The fourth cluster of criteria identified in this comparison of diagnostic categories is the presence of negative long-term consequences with continued involvement in the "addictive" activity. Restriction in social, occupational, and recreational activities, as well as regular physical and psychological difficulties, all appear to fall into this cluster.

Addiction is therefore defined as the persistent and repetitive enactment of a behavioral pattern (Walters, 1996a) in which one or more of the following four criterion clusters is observed: progression, preoccupation, perceived loss of control, and negative long-term consequences.

WHAT IS THE ADDICTION CONCEPT?

There are at least two things that should be kept in mind when evaluating the concept of addiction. First, the addiction concept is modeled after the definition of addiction described in the previous section. Second, it is conceptualized as a prototype that is manifest, to one degree or another, in nearly all major interpretations of addictive behavior. Like the definition of addiction delineated above, the addiction concept is comprised of four elements: progression, preoccupation, perceived loss of control, and negative long-term consequences or persistence. Behavior viewed to be addictive is accordingly perceived to reflect a progressively debilitating condition with which the individual becomes increasingly more preoccupied in terms of time and energy resulting in a loss of control that can only be rectified through reliance on an external agent (medication, higher power), which persists despite the presence of severe negative consequences.

It is also important to understand that the addiction concept is a prototype that is approximated but never achieved. Some formal interpretations of addictive behavior (e.g., the disease model) incorporate more elements of the prototypic addiction concept than others (e.g., biopsychosocial model), but it is unlikely that any one model provides equal coverage of all four elements. This book will accordingly provide a survey of major interpretations of addictive behavior by identifying the elements with which each model is most closely aligned with an eye toward identifying the limitations of each interpretation and each respective element of the addiction concept.

MARTIN: AN ILLUSTRATIVE CASE EXAMPLE

In order to illustrate some of the major concepts and ideas contained in this book, a single case study will periodically reappear in future chapters. The subject of this case study is a 38 year old white male with a history of multiple addictive involvements. Referred to here as Martin, this individual has had problems in the past with alcohol, tobacco, methamphetamine, gambling, and sex. He is currently serving a 10-year prison sentence for conspiracy to sell drugs and so we can add crime to the list of potential behaviors to which he appears to be "addicted." Martin has participated in traditional treatment programs for substance abuse and gambling but states that he received very little benefit from his involvement in these programs. Future chapters will describe how Martin's behavior might be conceptualized by different models based on the addiction concept and how this differs from a lifestyle view of Martin's behavior.

THE ORGANIZATION OF THIS BOOK

Although this book addresses the addiction concept as applied to a number of different behaviors, psychoactive substance abuse will serve as the prototypic addiction. The reason for this is two-fold. From a practical standpoint, there is probably more research addressing psychoactive substance dependence than all of the "activity addictions" combined. This is understandable as the addiction models of substance misuse have been in existence longer than addiction models of gambling, sexual preoccupation, and eating disordered behavior. Accordingly, there is significantly more information available on alcohol and drug misuse than on any of the "activity addictions."

A second reason for establishing psychoactive substance abuse as the prototypic addiction is strategic. Given the presence of an active agent, the drug itself, psychoactive substance abuse has an advantage over the "activity addictions" in that a clear physiological process seemingly drives drug-seeking behavior. Thus, if it can be demonstrated that the addiction concept does a poor job of modeling psychoactive substance misuse, then it is reasonable to assume that it probably also fails to account for behaviors with a less clearly defined activating agent. For this reason, in chapters probing the biological, psychological, and sociological roots of addiction, substance abuse will be considered first, followed by a review of the "activity addictions." In addition, each major section will include a "research focus" in which a relevant area of empirical study will be reviewed in greater detail than is typical of most textbooks.

The lifestyle model of addictive behavior is introduced in Chapter 2. In Chapters 3 through 6 the reader is afforded a glimpse of the major models of addictive behavior. Chapter 3 examines biological definitions of addiction, followed by psychological, sociological, and practical definitions in successive chapters. The logical, empirical, and practical limitations of the addiction concept are then explored in Chapters 7 through 9.

Rather than simply criticizing the addiction concept, the present book provides an alternative. The parameters of this alternative, referred to as the *lifestyle paradigm,* are outlined in Chapter 2. Chapter 10 describes how this alternative handles the logical, empirical, and practical limitations of the addiction concept. This is followed by a brief discussion of the lifestyle approach to intervention and change in Chapter 11.

In the final chapter of this book the constructional assets and liabilities of the addiction model are reviewed, the preponderance of evidence suggesting that the addiction concept may be inadequate to the task of explaining the actions of persons who abuse drugs, gamble incessantly, become sexually preoccupied, or engage in eating disordered behavior.

My intent in writing this book has been to stimulate interest in the scientific study of addictive behavior by introducing information and arguments helpful in evaluating the addiction concept. Perhaps this information can be used to reconcile ideas and philosophies that have too long served as points of contention and confusion, and move the addiction field in the direction of a more integrated philosophy of science.

2

THE LIFESTYLE MODEL
AS AN ALTERNATIVE
TO THE ADDICTION CONCEPT

It is understandable that people who feel compelled to overeat, drink, use drugs, gamble, or exercise would attribute their behavior to a compulsion or addiction. After all, the addiction concept ascribes such behavior to powerful addictive agents, monolithic host predispositions, and a variety of environmental influences, all of which appear to capture the driven quality of the person's actions. The lifestyle model, on the other hand, views these behaviors as a distorted expression of a person's survival instinct. According to this perspective, it is the person's perceptions of survival with respect to sundry aspects of the agent, host, and environment, not the agent, host, or environment directly, that drives the person to engage in these behaviors. This chapter defines the lifestyle concept, compares it to the addiction concept, offers a brief overview of the primary tenets of the lifestyle model, and explores how the model applies to Martin, our illustrated case example.

WHAT IS A LIFESTYLE?

Like the addiction concept, a lifestyle is a prototype that is approached rather than achieved. Unlike the addiction concept, the lifestyle concept applies to people rather than to ideas or abstractions. The behavior that defines a lifestyle is believed to conform to patterns with set rules, roles, rituals, and relationships. Rules are fixed principles or codes that regulate behavior. Roles are the functions and duties that people discharge, whereas rituals are rites, procedures, and actions people dramatize, often in a particular sequence. Finally, relationships characterize the nature, content, and quality of a person's interactions with others. These behavioral patterns become problematic when performed in situations for which they are clearly inappropriate.

The maintenance of behavioral patterns, either through one's associations, priorities, thinking, or identity, constitutes one's lifestyle. Hence, interacting with my clients as a psychologist or counselor may prove personally, professionally, or economically rewarding. Acting as a psychologist with my family, friends, or people I meet at a party is less beneficial and may actually inhibit my ability to form deep meaningful relationships with others and enjoy myself. By enacting a lifestyle, people limit what they can do and who they do it with (involvements), the goals they pursue (commitments), and their view of themselves and the surrounding environment (identity). The opposite of a lifestyle is adaptation wherein the person makes internal changes in order to meet the challenge of a constantly changing environment.

A COMPARISON OF THE ADDICTION AND LIFESTYLE CONCEPTS

There are several key factors that delimit the boundaries between the addiction and lifestyle concepts, four of which will be described in this section. First, the addiction concept tends to concentrate on one aspect of the community health model (i.e., agent–host–environment) to the exclusion of the other two aspects. Hence, the Washingtonians focused on the agent, adherents to the medical model on the host, and social psychologists on the environment. The lifestyle model takes an integrated, interactive approach in explaining addictive behavior, exploring how the host interacts with both the agent and environment and how each party to this interaction effects the others. In this way the lifestyle model is similar to the biopsychosocial model of addictive behavior proposed by Zucker and Gomberg (1986).

A second major difference between the addiction and lifestyle models is that whereas the former tends to label the host, agent, or environment as the primary cause of the problem, the latter concentrates on and labels the lifestyle that evolves from the host–agent–environment interaction. The lifestyle model practice of labeling the lifestyle rather than the person helps limit the negative influence of self-labeling or blaming attributions, neither of which are particularly helpful in establishing the proper conditions for change. These issues will be discussed further in a review of the practical limitations of the addiction concept.

The lifestyle model and most approaches with strong allegiance to the addiction concept also diverge on the issue of choice. The lifestyle model asserts that people choose to engage in addictive patterns of behavior, although they often do not understand the full ramifications of their choice. The addiction concept tends to disparage personal choice except in terms of a person's choice to "seek help" and "get better." The lifestyle model holds that choice is important in all phases of lifestyle development—from initiation, to transition, to maintenance, to desistance—and that change is made possible by the fact that a person can improve his or her choices and decisions.

A fourth difference between the addiction concept and lifestyle model is the latter's use of specific behavioral criteria. The behavioral patterns that serve as criteria are believed to be the result of a person's ongoing interactions with his or her environment. Lifestyle theory conceives of these patterns as falling along a continuum rather than forcing them into a rigid dichotomy (e.g., addicted–not addicted). Hence, it is more useful to speak of people's movement up and down the continuum in response to situational change as opposed to determining whether or not they possess the behavior in the form of a personality trait. A detailed description of the behavioral criteria that define a drug lifestyle are provided in Walters (1996d). Similar criteria are also available for the gambling lifestyle in Walters (1994d).

A BRIEF OVERVIEW OF LIFESTYLE THEORY

Lifestyle theory, with roots in evolutionary biology, existential philosophy, cognitive psychology, and social learning theory, assumes that all living organisms possess an instinct to survive, and that the environment is in a continual state of alteration. The interaction of the life instinct and continually changing environment gives rise to an organismic response designed to protect and further the organism's survival. This response is referred to as survival strain in organisms without a central nervous system, primal fear in organisms with a central nervous system, and existential fear in organisms with a central nervous system and rudimentary capacity for self-awareness. Experiences involving attachment, control, and self-image are particularly important in shaping existential fear (see Table 2–1).

Lifestyle theory (Walters, 1994d, 1996c, 1996d) proposes three primary mechanisms by which survival strain or fear is managed: overincorporating the change, underincorporating the change, and adaptation. The overincorporating mechanism is characterized by oversensitivity to environmental change in which openness to environmental experience, accommodation to change, and a tendency to increase rather than decrease system tension predominate. The underincorporating strategy, on the other hand, is marked by insensitivity to environmental change whereby the individual resists new environmental experience, assimilates change, and seeks to decrease rather

TABLE 2–1   Assumptions and Postulates of Lifestyle Theory

Major Assumptions
- All living organisms possess an instinct to survive.
- Environmental change is perpetual.

Fundamental Postulate
- An organism placed in a constantly changing environment experiences survival strain (organisms without a central nervous system), primal fear (organisms with a central nervous system), or existential fear (organisms with a central nervous system and the capacity for self-awareness).

Supplemental Postulates
- Survival strain, primal fear, and existential fear are shaped by environmental experience, particularly existential fear which responds to issues of attachment, control, and self-image.
- Survival strain, primal fear, and existential fear can be managed in one of three ways: overincorporating environmental change, underincorporating environmental change, or adapting.
- Humans with self-awareness (normally achieved by age 2) construct their own reality and then seek to defend this reality.
- In humans with self-awareness the overincorporating style entails oversensitivity to environmental change as characterized by tension induction motives, accommodation to change, and an emphasis on constructive over defensive thinking.
- In humans with self-awareness the underincorporating style entails a lack of sensitivity to environmental change as characterized by tension reduction motives, assimilation of change, and an emphasis on defensive over constructive thinking.
- In humans with self-awareness the adaptive style is characterized by balance in one's motives (tension induction–tension reduction), understanding (accommodation–assimilation), and thinking (constructive–defensive).
- The underincorporating style gives rise to behavioral patterns known as lifestyles, a lifestyle being a repetitive pattern of behavior habitually performed irrespective of its temporal or situational propriety.
- Each lifestyle has its own unique set of defining roles, rules, rituals, and relationships.
- The initiation of a behavioral pattern is a function of both incentive (existential fear) and opportunity (learning/availability).
- The transition from initiation to maintenance is mediated by outcome expectancies for the behavior that promise attainment of important life goals and the elimination of fear.
- A lifestyle is maintained by outcome expectancies, affective imbalance (person engages in the behavior in an effort to eliminate negative moods), enabling behavior on the part of others, changes in people's involvements (what they do and who they do it with), commitments (what goals and values they pursue), and identity (what they think, particularly about themselves).
- Reliance on lifestyles is reduced by increased life balance in motives (tension induction–tension reduction), understanding (accommodation–assimilation), and thinking (constructive–defensive).

than increase system tension. Learning to effectively blend these two opposing patterns constitutes the third mechanism—adaptation.

Through learning, reinforcement, and such social learning influences as the development of outcome expectancies, the individual finds comfort in interacting with his or her environment in a particular way. Excessive reliance on the underincorporating style is thought to give rise to a lifestyle or repetitive pattern of behavior comprised of specific roles, rules, rituals, and relationships. A lifestyle can form around any behavior, but the drug, gambling, sexual, and eating disordered lifestyles appear to capture the essence of addictive behavior. As people's involvements, commitments, and identifications become increasingly more congruent with the lifestyle, the patterns begin to maintain themselves. Like the addiction concept, a lifestyle is an ideal or caricature that many people approach but few people actually achieve.

It is hypothesized that all humans rely on one or more lifestyles as a way of managing existential fear. Problems arise, however, when a person becomes dependent on a particular lifestyle to cope with fear and the problems of everyday living. The way people reduce their dependence on lifestyles is by learning to balance their behavior and activities between a number of conflicting priorities, values, and goals. Thinking also plays a fundamental role in lifestyle theory. Constructive thinking is dedicated to making sense of the surrounding environment, while defensive thinking is designed to protect these constructions.

What is true of the individual also goes for professional organizations and disciplines. The development of a theoretical model or perspective is a constructional task, while application of the model requires defensive thinking. Problems arise when the constructional operations are not balanced between the four levels of construction (mythical, empirical, teleological, epistemological) or the defenses are so strong that they prevent proper evaluation of the model. The next four chapters will consider biological, psychological, sociological, and practical constructions of the addiction concept, but first it is important to consider how Martin's behavior might be construed by the lifestyle theorist.

MARTIN: A LIFESTYLE ANALYSIS

Martin was administered the Fear Checklist (Walters, 1996d), the results of which suggest that his existential fear has been largely influenced by issues of control. This fear appears to have served as Martin's incentive for lifestyle involvement. The opportunity for lifestyle development, on the other hand, can be traced to early learning experiences in the home and neighborhood. Observing his father's abuse of alcohol and mistreatment of his mother, receiving praise from peers for his ability to drink large quantities of alcohol without getting sick, hanging around the neighborhood pool hall, and securing money from local toughs for running errands supplied Martin with opportunities to learn all about the lifestyles that he would eventually embrace.

Initial experimentation with alcohol, marijuana, gambling, and anonymous sex in early to mid adolescence soon gave rise to a pattern of behavior by way of certain outcome expectancies. Martin believed that drinking alcohol and smoking marijuana would increase his status in the eyes of his peers, that gambling could provide him with the "respect" he craved, and that sex would grant him power over women. Each of these expectancies can be conceptualized as an attempt by Martin to overcome feelings of powerlessness and minimal control. Martin started using amphetamines in early adulthood, and while this afforded him a false sense of power and control, the amphetamines, like the alcohol, marijuana, gambling, and sex, failed to provide lasting satisfaction.

Caught in an escalating pattern of drug use, gambling, and sexual promiscuity, Martin began surrounding himself with others who thought and acted like he did. Now he could rationalize that there was nothing wrong with his behavior because everyone around him was doing the same thing. This pattern was maintained by a growing commitment to the drug, criminal, gambling, and sexual lifestyles in which the short-term benefits of these activities were emphasized and the negative long-term consequences ignored. His behavior was also maintained by a tendency to merge his identity with the negative behaviors to which he had grown accustomed. Hence, self-labels such as "doper" and "player" restricted his opportunities to engage in alternative behaviors.

There is more to lifestyle theory than can be written in a single chapter. What has been emphasized here and clarified using case study material is that a lifestyle develops in three phases. The inaugural phase of lifestyle development is known as initiation. The initiation phase is characterized by early experimentation and learning. The second phase of lifestyle development is transition, whereby the behavior becomes more habitual and patterned. Outcome expectancies play a vital role in the transition from initiation to maintenance. The third phase is maintenance wherein the behavior becomes self-reinforcing and self-perpetuating. The lifestyle is fully developed at this point. In many cases there follows a fourth phase—desistance or lifestyle termination.

3

ADDICTION AS A
BIOLOGICAL CONSTRUCT

Addiction is sometimes construed as a biological process driven by genetic or physiological forces. As such, the present chapter will delve into the genetic and physiological correlates of addictive behavior. Before this can be done, however, we must consider the form, content, and function of biological theories of addiction, two of which will be reviewed in this chapter. These theories, like all interpretations of addictive behavior, can be classified using the four elements of the addiction concept: progression, preoccupation, perceived loss of control, and persistence. Two theoretical versions of biological addiction will be examined in this chapter, one of which (the disease model) embraces all four elements of the addiction concept, but aligns itself most strongly with the progression and loss of control elements, and the other of which (the abuse liability model) highlights the persistence element of the addiction concept.

BIOLOGICAL CONSTRUCTIONS OF ADDICTION

Although the disease concept has its roots in the late eighteenth century writings of Dr. Benjamin Rush, the father of American psychiatry, it was not until official sanctioning of the disease model by the American Medical Association in 1956 and publication of E. M. Jellinek's book *The Disease Concept of Alcoholism* four years later that the disease model gained popular acceptance. Prior to this, people who misused alcohol were considered morally weak individuals who lacked proper willpower.

Alcoholics Anonymous (AA), a fellowship of recovering problem drinkers formed in the mid-1930s, has also helped shape the disease model of alcoholism. Comparing alcohol abuse to cancer or diabetes, the framers of the medical and twelve step disease models maintained that problem drinking was a disease of physical (medical) and spiritual (twelve step) proportions. Over time the medical and twelve step models have seemingly converged into a hybrid approach commonly referred to as the modern disease concept of addiction, although these two versions of the disease concept do not agree on all points.

The medical interpretation of the disease concept conceptualizes the abuse of alcohol as a physical disease confined to a subgroup of individuals afflicted with the condition (Vaillant, 1990). Other groups, like AA, take a more global view of substance misuse and apply the disease concept to a much larger audience of potential clients (Wallace, 1993). Spurred largely by proponents of the AA approach, the disease concept has been expanded to encompass an ever-growing number of behaviors: nonalcohol drug abuse (Talbott, 1986), gambling (Gamblers Anonymous, 1989), sexual preoccupation (Carnes, 1992), and eating disorders (Brumberg, 1988) being just some of the other behaviors to which this concept has been generalized.

Most disease models define addiction as a chronic, progressive, potentially fatal disease characterized by a genetic predisposition, loss of control, and persistence in the face of harmful consequences. A clinician following the medical disease model would likely view Martin's prior addictive involvement as evidence of an inherited predisposition to process alcohol and other drugs in ways different from most other people, in turn, leaving him vulnerable to loss of control in the presence of alcohol and other drugs. The AA version of the disease model, on the other hand, would stress the spiritual side of Martin's difficulties with substances, gambling, and sex. Both versions of the model would likely conceive of Martin's problem as slowly progressing and in need of treatment as a means of arresting the disease process.

In evaluating the disease concept it may be helpful to consider each element separately. First, the disease model holds that addiction is a chronic disorder rather than a transient or situationally-specific set of behaviors. Second, proponents of the disease model assert that addiction is a progressive condition that degenerates over time. Jellinek (1960), for instance, believed that the disease of alcoholism progressed through four phases—prealcoholic, prodrominal, crucial, and chronic—with each phase being more serious than its predecessor. A third element of this definition is that addiction is perceived to be potentially fatal. According to those subscribing to the disease model of alcohol misuse, a chronic drinking problem, left untreated, irrevocably leads to death (Maltzman, 1994).

A fourth aspect of the disease model definition of addiction is that there is a genetic component to this behavior that puts the individual at risk for future addictive involvement (Milam & Ketcham, 1983). Genetic research pertaining to this facet of the disease model will be reviewed in the next section of this chapter. A fifth aspect of this definition, loss of control, has sometimes been misinterpreted by critics of the disease model. According to Keller (1972), loss of control does not mean the person loses control each and every time he or she drinks, but rather, that he or she is unable to consistently refrain from the activity once initiated. The final major aspect of the disease model's definition of addiction is that the addicted individual continues to perform the addictive activity despite the presence of serious physical, social, and legal negative long-term consequences.

There are both strengths and weaknesses to the disease model of addiction. One of its primary strengths is its simplicity. This is probably why the traditional disease model of addiction continues to enjoy widespread popularity in this country, as well as in many other parts of the world (Wallace, 1993). A further advantage of the disease model is that it reduces the guilt commonly observed in people who abuse substances and which frequently stands in the way of change and help-seeking behavior. Before the disease concept came into existence, alcohol abuse was viewed as a sign of moral weakness. Needless to say, only a handful of people sought help for problem drinking during this period. By removing the social stigma associated with alcohol misuse, the disease concept encouraged problem drinkers to enter treatment.

Wallace (1993) contends that the disease concept was instrumental in stimulating funding for research on alcoholism and other forms of addictive involvement. A further advantage of the disease model sometimes mentioned by professionals affiliated with the medical field is that the disease concept gave medical practitioners primary responsibility for diagnosing and treating addictive forms of behavior. In spite of the perceived benefits of such an arrangement, some would argue that this is actually a disadvantage of the disease concept of addiction (Peele, 1989).

One of the great ironies is that many of the features that were once viewed as strengths of the disease concept are now seen as some of its most vexing weaknesses. Simplicity, as a case in point, is both a strength and weakness of the disease model. Although simplicity clearly facilitates understanding, the summarization of highly complex behaviors, like those observed in the abuse of cocaine, the preoccupation with sex, or the binge–purge cycle of bulimia, may result in a superficiality of understanding that ultimately stands in the way of a deeper and more comprehensive appreciation of the behavior under investigation. Furthermore, while the disease model may have once encouraged research on substance misuse, more recently it has served to impede meaningful empirical investigation. For one, its concepts are too global to be effectively operationalized, and for another, many of its proponents are unreceptive to external review.

Although the disease model does not normally avail itself of opportunities for empirical research, those aspects of the model that have been tested have not generally fared well (Chiauzzi & Liljegren, 1993). Other limitations of the disease concept include its potential as an excuse for illegal behavior, irresponsible decisions, and resistance to change (Wilbanks, 1989), and its role in promoting unnecessary treatment and hospitalization (Peele, 1989). The later limitation implies that addictive behavior might be better managed with resources that fall outside the bounds of the traditional medical system.

The disease concept is not the only biological view of addiction in existence. The abuse liability model also adopts a biological perspective on behavior believed to be addictive. Abuse liability is a procedure used to evaluate the abuse potential of various chemical compounds. The classic abuse liability paradigm involves having clients choose between two competing chemical compounds (one of which may be a placebo) or working for a certain dosage of an unknown chemical compound. Although more popular with researchers than clinicians, a counselor who adopts an abuse liability interpretation of addictive behavior would likely view Martin's addictive behavior as a sign of his growing physical and psychological dependence on substances and activities that promote certain chemical changes in his brain, particularly an increase in dopamine. These chemical interpretations of addictive involvement will be explored further in later sections of this chapter.

From the results of operant studies on abuse liability it has been determined that humans will work for low doses of alcohol (de Wit, Uhlenhuth, Pierri, & Johanson, 1987), marijuana (Mendelson & Mello, 1984), cocaine (Fischman & Schuster, 1982), morphine (Jones & Prada, 1975), and nicotine (Henningfield, Chait, & Griffiths, 1983). Dosage level clearly influences the willingness of subjects to work for a substance, with increased doses of pentobarbital (McLeod & Griffiths, 1983) and diazepam (Roache & Griffiths, 1987) being associated with higher rates of operant activity and increased doses of nicotine being followed by decreased levels of operant response (Henningfield & Griffiths, 1980). On the other hand, there may be no dose-response curve for cocaine, perhaps because it is highly reinforcing even at low doses (Fischman & Rachlinski, 1989). Additional research suggests that operant response tends to diminish with increased cost requirements (Bigelow, Griffiths, & Liebson, 1977) or an expanded response–reinforcement interval (Griffiths, Bigelow, & Liebson, 1976). Although narrow in scope, the abuse liability literature epitomizes how persistence can inform a biological model of addictive behavior.

GENETIC CORRELATES OF ADDICTION

An organism's genetic makeup at the time of conception is referred to as its *genotype*, whereas the physical appearance and actions of the organism that evolve from gene–gene and gene–environment interactions is referred to as its *phenotype*. The genotypes associated with addictive behavior have been studied using three primary methods: family studies, twin studies, and adoption studies. After reviewing family, twin, and adoption research on addictive behavior, studies probing the alleged association between one particular gene, the DRD2 polymorphism, and alcohol abuse will be surveyed.

Family Studies

In a review of 39 studies on alcohol misuse in the first-degree relatives of alcohol abusing patients, Cotton (1979) determined that the familial incidence of alcohol abuse was six times that of the general population and two times that of nonalcohol abusing psychiatric patients. From the results of her review, Cotton concluded that approximately one-third of all alcohol abusers have at least one parent who has experienced a problem with alcohol. Penick and her colleagues (1987) report that a group of patients who abused alcohol and acknowledged a family history of alcohol abuse (FH+) exhibited an earlier age of onset of abuse, increased severity of symptomatology, a greater number of legal and medical complications attributable to alcohol abuse, and more treatment contacts than patients with no family history of alcohol abuse (FH–). However, not all of the pertinent research supports the notion that a family history positive for substance misuse predicts a personal history of substance misuse (see Alterman, Searles, & Hall, 1989).

Besides substance abuse, there is some evidence that problem gambling (Lesieur, Blume, & Zoppa, 1986), transvestitism (Liakos, 1967), and eating disorders (Strober, Morrell, Burroughs, Salkin, & Jacobs, 1985) may also run in families. Since parents pass on both genes and experience to their progeny it is impossible to distinguish between the individual contributions of heredity and environment solely on the basis of family data. This has consequently encouraged greater use of the twin method in evaluating the heritability of addictive behavior.

Twin Studies

There are two types of twins: monozygotic (MZ) or identical twins and Dizygotic (DZ) or fraternal twins. Since a MZ birth occurs when a single ovum separates into two parts, MZ twins share the same exact genetic inheritance. DZ twins, on the other hand, derive from separate ova and share approximately 50% of their genes in common. The logic behind the twin method is that if a trait or behavior is genetic, then the *concordance* (agreement between twin pairs) for that trait or behavior will be higher for MZ twins than for DZ twins.

The twin method rests on several assumptions. First, it assumes that mating is random or nonassortative. However, this assumption may not hold true for alcohol abuse (Moskalenko, Vanyukov, Solovyova, Rakhmanova, & Vladimirsky, 1992). Whether it holds true for other forms of addictive involvement cannot be determined from data currently available. Consequently, the nonassortative assumption is open to question. A second assumption made by twin researchers, commonly referred to as the equal environments assumption, may be even more problematic in interpreting the results of twin studies.

The equal environments assumption presumes that the environmental experiences of DZ twins are no more variable than the environment experiences of MZ twins. Whereas this assumption has been empirically tested and found to be valid in many instances (Rowe, 1983), there is evidence that MZ twins experience greater mutual identity (Dalgard & Kringlen, 1976) and are more often mistaken for one another (Lester, 1988) than DZ twins. The fact that Garfinkel and Garner (1982) found greater concordance for anorexia nervosa in MZ, as compared to DZ, twins may mean nothing more than that environmental induction, operating perhaps through mutual identity channels, plays a leading role in the development of an eating disorder.

With the aforementioned caveats in mind, the reader is directed to Table 3–1 which lists twin studies on substance use, eating disorders, and gambling (the three addictive activities for which published MZ–DZ comparisons are currently available). A review of the data in this table reveals that the concordance rates for MZ twins are approximately twice that of the concordance rates for same-sex DZ twins. Such findings would normally indicate a moderate degree of heritability, were it not for possible violations of the nonassortative mating and equal environments assumptions and the presence of several additional methodological flaws.

Lester (1988) has reviewed twin studies on alcohol abuse and found that many are plagued by poorly defined criteria, sampling bias, and potentially unreliable methods of zygosity determination. With the exception of the Pickens et al. (1991) and Kendler, Neale, Heath, Kessler, and Eaves (1994) investigations, the criterion definitions used by researchers in this area have been arbitrary, vague, and contradictory. Kaij (1960), for instance, relied on the accounts of others, including the *proband twin* (a twin originally identified as alcoholic by the temperance registry), in diagnosing co-twins as alcoholic in what is often cited as one of the leading genetic studies on alcohol abuse. Kaij also counted 16 of the 48 MZ pairs twice because both twins were on the temperance registry he used to recruit subjects.

A further problem with twin research on substance misuse and eating disorders is that the majority of investigations have employed measures other than serological or blood tests to establish zygosity. A limitation specific to twin studies on substance misuse is that some of the subjects may not have passed through the age of greatest risk for substance abuse at the time the criterion diagnoses were made. Small sample sizes, on the other hand, plague twin research on eating disorders.

Adoption Studies

The adoption method partitions and compares the variance attributable to heredity and environment by correlating the behavior of persons adopted out of their biological homes at an early age with the behavior of their natural and adoptive parents. In an adoption study conducted in Denmark, 18% of a group of FH+ male adoptees (defined as having alcohol abuse in one or both biological parents) were diagnosed as "alcoholic" themselves. This contrasts with a 5% rate of "alcoholism" in FH– adoptees (Goodwin, Schulsinger, Hermansen, Guze, Winokur, 1973). There were no differences, however, when Danish FH+ and FH– female adoptees were compared (Goodwin, Schulsinger, Knop, Mednick, Guze, 1977).

Although the results of adoption studies suggest a possible role for heredity in the familial transmission of male alcohol abuse there are several additional issues that need to be addressed. First, the genetic effect did not extend to adoptees diagnosed as heavy or problem drinkers. In fact, if the problem drinking and alcoholic categories are combined into a single group the original genetic effect disappears (Murray, Clifford, & Gurling, 1983). Second, certain environmental factors may have influenced the outcome of this study, or at least made the sample unrepresentative. Searles (1988) reports that proband adoptees (FH+) experienced a divorce rate three times that of controls. Furthermore, approximately half the sample (probands + controls) experienced foster parent psychopathology and nearly two-thirds of the sample were younger than 30 years of age. The latter finding suggests that many of the subjects may not have progressed through the age of greatest risk for the development of alcohol problems (Searles, 1991).

The second major adoption study to address the heritability of addictive behavior examined alcohol use patterns in a large Swedish cohort. Like the Goodwin studies on Danish subjects, this investigation produced results congruent with the genetic hypothesis. In the initial phase of this project, Cloninger, Bohman, and Sigvardsson (1981) performed a cross-fostering analysis of 862 Swedish men adopted by nonrelatives prior to age 3. Using at least four entries on the Temperance Board Registry and compulsory treatment or hospitalization for alcohol misuse as signs of severe alcohol abuse, Cloninger and his colleagues identified an 8% incidence of severe alcohol

TABLE 3–1 Twin Studies on Substance Misuse, Eating Disorders, and Gambling

Study	Country	Criterion Diagnosis	Monozygotic			Dizygotic		
			N	Sex	Concord	N	Sex	Concord
Substance Misuse								
Kaij (1960)	Sweden	Alcohol abuse	58	M	.54	138	M	.28
		Chronic alcoholism	27	M	.71	60	M	.32
Partanen, Bruun, & Markkanen (1966)	Finland	Alcoholism	172	M	.26	557	M	.12
		Heavy alcohol use	198	M	.75	641	M	.63
		Heavy tobacco use	198	M	.73	640	M	.68
		Heavy caffeine use	198	M	.70	641	M	.60
Jonsson & Nilsson (1968)	Sweden	Alcoholism		M & F	.22		M & F	.16
Gurling, Murray, & Clifford (1981)	United Kingdom	Alcoholism	15	M	.33	20	M	.30
			13	F	.08	8	F	.13
Hrubec & Omenn (1981)	United States	Alcoholism	271	M	.26	444	M	.12
Pedersen (1981)	Sweden	Heavy alcohol use	39	M	.56	32	M	.15
			36	F	1.00	30	F	-.05
		Tranquilizer use	39	M	.26	32	M	.12
			36	F	.28	30	F	.17
Kaprio et al. (1987)	Finland	Beer consumption	841	M	.41	1885	M	.22
		Spirits consumption	841	M	.32	1885	M	.13
Pickens & Svikis (1988)	United States	Alcoholism	40	M	.70	53	M	.43
			24	F	.29	22	F	.36
		Problematic drug use	22	M	.55	47	M	.31
			15	F	.27	13	F	.23

Study	Country	Disorder	N	Sex	Concord	N	Sex	Concord
Carmelli, Swan, Robinette, & Fabsitz (1992)	United States	Cigarette smoking	890	M	.39	840	M	.34
Kendler et al. (1994)	United States	Alcoholism	590	F	.26	590	F	.12
Eating Disorders								
Holland, Sicotte, & Treasure (1988)	United Kingdom	Anorexia nervosa	25	F	.56	20	F	.05
Fichter & Noegel (1990)	Germany	Bulimia nervosa	6	F	.83	15	F	.27
Hsu, Chesler, & Santhouse (1990)	United States	Bulimia nervosa	6	F	.33	2	F	.00
Waters, Beumont, Touyz, & Kennedy (1990)	United States	Anorexia nervosa	5	F	.00	6	F	.00
Kendler et al. (1991)	United States	Bulimia nervosa	35	F	.23	23	F	.09
Walters & Kendler (1995)	United States	Anorexia nervosa	21	F	.10	18	F	.22
Gambling								
Winters & Rich (1996)	United States	Monthly gambling	75	M & F	.23	80	M & F	.21
		Weekly gambling	75	M & F	.08	80	M & F	.05
		SOGS[1] ≥ 1	75	M & F	.03	80	M & F	.01

[1]South Oaks Gambling Screen (SOGS: Lesieur & Blume, 1987).

N = Number of twin pairs

Concord = pairwise concordance (present/absent) of criterion diagnosis except for Kaprio et al. (1987) study in which intraclass correlations were used.

abuse in the adopted offspring of biological parents who appeared on the registry one or more times and a 5% incidence of severe alcohol abuse in adopted offspring of biological parents who were missing from the registry. A genetic effect was also noted in female adoptees, but was only significant for the mother–daughter relationship (Bohman, Sigvardsson, & Cloninger, 1981).

The Swedish adoption studies have been criticized for relying on the Temperance Board Registry as a criterion measure of alcohol abuse since such a practice may have created a sample in which criminally-oriented individuals were overrepresented (Littrell, 1988). An additional problem with the criterion measure used in this study is that it focused exclusively on the negative consequences of alcohol misuse, while ignoring the frequency and/ or severity of use. Finally, the results of this study indicate that alcohol abuse was seven times higher when assessed in the biological parents of Swedish adoptees than is typical of the general population of the United States. This implies that alcohol abuse is either substantially more common in Sweden, endemic to the biological parents of adopted children, or very loosely defined in this study.

In the only major adoption study to examine both alcohol and other drug abuse, Cadoret, Troughton, O'Gorman, and Heywood (1986) found higher rates of both alcohol (49%) and drug (26%) misuse in adoptees with evidence of alcohol abuse in a biological parent than in adoptees without any history of parental alcohol abuse (14% and 7%, respectively). This same group of investigators was unable to confirm the presence of a gene–environment interaction in male adoptees (Cadoret, O'Gorman, Troughton, & Heywood, 1985), but found evidence of such a relationship in a group of female adoptees (Cutrona et al., 1994).

Although the results of the Cadoret studies are consistent with the genetic hypothesis, each investigation's integrity is compromised by the use of vague diagnostic criteria (particularly in determining alcohol abuse in the biological parents), second-hand reports of paternal alcohol abuse, and failure to account for the effects of subject attrition on the outcome of this study. Although Cadoret used DSM–III criteria in diagnosing adoptees as alcoholic, he included subjects who satisfied the full syndrome and subjects who met some, but not all, of the criteria in the same group (Searles, 1991). Lastly, Cadoret's practice of using odds ratios to estimate genetic effects may have done more to confuse than clarify matters, since it has been noted that odds ratios tend to oversimplify complex relationships and often overlook subtle but important variations in the data (Searles, 1988).

Taken as a whole, family, twin, and adoption studies suggest a possible link between heredity and substance abuse, but the jury is still out on the heritability of eating disorders given the scarcity of data currently available on this population. Even with substance abuse, a great many questions remain to be answered before this connection can be viewed as a serious explanation for why people misuse drugs.

Research Focus: Alcoholism and the DRD2 Gene

The announcement that a group of researchers from the University of Texas Health Sciences Center at San Antonio (Blum et al., 1990) had isolated the gene for alcoholism created a tidal wave of interest in the news media. Since that time at least 16 studies have attempted to replicate these results. The original Blum study identified a mutant allele (A1) of the D_2 dopamine receptor (DRD2) in chromosome 11 to be three and one-half times more prevalent in 35 patients, examined postmortem, who during their lifetime had abused alcohol, compared to the postmortem results of 35 nonalcohol abusing control subjects (69% versus 20%). However, this conclusion has been challenged on both empirical and conceptual grounds.

In the original Blum et al. investigation, postmortem brain samples collected from 35 "chronic alcoholics" showed evidence of polymorphism in three of nine putative "alcoholism genes." A subsequent DNA probe revealed that only one of the polymorphisms correlated with alcohol abuse in this sample—the DRD2 gene. It is difficult to imagine that this group of investigators successfully isolated the gene responsible for alcohol abuse after considering just nine candidates from a pool of over 100,000 possible genes.

The original Blum et al. (1990) results are also limited by the fact that Blum and his colleagues used the outcome of their initial probe to validate their theory, rather than conducting a new series of analyses on an independent sample of subjects. Additional arguments leveled against the DRD2 as a putative genetic marker for alcoholism include sampling bias, ethnic group variations, exposure effects, lack of evidence for linkage, and problems with replication.

Sampling bias must be considered any time an investigator employs a nonrandom control group. Hence, in several studies addressing the DRD2 hypothesis the control group was purged of alcohol abusing subjects. Maintaining the separateness of the experimental and control groups is clearly desirable; however, the practice of screening and eliminating alcohol abusing subjects from the control group may actually introduce other sources of sampling bias into the investigation. Gelernter, Goldman, and Risch (1993) contend that the relatively large screened–unscreened discrepancies noted in the prevalence and frequency of the A1 allele cannot be attributed solely to the presence of alcohol abusing subjects in the control group. One possibility, then, is that the practice of screening control groups introduces nonrandom error into an experiment, which then makes the alcohol abusing and control groups dissimilar in more than just alcohol use history.

The fact that diagnoses have varied from study to study (Gelernter et al., 1993) further complicates interpretation of research studies on the A1 allele. The use of medical complications to diagnose alcohol dependence may be an additional source of error in that medical problems tend to correlate with age. Besides creating an unrepresentative sample, this procedure infuses extraneous variance into the experiment since the medical complications of alcohol abuse may have a genetic basis independent of the actual misuse of ethanol (Monteiro, Alves, & Santos, 1988).

Another major limitation of DRD2 research on alcohol abuse is that the A1 allele is known to vary widely by culture. Only 10% of Yemenite Jews test positive for the A1 allele (Grandy et al., 1989), as compared to 20%–25% of Europeans and Americans of European decent (Amadéo et al., 1993; Goldman et al., 1993; Schwab et al., 1991), 38% of African Americans (Goldman et al., 1993), 40%–50% of Asians (Arinami et al., 1993; Grandy et al., 1989), and 60%–80% of Native Americans (Goldman et al., 1993). These differences may be due to ethnicity, culture, or both.

Blum (cited in Horgan, 1993) has argued that cultural differences in DRD2 composition actually support the notion of an association between the A1 allele and alcoholism since, with the exception of the Asian samples, the ethnic groups in which the A1 allele is most prevalent also demonstrate the highest rates of alcohol misuse. He explains the discrepancy with Asians as being the consequence of the genetically-based oriental flush response. However, a fair percentage of Native Americans also experience flushing in response to alcohol (Reed, Kalant, Gibbons, Kapur, & Rankin, 1976) and concomitantly experience among the highest rates of alcohol abuse in the world.

Why, one might ask, are Asians protected by the oriental flush and Native Americans not? One possible explanation is that major cultural differences exist between these two groups, with Asian groups being less accepting of substance misuse than most Native American groups. It is also interesting that the three studies with the most ethnically homogeneous samples failed to demonstrate a connection between the DRD2 gene and alcohol abuse (i.e., Goldman et al., 1992; Goldman et al., 1993; & Schwab et al., 1991).

A further criticism of DRD2 research is that the A1 allele may be an effect, rather than a cause, of alcohol abuse. Heavy use of psychoactive substances can cause substantial changes in an organism's biophysiology, perhaps even to the point of producing genetic mutations. The chronic effects of alcohol abuse may therefore give rise to an increased prevalence of the A1 allele in persons diagnosed as alcoholic.

Like the P3 wave research reviewed later in this chapter, the only way to determine whether the increased presence of A1 alleles at the D_2 dopamine receptor is a marker for alcohol abuse is to study the issue longitudinally. Using this approach, children who have never experienced the effects of alcohol or other mood-altering substances could be tested for the A1 allele to be followed up several years later with an evaluation of their drug use patterns and proclivities. Given the abandon with which Blum et al. (1990), Noble (1993), and Cloninger (1991) have apparently interpreted preliminary findings, however, it is imperative that this relationship be adequately demonstrated with persons who have not yet altered their physiology through heavy drug usage, particularly in light of the potential ramifications of these findings should they prove legitimate.

There are two general strategies used to analyze genetic data at the cellular level. The association strategy simply evaluates the presence of a connection or correlation between the identified genetic marker and the behavior under investigation, in this case, alcohol abuse. The linkage strategy, on the other hand, requires that the gene be directly connected, in some measurable way, to the clinical syndrome under investigation and that it have a clearly defined mode of inheritance, penetrance, and onset.

The association strategy is much easier to implement than the linkage strategy and is the one adopted most frequently in research on the DRD2 gene and alcohol abuse. However, this strategy suffers from several noteworthy limitations. First, the association approach may yield chance results in small samples. Second, the association strategy is of limited value if important subpopulation differences exist for the genetic pattern being studied, a possibility borne out by research showing cultural variations in the DRD2 gene. Third, in using the association strategy one runs the risk of mistaking an association based on gene interaction for one that presumably identifies a genetic marker (Noble, 1993). These problems alone should make one skeptical of the results of association research. What is more, the three studies utilizing a linkage strategy have failed to demonstrate a connection between the DRD2 gene and alcohol abuse (Bolos et al., 1990; Goldman et al., 1993; Parsian et al., 1991). For a gene to be considered a "cause" of alcoholism it would need to be supported by both the association and linkage methods (Baron, 1993).

Failure to replicate the original Blum et al. study is also problematic for the DRD2 hypothesis. Table 3–2 outlines the major studies that have been published on this issue. This table tabulates the results accrued in these 17 individual investigations, as well as the results for the 15 replication studies, minus the two original Blum et al. (1990, 1991) investigations. Both the prevalence (proportion of subjects with at least one A1 allele) and frequency (the proportion of A1 alleles to the total number of alleles in the entire sample) of the putative pathognomonic allele are listed in Table 3–2. The Blum group has taken the prevalence route, whereas Goldman et al. (1993) prefer the frequency approach in the belief that the prevalence approach sacrifices important diagnostic information and may be inappropriate if the action of the mutation (dominant or recessive) is unknown.

TABLE 3–2 Prevalence and Frequency of the DRD2 A1 Allele in Published Research

Study	Alcohol Abusers						Control Subjects					
	N	A1A1	A1A2	A2A2	p(A1)	f(A1)	N	A1A1	A1A2	A2A2	p(A1)	f(A1)
Blum et al. (1990)	35	2	22	11	68.6%	37.1%	35	2	5	28	20.0%	12.8%
Bolos et al. (1990)	40	3	12	25	37.5%	22.5%	127	8	30	89	29.9%	18.9%
Blum et al. (1991)	89	3	39	47	47.2%	25.3%	31	0	6	25	19.3%	9.7%
Comings et al. (1991)	104	3	41	60	42.3%	22.6%	39	0	6	33	15.4%	7.7%
Gelernter et al. (1991)	44	1	18	25	43.2%	22.7%	68	3	21	44	35.3%	19.8%
Parsian et al. (1991)	32	0	13	19	40.6%	20.3%	25	0	3	22	12.0%	6.0%
Schwab et al. (1991)	45	0	11	34	24.4%	12.2%	69	8	14	47	31.9%	21.7%
Cook, Wang, Crowe, Hauser, & Freimer (1992)	20	0	6	14	30.0%	15.0%	20	1	4	15	25.0%	15.0%
Goldman et al. (1992)	46	0	14	32	30.4%	15.2%	36	2	11	23	36.1%	20.8%
Turner et al. (1992)	47	0	9	38	19.1%	9.6%	—	—	—	—	30.1%	—
Uhl, Persico, & Smith (1992)	75	—34—		41	45.3%	—	143	—43—		100	30.1%	8.1%
Amadéo et al. (1993)	49	3	18	28	42.8%	24.5%	43	0	7	36	16.3%	8.1%
Arinami et al. (1993)	78	9	45	24	69.2%	40.4%	35	2	19	14	60.0%	32.9%
Goldman et al. (1993)	22	11	10	1	95.4%	72.7%	24	14	7	3	87.5%	72.9%
Noble (1993)	73	—38—		35	52.0%	—	80	—24—		56	30.0%	—
Geijer et al. (1994)	74	3	20	51	31.1%	17.6%	81	5	24	52	35.8%	21.0%
Sander et al. (1995)	270	10	79	181	33.0%	18.3%	113	4	35	74	34.5%	19.0%
Totals	**1143**	**48**	**357**	**666**	**41.7%**	**22.8%**	**969**	**49**	**192**	**661**	**31.8%**	**19.4%**
Without Blum	**1019**	**43**	**296**	**608**	**40.3%**	**21.9%**	**903**	**47**	**181**	**608**	**32.7%**	**20.2%**

Note: A1A1, A1A2, A2A2 are the three genotypes possible through combination of the A1 and A2 alleles. Furthermore, p(A1) represents the prevalence of the A1 allele (total number of persons with A1 allele), whereas f(A1) represents the frequency of the A1 allele (total number of A1 alleles).

Comparisons: Alcohol versus Control for p(A1): $\chi^2(1) = 22.24$, $p < .001$.
    Alcohol versus Control for f(A1): $\chi^2(1) = 5.64$, $p < .05$.
    Alcohol versus Control (without Blum) for p(A1): $\chi^2(1) = 12.11$, $p < .001$.
    Alcohol versus Control (without Blum) for f(A1): $\chi^2(1) = 1.33$, $p > .10$.

Replication studies—excluding the two early Blum et al. (1990, 1991) investigations—would seem to provide the best estimate of the replicability of the original findings. An analysis of the results obtained from the 15 replication studies indicates that the A1 allele was significantly more prevalent in alcohol abusing subjects than in control subjects, but that the two groups did not differ in the frequency of the A1 allele.

Preliminary results from two studies suggest that the A1 allele may not only be associated with alcohol abuse, but with cocaine (Noble et al., 1993) and polydrug (Smith et al., 1992) abuse as well. However, before these, or any other genetic finding, can be taken seriously, the aforementioned problems must be addressed and rectified.

There are at least two questions that must be answered before the DRD2 hypothesis can be viewed as anything more than speculative. First, if the DRD2 gene is a potent marker of alcohol abuse, why is it present in less than half the identified alcohol abusing subjects? Second, if alcohol abuse is intimately tied to dopamine metabolism, then why does the DRD2 gene fail to correlate with dopamine metabolites in the cerebrospinal fluid of chronic alcoholics (Goldman et al., 1992)? Perhaps the most prudent conclusion at this point in time is that there is no compelling evidence to suggest that the DRD2 gene is a marker for or meaningfully linked to future substance abuse difficulties. Additional research will be required to ascertain the robustness of the DRD2 hypothesis and determine whether there are other candidate genes capable of shedding light on the complex problem of substance misuse.

An Alternate View

The perspective being advanced in this book is that behaviors traditionally viewed as addictive may be more usefully conceptualized as lifestyles. This does not mean, however, that heredity plays no part in lifestyle development. As a matter of fact, heredity and other biological factors are believed to be critical in the development of a drug or other kind of lifestyle. The problem is not with the idea that genetics contribute to addictive behavior, but with oversimplified application of genetic findings in the development of popular theories of addictive behavior. This appears to be the case with the medical disease model of addiction, but may also be true of several mainstream scientific approaches to addictive behavior. One of the more highly respected scientists in the field, Robert Cloninger (1991), has gone so far as to assert that genetic interpretations of alcohol abuse have been "confirmed." However, as the present review suggests, alcohol abuse, like any of the so-called addictions, has a plethora of possible causes, some genetic, others environmental, and many more interactive. To suggest otherwise is to ignore the vast literature on the genetic correlates of substance misuse.

Although Cadoret and his colleagues (1985) were unable to identify a gene–environment interaction in male adoptees, they did witness an interaction between genes and environment in female adoptees. Women with at least one alcohol abusing biological parent were at increased risk for alcohol abuse and dependence provided they were raised in an adoptive home marked by conflict or parental psychopathology (Cutrona et al., 1994). The negative results obtained with males may indicate that heredity and environment covary without interacting, a possibility suggested in an article by Searles (1988).

The first category of gene–environment correlation proposed by Searles is passive association whereby the environment and genotype correlate because of their common association with some third variable (e.g., parents). A second major category of gene–environment correlation is the reactive–evocative pattern in which genetically-based characteristics (e.g., hyperactive temperament) elicit a predictable response from the environment (i.e., rejection). A third way heredity and environment may correlate is through an active/niche seeking process in which the person actively pursues an environment that complements his or her genotype. Researchers are advised to consider both the interaction and correlation of genes and environment in their attempts to decipher the genetic bases of human behavior.

PHYSIOLOGICAL CORRELATES OF ADDICTION

One of the limitations of genetic research on addictive behavior is that it offers little insight into the predispositions and characteristics presumed to increase a person's future risk of addictive involvement. As the research reviewed in the first part of this chapter denotes, a relationship between heredity and addictive behavior is implied in the literature, but has not been conclusively demonstrated. In the event such an association can be established, the next step will be to elucidate the physiological mechanisms that subserve this association. However, these physiological mechanisms may be important in their own right, regardless of their origin. With this in mind, a survey of major areas of physiological interest to a biological interpretation of addictive behavior will be conducted.

Physiological Vulnerability to Addiction

The high risk approach to addictive behavior focuses on subjects who have not yet displayed the behavior in question but are perceived to be at risk for future involvement by virtue of a family history of that particular disorder. Schuckit and Rayses (1979) utilized this approach and found significantly higher levels of acetaldehyde in the sons of alcoholics following ethanol dosing.

Physiological response to a chemical substance or addictive activity has also been studied using the high risk method. As a case in point, Schuckit (1985) observed significantly less static ataxia (body sway) in FH+ males following ethanol dosing than in a comparable group of FH– males. Nagoshi and Wilson (1987), on the other hand, were unable to replicate these findings. Similar to the Schuckit (1985) data on body sway, Leon, Fulkerson, Perry, and Early–Zald (1995) determined that poor interoceptive awareness (i.e., ignoring cues associated with hunger and pain) predicted future eating disordered behavior in a group of Minnesota schoolgirls.

Autonomic response is a third possible identifier of future risk for addictive involvement. Adolescent boys at risk for future alcohol abuse displayed greater cardiovascular reactivity than low risk boys in a recent Canadian study (Harden & Pihl, 1995). A fourth physiological response that has been studied using the high risk method of investigation is the subject of our next research focus.

Research Focus: The P3 Wave

Event-related potentials (ERP) are electroencephalographic (EEG) recordings of brain wave activity obtained from subjects responding to a discrete stimulus event. When chronic alcoholics are exposed to auditory and visual stimuli their ERPs exhibit several abnormalities, including decreased amplitude of the P300 or P3 wave (Porjesz & Begleiter, 1981). In an effort to rule out the acute effects of alcohol misuse on EEG performance, currently abstinent alcoholics were studied. Similar to what had been observed with active alcohol abusers, currently abstinent misusers of alcohol registered abnormal EEG readings in response to a stimulus, including decreased amplitude of the P3 wave (Pfefferbaum, Horvath, Roth, & Koppell, 1979; Porjesz, Begleiter, & Garozzo, 1987). Although the vast majority of studies in this area have been conducted on male alcohol abusers, recent studies have also found reduced amplitude P3 waves in alcohol abusing females (Hill & Steinhauer, 1993) and former users of cocaine and heroin (Branchey, Buydens–Branchey, & Horvath, 1993).

Whereas acute alcohol intoxication and misuse can be eliminated as possible alternative explanations for the P3 wave abnormalities obtained from current and former problem drinkers, it is not possible to rule out the chronic effects of alcohol abuse using this procedure. This has led to implementation of the high risk paradigm wherein the ERPs of FH+ subjects, typically sons of alcohol abusers naive to the effects of alcohol, are compared with the results obtained by FH– subjects.

In the first ERP study to employ a high risk methodology, Elmasian, Neville, Woods, Schuckit, and Bloom (1982) surmised that a group of 18 to 26 year old nonalcohol abusing FH+ men displayed smaller P3 amplitudes after consuming an alcohol placebo than a group of FH– men. Two years later, Begleiter, Porjesz, Bihari, and Kissin (1984) observed a diminished P3 ERP response in a group of FH+ boys ages 7 to 13. A third ERP high risk study failed to find evidence of a relationship between P3 performance and a family history of alcohol abuse in nonalcohol abusing males (Polich & Bloom, 1988).

Conducting a meta-analysis of 20 studies in which the sons of alcoholics and nonalcoholics were compared, Polich, Pollock, and Bloom (1993) identified a pattern in which high risk subjects exhibited significantly lower P3 amplitudes than low risk subjects. There were also several interesting moderator variable effects observed in this meta-analysis. For one, the effect sizes were stronger for samples under the age of 18. This could be used to support a developmental lag interpretation of the P3 effect, or may simply reflect increased homogeneity, and the associated restriction in the range of intellectual performance, in the older sample since these groups were comprised mostly of college students.

The risk–P3 relationship may also be moderated by the nature and/or difficulty of the task. More difficult visual tasks do a better job of distinguishing between high and low risk subjects than less difficult visual tasks or auditory tasks of either high or low difficulty. Further research is required to determine whether it is the modality (visual–auditory) or the difficulty (high–low) that moderates the risk–P3 relationship since the visual tasks used in these studies have tended to be more difficult than the auditory tasks.

Before concluding this discussion of the relationship between the P3 waveform and alcohol abuse, the possible implications of this research need to be considered. First and foremost, it should be noted that diminished P3 amplitude is not restricted to alcoholics and the sons of alcoholics. Reduced P3 amplitudes have also been observed in schizophrenics (Pritchard, 1986), the biological relatives of schizophrenics (Kidogami, Yoneda, Asaba, & Sakai, 1992), depressed patients (Diner, Holcomb, & Dykman, 1985), and children with attention deficit disorder (Holcomb, Ackerman, & Dykman, 1985). Consequently, the P3 effect is not specific to alcohol abuse.

A second issue that needs to be addressed is the functional significance of the P3 effect. It has been speculated that the P3 wave provides a general index of a person's ability to allocate cognitive resources to the processing of new stimuli or the updating of old memories (Donchin, Karis, Bashore, Coles, & Gratton, 1986). It may well be, then, that the P3 wave signals a person's ability to process, store, and recall complex information. Although this relationship would appear to be independent of the acute and chronic effects of alcohol, there is insufficient evidence at this time to conclude that it is necessarily genetic.

Finally, in order to demonstrate that P3 abnormalities cause alcohol abuse rather than the other way around, follow-up studies comparing pre-alcohol EEG results with later substance misuse must be carried out. In a preliminary study on this issue, Berman, Whipple, Fitch, and Noble (1993) unveiled a connection between P3 performance and self-reported substance use four years later.

Physiological Protection against Addiction

In contrast to the wealth of information available on biological risk factors, influences that potentially decrease a person's vulnerability to future addictive involvement, commonly termed protective factors, have received far less attention. One of the few studies to address this issue was carried out on a group of Hawaiian youth (Werner, 1986). In this study children believed to be at risk for future alcohol involvement, owing to the presence of certain adverse environmental conditions (e.g., growing up in a home with an alcoholic parent), were themselves much less likely to develop a problem with alcohol if they projected a positive self-image, possessed good verbal skills, and displayed a temperament that invoked affiliative responses from a primary caregiver.

Situational factors that shielded these children from future problem drinking included positive attention from a primary caregiver, youngest child status for at least two years prior to the birth of the next youngest sibling, and freedom from any major family or domestic problems prior to age two (Werner, 1986). A physiologically-based protective mechanism was observed in a group of adolescents who failed to develop subsequent problems with tobacco after experiencing an adverse reaction to initial cigarette smoking (Kozlowski & Harford, 1976). A physiologically-based mechanism has also been proposed for the so-called oriental flush.

Research Focus: The Oriental Flush

There is a large body of research to suggest that oriental populations experience among the lowest rates of alcohol abuse in the world (see Cheung, 1993). Although sociocultural factors likely contribute to this phenomenon, physiological mechanisms may also be at work. It has been estimated, for instance, that approximately half the world's population of Japanese, Chinese, and Koreans experience an unpleasant physiological reaction to ethanol (Wolff, 1973). Termed the oriental flush, this response is characterized by a rapid increase in blood flow to the face, neck, and chest, elevated heart rate, decreased blood pressure, headaches, and nausea. These symptoms are similar to those experienced when persons on disulfiram (antabuse) consume a quantity of alcohol.

In line with learning theory, which holds that more proximal and consistent consequences exert a more powerful effect on behavior than more distant and unreliable consequences, research indicates that a fast flushing response exerts a more powerful effective than a slow flushing response (Park et al., 1984) and a partial or atypical flushing response may actually be more detrimental than no response at all (Higuchi, Parrish, Dufour, Towle, & Harford, 1992). These research studies, as well as centuries of observation, have led some investigators to conclude that the flushing response protects many Asians from developing problems with alcohol. This has persuaded some researchers to examine the biochemistry of the oriental flush response.

Research has established that the flushing response is associated with elevated levels of acetaldehyde in the blood (Mizoi et al., 1983). It is important to understand that ethyl alcohol is metabolized into acetaldehyde, a noxious chemical, by the liver enzyme alcohol dehydrogenase (ADH). Under normal circumstances the acetaldehyde has little effect on the body because it is rapidly metabolized by a second liver enzyme, aldehyde dehydrogenase (ALDH), into acetate or acetic acid.

ADH and ALDH have both been implicated in the oriental flush. A highly efficient form of ADH is believed to convert alcohol into acetaldehyde at a rate that exceeds the capacity of ALDH to transform acetaldehyde into acetate (Bosron & Li, 1987). Additionally, a reduction in the ability of ALDH to convert acetaldehyde into acetate has also been implicated in this response and has been traced to a mutant gene referred to as the ALDH2*2 allele. Research shows that this gene is dominant and finds its greatest concentration in Asian populations (Crabb, Edenberg, Bosron, & Li, 1989).

In line with the hypothesis that genes are responsible for the flush response, people with the ALDH2*2 allele register blood acetaldehyde levels 10 times the rate found in people lacking this mutant gene (Enomoto, Takase, Yasuhara, & Takada, 1991). Furthermore, this allele is significantly less common in Japanese "alcoholics" (Harada, Agarwal, Goedde, & Ishikawa, 1983). Thomasson, Crabb, Edenberg, and Li (1993) recently examined this issue in a group of Chinese alcohol abusers and surmised that 50% of the control subjects possessed the ALDH2*2 allele as compared to 12% of the problem drinkers. These authors also identified two mutant ADH genes that were significantly less common in the alcohol abusing group.

Although the relationship between the ALDH2*2 allele and the oriental flush is well established, there are those who would argue that the oriental flush is an insufficient explanation for the low rate of problem drinking observed in persons of Asian descent. Cheung (1993) finds the flush hypothesis inadequate for the purpose of explaining Asian alcohol use and contends that the flush response cannot account for the large group differences in alcohol consumption that occur between immigrant and American-born Asians and between different generations of Chinese, Japanese, and Koreans.

Kitano, Chi, Rhee, Law, and Lubben (1992) studied the effects of culture on Asian drinking practices by reviewing the alcohol consumption patterns of Japanese subjects living in Japan, Hawaii, and California. The results of this study showed that the amount of alcohol consumed conformed to the dominant cultural norms and values of the area in which the subject resided, despite the fact that these groups were presumably equivalent in terms of their ability to generate a flushing response.

Studying the flushing responses of Japanese, Chinese, Filipino, and Hawaiian subjects, Schwitters, Johnson, McLearn, and Wilson (1982) observed an inverse correlation between flushing and alcohol consumption in subjects of Japanese ancestry only. Thus, while it may be true that the oriental flush response protects certain groups and persons from future problems with alcohol, other factors need to be considered in explaining the relatively low rates of alcohol abuse found in Asian populations.

Physiological Mechanisms that Serve Both a Vulnerability and a Protective Function

Certain physiological mechanisms appear to increase a person's vulnerability to future addictive involvement, whereas other mechanisms protect the individual against such involvement. Some physiological mechanisms may, in fact, do both. The same variable may serve a risk function in one situation and a protective function in another situation, or act as a risk factor for one person and as a protective factor for a second individual. This speaks to the complexity of human physiology as represented by research on neurotransmitters and neuromodulators.

Even though reduced levels of the neurotransmitter serotonin have been found in alcohol-preferring rats, problem drinkers, and persons at risk for future alcohol use difficulties (Walters, 1994c)—not to mention the fact that administration of serotonin agonists often alleviates the subjective urge to drink (LeMarquand, Pihl, & Benkelfat, 1994)—the nature of the serotonin–alcohol abuse relationship is enigmatic. In research conducted on eating disorders, changes in norepinephrine and serotonin have been observed in both anorexics and bulimics, although the effect may vary according to the situation or context in which the behavior takes place (Fava, Copeland, Schweiger, & Herzog, 1989). The complexity of neurophysiological correlates of gambling behavior is explored in the next section.

Research Focus: The Neurophysiology of Gambling

A handful of researchers have examined the putative neurophysiological substrates of pathological gambling, the results of which are summarized in Table 3–3. Consistent with the hypothesis that problem gambling is an

TABLE 3–3 Neurophysiological Studies on Problem Gambling

Study	Country	Gamblers		Controls		Results of Study			
		N	Sex	N	Sex	GABA	NE	5-HT	BE
Blaszczynski, Wilson, & McConaghy (1986)	Australia	39	M	35	M				G = C
Roy et al. (1988a)	United States	20	M	20	M		G > C	G = C	
Roy et al. (1989a)	United States	17	M	13	M	G = C			
Roy et al. (1990)	United States	19	M	13	M		*		
Moreno et al. (1991)	Spain	8	M & F	8	M & F			G < C	
Blanco (1996)	Spain	27	M	27	M			G < C[1]	

Note: GABA = gamma-aminobutyric acid; NE = norepinephrine; 5–HT = serotonin; BE = beta-endorphin; G = gambling group; C = control group.
*nonsignificant trend suggesting that problem gamblers showed an inverse relationship between CSF levels of NE and galanin (a putative cotransmitter that has been shown to enhance the release of NE in rats).
[1]platelet monoamine oxidase (MAO) activity served as the dependent measure.

impulse control disorder, it has been shown that norepinephrine is elevated and serotonin reduced in some problem gamblers. Several additional factors must be kept in mind, however. Besides the small sample sizes used in these studies, many of the subjects were atypical with respect to their level of non-gambling psychopathology. Seventy nine percent of the gamblers participating in the Roy et al. (1988a) study, for instance, satisfied DSM–III criteria for one or more additional psychiatric diagnoses.

Additional evidence suggests that disposition or behavioral style may mediate the relationship between problem gambling and neurophysiology. In addressing this issue, Roy, De Jong, and Linnoila (1989b) observed a significant relationship between extraversion, on the one hand, and CSF levels of the norepinephrine metabolite 3-methoxy-4-hydroxyphenylglcol (MHPG) and urinary output of norepinephrine, on the other.

A final issue requiring resolution involves the contradictory outcomes registered with serotonin. Roy et al. (1988a), in contrast to Moreno, Saiz–Ruiz, and Lopez–Ibor (1991), failed to uncover evidence of reduced serotonergic activity in problem gamblers. Two of the more likely explanations for this discrepancy are sociocultural factors, since the Roy study was conducted in the United States and the Moreno study in Spain, and methodological variations. With respect to the latter, the Roy study used the relatively unreliable method of estimating CSF serotonin from peripheral and CSF levels of the serotonin metabolite, 5-hydroxyindoleacetic acid (5-HIAA), whereas Moreno and his colleagues used a far more reliable procedure—chlomipramine (CMI) as a serotonin probe administered in half hour intervals. It is also possible that the effect of serotonin on gambling behavior varies by cortical site or is influenced by the action of another neurotransmitter or neuromodulator.

The results of studies exploring the neurochemical correlates of problem gambling suggest that certain neurotransmitters may be altered in persons who engage in problematic gambling behavior. It is impossible to tell from data currently available, however, whether these biochemical abnormalities are a cause of problem gambling, an effect of problem gambling, or the consequence of some third variable. In addressing this issue it may be helpful to consider a more general model of neurobiological learning, such as the one proposed by Cloninger (1987).

Cloninger posits three primary neurogenetic adaptive mechanisms, each of which is believed to be controlled by a different neurotransmitter. Behavioral activation (novelty seeking) is presumed to be under the control of the dopamine neurotransmitter system where it gives rise to exploratory conduct, appetitive approach behaviors, escape from punishment, and active avoidance of monotony or conditioned signals for punishment. Behavioral inhibition (harm avoidance) is believed to be modulated by the serotonin system and calls for passive avoidance of punishment or novelty and extinction of responses that are not reinforced. Norepinephrine is the principal monoamine neurotransmitter involved in behavioral maintenance (reward dependence) and is believed to modulate resistance to extinction of behaviors that have been previously reinforced.

Although the Cloninger system is clearly speculative, it provides a framework that may be useful in exploring gambling behavior from initiation (behavioral activation), to escalation and maintenance (behavioral maintenance), to cessation (harm avoidance). By measuring the levels of dopamine, norepinephrine, and serotonin in problem and nonproblem gamblers engaged in an ongoing wagering activity, one might be in a position to decipher the physiological underpinnings of the gambling experience.

An Alternate View

Physiological research in the addictions field has traditionally focused on how a person's physiology acts to increase or decrease future risk of addictive involvement. While the impact of physiology on addictive involvement cannot be denied, the converse effect—of involvement on physiological activity—cannot be ignored. The lifestyle model adheres to a reciprocal effects view of human behavior in that the lines between cause and effect are blurred by the reciprocal relationships that form between variables.

Tonnesen (1992), for one, notes that regular alcohol usage exerts acute effects on the hemostatic and immune systems of the human body that may persist for up to two months. Prominent effects of chronic alcohol abuse, on the other hand, include atrophy of the cerebral cortex, cirrhosis of the liver, and severe gastrointestinal problems (Talbott, 1986). The chronic effects of morphine on physiology include changes in the postsynaptic opiate receptors (Ackerman, Womble, & Moises, 1994), and, if used intravenously, increased risk of hepatitis and HIV (Miller & Gold, 1990).

Even when a chemical substance is not consumed, an addictive activity can still effect physiology. Turner and Shapiro (1992) note that numerous physiological changes, occurring as a result of starvation, may account for some of the symptomatology of anorexia nervosa. Physiological sequela of the binge–purge cycle of bulimia have also been observed (Goldbloom, Garfinkel, & Shaw, 1991).

Perhaps the most interesting physiological effects, however, are those that show changes in the activity of the central nervous system. Edythe London and her colleagues at the National Institute on Drug Abuse have observed metabolic changes in the human brain following morphine (London et al., 1990a) and cocaine (London et al., 1990b) ingestion. Employing positron emission tomography (PET) to visualize and measure the brain's use of glucose, London and her associates recorded decrements of 5% to 25% in the metabolic activity of the neocortex, basal ganglia, thalamus, midbrain, and hippocampus following consumption of these substances. There is evidence that chronic substance use suppresses brain dopamine to the point where the person is compelled to continue using just to avoid feeling bad (White, 1996).

Whereas concentrating on high risk populations to the exclusion of protective and reciprocal effects has limited the scope of research on addictive behavior, the field's preoccupation with pathology seems to have limited its ability to appreciate the motivational bases of human behavior. Lifestyle theory contends that there may be nothing abnormal about the motives that encourage a person to seek solace in a drug, gambling, sexual, or eating disordered lifestyle. It is not the motive that differentiates between a lifestyle and adaptation, but how the individual pursues this motive.

The source of all motivation, according to the lifestyle model, is the conflict that arises between the organism's "life instinct" and a constantly changing environment. Such conflict is believed to exist in all living things, but in humans beyond the age of two it manifests itself as existential fear. In confronting this fear, the person can either modify his or her thinking and behavior (constructive function and the pursuit of novelty) or perform stereotypic actions designed to temporarily ward off the fear (defensive function and the pursuit of familiarity). Adaptive living requires the reconciliation of these two cognitive–behavioral trends, as opposed to a lifestyle in which the defensive function predominates.

It is interesting that Edythe London and her associates at the National Institute on Drug Abuse not only observed decreased metabolic activity in the brains of rats that were administered phencyclidine, but also an increase in stereotypic behavior (Weissman, Dam, & London, 1987). From the perspective of lifestyle theory, the human organism is motivated by a desire to manage existential fear, a desire that is closely linked to the reward systems of the brain. Although these reward systems may be mediated by the release of dopamine in the nucleus accumbens and ventral tegmentum (Carlson, 1994), we would be well advised to consider the contributions of serotonin and norepinephrine to this process as well.

It is difficult to critique biological theories of addiction without being accused of constructing a straw man. The majority of models in this area are often so one-dimensional that they leave themselves open to scathing criticism. The abuse liability model, for instance, centers on the physiological effects of chemical substances to the exclusion of the sociocultural, familial, and general environmental features of addictive involvement. In all fairness to the abuse liability model, however, it was never meant to serve as a comprehensive explanation of addictive involvement, just as a tool for evaluating the abuse potential of various chemical compounds. Unfortunately, the same cannot be said of the disease concept.

Many proponents of the disease model, whether of the medical or spiritual variety, fancy this model a complete and comprehensive explanation for addictive behavior (see Maltzman, 1994). However, as many researchers and clinicians have come to realize, this model has many supporters, but few testable hypotheses. For this reason alone it should be viewed skeptically. In the final analysis, the disease model may be helpful to some clients, but the manner in which it has been construed (imprecise definition of terms, contradictory tenets, overall lack of coherence) makes it less than adequate for scientific study. What is more, those aspects of the theory that have been empirically evaluated have met with largely negative outcomes. Other models must therefore be considered. One group of alternative theories conceptualizes addiction as a psychological process. This perspective on addictive behavior forms the nucleus of the next chapter.

4

ADDICTION AS A PSYCHOLOGICAL CONSTRUCT

Psychological constructions of addictive behavior, like their biological counterparts, focus on internalized processes, and like their biological analogues, can be classified using the four primary elements of the addiction concept. The first psychological construction of addictive behavior to be described in this chapter, the self-medication hypothesis, highlights the progression element of the addiction concept based on Khantzian's (1985) assertion that the ego deficit that marks addictive behavior is a slowly progressive condition. Preoccupation is the element emphasized by theorists who view addiction as a component of the obsessive–compulsive spectrum, the second psychological construction of addiction to be discussed in this chapter. The third psychological construction of addiction reviewed here conceives of addiction as a personality construct in which persistence is the featured element. The three major sections of this chapter are accordingly devoted to these three psychological constructions of addiction, beginning with the view that addiction is a form of self-medication.

ADDICTION AS SELF-MEDICATION

The clinical observation that addictively involved clients tend to be more anxious, depressed, and angry than the norm served as a catalyst for development of the self-medication hypothesis. This hypothesis, with roots in psychoanalytic theory, holds that drugs are used and other addictive activities engaged in for the express purpose of alleviating psychiatric symptomatology and painful emotional states (Wurmser, 1974). Martin's alcohol, drug, gambling, and sexual problems would consequently be viewed as an expression of underlying emotional issues by therapists adopting a self-medication model of addictive behavior.

An assumption central to most versions of the self-medication hypothesis is that people use different drugs (or addictive activities) to medicate against specific emotions, issues, and problems (Khantzian, 1985). According to the self-medication hypothesis, a depressed person will be attracted to a central nervous system stimulant like cocaine, whereas an anxious person will seek relief through a central nervous system depressant like alcohol or valium. The relationship between negative affect and addictive involvement is reviewed next, followed by a survey of research on the direction of this relationship, the effect of addictive involvement on a person's mood, and the psychopharmacological specificity tenet of the self-medication hypothesis.

The Relationship between Negative Affect and Addictive Involvement

It is generally agreed that people who abuse substances characteristically exhibit higher levels of anxiety (Clark & Sayette, 1993) and depression (Mayfield, 1985) than those who do not abuse substances. Likewise, people diagnosed with anxiety disorders (Helzer, Burnam, & McEvoy, 1991) and major depression (Davidson & Ritson, 1993) are at elevated risk for concurrent drinking and other substance misuse problems. Whereas these findings confirm the presence of a relationship between substance misuse and negative affect, the results of research on juvenile drug use are less clear.

Swaim, Oetting, Edwards, and Beauvais (1989), for instance, surveyed a large group of eleventh and twelfth grade high school students and surmised that emotional distress and negative affect (anxiety, depression, anger, low self-esteem, blame–alienation) accounted for only 4.8% of the variance in drug use behavior. Furthermore, except for a small residual path from anger to drug use, the vast majority of variance attributable to emotional distress and negative affect was mediated by peer relations. This same group of investigators recorded similar outcomes in a group of Native American youth, but in this sample anger was linked to higher self-esteem and lower levels of drug use (Oetting, Swaim, Edwards, & Beauvais, 1989). Based on these results, Oetting, Beauvais and their colleagues concluded that emotional distress produces small, largely indirect, effects on drug use in adolescents, irrespective of their ethnic identity.

Heightened levels of depression have been observed in problem gamblers (McCormick, Russo, Ramirez, & Taber, 1984), anxiety is customary for sexually preoccupied persons (Quadland, 1985), and both depression (Hinz & Williamson, 1987) and anxiety (Bulik, Beidel, Duchmann, Weltzin, & Kaye,

1991) work their way into the profiles of eating disordered clients. Nineteen out of 20 compulsive buyers in one study could be assigned a DSM–III–R lifetime major mood disorder diagnosis (McElroy, Keck, Pope, Smith, & Strakowski, 1994). However, these findings are open to alternate explanations.

One possibility is that psychological distress is the consequence rather than cause of a person's involvement in addictive behavior. A second possibility is that the relationship between addictive behavior and emotional disturbance is caused or mediated by a third variable known to correlate with both addictive involvement and a person's level of psychological distress. Attempting to control for this possibility through the use of temporally concurrent measures of affect and gambling involvement, Dickerson, Cunningham, Legg England, and Hinchy (1991) examined the correlates of persistent gambling in a setting of the subject's own choosing, with observations recorded on an ongoing basis. The results of this study, however, failed to identify any mood or heart rate differences between high- and low-rate gamblers.

Kafka and Prentky (1994) studied the lifetime prevalence of DSM–III–R Axis I diagnoses in 34 individuals seeking treatment for a paraphilia (e.g., exhibitionism, pedophilia, voyeurism) and 26 individuals seeking treatment for a paraphilia-related disorder (e.g., protracted promiscuity, dependence on pornography, excessive masturbation) in an effort to understand the etiology of sexual impulsivity. Although there were no significant group differences in DSM–III–R Axis I diagnoses, both groups displayed high rates of lifetime mood (77%), anxiety (47%), and substance misuse (47%) disorders. In addition, the outpatient subjects participating in this study reported multiple paraphilias and/or paraphilia-related disorders, rather than restricting themselves to any one particular form of sexual deviance.

The lack of differentiation between persons displaying paraphilic and paraphilia-related disorders implies a lack of specificity in sexually deviant behavior and is interpreted by Kafka and Prentky as evidence that sexual impulsivity is a diverse phenomenon that embodies both culturally "deviant" and culturally "normative" behaviors. From these results, the authors conclude that negative affect may be more instrumental in maintaining sexual preoccupation than in initiating it. This supports the results of a study on alcohol and anxiety in which a group of inpatient alcohol abusers reported that anxiety played a more important role in maintaining than in initiating their usage (Chambless, Cherney, Caputao, & Rheinstein, 1987).

The anxiety model of bulimia nervosa postulates that binge eating is precipitated by negative affective states and that the fear of weight gain following a binge creates anxiety that the individual learns to control by purging (Rosen & Leitenberg, 1982). In support of this model, Leitenberg, Gross, Peterson, and Rosen (1984) witnessed elevated subjective ratings of anxiety in bulimics after consumption of a large test meal that subjects were prevented from purging. Janata, Klonoff, and Ginsberg (1985) likewise noticed heart rate increments in bulimics following their consumption of food that fell as soon as they purged. Additional confirmation is found in a laboratory study where psychologically induced negative affect stimulated overeating in restrained eaters but had no effect on a group of control subjects (Ruderman, 1985).

A study by Williamson, Goreczny, Davis, Ruggiero, and McKenzie (1988) obtained mixed results with respect to the anxiety model of bulimia nervosa in which the physiological responses of bulimic, obese, and control women were measured before and after eating. Exposing bulimic and control subjects to six food-related scenes and one pleasant scene, French, Nicki, and Cane (1993) revealed minimal support for a strict behavioral interpretation of the relationship between anxiety and bulimia. Whereas bulimics acknowledged a desire to ingest more food in situations where opportunities for purging were available, there were no systematic bulimic–control differences on subjective or physiological measures of anxiety. French, Nicki, and Cane speculate that bulimics may employ a hierarchy of cognitive control strategies designed to weigh opportunities for purging and formulate alternative plans of food regulation, both of which may mediate the level of anxiety experienced.

The Direction of the Relationship between Negative Affect and Addictive Behavior

For negative affect to be considered a cause of addictive involvement it must precede addictive involvement. The retrospective accounts of persons achieving high scores on anxiety and alcohol misuse, in fact, suggest that in many cases the anxiety disorder is believed to have predated the alcohol abuse and that many such individuals perceived that they began drinking as a way of alleviating anxiety (Bibb & Chambliss, 1986). Investigators probing the relationship between negative affect and alcohol abuse using a prospective or longitudinal design arrive at a different conclusion. McCord and McCord (1960), for instance, note that future alcohol abusers were no more phobic, worrisome, or dependent during childhood than nonalcohol abusers.

In a second prospective study, Loper, Kammier, and Hoffmann (1973) ascertained that future alcohol abusers were more self-confident, aggressive, and heterosexually-oriented during college and before they developed a drinking problem than their nonalcohol abusing peers. Directing a prospective analysis of 456 persons who had served as nondelinquent controls in the Glueck and Glueck (1968) studies on delinquency, Vaillant (1983) determined that childhood emotional problems contributed no unique variance to future alcohol abuse difficulties once pre-existing differences in ethnicity and family alcohol use were controlled. Upon witnessing fundamental differences in the symptom patterns produced by bulimic and clinically depressed patients, Cooper and Fairburn (1986) deduced that the anxiety and depressive symptomatology regularly observed in bulimia nervosa may be a consequence of the eating disorder rather than its cause.

If emotional difficulties cause addictive involvement, then alleviating the emotional difficulties should lead to reduced addictive involvement. However, antidepressant medications, in general, are of limited value in controlling the alcohol use patterns of problem drinkers (Schuckit, 1979), although one study found antidepressants effective in reducing opiate consumption in a group of chronic heroin users (Woody, O'Brien, & Rickels, 1975). A recent double-blind placebo controlled study on the use of buspirone (a nonbenzodiazepine anti-anxiety agent) in a group of highly anxious problem drinkers revealed no benefit in terms of either anxiety reduction or amount of alcohol consumed (Malcolm et al., 1992).

Another way emotional distress may be dampened is through the formation of social support networks. After all, it has been demonstrated that social support frequently buffers a person against stress (Kessler, Price, & Wortman, 1985). Goehl, Nunes, Quitkin, and Hilton (1993) tested this possibility in a group of 70 methadone-maintained outpatients given weekly drug screens for three months. Whereas the results of this study revealed that negative affect rose as stress mounted and positive affect climbed in response to increased social support, none of these variables predicted drug use outcome. The presence of another drug user in a subject's social network, however, greatly enhanced the subject's chances of producing a urine screen positive for drugs. Therefore, while social support may reduce negative emotions and social isolation, it can also increase the odds of relapse if drug users are part of that social network.

In contrast to studies denoting that reductions in negative affect have minimal impact on future drug use, the alleviation of alcohol and drug use problems may have a beneficial effect on a person's psychological well-being. O'Connor, Berry, Morrison, and Brown (1992) observed a reduction in psychiatric symptomatology and emotional distress following the cessation of drug use in a recovering population. Udel (1984) and Roy, Custer, Lorenz, and Linnoila (1988) likewise conceive of emotional difficulties as the consequence, rather than the cause, of people's involvement in problem drinking and gambling, respectively. In line with these suppositions, Rounsaville, Kosten, and Kleber (1986) recorded decreasing rates of depression in opiate addicts as the amount of time spent in treatment increased.

Based on the results of prospective and intervention studies, it would seem that negative affect may be more a consequence than a cause of addictive involvement. However, it is more likely that negative affect and addictive involvement are both a cause and effect of one another. The complex, bidirectional relationship existing between negative affect and addictive involvement was first described two decades ago by Kandel, Kessler, and

Margulies (1978) wherein it was proposed that emotional difficulties put a person at initial risk for drug involvement and that escalating drug usage then serves to exacerbate the person's emotional difficulties. It is also possible that instead of directly causing drug use, negative mood states trigger a craving for drugs that then leads to drug usage. Support for this possibility is provided in a study by Childress and her colleagues (1994) in which hypnotically-induced mood states were found to elicit craving and other drug-related conditioned responses in detoxified opiate abusers.

The Effect of Addictive Behavior on Mood

The self-medication hypothesis holds that there is a meaningful connection between negative affect and addictive involvement, that negative affect causes addictive involvement, and that this effect is a function of the addictive agent's ability to directly reduce negative affect. In testing this supposition, Tamerin and Mendelson (1969) ascertained that a group of alcohol abusing subjects experienced momentary mood elevation after consuming small amounts of alcohol in a controlled experimental setting, but that mood worsened as the level of alcohol consumption increased.

Post, Kotin, and Goodwin (1974) evaluated this hypothesis in a group of 23 depressed patients who were administered cocaine under experimental conditions. Upon receiving low to moderate doses of cocaine, one-third of the sample experienced mood elevation, one-third experienced mood deterioration, and one-third experienced no mood change whatsoever. The eight nonresponding subjects were subsequently administered larger doses of cocaine, the results of which showed mood elevation in one case and either no change or a deterioration in mood for the remaining seven subjects.

Neither high nor low anxiety volunteers found diazepam (valium) in 5 or 10 mg. doses to be more reinforcing than the placebo (de Wit, Uhlenhuth, Hedeker, McCracken, & Johanson, 1986), although in a later study subjects with a prior history of substance misuse preferred diazepam over the placebo (de Wit, 1991). This implies that a history of substance misuse may be more portentous than the anxiety-reducing properties of the substance in initiating, if not maintaining, substance misuse.

Castaneda, Galanter, and Franco (1989) determined that while subjects who abused central nervous system depressants like alcohol and heroin reported drug-induced improvement in their psychiatric symptoms, subjects who abused cocaine experienced a drug-induced aggravation of psychiatric symptomatology. In a later study administered by this same group of investigators, self-reported alleviation of psychiatric symptomatology and cognitive dysfunction were acknowledged by a group of heroin abusers, but cocaine users reported exacerbated symptomatology and cognitive dysfunction in response to their drug of choice and problem drinkers recalled variable symptom effects and deteriorating cognitions in response to their drug of choice (Castaneda, Lifshutz, Galanter, & Franco, 1994).

The results of a three-wave longitudinal panel study provide partial support for the self-medicating effects of alcohol (Schutte, Moos, & Brennan, 1995). With 951 late middle-aged male and 621 late middle-aged female community residents (aged 55 to 65) participating in this study, heavier alcohol consumption predicted lower levels of depression one and three years later in female subjects, but higher levels of depression predicted lighter subsequent alcohol consumption in male subjects. One possible interpretation of this finding is that self-medication is more instrumental in maintaining alcohol usage than in initiating it. A second possibility is that self-medication is more descriptive of female alcohol use patterns than male alcohol use patterns.

Research Focus: Psychopharmacological Specificity

A founding tenet of the self-medication hypothesis is that self-medication is specific to the substance consumed. This is another way of saying that proponents of the self-medication hypothesis place a great deal of emphasis on a subject's alleged drug of choice. One of the principal arguments against the psychopharmacological specificity tenet of the self-medication hypothesis, however, is research showing a minimal degree of drug use specificity and a growing trend away from a clearly defined drug of choice.

Studies indicate that the rate of dual dependency and polydrug abuse has risen dramatically in recent years (Gawin & Ellinwood, 1988). Employing a liberal definition of drug of choice and file information on a group of incarcerated drug users, Walters (1994b) identified a primary drug of abuse or drug of choice in just 46% of the group. Furthermore, only 57% of the subjects in this sample could be classified as having a drug of choice when results from an extensive clinical interview replaced the file information as the dependent measure for this study.

Research conducted on sexual deviations also reveals substantial overlap between the different paraphilias, from voyeurism to exhibitionism (Abel & Osborn, 1992; Bradford, Boulet, & Pawlak, 1992). Similarly, less than half the problem gamblers interviewed by Blaszczynski and McConaghy (1989) displayed a clear preference for one specific division or category of gambling. The fact that only about half the individuals who become involved in an addictive activity have a drug (or abuse) of choice brings the psychopharmacological specificity tenet of the self-medication hypothesis into serious question.

Weiss, Mirin, Griffin, and Michael (1988) unearthed preliminary support for the psychopharmacological specificity prediction in a large sample of inpatient drug users. This team of investigators determined that patients listing tranquilizers as their primary drug of choice more often presented with anxiety disorders, whereas those who viewed cocaine as their primary drug of choice evinced a higher rate of affective disorder and those who designated heroin as their primary drug of choice exceeded the population base rate for antisocial behavior and conduct disorder. A more recent investigation carried out on subjects from this same hospital, however, failed to find evidence of psychopharmacological specificity (Weiss, Griffin, & Mirin, 1992).

While it is true that persons diagnosed with major depression acknowledged greater drug use in response to depression relative to nondepressed patients, drug of choice—cocaine, sedative–hypnotics, opioids—had no bearing on self-medication, highlighted by the fact that nearly all of the drugs were effective in elevating the user's mood (Weiss, Griffin, & Mirin, 1992). Lemere and Smith (1990), in fact, report that a substance like cocaine may be used more to enhance a pre-existing mood (e.g., hypomania) than to mediate against a converse emotion (e.g., depression).

In a study reviewed earlier, Castaneda, Lifshutz, Galanter, & Franco (1994) concluded that persons exhibiting related psychopathology used different drugs, experienced dissimilar effects, and formed divergent expectancies concerning the anticipated impact of the drug on their mood. Psychometric studies have also failed to generate support for the psychopharmacological specificity tenet of the self-medication hypothesis (Greene, Adyanthaya, Morse, & Davis, 1993; Schinka, Curtiss, & Mulloy, 1994).

Extending the psychopharmacological specificity hypothesis to nondrug behavior, Blaszczynski and McConaghy (1989) predicted that exclusive horse race gamblers would display more anxiety and depression than exclusive poker machine players based on the results of an earlier study showing ß-endorphin level differences between horse race enthusiasts and poker machine aficionados (Blaszczynski, Winter, & McConaghy, 1986). The results of the more recent investigation, however, failed to identify any significant group differences between horse race and poker machine players on measures of trait anxiety, state anxiety, or depression.

An Alternate View

There is little question that a relationship exists between addictive involvement and emotional distress. More at issue are the relationship's direction, the consistency of an addictive activity's effect on mood, and the validity of the pharmacological specificity tenet of the self-medication hypothesis. As described earlier in this chapter, the relationship between addictive involvement and emotional disturbance may be bidirectional. A reciprocal effects model, in which the variables are both a cause and effect of one another, may prove more useful than a simple unidirectional approach.

The impact of addictive involvement on mood may also not be as simple as proponents of the self-medication hypothesis would have us believe.

There are those who continue abusing drugs, laying down bets, calling 1-900 sex lines, and restricting their food intake long after the self-medicating effects of the addictive behavior have worn off. Although this alone does not invalidate the self-medication hypothesis, it does demand explanation. To be useful, the self-medication hypothesis must account for the functionally autonomous (Allport, 1961) shift in motivation that occurs with prolonged involvement in an addictive activity.

Also, the psychopharmacological specificity tenet of the self-medication hypothesis has received minimal support in empirical studies on the subject. Current data suggest broad generality within different addiction categories (i.e., substance abuse, problem gambling, sexual preoccupation). Whether or not these different categories exhibit significant intercorrelation will be discussed shortly.

Before entertaining the possibility of overlap between different categories of addictive involvement, it is imperative that we consider the implications of research on addictive involvement beyond self-medication. While it is true that some individuals begin using drugs or participating in other forms of addictive activity in an effort to relieve feelings of anger, anxiety, or depression, many other individuals enter into such activities for reasons other than self-medication. Thus, self-medication is but one of many reasons for initially becoming involved in an addictive behavior.

To the extent that maintenance factors are what drive a person to participate in an addictive behavior, concentrating on variables that may have initiated this behavior will be of little value. It is at this point that the behavioral pattern becomes a lifestyle and it is the thoughts and actions that promote and protect the lifestyle that must be confronted if meaningful change is to occur. Diversity, as the reader may recall, is the antithesis of a lifestyle. By encouraging greater diversity of thought and behavior, increased sensitivity to new information, and greater flexibility in response to continually shifting internal and external contingencies, adaptation affords the individual an opportunity to reverse the stagnation of behavioral patterns that are no longer functional.

ADDICTION AS OBSESSIVE–COMPULSIVE DISORDER

Obsessive–compulsive disorder (OCD) is characterized by recurrent thoughts (obsessions) and/or actions (compulsions) that are time consuming, distressing, and interfere with the person's everyday functioning (APA, 1994). Armed with the knowledge that OCD may be a distinct nosological disorder, some investigators have sought to map the obsessive–compulsive spectrum onto which OCD, trichotillomania, body dysmorphic disorder, Tourette's syndrome, and sundry compulsive behaviors are placed (Hollander, 1991). Therapists committed to an OCD view of addictive behavior would likely conceptualize Martin's involvements with drugs, gambling, and sex as an expression of an underlying obsessive–compulsive disorder. The prescribed treatment would accordingly consist of a behavioral technique like thought stopping or a trial on one of the Specific Serotonin Reuptake Inhibitor (SSRI) medications.

OCD theories of substance abuse (Fals–Stewart & Schafer, 1992), sexual preoccupation (Coleman, 1991), and eating disordered behavior (Rothenberg, 1990) have been proposed. One of the principal arguments against such theories, however, is that whereas the obsessional thoughts and compulsive behaviors germane to OCD are ego-dystonic (distressing), the thoughts and actions of someone "addicted" to drugs, gambling, sex, exercise, food, or shopping are often a source of personal pleasure (Barth & Kinder, 1987). Hence, these behaviors may be more impulsive than compulsive. OCD theories of addiction can also be evaluated by taking a look at familial transmission patterns, obsessive–compulsive symptomatology in persons presumed to be addicted, and addictive behavior in persons diagnosed with OCD.

Familial Transmission of OCD and Addictive Behavior

Research on the familial transmission of addictive behavior demonstrates that the prevalence of alcohol and other drug abuse (Black, Noyes, Goldstein, & Blum, 1992), problem gambling, and eating disorders (Black, Goldstein, Noyes, & Blum, 1994) is no greater in the first-degree relatives of OCD patients than it is in the first-degree relatives of control subjects. The primary strength of these studies is that relatives were interviewed directly using a procedure known as the family study method.

Halmi and her colleagues (1991) used the family study method to examine the lineage of anorectic patients and discovered that the mothers of these patients registered higher rates of OCD than the mothers of control subjects. Employing the less reliable family history method, in which the behavior of first-degree relatives is assessed second-hand using data provided by the patient, Linden, Pope, and Jonas (1986) witnessed an increased rate of primary affective disorder and alcohol abuse in the first-degree relatives of 25 pathological gamblers. However, these authors failed to provide data on (or failed to find evidence of) familial OCD. These results suggest that with the possible exception of eating disorders, there is no discernible familial link between OCD and addictive behavior.

Obsessive–Compulsive Symptomatology in Addictive Disorders

Since surveys place the lifetime prevalence of OCD at 1% to 2% (Robins et al., 1984), a subgroup prevalence in excess of 2% is potentially significant.

Weiss and Rosenberg (1985) surmised that 25% of the 84 chronic alcohol abusers they interviewed satisfied DSM–III criteria for anxiety disorder, but none could be classified as OCD. Four years later, Eisen and Rasmussen (1989) determined that 6% of a group of 50 inpatient alcohol abusers satisfied DSM–III–R criteria for lifetime OCD. More recently, Fals–Stewart and Angarano (1994) diagnosed OCD in 11% of patients participating in a community-based treatment program for substance misuse. Investigating the rate of OCD in an independent group of substance abusers, Hasin and Grant (1987) discerned that 10% of the cases received a concurrent DSM–III–R diagnosis of OCD using the Diagnostic Interview Schedule (DIS), but only 3% of the cases registered a concurrent OCD diagnosis using the Research Diagnostic Criteria (RDC).

One possible explanation for these conflicting findings is that the relationship between substance misuse and OCD varies as a function of which measures are employed. The DIS and the Structured Clinical Interview for DSM–III (Spitzer & Williams, 1983) employed in the Eisen and Rasmussen (1989) and Fals–Stewart and Angarano (1994) studies may identify subclinical cases of OCD that would not be considered significant using a more conservative system of diagnosis like the RDC; or it may be that the DIS and Structured Clinical Interview for DSM–III, by furnishing the interviewer with specific examples of the types of symptoms indicative of OCD, render a more complete evaluation of obsessive and compulsive symptomatology.

In interviews conducted with 25 pathological gamblers, Linden, Pope, and Jonas (1986) ascertained that 5 (20%) satisfied DSM–III criteria for OCD. Raviv (1993), on the other hand, was unable to identify an increased rate of obsessionality in a group of 32 pathological gamblers relative to a group of 38 control subjects on the obsessive–compulsive subscale of a multi-symptom problem checklist, although obsessive–compulsive symptomatology was more common in a group of 32 sexually preoccupied subjects relative to this same group of 38 control subjects.

O'Guinn and Faber (1989) report that a group of 386 self-identified compulsive buyers scored significantly higher than a group of 250 general consumers on a 5 item obsessive–compulsive measure derived from the Psychasthenia scale of the Minnesota Multiphasic Personality Inventory (MMPI). Excessive exercising has also been shown to correlate with obsessive–compulsive symptomatology, but only in men (Davis, Brewer, & Ratusny, 1993).

A link between OCD and eating disorders has also been insinuated, but again, the evidence is inconclusive. Studies employing the Leyton Obsessional Inventory (LOI) show an increased incidence of obsessional thinking on the part of anorectic patients (Solyom, Freeman, & Miles, 1982), but studies using other self-report measures, like the Maudsley Obsessive Compulsive Inventory (MOCI), have yielded largely negative results in both anorectic and bulimic populations (Fahy, 1990). Administering the Diagnostic Interview Schedule to a group of 62 anorectic patients, Halmi et al. (1991) identified lifetime and concurrent diagnosis of OCD in 26% and 11% of the subjects in their sample, respectively.

In a recently completed study, Thiel, Broocks, Ohlmeier, Jacoby, and Schübler (1995) determined that 37% of a group of 93 female German eating disordered inpatients met DSM–III–R criteria for OCD and displayed signs of obsessive preoccupation unrelated to dieting or body image. Although the results of several of these studies suggest that a relationship may exist between OCD and eating disorders, it needs to be understood that in a majority of cases, subjects were recruited from inpatient settings where psychopathology may be more pronounced than outside the hospital environment. Furthermore, a group of investigators from Milan, Italy found that OCD and eating disorders present different personality disorder profiles, with OCD patients appearing more avoidant and paranoid and eating disordered patients demonstrating more borderline, histrionic, and dependent symptoms (Bellodi et al., 1992).

Addictive Involvement in Persons Diagnosed with OCD

A team of researchers from Greece detected alcohol abuse in 23 of 87 (26.4%) OCD patients (Dimitriou, Lavrenthiadis, & Dimitriou, 1993). However, there were no significant differences noted between alcohol abusing and nonalcohol abusing OCD patients with respect to either a family history of OCD or clinical course of the disorder. These investigators did find, nevertheless, that alcohol abuse predicted a longer duration of OCD symptomatology and a greater number of OCD-related precipitating conditions. Alcohol abuse status, on the other hand, failed to impact on treatment outcome, except for the fact that the alcohol abusing OCD patients were more apt to demonstrate new OCD symptomatology following treatment than nonalcohol abusing OCD patients.

Assessing alcohol abuse in a group of 25 male and 25 female OCD patients with a structured interview, Rieman, McNally, and Cox (1992) identified a lifetime prevalence of alcohol dependence in 16% of the OCD men and 4% of the OCD women, rates that do not appear to deviate significantly from rates found in the general population. They did, however, note an increased prevalence of OCD symptomatology in a group of alcohol abusers. These authors conclude that the level of commonality between OCD and alcohol abuse may depend on certain characteristics of the sample being investigated.

Scrutinizing the sexual behavior of OCD patients, a team of investigators observed that three of 25 males with severe OCD registered comorbid diagnoses for pedophilia and a fourth man acknowledged a history of transvestitism (Monteiro, Noshirvani, Marks, & Lelliott, 1987). A moderately high degree of sexually-related obsessionality was observed in a group of white male and female outpatients diagnosed with OCD (Freund & Steketee, 1989). However, these thoughts were, for the most part, highly distressing and not something from which the subjects participating in this study derived pleasure or excitement. Rather than acting out sexual fantasies or obsessions, as is often the case with sexual preoccupation, the majority of these OCD patients were socially withdrawn and isolated. Wherefore this group demonstrated a high degree of sexually-related obsessionality, their thinking differed qualitatively from the thinking of persons viewed to be preoccupied with sex since their fantasies were disturbing rather than pleasurable and virtually none of these sexual obsessions were acted out behaviorally.

As with research on family transmission and obsessive–compulsive symptomatology, eating disorders provide the best evidence of an OCD–addiction link. Reviewing case notes on 151 female OCD patients admitted to Bethlem/Maudsley Hospital in London, England, Kasvikis, Tsakiris, Marks, Basoglu, and Noshirvani (1986) detected a past history of anorexia in 11% of the cases. Identical results were obtained in a review of case notes written on 105 females subsequently admitted to these same hospitals (Fahy, Oscar, & Marks, 1993). Interviewing a group of 100 OCD patients sequestered in a university-based hospital in the United States, Rasmussen and Eisen (1989) identified a coexisting eating disorder in eight of these patients. Using an outpatient sample, Rubenstein, Pigott, L'Heureux, Hill, and Murphy (1992) recorded a lifetime diagnosis of anorexia nervosa, bulimia nervosa, or both in 13% of a group of male and female patients diagnosed with OCD using DSM–III–R criteria.

Research Focus: Serotonin Reuptake Inhibitors and Sexual Preoccupation

We now know that OCD responds differentially to drugs that block serotonin reuptake in the central nervous system (Hollander, 1991). Chemical compounds possessing a strong serotonin reuptake inhibitory effect used in the treatment of OCD include clomipramine (Anafranil), fluoxetine (Prozac), fluvoxamine (Luvox), paroxetine (Paxil), and sertraline (Zoloft). Assuming that sexual preoccupation and the other addictive behaviors lie along the obsessive–compulsive spectrum, it stands to reason that they too should respond to these agents. A series of case studies have, in fact, suggested that fluoxetine (Perilstein, Lipper, & Friedman, 1991), fluvoxamine (Zohar, Kaplan, & Benjamin, 1994), and clomipramine (Rubey, Brady, & Norris, 1993) are effective in alleviating symptoms of paraphilia and nonparaphilic sexual preoccupation. Larger scale open trials of serotonin reuptake inhibiting drugs, on the other hand, have produced mixed results.

In one of the larger studies to assess the treatment potential of the SSRIs in interventions with sexually preoccupied clients, Kafka and Prentky (1992b) witnessed large reductions in depression and unconventional sexual behavior on the part of 20 men diagnosed with a paraphilia or nonparaphilic "sexual addiction" following a 12-week trial on fluoxetine. The results of a study published the same year as the Kafka and Prentky investigation, however, failed to substantiate the therapeutic value of SSRIs in the treatment of sexual preoccupation. Stein and a group of colleagues (1992) found fluoxetine, clomipramine, and fluvoxamine marginally effective in managing the sexual obsessions of nonparaphilic sexually addicted men and largely ineffective in alleviating paraphilic behavior.

Whereas results from the Kafka and Prentky (1992b) and Stein et al. (1992) studies conflict, the only definitive test of the putative serotonin reuptake inhibition–sexual preoccupation connection is a double-blind placebo controlled study. Such a strategy was adopted by Kruesi, Fine, Valladares, Phillips, and Rapoport (1992) in a survey of 15 subjects receiving a single-blind 2-week trial of placebo, followed by a double blind 5-week trial of either clomipramine or desipramine (an antidepressant medication with weak serotonin reuptake inhibiting properties), and ending with a 5-week cross-over trial of the drug subjects did not receive during the previous five weeks. Paraphiliac behavior was evaluated at baseline, following administration of the placebo, and after each of the two 5-week trials on active medication with a semi-structured interview.

Four subjects were removed from the Kruesi et al. (1992) study because they displayed 50% or more improvement after the 2-week placebo trial. This makes for a placebo response rate of 27%. Three additional subjects dropped out over the next 10 weeks of the study, leaving eight subjects to complete the study. These eight subjects experienced reduced paraphilic symptomatology over baseline and placebo in response to either clomipramine or desipramine, but there were no response variations between the two active drugs. That the paraphilias do not fall along the obsessive–compulsive spectrum is further suggested by the fact that the placebo response rate obtained in this study (27%) was closer to the placebo response rate found for anxiety disorders (25%, Coryell & Noyes, 1988) than the rate normally associated with OCD (5%, Montgomery, 1993).

Double-blind placebo controlled studies assessing the effect of serotonin reuptake inhibitors on other forms of addictive involvement are no more encouraging than those observed with sexual preoccupation. Grabowski and his colleagues at the University of Texas Health Sciences Center in Houston (1995) probed the efficacy of fluoxetine in large groups of cocaine and cocaine–heroin abusers and found that retention in concurrent individual therapy was highest in the placebo condition and lowest in the group receiving the largest dose of fluoxetine (40 mg per day). Moreover, there were no significant group differences in cocaine usage or cocaine-related craving. Serotonin reuptake inhibitors also appear to be no more effective than placebos in reducing people's involvement with alcohol (Kranzler et al., 1995), tobacco (Dalack, Glassman, Rivelli, Covey, & Stetner, 1995), and PCP (Covi, Hess, Kreiter, & Jaffee, 1993).

These agents also appear to have little effect on the physical and psychological status of anorectic patients (Lacey & Crisp, 1980). Double-blind research on the use of fluoxetine with bulimic patients has been encouraging but is limited by a lack of post-study follow-up (Fluoxetine Bulimia Nervosa Collaborative Study Group, 1992). A double-blind placebo controlled investigation that did include a follow-up found clomipramine to be significantly more effective than the placebo in reducing the gambling involvement of a female problem gambler (Hollander, Frenkel, DeCaria, Trungold, & Stein, 1992). Unfortunately, it is difficult to generalize from a single case study, no matter how well designed.

An Alternate View

Of the addictive behaviors thus far reviewed, the best case for an addictive contribution to the obsessive–compulsive spectrum can be made for eating disorders. Given the documented superiority of serotonin reuptake inhibitors in the treatment of OCD, the serotonin hypothesis of eating disordered behavior would seem to have found some support in this review. The serotonin hypothesis of eating disordered behavior, as advanced by several different research groups, attributes anorexia and bulimia to serotonergic hypoactivity of the central nervous system (Pirke, Vandereycken, & Ploog, 1988). However, research studies addressing this hypothesis have tended to yield mixed outcomes (Goldbloom & Garfinkel, 1990; Hsu, Kaye, & Weltzin, 1993).

A group of investigators from the University of Pittsburgh discovered reduced levels of 5-hydroxyindoleactic acid (5-HIAA), the main serotonin metabolite, in the cerebral spinal fluid of weight-recovered bulimic anorexics relative to nonbulimic anorexics and normal controls (Kaye, Ebert, Gwirtsman, & Weiss, 1984), but were unable to replicate these findings in a later study (Kaye et al., 1990). The relationship between serotonin and eating disorders is complicated by the fact that abnormal eating may alter brain serotonin (McCargar, Clandinin, Fawcett, & Johnson, 1988). One inference that might be drawn from this is that reduced serotonin may be the consequence, rather than the cause, of eating disordered behavior. As such, the serotonin hypothesis of eating disordered behaviors requires additional study before it can be accepted at face value.

Despite the apparent relationship between obsessive–compulsive symptomatology and addictive behavior, the lifestyle model does not subscribe to the view that addictive behavior falls along the obsessive–compulsive spectrum. In formulating an alternate hypothesis of the relationship between OCD and addictive behavior the lifestyle approach focuses on the dynamics of lifestyle socialization.

A lifestyle is said to be a consequence of socialization whereby the individual becomes increasingly more involved in addictive activities, committed to addiction-related goals, and identified with addictive behavior. Behaviors considered addictive are those that provide pleasurable short-term outcomes. By focusing on short-term gratification people often ignore many of the negative long-term consequences of their continued involvement in habitual drug use, gambling, sex, or disordered eating. As the individual becomes progressively more preoccupied with the short-term goals and expectancies of a drug, gambling, sexual, or eating disordered lifestyle, his or her behavior becomes increasingly more stereotypic.

Given an atmosphere of expanding involvement, commitment, and identification with activities that lead to immediate gratification, it is no wonder the individual's actions take on an obsessive–compulsive quality. However, rather than reflecting true OCD, these findings depict an ingrained pattern of behavior that provides short-term pleasure and lends itself to repetition and ritualization, thereby making it possible to downplay, ignore, or discount the behavior's negative long-term consequences.

THE ADDICTIVE PERSONALITY: TWO MYTHS IN ONE?

The observation that some people engage in multiple "addictions" or switch from one addictive behavior to another has been used to prove the existence of an addictive personality. This is one way to conceive of Martin's involvement with drugs, sex, and gambling. In other words, Martin's propensity for multiple "addictions" is actually a reflection of an underlying addictive personality. Several theorists have attempted to construct a personality theory of addiction, two of which are described below.

Jacobs (1986), in offering a general theory of addictive behavior, considers the role of personality in the development of these behaviors. Personality factors figure even more prominently in Nakken's (1988) addictive personality model. Emphasizing the consequences of shame in the formation of this particular personality configuration, Nakken discusses the stages of addictive personality development, forms of addictive logic, family precursors, and sundry rituals believed to support addictive involvement. However, the addictive personality is never really defined by Nakken, at least not in a way that permits logical, let alone empirical, analysis of the underlying tenets of his proposition.

Because many of Nakken's observations can be accounted for without resorting to a personality-based construction of reality, the present section begins with a brief review of the controversy surrounding the general concept of personality, followed by a survey of the personality correlates of addictive behavior and evidence pertaining to the addictive personality concept. The research focus will then consider data on dual dependency (involvement in more than one addictive activity at a time) and what this informs us about the prospect of an addictive personality. Finally, as is the case with all sections of this book dealing with traditional models of addictive behavior, an alternate view is presented.

What Is Personality?

Various researchers have defined personality in diverse and multifarious ways. For our purposes, personality will be defined as relatively enduring patterns of behavior that are reasonably consistent across time and situations. The personality construct has generated more than its share of controversy in the field of psychology as exemplified by the person–situation debate. The question posed by this debate is whether human behavior is a function of individual traits or situational contingencies.

Early research relevant to the person–situation debate suggested that situational factors may be more important than personality traits in predicting behaviors like honesty (Hartshorne & May, 1928). These and more contemporary findings led Mischel (1968) to reject the notion of broad personality dispositions in favor of a social learning interpretation that stressed the situational context of human behavior. Mischel later modified his position in response to criticism from Bem (1977) and Epstein (1977), but has remained adamant in his belief that situational factors are the predominant force in human psychology (Mischel & Peake, 1982).

Given the fact that both dispositional and situational factors appear to act on a person's behavior, it may be more helpful to consider the manner in which the person and situation interact rather than focusing exclusively on one or the other. This is the position adopted by lifestyle theory and one to which we will return later in this discussion.

Personality Correlates of Addictive Behavior

Studies assessing the personality characteristics of people who abuse alcohol have failed to identify a core set of personality attributes unique to this group of individuals (Cox, 1985; Gaines & Connors, 1982). Research conducted with the Minnesota Multiphasic Personality Inventory (MMPI) also suggests that there is no single pattern associated with problem drinking (Graham & Strenger, 1988). This appears to apply to other forms of drug abuse as well (Johnson, Tobin, & Cellucci, 1992). To make matters worse, the small number of personality correlates that have been identified may actually be the consequence, rather than the cause, of problem drinking. Testing this hypothesis using the high risk method, Schuckit (1983) was unable to find significant differences between 32 FH+ nonalcoholic men and a matched group of FH– men on the extroversion and neuroticism scales of a popular personality inventory.

In a review of the literature on personality and alcohol abuse, Nathan (1988) concluded that only a history of antisocial behavior had any degree of predictive utility when it came to forecasting a person's proclivity to misuse alcohol. This conclusion has been confirmed in several longitudinal studies (Stein, Newcomb, & Bentler, 1987). Although Labouvie and McGee (1986) unearthed evidence of a relationship between putative measures of personality and drug use in a longitudinal investigation of New Jersey adolescents, protective personality factors were as effective in predicting low drug use as risk or "addiction" personality factors were in predicting high drug use.

Sensation seeking behavior has been advanced as a major etiological factor in problem gambling (Anderson & Brown, 1984). There is, however, little evidence of a robust association between sensation seeking and persistent or problem gambling. Some studies show a positive relationship between sensation seeking and problem gambling (Coventry & Brown, 1993), other studies suggest a negative relationship (Blaszczynski, Wilson, & McConaghy, 1986), and still other studies find no relationship at all (Dickerson, Cunningham, Legg England, & Hinchy, 1991). Kusyszyn and Rutter (1985) failed to uncover any significant group differences when comparing heavy gamblers, light gamblers, and nongamblers on a series of personality measures.

In another study investigating the personality correlates of problem gambling, Roy, Custer, Lorenz, and Linnoila (1989) recorded significantly higher scores on measures of neuroticism, psychoticism, and hostility in problem gamblers relative to a group of normal controls. However, whereas the controls were screened for psychopathology and removed from the study if they acknowledged any past or present episodes of psychological disorder or family history of psychiatric disturbance, subjects in the gambling group were only removed from the study if they had a current alcohol or drug abuse problem or had been diagnosed with an antisocial personality disorder. The significant group differences noted in this study may therefore be attributable to greater psychiatric disturbance on the part of subjects in the gambling condition.

Surveying the behavior of problem gamblers, sexually preoccupied persons, and control subjects, Raviv (1993) discerned higher levels of interpersonal sensitivity in the sexually preoccupied group, but failed to identify significant group differences on sensation seeking or self-defeating personality disorder. In a study exclusive to sexual preoccupation, Quadland (1985) failed to uncover any significant group differences on a personality measure of neuroticism between gay and bisexual men enrolled in treatment for sexually "compulsive" behavior and a matched group of control subjects. There were also no significant group differences noted between self-labeled television addicts and nonaddicted TV viewers on measures of neuroticism, extroversion, sensation seeking, or dependency (McIlwraith, Jacobvitz, Kubey, & Alexander, 1991).

Studies inspecting the personality characteristics of eating disordered patients confirm clinical descriptions of anorexic individuals as constricted, conforming, and obsessional, and bulimic patients as unstable and impulsive (Vitousek & Manke, 1994). More work remains to be done in these areas, however, since it is uncertain whether the few personality correlates that have been identified are the cause or consequence of addictive involvement.

Evidence Regarding the Existence of an Addictive Personality

Paralleling developments in the more general field of addictions, the concept of an addictive personality owes its existence to a forerunning construct known as the alcoholic personality (Landis, 1945). Most reviewers of the research literature on alcohol abuse conclude that there are virtually no traits or patterns common to people who drink excessively besides those that are secondary to the abuse of alcohol (Nathan, 1988). Much the same can be said for the prospect of an addictive personality (Pols, 1984). However, only a few direct tests of the addictive personality construct have been carried out. Gendreau and Gendreau (1970) were perhaps the first investigators to empirically evaluate the possibility of such a personality. Administering the MMPI to 51 penitentiary inmates reporting a chronic pattern of substance misuse and 82 penitentiary inmates with no history of misuse, the Gendreaus were unable to discern any significant group differences on the standard MMPI scales.

Comparing persons heavily involved with alcohol, cigarettes, gambling, or jogging, Kagan (1987) also found little uniformity in the pattern of scores produced by these three groups on the six subfactors of the MacAndrew Alcoholism scale of the MMPI. In a survey of self-reported alcohol, tobacco, illicit drug, and sexual involvement, Miller, Plant, Plant, and Duffy (1995) identified five distinct clusters of risk-taking behavior but failed to find evidence of a global addictive personality. Likewise, Lavelle, Hammersley, and Forsyth (1991) determined that adolescents who used drugs for the purpose of self-medication or who recorded elevated scores on personality measures of antisocial behavior and neuroticism were no more likely to be "dependent" on drugs one year later than adolescents who did not use drugs to self-medicate or did not elevate these personality scales.

Shisslak, Schnaps, and Crago (1989) administered the MMPI to women with bulimia, women who misused substances, and bulimic women who misused substances and discovered that women in the bulimia and bulimia + substance misuse conditions produced widely disparate scores on the MMPI. A prospective analysis of young adult males administered a series of personality measures and followed for an average of 9 years failed to disclose a link between premorbid personality and subsequent alcohol abuse difficulties (Schuckit, Klein, Twitchell, & Smith, 1994).

In a study more congruent with the underlying tenets of the addictive personality construct, Blaszczynski, Buhrich, and McConaghy (1985) compared pathological gamblers, heroin users, and controls on the Eysenck Personality Questionnaire (EPQ: Eysenck & Eysenck, 1975) and discovered that both "addiction" groups scored significantly higher on the EPQ Addiction scale than control subjects. DeSilva and Eysenck (1987) conducted a similar study on bulimia nervosa and determined that this group's scores on the EPQ Addiction scale corresponded with scores indicative of drug dependence. Using a sample of female subjects, Davis (1990) witnessed a positive correlation between the EPQ Addiction scale and several subscales from the Eating Disorder Inventory. It should be noted, however, that the EPQ Addiction scale loads heavily on anxiety and depression. As such, the results of these three studies may reflect negative affect secondary to a person's involvement in substance misuse, heavy gambling, or an eating disorder, rather than premorbid personality differences between index and control subjects.

The most direct test of the addictive personality hypothesis to date appears to have been a study by Rozin and Stoess (1993) wherein a group of undergraduate students from the University of Pennsylvania and their parents were asked to rate 10 substances and activities (coffee, tea, cola beverages, favorite alcoholic beverage, chocolate, nonchocolate sweets, hot chili pepper on food, cigarettes, gambling, and video games) on four dimensions of addiction (craving, withdrawal, lack of control, tolerance). Each dimension was rated on a 3 point scale (3 = strong, 2 = weak, 1 = none) and the ratings combined to form a total addiction score for each substance or activity. An intercorrelational matrix was then constructed from these data, the results of which indicated modest positive association between the different substances and activities. However, only a quarter of the correlations exceeded .20 and only one of the 45 correlations surpassed the .30 mark. Rozin and Stoess surmised that while involvement with one addictive substance or activity may increase a person's chances of becoming involved in other addictive substances and activities, the pattern of results is not consistent with the concept of an addictive personality. The overlap that exists between the four addictive activities highlighted in this book (substances, gambling, sex, and eating disorders) is examined next in a research focus.

Research Focus: Dual Dependencies

Dual dependency can be defined as simultaneous involvement in two or more addictive behaviors. In over 100 studies addressing this issue, there is evidence of moderate to high overlap between the various addictive behaviors, although few of these studies have made use of an appropriate control group. It should also be noted that crime and delinquency show signs of correlating with these traditional indices of addictive involvement. In a study testing Jessor and Jessor's (1977) problem behavior theory, Farrell, Danish, and Howard (1992) detected a robust relationship between cigarette smoking, drinking, marijuana use, delinquency, and sexual intercourse in a large group of seventh and ninth grade students. Other studies show that this overlap persists into adulthood (McGee & Newcomb, 1992).

Table 4–1 lists recent studies (published after 1980) providing a controlled comparison (i.e., a control group is included) of the overlap presumed to exist between substance misuse, problem gambling, sexual preoccupation, eating disorders, and delinquency or crime. As this table illustrates, controlled studies are available for only a minority of the 20 cross-addiction combinations theoretically possible between the five behaviors. By summing the observed prevalences for each of the five behaviors outlined in Table 4–1 and contrasting these prevalences with their respective control prevalences, a meta-analysis of the overlap believed to exist between the so-called addictions (plus delinquency and crime) was performed. The results of this meta-analysis (see Table 4–2) indicate that the cross-addiction prevalence exceeds the control prevalence in each case and that the amount of overlap is fairly consistent across the five behaviors, although the sexual preoccupation effect failed to attain statistical significance due to the low number of controlled comparisons available.

An Alternate View

As the results of research on dual dependency suggest, there is substantial overlap between the different addictive behaviors. However, if this is evidence of an addictive personality, then we must include crime in our definition of addiction given the equivalence of cross-prevalences achieved by the five groups surveyed in Table 4–1. Another way to look at this outcome is that rather than enlisting support for the presence of an addictive personality, these high cross-prevalences point to the possibility of a common lifestyle process shared by these five problem behaviors. Few people would be willing to consider crime an addiction, but the research reviewed in this section suggests that it correlates as well with four traditional categories of "addiction" as these four categories of "addiction" correlate with one another. It may therefore make more sense to attribute this overlap in behavior

TABLE 4–1 Controlled Comparisons Investigating the Cross-Prevalence of Substance Misuse, Problem Gambling, Sexual Preoccupation, Eating Disorders, and Delinquency or Crime

Substance Misuse in Problem Gambling Populations

| | Sample Characteristics | Measures | | Prevalence | |
	Index and Control Subjects	Criterion	Outcome	Index	Control
Study					
Pina et al. (1991)	57 adult pathological gamblers 115 age- and sex-matched controls	SOGS[1] ≥ 5	Cage's Test[2]	.40	.19
Walters (1997)	46 problem gambling federal prisoners 317 nonproblem gambling federal prisoners	SOGS[1] ≥ 3	self-report of alcohol/drug abuse	.80	.46

Substance Misuse in Eating Disordered Populations

| | Sample Characteristics | Measures | | Prevalence | |
	Index and Control Subjects	Criterion	Outcome	Index	Control
Study					
Pyle et al. (1983)	45 bulimic college students 540 nonbulimic college students	DSM–III	self-report of alcohol/drug abuse	.13	.04
Stern et al. (1984)	27 bulimic outpatients 27 noneating disordered subjects	DSM–III	RDC substance use disorder	.30	.04
Toner, Garfinkel, & Garner (1986)	55 anorexic patients 26 nonanorexic subjects	DSM–III	DSM–III substance use disorder	.33	.15
Bulik (1987)	35 bulimic patients 35 nonbulimic subjects	DSM–III	DSM–III alcohol abuse disorder DSM–III drug abuse disorder	.49 .26	.09 .00

Killen et al. (1987)	117 10th grade bulimics and purgers 444 noneating disordered 10th graders	interview	gets drunk at least once a month smokes marijuana at least once a month	.23 .13	.18 .06
Keck et al. (1990)	120 bulimic outpatients 52 noneating disordered subjects	DSM–III–R	DSM–III–R alcohol use disorder DSM–III–R drug use disorder	.23 .30	.10 .13
Stuart, Laraia, Ballenger, & Lydiard (1990)	30 bulimic patients 100 nonpsychiatric control subjects	DSM–III–R	self-report of childhood alcohol abuse self-report of childhood drug abuse	.13 .20	.00 .00
Halmi et al. (1991)	62 anorectic patients 62 age- and sex-matched control subjects	DSM–III–R	DSM–III–R diagnosis of substance abuse	.18	.26

Substance Misuse in Delinquent or Criminal Populations

	Sample Characteristics	Measures		Prevalence	
Study	Index and Control Subjects	Criterion	Outcome	Index	Control
Temple & Ladouceur (1986)	101 former delinquents with adult charges 99 former delinquents with no adult charges	charged as an adult with a felony	self-report of heavy drinking	.57	.41
Watts & Wright (1990)	89 delinquent males 348 nondelinquent high school students	adjudication as a delinquent	self-report of regular drinking self-report of marijuana use	.42 .51	.25 .13

(continued)

TABLE 4-1 Continued

Problem Gambling in Substance Misusing Populations

Study	Sample Characteristics Index and Control Subjects	Measures Criterion	Measures Outcome	Prevalence Index	Prevalence Control
Lesieur & Heineman (1988)	100 adolescent/young adult drug abusers 1771 college and university students[3]	therapeutic community	SOGS[1] ≥ 3	.28	.15
Lesieur & Blume (1990)	36 substance abusing psychiatric inpatients 69 nonsubstance abusing psychiatric inpatients	DSM–III–R	SOGS[1] ≥ 5	.11	.04
Elia & Jacobs (1993)	85 VA inpatient alcohol abusers National Prevalence Estimate[4]	DSM–III–R	SOGS[1] ≥ 3	.29	.04
Ladouceur, Pubé, & Bujold (1994)	79 alcohol abusing adolescents 1383 control adolescents	health survey	SOGS[1] ≥ 3	.37	.07

Problem Gambling in Eating Disordered Populations

Study	Sample Characteristics Index and Control Subjects	Measures Criterion	Measures Outcome	Prevalence Index	Prevalence Control
Ladouceur et al. (1994)	24 bulimic adolescents 1425 control adolescents	health survey	SOGS[1] ≥ 3	.38	.08

Problem Gambling in Delinquent or Criminal Populations

	Sample Characteristics	Measures		Prevalence	
Study	Index and Control Subjects	Criterion	Outcome	Index	Control
Ladouceur et al. (1994)	145 adolescents with criminal arrests	health survey	SOGS[1] ≥ 3	.13	.07

Sexual Preoccupation in Delinquent or Criminal Populations

	Sample Characteristics	Measures		Prevalence	
Study	Index and Control Subjects	Criterion	Outcome	Index	Control
Lang, Langevin, Checkley, & Pugh (1987)	34 genital exhibitionist forensic unit inmates 20 nonviolent, nonsex forensic unit inmates	DSM-III	transvestitism voyeurism	.47 .71	.05 .15

(continued)

TABLE 4–1 *Continued*

Delinquency or Crime in Substance Misusing Populations

	Sample Characteristics	Measures		Prevalence	
Study	Index and Control Subjects	Criterion	Outcome	Index	Control
Tuchfeld, Clayton, & Logan (1982)	575 heavy drinking junior and senior high students	self-report	breaking and entering theft	.40 .63	.15 .32
	4820 abstinent or moderate drinking students				
	933 heavy drinking adults	self-report	breaking and entering theft	.18 .56	.09 .37
	1576 abstinent or moderate drinking adults				

Delinquency or Crime in Problem Gambling Populations

	Sample Characteristics	Measures		Prevalence	
Study	Index and Control Subjects	Criterion	Outcome	Index	Control
Walters (1997)	363 medium security federal prisoners National Prevalence Estimate[4]	Incarceration	SOGS[1] $\geq$ 3	.13	.04

[1]South Oaks Gambling Screen (SOGS: Lesieur & Blume, 1987).
[2]Borrell (1988).
[3]Estimated from students at six colleges and universities in five states (Lesieur et al., 1991).
[4]Estimated from samples in California, Iowa, Maryland, Massachusetts, New Jersey, and New York (see Volberg, 1993).

70

TABLE 4–2 Mean Cross-Prevalences of Index
and Control Groups for Substance Misuse,
Problem Gambling, Sexual Preoccupation,
Eating Disorders, and Delinquency or Crime

Activity	Number of Comparisons	Index Prevalence[1]		Control Prevalence[2]		Comparison	
		Mean	SD	Mean	SD	*t* test[3]	sig
Substance Misuse	25	.33	.19	.15	.13	7.29	.000
Problem Gambling	9	.33	.23	.13	.14	5.01	.001
Sexual Preoccupation	2	.59	.17	.10	.07	7.00	.090
Eating Disorders	13	.25	.11	.09	.08	4.85	.000
Delinquency or Crime	11	.43	.20	.18	.13	5.11	.000

[1]percentage of persons with this diagnosis who displayed cross-prevalence for a second "addictive" disorder.
[2]percentage of control subjects in studies on this diagnosis who displayed prevalence for a second "addictive" disorder.
[3]paired *t* tests.

to a commonality in lifestyles rather than ascribing it to stable response dispositions that manifest themselves in an addictive personality.

Lifestyle theorists contend that behavioral overlap, both within (e.g., different forms of sexual preoccupation) as well as between (e.g., substance abuse and gambling) categories, increases over time. This is another way of saying that generality and cross-over are greater during the maintenance or lifestyle phase of a problem behavior than during the initiation phase. One could test this hypothesis by following a group of subjects displaying different addictive behaviors over time using a multi-addiction assessment instrument.

Although the addictive personality construct has not been corroborated empirically, the more general concept of personality is more difficult to reject given research documenting the presence of five robust personality factors (Paunonen, Jackson, Trzebinski, & Forsterling, 1992) and broad response dispositions when aggregated data are used (Epstein & O'Brien, 1985). Proponents of the lifestyle model acknowledge the existence of behavioral consistency but view it within a person × situation interactive framework. One interaction that supports behavioral consistency is the pursuit of familiarity. Ainsworth (1979) writes that infants display a strong drive for exploration (pursuit of novelty), but balance this with an equally strong drive for security and protection (pursuit of familiarity).

The drive for security and protection is one device that gives birth to behavioral consistency since it encourages humans to seek familiar surroundings. Self-regulation is a second factor that contributes to behavioral consistency. By following self-selected goals, controlling and modifying one's behavior in response to feedback, and engaging in self-reinforcement and self-punishment, the individual establishes routines and achieves a certain degree of behavioral consistency (Bandura, 1986). A third process, self-verification, is driven by attempts to confirm one's self- and world-views even when these views are negative (Swann, Stein–Seroussi, & Giesler, 1992). Self-verification facilitates behavioral consistency by encouraging people to interpret situations in a manner consistent with their current self- and world-views. These three interrelated processes merge to create a reasonably predictable and consistent environment, that then interacts with certain personal dispositions to produce behavioral consistency.

5

ADDICTION AS A
SOCIOLOGICAL CONSTRUCT

Like biological and psychological constructions of addiction, sociological constructions are drawn to predisposing and initiating explanations for addictive behavior. Unlike biological and psychological constructions of addiction, sociological constructions are equally interested in how this behavior maintains itself. One way that sociologically-minded investigators construe maintenance is through the construct of enabling. Enabling involves providing someone with the means to avoid the natural consequences of his or her behavior. Family members and mental health professionals commonly act as enablers, but are not the only groups capable of sabotaging the natural change process. The supervisor who supplies an alcohol abusing subordinate with an alibi or the friend who covers for a carousing coworker are just as guilty of enabling as the parents who ignore their daughter's sudden weight loss or the therapist who fails to confront the irresponsible actions of a client preoccupied with gambling. Two sociological constructions of addictive behavior will be reviewed in this chapter—the social mold perspective and addiction as codependence. The first stresses loss of control in its view of addictive behavior, and the second accentuates the preoccupation element.

THE SOCIAL MOLD PERSPECTIVE ON ADDICTION

The social mold perspective conceives of addictive behavior as a socialization process in which a person is taught the attitudes, values, and beliefs of a particular group or culture. The concept of socialization is normally discussed with respect to a person's compliance with normative social practices and behaviors. However, deviant patterns of behavior are also acquired through socialization. Addictive behavior is therefore construed as a person's socialization to culturally aberrant definitions of behavior and failed socialization to conventional definitions of behavior. A third socialization effect has also been proposed: namely that conventional attitudes and beliefs taken to an extreme can lead to the formation of unconventional attitudes and beliefs à la the sociocultural theory of eating disordered behavior.

There is little question that socialization influences the development of the behavioral patterns people adopt. Social mold theories of addiction assume that addiction is a manifestation of failed or deviant socialization and the person's helplessness in the face of outside influences (hence, the rationale for classifying it under loss of control). A social mold theorist would therefore likely view Martin's behavior as a reflection of early family and peer relationships in which he was socialized to accept certain deviant practices (i.e., sexual promiscuity, drug use, heavy gambling) and reject more conventional activities (school, work, marriage). In this section, three major sources of socialization influence will be considered—family, peers, and the media—followed by a review of research on sexual abuse in the development of an eating disorder.

Family-Related Correlates of Addictive Involvement

The family is a particularly potent source of socialization influence. As such, family factors are frequently emphasized in social mold theories of addictive behavior. Five areas of familial influence will be considered in this section: family structure, family relations, modeling of parental and sibling behavior, attachment, and parenting style.

Family Structure

Reviews have consistently demonstrated that family structure, as exemplified by research on family size, birth order, and broken homes, has little effect on a person's propensity to misuse drugs (Glynn, 1984). Certain moderating variables, however, may convey some measure of influence over substance use outcomes. The age at which the home of origin was broken by divorce or death, for instance, was found to moderate the broken home–substance misuse relationship in at least two studies on this issue, with the loss of a parent before age 12 having no apparent effect on future substance misuse and the loss of a parent after age 12 exerting a major impact on subsequent drug-seeking behavior (Binion, 1979; Kolb, Gunderson, & Nail, 1974). More recent studies have also failed to detect a relationship between family structure and indices of substance involvement (Coombs & Paulson, 1988; Piercy, Volk, Trepper, Sprenkle, & Lewis, 1991). Equally disappointing

results have been recorded in studies scrutinizing the family structure correlates of eating disordered behavior (Kog & Vandereycken, 1985).

Family Relations
According to clinical lore, the mothers of substance abusing adults and adolescents are overprotective and pampering and the fathers underinvolved
and distant (Kaufman, 1981). However, there is some evidence that the
fathers of substance abusers may be just as overindulgent as the mothers
(Alexander & Dibb, 1977). Searight and his coworkers (1991) administered a
family atmosphere scale to adolescents housed in a residential drug treatment center and determined that these youths viewed their parents as emo-
tionally constricted, distant, and critical. On the basis of these findings, the
authors concluded that the parents of substance abusing youth may have
trouble balancing the autonomy and emotional–expressive needs of their
offspring.

In a study comparing drug users classified by drug type ("hard" versus
"soft"), frequency ("heavy" versus "light"), and number ("poly" versus "single"), family cohesion was found to be low in persons classified as "hard" or
"heavy" users (Piercy et al., 1991). A 3-year longitudinal investigation conducted by Needle, Lavee, Su, Brown, and Doherty (1988) showed that stressors increased and family cohesion decreased in a group of mid-adolescent
youth, regardless of their drug use status. Factors correlating with future
substance misuse in this sample included early disengagement from the
family and early involvement with drug-using peers. Lesieur, Blume, and
Zoppa (1986) note that problem gamblers also recall a relatively large number of relationship problems in their families of origin.

Attie and Brooks–Gunn (1989) determined that girls exhibiting negative
body images were significantly more likely to report subsequent eating disorder symptomatology than girls projecting a more positive body image.
However, family relations did not predict eating disorder symptomatology
in this sample. Similar results were obtained in a study evaluating the relationship between the Eating Attitudes Test (EAT: Garner, Olmstead, Bohr,
and Garfinkel, 1982) and a measure of family functioning (Gibbs, 1986).
Bulik and Sullivan (1993) likewise failed to detect any significant bulimia–
control differences in family environment, although the fathers of bulimic
patients were described as more seductive and the mothers as more neurotic
relative to the parents of control subjects.

Laura Humphrey has identified a number of deficits in the parent–child
relationship that may put a child at risk for future eating disordered behavior.
In one study, Humphrey (1989) videotaped role plays performed by 74 family
triads (a teenage daughter and her two parents) and asked raters to evaluate
the content and process of these interactions. The raters viewed triads with
an eating disordered daughter as more neglectful, blaming, belittling, and

sulking than triads in which the daughter displayed normal eating behavior. Although good interrater reliability was obtained in this study, the reader is left to wonder whether eating- and weight-related issues were discussed in these role plays, and if so, what effect this may have had on a rater's evaluation of family functioning.

Modeling of Parental and Sibling Behavior
A powerful link has been observed between parental alcohol use and offspring drug use (Barnes, Farrell, & Cairns, 1986). Problem gambling (Browne & Brown, 1994) and eating disorders (Kog & Vandereycken, 1985) also appear to run in families. Children, it would seem, imitate and model the drug use, gambling, and eating habits of their parents, siblings, and other relatives. Modeling effects are exceedingly complex, however. In one study a counter–imitation effect was observed in the opposite sex offspring of high volume problem drinkers, but not in same sex offspring (Harburg, DiFrancisco, Webster, Gleiberman, & Schork, 1990). Likewise, McCord (1988) reports that fathers who drank excessively exerted a stronger modeling effect on male children if they themselves were held in high esteem by the mother.

Research on the modeling of parental eating behavior has also produced contradictory results. For instance, while one set of investigators observed disordered eating attitudes on the part of mothers whose daughters displayed bulimic symptomatology (Pike & Rodin, 1991) and a second group of investigators identified a positive association between dieting in adolescent girls and dieting in one or both parents (Paxton et al., 1991), a third team of investigators failed to unearth evidence of a relationship between the EAT scores of adolescent girls and the EAT scores of their mothers (Attie & Brooks–Gunn, 1989).

Attachment
It has been suggested that mutual attachment between a child and parent may protect the child against future substance misuse outcomes (Brook, Brook, Gordon, Whiteman, & Cohen, 1990). Reviewing the results of several ongoing studies, Kandel and Davies (1992) identified an inverse association between marijuana usage and the adolescent's stated degree of closeness to his or her parents. This implies that a strong child–parent bond may insulate the child from drug-using peers and other drug-related influences (Coombs, Paulson, & Richardson, 1991).

A lack of parental attachment, as measured by weak identification with one's mother and father, may also characterize the social relationships of incarcerated rapists and pedophiles (Levant & Bass, 1991). As was already mentioned, adverse interpersonal experiences are commonly observed in the backgrounds of problem gamblers (Lesieur, Blume, & Zoppa, 1986). It is possible that negative relationships within the family increase a child's chances of becoming involved in sexual acting out behavior or problem gambling later on in life by virtue of the disruptive influence these relationships have on the child's ability to connect and empathize with others.

One of the earliest theories on anorexia held that it grew out of a young woman's struggle with individuation from her family of origin (Bruch, 1973). Although data exist in support of the separation–individuation hypothesis (Heesacker & Neimeyer, 1990), other evidence implies that attachment may be as important as individuation in the development of anorexia. From an early age women are taught to value interpersonal relationships, yet as they progress through adolescence they are encouraged to relinquish their prized relationship with their parents.

Preliminary support for the attachment–individuation supposition was obtained in a study by Armstrong and Roth (1989). In that study, 96% of a group of inpatient eating disordered women indicated anxious attachment on a semi-projective technique. The results of a study by Kenny and Hart (1992) further revealed that eating disordered patients were less securely attached to their parents than control subjects. Relative to the control group, the eating disordered patients characterized their parents as less supportive and more negative. Rhodes and Kroger (1992) unearthed additional evidence that substantiates the attachment–individuation hypothesis by way of increased separation anxiety and significantly lower individuation in eating disordered patients relative to a group of noneating disordered controls.

Parenting Style
Laissez-faire and authoritarian styles of parenting tend to correlate with higher levels of drug misuse in offspring. Moderate parental control and high support, on the other hand, typically predict lower levels of substance misuse (Barnes, Farrell, & Cairns, 1986). Chassin, Pillow, Curran, Molina, and Barrera (1993) discerned that parental alcohol misuse predicted small to moderate increments in offspring substance use. A path analysis of these data revealed that reduced parental monitoring was a key mediating variable in the parental–offspring alcohol misuse relationship.

Employing a standardized measure of recollected family relations and parenting style—the EMBU (Perris, Jacobsson, Lindstrom, Von Knorring, and Perris, 1980)—Emmelkamp and Heeres (1988) determined that compared to control subjects, drug abusers perceived their fathers as more rejecting and their mothers as more overprotective. Kokkevi and Stefanis (1988) administered the EMBU to 91 incarcerated drug users and noted that these subjects perceived both parents as less rejecting and more permissive, their fathers as more inconsistent, and their mothers as more overprotective than general population respondents. Administering the EMBU to eating disordered patients and noneating disordered controls, Esparon and Yellowlees (1992) cataloged recollections of reduced consistency and emotional warmth and increased rejection in the parenting styles to which the eating disordered patients were exposed.

Peer-Related Correlates of Addictive Involvement

Recognizing the role of peers in the initiation and maintenance of addictive involvement is central to understanding socialization effects. This section explores research on peers and substance use, peers and other forms of addictive involvement, family versus peer influence, and various interpretations of the peer effect.

Peers and Substance Use

It is fairly evident that drug users tend to associate with other drug users (Elliott, Huzinga, & Ageton, 1985). In one study, treatment-seeking and non-treatment-seeking adolescents involved with drugs were more apt to associate with peers who used drugs than with peers who did not use drugs (Needle et al., 1988). Napier, Goe, and Bachtel (1984) ascertained that drug usage by friends, the desire to be accepted by a peer group, and identification with certain types of "pothead" and rock music listening groups were powerful predictors of drug use in a large group of junior and senior high school students.

Studying the marijuana use habits of 987 college students and their four closest friends, James Orcutt (1987) discovered that students holding negative views of marijuana usage were unlikely to be semi-regular users of marijuana themselves unless all four of their closest friends were also semi-regular users. Conversely, students espousing opinions favorable to marijuana ingestion were likely to be semi-regular users of this substance themselves if at least one of their four closest friends smoked marijuana semi-regularly. However, in students expressing neutral views toward marijuana, the rate of personal marijuana usage rose from 9% to 24% to 50% when none, one, and two or more of the student's four closest friends, respectively, used marijuana on a semi-regular basis. This suggests that peer effects may be strongest for persons who do not have clearly formulated attitudes and opinions on a particular subject.

The founding tenet of peer cluster theory is that the effects of family, neighborhood, role models, negative affect, and availability are mediated by one's peer group (Oetting & Beauvais, 1987). While this supposition has received some empirical support (Dielman, Butchart, & Shope, 1993), the peer–drug use relationship may not be as invariant as proponents of peer cluster theory have proposed in the past.

Stattin, Gustafson, and Magnusson (1989) interviewed male and female Swedish adolescents at three different points in time (age 14, age 15 to 16, and age 26). Considerable variability was observed in the peer–alcohol use relationship. Thus, while associating with younger peers was found to presage a lower rate of drinking and drunkenness at ages 14 and 15 to 16 and associating with older peers predicted a higher prevalence of drinking and drunkenness at these ages, peer relations at age 14 failed to correspond with drinking practices at age 26. As the results of this study insinuate, researchers would be well advised to take certain facets of a reference group into account when investigating the drug–peer relationship. These results also indicate that adolescent peer relations may have minimal impact on early adult drinking. The latter outcome is consistent with lifestyle theory's assertion that the motivation for initial drug use (peer influence) differs widely from the motivation that maintains this usage once it is established.

Peers and Other Forms of Addictive Involvement

Peer relations may be as instrumental in encouraging youthful gambling (Browne & Brown, 1994) and sexual activity (Whitbeck, Conger, & Kao, 1993) as they are in promoting teenage drug use. Eating disorders also appear to respond to peer-related influences. Nearly half the bulimics interviewed by Mitchell, Hatsukami, Pyle, and Eckert (1986) acknowledged that they started binging and purging in response to weight-related pressure from friends. Similarly, Crandall (1988) determined that sorority members who binged had close friends who also binged.

Consistent with the notion that peers may not only encourage initiation of disturbed eating patterns but maintain them as well, anecdotal evidence supplied by a college gymnast suggests that in one case, ritualistic team binging and purging would frequently occur after a meet (Noden, 1994). Finally, certain features of bulimia may be more susceptible to peer influence than others. In this regard, bulimics who exhibit depressive and avoidant personality features appear to be more profoundly influenced by peer relations and expectations than bulimics who display borderline personality features (Wonderlich, Ukestad, & Perzacki, 1994).

Family versus Peer Influence

In a survey of 768 adolescents, Johnson, Marcos, and Bahr (1987) discerned that subject drug use matched peer drug use more closely than parental drug use. Rather than simply imitating peer drug use behavior, the adolescents in this study felt situational pressure to participate in the use of substances or risk social rejection. Swadi (1988) likewise determined that when a close friend used drugs but a family member did not, 60% of the youth engaged in some form of drug taking behavior. This compares with a 35% rate of reported drug usage when the youth's closest friends did not use drugs but a family member did. The Johnson et al. and Swadi studies indicate that while family factors correlate robustly with drug use in adolescent populations, peer factors may play an even more critical role in the drug use activities of adolescents. The results of a third study, however, support the converse position in which parents exercised greater control than peers over drug using and nondrug using teens (Coombs, Paulson, & Richardson, 1991). The equivocal nature of these findings imply that the question of family versus peer contributions to addictive involvement may need to be rethought.

Instead of pitting family members against peers in the derivation of addictive patterns of behavior, a more productive strategy may be to consider how these two variables interact. Addressing this very question, Simons and Robertson (1989) verified that both parental rejection and deviant peer associations effectively predicted drug use in a large group of adolescents. However, a path analysis of these data incisively demonstrated that parental rejection contributed to heightened levels of aggressiveness that then encouraged association with a deviant peer group. It is also possible that in some cases parental rejection is the consequence, rather than cause, of aggressiveness and drug involvement. In the Coombs, Paulson, and Richardson (1991) study cited earlier, parents exerted greater influence over the drug use activities of their offspring than peers. However, users, perhaps because they perceived rejection from their parents, were more influenced by peers than nonusers, whose relationship with parents served as a buffer against negative peer influence. Along similar lines, poor parental monitoring has been found to have both direct and indirect (by encouraging deviant peer associations) links to risky sexual behavior (Metzler, Noell, Biglan, Ary, & Smolkowski, 1994).

Peer Influence versus Selection
The relationship between peers and drug use is often attributed to social pressure and modeling. However, this may also reflect the tendency on the part of many substance users to select other substance users as friends. Fisher and Bauman (1988) contend that approximately half the commonality in friends' use of alcohol and tobacco is traceable to selection factors. This is because people choose friends who think and act like they do, friendships dissolve when drug use behavior becomes dissimilar, and peer groups restrict membership to like-thinking members (Bauman & Ennett, 1994).

Contrary to the predictions of peer cluster theory, social network analysis suggests that one-third of all adolescents are isolates and that being an isolate is a more potent predictor of substance misuse than interacting with drug-using peers (Ennett & Bauman, 1993). Similar results are reported by Simons, Whitbeck, Conger, and Melby (1991) in which adolescents with poor social skills and weak prosocial value commitments encountered interpersonal, disciplinary, and academic problems and so selected one another as friends through associative pairing. Unlike the social influence model of peer effects in which peer relations are viewed as a cause of addictive involvement, the selection model asserts that addictive involvement leads to certain peer relationships.

It is also possible that adolescents project their own thoughts and beliefs onto friends. Fisher and Bauman (1988) entertained this possibility and witnessed a noticeable drop in the correlation between self and friend drug use when subject estimates of friend drug use were replaced by reports solicited directly from friends.

Media-Related Correlates of Addictive Involvement

Research indicates that many preschoolers in the United States spend more time in front of a television set than with their parents (Comstock, 1980). This demonstrates the influence the media has over the socialization process. The commercial media's messages of violence and self-indulgence are seen by some as powerful facilitators of youth alienation, drug use, and eating disorder (Whitaker, 1989). The entertainment media's unsophisticated treatment of complex problems may have spawned an entire generation of citizens looking for a "quick fix" to the problems of everyday living.

The news media, like the commercial and entertainment medias, influences people's perceptions, goals, and expectancies. It has also been accused of spreading misinformation. Eiseman (1993) asked college undergraduates to indicate whether they believed drug use had increased or decreased in recent years. The outcome of this study revealed that 70% of the students surveyed believed that drug use was on the rise despite national estimates of a downward trend. Eiseman attributes this difference in perspective to the media's expanded coverage of the "war on drugs." Such a conclusion is speculative, however, since Eiseman failed to employ a direct measure of media exposure. A more adequate test of this hypothesis would require a longitudinal analysis of attitudes and level of exposure to specific media messages.

The media may wield a substantial effect on the frequency of gambling behavior by promoting wagering activities (e.g., casino gambling, off-track betting, state lotteries) in advertisements and inducements (Hraba, Mok, & Huff, 1990). Although media promotion of gambling may tend to increase the rate of problem gambling, the actual extent of such an effect is unknown. Nonetheless, this highlights the responsibility that the media, state and national governments, and gaming industry have to present a balanced view of gambling, minimize the exploitation of vulnerable individuals, and alert the public to the potential hazards of excessive gambling.

In the wake of Ted Bundy's admission that pornography caused him to commit heinous crimes against women, there has been growing speculation that sexually explicit films may be responsible for a portion of the sexual violence witnessed in this country every year. It has traditionally been assumed that rapists are aroused by depictions of rape and consensual sexual activity, but that nonrapists do not respond to simulated rape scenes (Abel, Barlow, Blanchard, & Guild, 1977). However, Malamuth, Heim, and Feshbach (1980) note that male and female sexual interest and arousal are enhanced by simulations that portray the victim of a sexual assault as enjoying the experience.

Males with no record of sexual assault have been asked to state whether they would be willing to rape if they knew there would be no negative repercussions to their actions. A group of college students who indicated their willingness to rape if they knew they would not get caught, referred to as the high-likelihood of raping (LR) group, were less aroused by descriptions of rape than by descriptions of consensual intercourse when the female victim was depicted as disgusted by the encounter (Malamuth & Check, 1983). However, when the vignette was modified so that the victim was portrayed as experiencing an orgasm during the assault, sexual arousal in low-LR subjects was comparable across the consenting and nonconsenting scenes and was significantly higher for the nonconsenting scene in high-LR subjects.

Exposing 156 college-age men to sexually degrading R and X rated movies, Linz, Donnerstein, and Penrod (1988) observed reductions in anxiety, depression, and empathy toward rape victims with continued exposure to R rated violent ("slasher") movies. Subjects exposed to R and X rated nonviolent films failed to differ from the no-exposure control group on these measures.

Despite the attitudinal changes that occur with exposure to violent and nonviolent pornography, it is still uncertain whether this translates into aggressive behavior. Zillman and Bryant (1982), in fact, report that long term exposure to nonviolent pornography may actually reduce aggression. There is obviously a great deal more that needs to be learned about the effects of sexually explicit material on human behavior. In an exhaustive review of the literature on this topic, Davis and Bauserman (1993) conclude that "although most of the commonly available material has the short-term effect of producing sexual arousal, whether that arousal is carried over to overt sexual behavior depends largely on the predispositions of the viewer toward the behavior, the immediate affective response to the material, and the opportunity to engage in the behavior" (p. 199). This would suggest that people are not simply pawns of environmental influence and the situational agents that direct this influence.

Despite its facility in promoting attitudes and behaviors favorable to substance misuse, gambling, and sexual preoccupation, the media may play its most dramatic role vis-a-vis eating disorders. Garner, Garfinkel, Schwartz, and Thompson (1980) note that between 1959 and 1978 the average weight-to-height ratio of Playboy centerfolds and the average weight of Miss America contestants dropped, while the number of diet articles appearing in women's magazines rose. Likewise, the bust-to-waist ratio of models gracing the pages of women's magazines fell dramatically between 1950 and 1981 (Silverstein, Perdue, Peterson, & Kelly, 1986). This corresponds with a reported increase in the rate of eating disorder diagnoses over this same time period (Szmukler, McCance, McCrone, & Hunter, 1986).

Another interesting media effect that parallels the known demographics of eating disordered behavior is that women's magazines contain 10.5 times more articles and advertisements on weight loss than men's magazines, a rate that corresponds roughly to the gender ratio for eating disordered behavior (Anderson & DiDomenico, 1992). The influence of the media on eating-related socialization is further demonstrated by studies identifying the news media as the single most important source of information on eating disorders for general population respondents (Murray, Touyz, & Beumont, 1990). These and other findings insinuate that the media may reflect and shape current views on femininity, which in modern American culture emphasize a thin physique.

Whether the media shapes views on femininity, reflects views on femininity, or does both is an important research question for which there is no clear-cut answer at this time. However, several studies touch on this issue. Stice and Shaw (1994), for instance, established that female undergraduates exposed to pictures of thin models were more inclined to report depression, shame, stress, and body dissatisfaction than female undergraduates shown pictures of average sized women or control photos of inanimate objects. Likewise, after logging the level of media exposure reported by a group of undergraduate women, Stice, Schupak–Neuberg, Shaw, and Stein (1994) ascertained that media exposure exerted both a direct and indirect effect on eating disordered behavior. The indirect link ran from media exposure to acceptance of gender role stereotypes, to internalization of ideal body expectations, and to body dissatisfaction, and culminated in an increased rate of eating-related concerns. In a third study bearing on this issue a clinical sample of 24 women with DSM–III–R eating disorder diagnoses were more likely to overestimate their body proportions when viewing pictures of thin models than when viewing control stimuli, whereas a comparison group of 24 noneating disordered women demonstrated no such effect (Hamilton & Waller, 1993).

Findings such as these have encouraged development of a sociocultural theory of eating disordered behavior, the founding premise of which is that eating disorders are shaped, in part, by cultural expectations (Stice, 1994). Levine, Smolak, and Hayden (1994) studied 48 middle school girls who reportedly received strong weight and shape messages from family, peer, and media sources and determined that these girls exhibited more disturbed patterns of eating and a stronger drive for thinness than 337 middle school girls receiving less apparent weight and shape messages. The two most reliable correlates of disturbed eating in this sample were exposure to magazines that emphasized attractive body shape and weight management and weight- or shape-related criticism from family members.

The results of research on the sociocultural correlates of eating disordered behavior not only underscore the relevance of all three sources of socialization to the development of eating-related concerns, but also illustrate how conventional cultural messages contribute to "addictive" patterns of behavior. Hence, anyone who accepts common cultural myths about thinness being a major criterion for attractiveness and attractiveness leading to success and who is then able to remain thin without purging or becoming dangerously underweight is the recipient of praise and adoration. Alternately, people who take cultural messages for thinness to an extreme by severely restricting their intake of food, compulsively engaging in exercise, or purging on a regular basis are more commonly labeled addicted, disordered, or diseased and are prescribed a course of psychological treatment.

Research Focus: Childhood Sexual Abuse and Eating Disorders

Some clinicians have long believed that childhood sexual abuse is a major risk factor for eating disordered behavior. Whereas this appears to make good intuitive sense, it is based largely on clinical lore, case studies, and prescientific speculation (Crisp, 1984). In fact, up until just recently there were only a handful of empirical studies on this issue. The results of a literature review on eating disorders and childhood sexual abuse insinuate that childhood sexual abuse is no more common in eating disordered populations (30%) than in the general population and may actually be lower than that observed in other patient groups (Connors & Morse, 1993).

Table 5–1 outlines empirical studies contained in the Connors and Morse review, as well as several more recent investigations. As a group, these findings provide minimal support for sexual victimization as a principal cause of eating disordered behavior. A recent cross-national investigation conducted on American, Austrian, and Brazilian women arrived at a similar conclusion (Pope, Mangweth, Negrao, Hudson, & Cordas, 1994). There is some evidence, however, that family conflict may magnify the influence of sexual abuse on eating disordered behavior (Mallinckrodt, McCreary, & Robertson, 1995). One possibility, then, is that childhood sexual abuse is only a risk factor for girls raised in chaotic home environments. To more thoroughly investigate this possibility the definitional and design problems that have plagued studies in this area must be addressed and rectified (see Connors & Morse, 1993).

Although it is debatable whether a meaningful link exists between childhood sexual abuse and eating disordered behavior, if a relationship does exist, it is stronger for bulimia than anorexia. This is because studies signaling the possibility of an abuse–eating disorder relationship have nearly always been carried out on bulimic samples. In one of the better designed studies of this sort, Steiger and Zanko (1990) ascertained that restricting anorexics recorded lower rates of sexual abuse (6%) than bulimics with no history of anorexia (46%). It may also be significant that several studies, while failing to find evidence of an association between intrafamilial sexual abuse and eating-related concerns, note the presence of a relationship between extrafamilial sexual abuse, typically after age 12, and bulimia (Beckman & Burns, 1990; Hastings & Kern, 1994; Smolak, Levin, & Sullins, 1990).

The one study showing an increased rate of post-age 12 sexual experience with adult relatives notes that in two-thirds of the cases the relative was a cousin (Miller, McCluskey–Fawcett, & Irving, 1993). A plausible alternative explanation of the proposed bulimia–sexual abuse connection is that the bulimic lifestyle, in which sexual acting out and substance misuse predominate (Bulik, 1992), places the individual at an increased risk for sexual victimization. Although it is imperative that the potential effects of sexual victimization not be trivialized, neither should we jump to the conclusion that sexual abuse is a major cause of eating disordered behavior in the absence of firm evidence.

An Alternate View

The social mold theory of addiction is limited by its simplistic approach to cause-and-effect. Any perspective that considers people victims of their social circumstances fails to explain many common occurrences, several of which come immediately to mind. How is it that only one out of a group of several children growing up in the same household develops an eating disorder? Why do certain children fall prey to pressure from a drug using peer group, when nearly all children are exposed to such influence? Where is the effect of the media for those millions of Americans who view advertisements for the state lottery or Super Bowl yet do not wager large sums of money on these events? These and related questions are often ignored by social mold theorists.

While there are no simple answers to the aforementioned questions, there are several ways in which the lifestyle approach accounts for the complexity of human behavior. First, the lifestyle approach asserts that social factors do not function independently, but interact with one other and with various characteristics of the individual. Second, the lifestyle model holds that some people are more resistant to negative social influences than others. Third, the lifestyle perspective makes allowances for reciprocal influences in which behavior is seen as having as much impact on social conditions as social conditions have on behavior (Bandura, 1986).

The reciprocity principle holds that important relationships are bidirectional. Parenting behavior not only influences the actions of a child, the

TABLE 5–1 Studies Probing the Relationship between Childhood Sexual Abuse and Eating Disordered Behavior

Study	Sample		SA Measure	ED Measure	Outcome
Finn, Hartman, Leon & Lawson (1986)	87	F outpatients	SASC + Interview	DSM–III	No relationship between CSA & ED
Bulik, Sullivan, & Rorty (1989)	35	F bulimic patients	Interview	DSM–III	No relationship between CSA & ED
Hall, Tice, Beresford, Wooley, & Hall (1989)	158	inpatients	Interview	DSM–III	SA in 50% of ED SA in 28% non-ED
Baily & Gibbons (1989)	294	F undergraduates	Interview	DSM–III	CSA failed to correlate with bulimia
Calam & Slade (1989)	130	F undergraduates	SLEQ	EAT	CSA correlated with EAT
Beckman & Burns (1990)	340	F undergraduates	SLEQ	BULIT	Bulimics reported more SA after age 12
Smolak & Sullins (1990)	298	F undergraduates	SLEQ	EDI	Correlation between CSA and EDI
Steiger & Zanko (1990)	94 24	F outpatients F normal controls	Interview	DSM–III	30% CSA in ED 33% CSA in psych. control 9% CSA in normal control
Abramson & Lucido (1991)	16 47	F bulimics F nonbulimics	SLEQ	BULIT	69% CSA in bulimics 70% CSA in nonbulimics
Palmer & Oppenheimer (1992)	158 115	F ED outpatients F non-ED outpatients	Interview	DMS–III–R	SA in 31% of ED SA in 50% of non-ED

Study	N	Sample	Abuse Measure	ED Measure	Results
Folsom et al. (1993)	102 49	F ED inpatients F non-Ed inpatients	SLEQ	DSM-III-R	SA in 69% of ED SA in 80% of non-ED
Miller, McCluskey-Fawcett, & Irving (1993)	144	F undergraduates	SLEQ	BITE	Bulimics reported more SA with relative after age 12 (40%) than nonbulimics (29%)
Hastings & Kern (1994)	786	F undergraduates	CSAQ	BULIT	43% CSA in bulimics 14% CSA in subclinical-bulimia 9% CSA in nonbulimics
Kinzl, Traweger, Guenther, & Biebl (1994)	202	F undergraduates	SLEQ	EDI	EDI and CSA did not correlate
Welch & Fairburn (1994)	50 50 100 59	F BN community residents F BN patients F community residents F other diagnoses	Interview	DSM-III-R	SA of 26% in BN SA of 24% in other diagnoses SA of 10% in community residents
Mallinckrodt et al. (1995)	102	F undergraduates	USE	EAT	19% CSA in ED 17% CSA in non-ED

Note: BITE = Bulimic Investigatory Test, Edinburgh (Henderson & Freeman, 1987); BULIT = Bulimia Test (Smith & Thelan, 1984); CSA = childhood sexual abuse; CSAQ = Child Sexual Abuse Questionnaire (Walters et al., 1987); EAT = Eating Attitudes Test (Garner et al., 1982); ED = eating disordered; EDI = Eating Disorder Inventory (Garner et al., 1983); F = female; SA = sexual abuse; SASC = Sexual Abuse Screening Checklist (Finn et al., 1986); SLEQ = Sexual Life Events Questionnaire (Finkelhor, 1979); USE = Unwanted Sexual Events Scale (Russell, 1986).

actions of a child also impact on parenting (Lerner & Spanier, 1978). The majority of studies in the addictions field touching on the issue of reciprocity confirm the bidirectional nature of the behavior–environment relationship. Downs (1987), for instance, unearthed evidence of a reciprocal effect for adolescent drinking and alcohol use in close friends. Farrell and Danish (1993) likewise devised a 3 wave longitudinal panel study to explore reciprocal relations between peer drug associations, emotional restraint, and gateway drug use and determined that a reciprocal effects model provided a significantly better fit for the data than the two alternative unidirectional models they considered.

Reciprocity has also been observed between adolescent substance use and parental support and control (Stice & Barrera, 1995) and between adolescent alcohol use and peer drinking behavior (Curran, Stice, & Chassin, 1997). In one of the few studies to show less than a full reciprocal effect, Newcomb (1994) determined that drug use had a significantly stronger impact on social relations than social relations had on drug use. Taken as a whole, however, research on reciprocity intimates that social conditions and behavior form relationships that are bidirectional and complex rather than unidirectional and simple.

ADDICTION AS CODEPENDENCE

Codependence can be viewed as an addiction unto itself. People intimately involved with an addictively preoccupied person are said to be "addicted" to the relationship they form with this other person. Codependence theorists would point to the fact that Martin's father died of alcohol-related causes after many years of heavy drinking in accounting for Martin's own problems with addictive behavior. They might go on to state that Martin developed a codependent relationship with his alcohol abusing father which, in turn, interfered with his ability to feel good about himself and form healthy relationships. It was Martin's reaction to his father's alcohol abuse, then, that is responsible for his problems with drugs, gambling, and sex.

Since its inception, the codependency construct has steadily grown in popularity to the point where it is now applied to a much wider audience of clients than was initially intended. Although it likely touches on all four elements of the addiction concept (progression, preoccupation, perceived loss of control, and persistence), the codependency construct emphasizes the preoccupation element. This section begins with a review of definitional issues, followed by consideration of the empirical literature on codependency, the criticisms that have been leveled against the concept, and research on the children of alcoholics (COAs) as a group distinct from the children of nonalcoholics.

Defining Codependence

Codependency means different things to different people. To Schaef (1986) codependency signifies a disease process marked by a clearly defined onset, course, and outcome. To Cermack (1984), codependency is an Axis II mixed personality disorder with features similar to those observed in substance misuse, dependent personality disorder, histrionic personality disorder, borderline personality disorder, and post traumatic stress disorder (PTSD). To Beattie (1987) codependency is a disease of relationships in which the person becomes obsessed with controlling the behavior of someone engaged in a substance or activity addiction. These definitions imply that codependency incorporates aspects of both an environmental and host nature. However, lack of consensus on a definition and imprecise terminology have hampered empirical evaluation of the codependency concept.

The argument that anyone who associates with someone actively involved in an addictive behavior is codependent (Schaef, 1986) has led to national estimates reaching upwards of 96% (Wegscheider–Cruse, 1985). It is uncertain whether codependency is the scourge of the 90s or simply a magnet for enterprising mental health professionals who wish to make a name for themselves and build large caseloads. In the section that follows, research addressing the empirical validity of the codependency construct is surveyed.

Empirical Studies on Codependence

The uniformity principle assumes that people classified as codependent form a homogeneous group. However, research support for this assumption is lacking. In an early review of the literature on the wives of problem drinkers, Edwards, Harvey, and Whitehead (1973) found no evidence of increased psychopathology on the part of these women. Edwards and his colleagues, along with Steinglass (1987) in a more recent review, concluded that the wives and families of alcohol abusers are heterogeneous. While Gierymski and Williams (1986) observed greater emotional distress in the wives of alcohol abusers compared to the wives of nonalcohol abusers, wide discrepancies in emotional adjustment were observed in both groups.

Other studies indicate that many of the adjustment difficulties reported by the spouses of problem drinking males reflect these women's attempts to cope with the alcohol-influenced behavior of their husbands (Asher & Brissett, 1988). In some cases, the manner in which the wife of an alcohol abuser copes with her situation can lead to the formation of an independent, rather than codependent, lifestyle (Wiseman, 1975). Furthermore, there is no empirical support for the clinically-based assumption that the wives of problem drinkers psychologically decompensate in response to a reduction in the consumption of alcohol by their partners (Moos, Finney, & Cronkite, 1990).

O'Brien and Gaborit (1992) witnessed increased levels of depression in persons who had formed a relationship with a drug or alcohol abusing intimate, but failed to identify an association between depression and scores on a measure of codependency.

Direct tests of the codependency concept have also proved inconclusive. One common assumption made by codependency theorists is that people who enter into codependent relationships early in life are drawn to the helping professions. However, Clark and Stoffel (1992) surmised that a group of occupational therapy students actually achieved lower codependency scores than a group of health information administration students, despite the fact occupational therapy is more of a helping profession than health information services.

A second study explored the hypothesis that codependents have trouble establishing mature intimate adult relationships. Contrary to the predictions of codependency theorists, the wives of alcohol abusing men were no less likely to have established "best or close" friendships than the wives of non-alcohol abusing men (Troise, 1992).

It has been argued that codependency may serve as a defense against the overly controlling behavior of a substance abusing parent (Schaef, 1986). Probing the relationship between codependency and parenting styles, Fischer and Crawford (1992) determined that male college students raised by authoritarian fathers scored higher on a codependency measure than male college students raised by uninvolved fathers; in this same study, female college students raised by authoritarian fathers achieved higher codependency scores than female college students raised by permissive fathers. However, there were no significant differences between males growing up with authoritarian, democratic, or permissive fathers, or between females growing up with authoritarian, democratic, or uninvolved fathers.

Arranging for female undergraduates to interact with an experimenter portrayed as either exploitative or nurturant, Lyon and Greenberg (1991) determined that students with alcohol abuse in at least one parent volunteered significantly more time to a fictitious study in which the experimenter was characterized as exploitative than when the experimenter was described as nurturant. In contrast, students who reported no history of parental alcohol abuse volunteered more time to the study when the experimenter was described as nurturant. These results, tending to corroborate the codependent view that people raised in an alcohol abusing home seek to assist those they view as exploitative, surfaced irrespective of a subject's liking for the experimenter or estimated level of self-esteem. It seemed, at least to Lyon and Greenberg, that the daughters of problem drinkers perceived the exploitative experimenter as needing nurturance. Although these results support a codependent view of family relationships, it is incumbent upon researchers to pursue this relationship outside the artificial confines of an analog laboratory setting and consider the possibility that this effect is not specific to children growing up in alcohol abusing homes.

Criticisms of the Codependency Concept

A number of criticisms have been leveled against the concept of codependence. First, definitions of codependency tend to be imprecise, broad, and overly inclusive. Overinclusive definitions may achieve face validity by creating a Barnum effect, in that the descriptions are sufficiently vague to be nearly universal. However, this tends to detract from the concept's usefulness. In a penetrating analysis of the codependency concept, Logue, Sher, and Frensch (1992) recorded a Barnum effect in college students asked to evaluate the applicability of an adult children of alcoholics (ACOA) personality profile to themselves and others.

Codependency advocates have also been taken to task for ignoring the complex interaction of variables that apparently encourages preoccupation with an addicted associate, friend, or family member (Watson, 1991).

A third criticism of the codependency construct is that it demonstrates poor conceptual integrity (Gomberg, 1989). Many of the underlying tenets of the codependency model are poorly elaborated, not to mention logically inconsistent (Myer, Peterson, & Stoffel–Rosales, 1991).

Finally, the codependence concept has been rebuked for its white, middle-class bias (Kaminer, 1992) and its supporters chided for pathologizing culturally prescribed female gender role behavior (Gilligan, 1982). As the argument goes, women are socialized to act in a specific way (e.g., nurturing, concerned), but when they conform to these cultural expectations, they are then labeled codependent.

Research Focus: Adult Children of Alcoholics

Investigators scrutinizing the long-term adjustment of children of alcoholics (COAs) and adult children of alcoholics (ACOAs) take a codependent view of addiction. Claudia Black (1981) contends that growing up in an "alcoholic" home nearly always has a devastating effect on a person; so much so that Black characterizes good adjustment on the part of an ACOA as a defense against the person's "true" feelings. Contrasting 409 ACOA patients with 179 controls, Black and her associates (1986) detected increased levels of mistrustfulness, weak emotional expressiveness, and lack of sensitivity to personal needs in the ACOA group. However, this study suffers from sampling bias in that subjects were recruited from advertisements posted in two alcohol or drug journals and one family journal. This study, as is the case with many of the early studies on ACOAs and COAs, relied on an unrepresentative clinical sample.

There is some evidence that what has traditionally been ascribed to the ACOA experience may actually be the result of exposure to ACOA self-help groups (Fiese & Scaturo, 1995). In a study that distinguished between treatment-seeking and nontreatment-seeking ACOAs, Hinson, Becker, Handal, and Katz (1993) observed no differences between ACOA and non-ACOA subjects on a measure of psychological distress, but did note that treatment-seeking subjects, whether ACOA or non-ACOA, recorded significantly higher levels of distress than nontreatment seeking subjects.

Mindful of the problems that can be incurred with the use of clinical samples, more recent investigators have used community and student samples. College students with at least one alcohol abusing parent recall more parental inconsistency (Jarmas & Kazak, 1992) and communication problems (Jones & Houts, 1992) in their families of origin than college students with no parental history of alcohol misuse. The adult offspring of heavy drinkers also report more negative childhood experiences (Velleman & Orford, 1990) and exhibit stronger alcohol expectancies (Sher, Walitzer, Wood, & Brent, 1991) than the offspring of light drinkers.

Research on the transmission of problem drinking across generations, however, is inconclusive. Accordingly, some research studies note an increased rate of subsequent drug misuse on the part of ACOA subjects (Wright & Heppner, 1993), whereas other investigators report being unable to detect a difference in drug use between ACOAs and controls (Alterman, Searles, & Hall, 1989). Harvey and Dodd (1993) witnessed ACOA–control differences on four of 15 personality scales, but were unable to identify any group variations in problem drinking. Using a racially and ethnically mixed community sample of 1,784 adults, Neff (1994) found comparable results for ACOA and control subjects in the quantity and frequency of alcohol consumed. Exploring the effect of ACOA status on eating behavior and drug use, Mintz, Kashubeck, and Tracy (1995) identified only one ACOA–control difference on the Eating Disorder Inventory and no ACOA–control differences in substance use or problem drinking.

Jacob and Leonard (1986) compared children with normal, depressed, and alcohol abusing fathers and found that teacher and parent ratings reflected a propensity for disruptive behavior on the part of children raised by alcohol abusing fathers, although "severe" impairment was rare in this sample. Contrasting the children of alcohol abusing parents with the offspring of nonalcohol abusing parents, Murphy, O'Farrell, Floyd, and Connors (1991) were unable to discern an increased incidence of academic or school conduct problems in the former group.

The daughters of problem drinkers participating in one study were less self-confident, more prone to guilt, and more willing to assume responsibility for others than the daughters of nonalcohol abusers (Jackson, 1985). Although Jackson was unable to detect an increased incidence of depression in his sample of ACOA females, Jarmas and Kazak (1992) identified a trend on the part of the ACOA students that revealed greater introjective depression (guilt-prone, self-critical) and increased reliance on aggressive defenses. ACOA adults drawn from clinical settings are more apt to experience divorce, marital conflict (Kerr & Hill, 1992), sexual dysfunction, and low self-esteem (Currier & Aponte, 1991). However, studies conducted in community settings have failed to document ACOA–control differences in self-esteem (Lyon & Greenberg, 1991; Neff, 1994), distress, or fear of intimacy (Giunta & Compas, 1994). Studying a group of college students, Jones and Kinnick (1995) failed to detect any significant ACOA–control differences on a measure of psychosocial development.

Reviewing personality data on 860 undergraduate students, Berkowitz and Perkins (1988) surmised that measures of impulsivity, anxiety, control, sociability, need for social support, and other-directedness were incapable of discriminating between ACOA subjects and their non-ACOA counterparts. On the other hand, female ACOAs reported greater self-depreciation than female non-ACOAs, whereas male ACOAs reported significantly greater autonomy than their same-sex non-ACOA counterparts.

Findings more congruent with the ACOA hypothesis were recorded in a study by Bensley and Spieker (1992) whereby adult children of alcoholics displayed a tendency to enter into caretaking relationships. Both ACOA subjects and persons raised in families marked by nonsubstance abuse difficulties (divorce, parental death, physical abuse, sexual abuse) scored significantly higher on a personality measure believed to assess one's capacity for creative thinking (Fisher, Jenkins, Harrison, Jesch, 1993).

Clair and Genest (1987) state that whereas a group of young adult ACOAs acknowledged accelerated levels of family conflict and avoidant coping relative to the offspring of nonalcohol abusers, the majority of ACOA subjects were functioning at, or above, the level obtained by children raised in nonalcohol abusing homes. In light of recent studies showing a substantial number of offspring of alcohol abusing parents functioning reasonably well as adults (see Neff, 1994), Black's (1981) assertion that positive outcomes in ACOAs invariably reflect defensiveness seems in error.

Although studies investigating possible ACOA–control differences on various measures of adult functioning have yielded mixed outcomes, studies probing specific tenets of the ACOA hypothesis have produced largely negative results. Woititz (1983), for instance, postulates that ACOAs demonstrate 13 characteristics:

- judge selves without mercy
- feel different from other people
- are extremely loyal
- lie when they could just as easily tell the truth

- overreact to situations over which they have minimal control
- have difficulty following through on a project
- guess at what constitutes normal behavior
- tend to be impulsive
- take selves too seriously
- find it difficult to have fun
- desire approval and affirmation
- become either super responsible or super irresponsible
- have problems with intimate relationships

Seefeldt and Lyon (1992) compared ACOA and non-ACOA college students on 11 personality scales designed to measure 12 of these characteristics and failed to identify a single significant difference.

Lyon and Seefeldt (1995) subsequently replicated the results of the Seefeldt and Lyon study in an independent sample of 139 undergraduate and graduate students using personality scale analogues of all 13 criterion characteristics proposed by Woititz. The outcome was such that Lyon and Seefeldt were unable to discern a single significant group difference, except for one that ran counter to Woititz's predictions. There was also no evidence of a relationship between ACOA status in college students and scores on a 19 item instrument designed to measure Woititz's 13 characteristics (Havey, Boswell, & Romans, 1995).

Wegscheider (1981) offers a view of ACOAs that finds such individuals assuming dysfunctional roles in an attempt to cope with parental alcohol abuse. Some of the more popular roles listed by Wegscheider include the hero role, the scapegoat role, the lost child role, and the mascot. Jenkins, Fisher, and Harrison (1993) studied these roles in a solicited community sample of 174 adults in which 56% of the subjects surveyed reported that they had been raised in homes where at least one parent abused alcohol, 21% of the sample stated that they had been raised in a home marked by problems other than alcohol abuse (divorce, parental death, physical abuse, sexual abuse), and 23% of the sample indicated that they had been raised in a family with no major problems. The bulk of both the ACOA and other problem subjects adopted one or more of the roles proposed by Wegscheider, suggesting that such role adoption is not specific to adult children of alcoholics. ACOAs were also more likely to have adopted two or more specific roles than subjects in the other two conditions, implying reasonable flexibility in the use of social roles.

Studying these same three groups, Fisher, Jenkins, Harrison, and Jesch (1993) identified differences between the ACOA and no problem groups on 9 of 28 scales from the California Personality Inventory (CPI). However, there were no significant CPI scale differences between the ACOA and other problem groups.

The potential debilitating effects of labeling someone an ACOA are illustrated in the results of two studies by Burk and Sher (1990). In the first of these two investigations, 1,570 high school students rated six different roles—male and female typical teenagers, male and female COA teenagers, and male and female mentally ill teenagers—on 11 bipolar adjective pairs. The COAs were rated less favorably than the typical teenagers on all 11 adjectives and received ratings closer to those assigned to the mentally ill teenagers on 9 of the 11 pairs. Burk and Sher conducted a follow-up to this study in which 80 mental health professionals viewed a videotaped interview held with an adolescent whose family background (ACOA or non-ACOA) and current level of functioning (class leader or behavior problem) were manipulated. The mental health professionals participating in this study assigned higher ratings of pathology to the condition in which the adolescent was portrayed as a COA, regardless of the youth's current level of functioning. These data imply that an ACOA or COA label may stigmatize an individual despite evidence of good functioning. There is also some indication that self-definitions may mediate the relationship between ACOA status and psychopathology (Drozd & Dalenberg, 1994). Hence, the effects of labeling on self-definitions may actually result in a self-fulfilling prophesy whereby the person's behavior becomes a reaction to the ACOA or COA label.

An Alternate View

The lifestyle paradigm differs from the social mold perspective in its emphasis on reciprocal relationships. It diverges from the codependency concept in its respect for human resiliency and faith in people's ability to transcend negative life circumstances. The majority of people raised in homes characterized by heavy adult drinking do not develop serious emotional, behavioral, or substance use problems. Such resiliency was chronicled in a longitudinal investigation of 49 youth born on the Hawaiian island of Kauai (Werner, 1986). All of the subjects participating in this study grew up with at least one alcoholic parent and most were raised in an impoverished home environment. However, only 41% of the sample could be classified as suffering from serious coping problems at age 18.

Werner contrasted resilient subjects with problem subjects in an effort to identify the conditions and characteristics that may have protected the former group from developing serious coping difficulties. Whereas socioeconomic status did not differentiate between the groups, resilient adolescents registered higher levels of intelligence, better self-esteem, and had been exposed to fewer episodes of family conflict during the first two years of life than less resilient adolescents. It is important to understand, however, that resiliency may vary by gender as suggested in the results of a study in which independence served as a protective factor for female ACOAs, while financial security served as a protective factor for male ACOAs (Schissel, 1993).

Resilience is not simply a characteristic of the individual, but is also effected by one's current situation and the interaction that forms between a person and his or her environment. Person characteristics that appear to support resilience include intelligence, achievement motivation, responsibility, a positive self-image, a belief in self-help, an internal locus of control (Werner, 1986), and high self-efficacy (Garmezy, 1985). Valentine and Feinauer (1993) uncovered themes of high self-regard, spirituality, internal locus of control, and externalization of blame in the reports of 22 women who successfully overcame childhood sexual abuse. The family, on the other hand, is a major situational facilitator of resiliency.

Students in two urban Chicago high schools were much less likely to have problems with drugs if their parents modeled the socially appropriate use of alcohol and supplied the adolescents with ample amounts of support and supervision (Rhodes & Jason, 1990). The maintenance of family rituals and routines may also protect offspring against future substance abuse difficulties (Bennett, Wolin, & Reiss, 1988). Another family situation variable that may contribute to offspring resiliency is the mother's reaction to an alcohol abusing father. McCord (1988) notes that in situations where mothers expressed high esteem for an alcohol abusing father, a majority of the male offspring abused alcohol themselves in comparison to boys growing up in homes where the mother showed low esteem for her alcohol abusing spouse.

After reviewing the family literature on resiliency, Ullman and Orenstein (1994) concluded that the cross-generational transmission of alcohol abuse is much less likely to occur in situations where the alcohol abusing parent has limited power in the family system. Accordingly, children from low transmitting families tend to disengage from an alcohol abusing parent (Steinglass, 1987) and frequently select a spouse from a nonalcohol abusing family, often attaching themselves instead to the spouse's family (Bennett, Wolin, Reiss, & Teitelbaum, 1987). These findings illustrate the potential impact of the person × situation interaction in the production of resiliency.

Werner (1986) unearthed preliminary evidence of an interactive effect in her own groundbreaking research on this topic. Subjects in the Werner study who enjoyed a temperament that elicited positive attention from a primary caretaker were the individuals most likely to avoid serious coping problems at age 18. Although Werner did not directly test the interaction of these two variables (temperament, behavior of primary caretaker), it is possible that temperament interacted with caretaker behavior rather than either variable being the exclusive cause of the other. An interaction of early medical problems and family environment was observed in the formation of a resilient attitude on the part of children born to methadone-maintained mothers

(Johnson, Glassman, Fiks, & Rosen, 1990). Resiliency, it would seem, is not simply a personal trait or a fortunate set of circumstances, but an active attempt by the individual to influence his or her surrounding environment.

Like biologically and psychologically informed constructions of addiction, sociological constructions are of limited value in forming a consummate understanding of addictive behavior. As discussed in the initial section of this chapter, the environment–behavior relationship may be more complex than is commonly acknowledged by social mold theorists. Furthermore, people may be more resilient in the face of negative environmental experience than codependency advocates are willing to acknowledge. This does not preclude the possibility of simple relationships or the effect of isolated social conditions on behavior. As a comprehensive explanation for addictive behavior, however, sociological constructions of addictive behavior fall short of their mark.

6

ADDICTION AS A
PRAGMATIC CONSTRUCT

Some clinicians believe that addiction can serve a practical or pragmatic function by supporting prevention, intervention, or behavioral maintenance. Proponents of this perspective are less interested in proving the existence of addiction as they are in using it to inspire change. Pragmatic models of addiction accordingly adopt a practical view of addiction. Vaillant (1983), in fact, states that it is unimportant whether or not alcohol abuse is a physical disease, so long as the concept convinces people to seek treatment and insurance companies to pay for the services. According to this thinking, labeling Martin's problem an addiction will encourage him to seek help.

Three pragmatic models of addiction will be reviewed in this chapter. First, we will consider the role of addiction in preventing substance misuse, problem gambling, sexual preoccupation, and eating disorders. Next, we will evaluate the addiction concept as a treatment construct. The treatment section of this chapter will probe the relationship between intervention intensity and client outcome, the value of treatment–client matching, and the notion of a drug cure. The third and final pragmatic construction of addiction explored in this chapter is one that approaches the addiction concept as a maintenance strategy.

PREVENTION

Prevention is normally conceptualized as either primary, secondary, or tertiary. Whereas primary prevention is designed to reduce the prevalence of an identified disorder, secondary prevention seeks to reduce the duration of an existing disorder. Tertiary prevention, on the other hand, is designed to reduce the impairment associated with an established disorder. Prevention follows a medical or mental health definition of addiction by assuming that drug misuse, gambling, sexual preoccupation, and eating-related concerns are mental disorders amenable to prevention. Although prevention programs are less affiliated with the addiction concept than are the biological, psychological, and sociological constructions previously described, they nonetheless conceive of addictive behavior as a condition or disorder that persists despite growing negative consequences. For this reason, they will be treated as models affiliated with the addiction concept.

Early efforts to prevent the misuse of alcohol and other drugs through knowledge acquisition were largely unsuccessful (Elder et al., 1987). Resistance skills training was consequently introduced as an alternative to traditional drug education prevention programs. Gersick, Grady, and Snow (1988) determined that resistance skills training improved decision-making competence and reduced adolescent tobacco smoking, although there was no discernable effect of training on alcohol, marijuana, or other illegal drug usage. Johnson, Pentz, Weber, Dwyer, Baer, MacKinnon, Hanson, and Flay (1990) incorporated drug-resistance training into a community-based program of primary prevention and determined that teenage tobacco and marijuana usage grew at a substantially slower rate than control comparisons, although there were no experimental–control differences in teen alcohol usage.

In a three year study of a primary prevention program targeting preadolescent drug use, Botvin, Baker, Dusenbury, Tortu, and Botvin (1990) found resistance skills training to have a positive effect on cigarette smoking, marijuana inhalation, and immoderate alcohol use. Gaboury and Ladouceur (1993) report that a primary prevention program aimed at preventing problem gambling effectively improved participants' knowledge about gambling and general cognitive coping skills but failed to alter subjects' gambling behavior and attitudes.

Despite the documented superiority of resistance skills training over traditional drug education programs, this training must be generalizable to have any practical value. Hays and Ellickson (1990) addressed this issue in a large group of adolescents evaluated at three points in time. The results of this study showed that while self-efficacy and the perceived pressure to use drugs were generalizable across substances (alcohol, tobacco, and marijuana), there was greater individuality in subjects' perceived ability to rebuff drug offers in different social situations. As might reasonably be anticipated, subjects experienced the least amount of self-efficacy in situations where the social pressure to use drugs was strong. Thus, adolescents taught to resist one type of drug will, in most cases, be able to use these skills to refuse related substances. However, it may be more difficult to generalize these skills to new situations.

The results of the Hays and Ellickson study suggest that it may be necessary to provide students with multiple scenarios and arrange for them to practice their skills across different situations. Hays and Ellickson also recommend including an environmental management component in prevention programs as a way of teaching students to avoid, reduce, and minimize social pressure. Additional evidence from a Norwegian study denotes that prevention programs are more effective when teachers and peer leaders are given specific instructions on how they might present the material to student participants (Wilhelmsen, Laberg, & Klepp, 1994).

Although resistance skills training may be more effective than traditional educational programs, several studies intimate that this approach may be more effective if used as a high risk or secondary prevention strategy. Shope, Dielman, Butchart, Campanelli, and Kloska (1992), for instance, conducted a 26 month follow-up of fifth and sixth graders exposed to a resistance skills curriculum and determined that participating students improved their knowledge on alcohol and other drugs but were no different from controls in their use of substances. A secondary prevention effect was nonetheless found for students who had experienced supervised or unsupervised alcohol use prior to the prevention program.

Killen and associates (1993) obtained results similar to those of Shope et al. in a group of sixth and seventh grade girls randomly assigned to an experimental healthy weight regulation program in which the dangers of unhealthy weight regulation, the benefits of healthy weight regulation, and the importance of resisting the societal message to be thin were emphasized. Relative to girls enrolled in a nonintervention control class, girls exposed to the experimental program increased their knowledge of nutrition and eating disorders but realized no additional benefit in terms of eating attitudes, weight regulation, or body mass. When analyses were restricted to girls with above average weight concerns, however, program participants showed less dramatic increases in body mass than control subjects. These findings suggest that the prevention of addictive behaviors may be more cost effective when applied to high risk populations.

There is some concern that in addition to being less than maximally cost-effective, primary prevention programs may actually promote the very behaviors they are designed to prevent. Both Goodstadt (1984) and Hanson (1982) report that general educational substance abuse programs may encourage drug use. Garner (1985) has raised similar concerns about primary prevention programs for eating disorders. He speculates that such programs may actually inspire young girls to experiment with restricting and purging activities as a means of managing societally induced body image anxiety. Chiordo and Latimer (1983) report that many eating disorder patients acknowledge learning unhealthy weight control practices from family, peer, and media sources. In fact, Murray, Touyz, and Beumont (1990) identified a small group of general population respondents who indicated that they experimented with eating disorder techniques to loose weight after hearing about them in the media. Addictive behaviors may therefore be more practically managed using a high risk or secondary prevention strategy.

Secondary prevention is apparently more cost-effective than primary prevention, and since it is confined to high risk populations, it may produce fewer iatrogenic effects. On the other hand, a case could be made for primary prevention with high frequency behaviors like alcohol consumption. In light of the fact that a medical interpretation of addictive behavior may be less useful than alternative viewpoints, however, the entire prevention scheme may be unnecessary, impractical, and potentially damaging. Before we can seriously entertain this possibility, it is important that we consider the matter of tertiary prevention. This approach, which seeks to reduce the impairment created by an existing disorder, is considered next under the heading of treatment.

TREATMENT

Tertiary prevention or treatment is designed to ameliorate the problems created by an existing disorder. The notion that people lose control over their "addiction" and that control can only be restored by an outside agent is perhaps the cornerstone of treatment constructions of addictive behavior. Consequently, the loss of control element plays a major role in treatment-related interpretations of the addiction concept. Numerous treatments have been proposed for addictive behavior and most reflect the underlying assumptions of their supporting theoretical models. Although a comprehensive review of the treatment literature on addictive behavior is beyond the scope of this book, several topics are of considerable importance to those subscribing to a philosophy of treatment. The present section will focus on three such topics: intervention intensity, client–treatment matching, and the notion of a drug cure.

Intervention Intensity

Mattick and Jarvis (1994) reviewed the literature on the intensity of intervention with substance abusing populations and discovered that more treatment does not necessarily mean better outcomes, that outpatient therapy may be as effective as inpatient treatment, and that day programs may produce results superior to those attained with hospitalization. Table 6–1 lists the controlled studies included in the Mattick and Jarvis review, wherein subjects were randomly assigned to treatment and control conditions, as well as several additional randomized controlled studies not cited in the Mattick and Jarvis paper.

TABLE 6-1 Randomized Controlled Studies on Treatment Intensity and Outcome

Study	Sample	Comparison Groups	Outcome
Length of Treatment			
Pittman & Tate (1969)	250 alcohol abusers	3–6 weeks of inpatient 7–10 days of inpatient	No significant group differences in drinking 1 year after treatment
Willems, Letemendia, & Arroyave (1973)	69 alcohol abusers	82 days of inpatient 20 days of inpatient	No significant group differences in outcome 1 and 2 years later
Mosher, Davis, Mulligan, & Iber (1975)	200 alcohol abusers	30 days of inpatient 9 days of inpatient	No significant group differences in alcohol usage 3 and 6 months after treatment
Edwards et al. (1977)	100 alcohol abusers	6 weeks of treatment 1 session brief advice	No significant group differences in alcohol usage 1 and 2 years after treatment
Smart & Gray (1978)	510 alcohol abusers	1 outpatient contact ≤ 6 months outpatient > 6 months outpatient	More long term subjects remained abstinent after 1 year, but no group differences on other measures of adjustment
Page & Schaub (1979)	86 alcohol abusers	5 weeks of treatment 3 weeks of treatment	No significant group differences in drinking behavior
Miller, Gribskov, & Mortell (1981)	31 problem drinkers	eval + feedback session eval + 10 sessions	Significant reductions in drinking at 3 months for both groups but no group differences
Rounsaville, Glazer, Wilbur, Weissman, & Kleber (1983)	73 opiate abusers	drug counseling + IP drug counseling	No significant group differences in opiate usage
Walker, Donovan, Kivlahan, & Leary (1983)	245 alcohol abusers	2 counseling sessions 7 counseling sessions	No significant group differences 3–9 months after treatment

(Continued)

103

TABLE 6-1 *Continued*

Study	Sample	Comparison Groups	Outcome
Woody et al. (1983)	110 opiate abusers	counseling + SET counseling + CBT counseling	Subjects in two more intensive interventions improved more than those in counseling alone
Robertson et al. (1986)	37 problem drinkers	CBT for 9 sessions 3–4 sessions of advice	Subjects in more intensive intervention displayed lower consumption levels and more abstinence days than subjects in brief intervention after 15 months
Chick, Ritson, Connaughton, Stewart, & Chick (1988)	152 alcohol abusers	"extended" treatment 1 session of advice	Extended treatment clients were better functioning 2 years after treatment; no group differences in abstinence
Zweben, Pearlman, & Li (1988)	116 couples with one alcohol abusing member	conjoint therapy 1 session of advice	Both groups showed significant improvement in drinking-related outcome, but no significant differences between groups
Baer et al. (1992)	132 alcohol abusers	6 weeks of treatment 1 session of advice	No significant group differences in self-reported drinking 2 years after treatment
Project Match Research Group (1997)	952 alcohol abusers	CBT for 12 sessions TSF for 12 sessions MET for 4 sessions	Significant reductions in the number of drinking days and drinks per day for all three groups, but no significant differences between groups
Inpatient versus Outpatient			
Edwards & Guthrie (1966)	40 alcohol abusers	8 weeks of inpatient 8 sessions of outpatient	Slight advantage for outpatient treatment
Stein, Newton, & Bowman (1975)	58 alcohol abusers	25 day inpatient outpatient treatment	No significant group differences in alcohol usage or adjustment 13 months after treatment

Study	Sample	Conditions	Outcome
Smart, Finley, & Funston (1977)	72 alcohol abusers	inpatient treatment outpatient treatment	50% of outpatients experienced good outcomes after 6 months compared to 25% of inpatients
Wilson, White, & Lange (1978)	90 alcohol abusers	inpatient hospitalization community program	Community program subjects displayed fewer signs of alcohol abuse than inpatient subjects after 5 months; no group differences after 10 and 15 months
Gossop, Johns, & Green (1986)	60 opiate abusers	inpatient treatment outpatient treatment	81% of the inpatients became drug-free; 17% of the outpatients became drug-free
Potamianos, Meade, North, Townsed, & Peters (1986)	151 alcohol abusers	inpatient treatment community program	Subjects in community program consumed less alcohol than subjects in hospital program
Chapman & Huygens (1988)	113 alcohol abusers	6 weeks of inpatient 6 weeks of outpatient 1 session of advice	No significant group differences in alcohol usage 6 and 18 months after treatment
Walsh et al. (1991)	227 alcohol abusers	inpatient treatment AA attendance	Inpatient treatment superior to AA in reducing alcohol intake and drug use; no significant group differences on job-related outcome measures
Hospital versus Day Program			
McLachlan & Stein (1982)	100 alcohol abusers	4 weeks of inpatient 4 week day program	No significant group differences in alcohol usage, but day program subjects used fewer subsequent medical services
Longabaugh et al. (1983)	174 alcohol abusers	behavioral inpatient behavioral day program	No significant group differences in alcohol usage 6 months after treatment, but day program subjects had more abstinent days 24 months after treatment

Note: IP = Interpersonal Psychotherapy; SET = Supportive Expressive Therapy; CBT = Cognitive Behavioral Therapy; TSF = Twelve-Step Facilitation; MET = Motivational Enhancement Therapy; AA = Alcoholics Anonymous.

The eating disorders literature also implies that intervention intensity may have little bearing on treatment outcome. In one of the better designed studies on this issue, Hall and Crisp (1987) randomly assigned 30 anorectic outpatients to 12 sessions of individual and family therapy or 12 sessions of dietary advice. Both groups displayed weight increases but only the gains of the dietary advice group were statistically significant. The psychotherapy group, on the other hand, achieved superior outcomes on measures of social and sexual adjustment.

Research failing to confirm evidence of a link between treatment intensity and outcome can be interpreted in one of two ways. Either all forms of intervention are equally effective or all forms of intervention are equally ineffective. Given the fact that several studies show intervention subjects (regardless of intensity) improving significantly more than no-treatment control subjects (see Timko, Moos, Finney, & Moos, 1994), the first conclusion—that interventions of varying degrees of intensity are equally effective—seems more justified.

Client–Treatment Matching

According to Hester and Miller (1988), two attitudes have traditionally inhibited research on client–treatment matching. One attitude reflects a belief in the uniformity principle whereby all cases of substance misuse or addictive involvement are viewed as sharing a common underlying etiology, thus eliminating the need for alternative interventions. For clinicians subscribing to the uniformity principle, the goal becomes identifying the one "true" universally effective intervention.

Program dogmatism is a second attitude that hinders research on client–treatment matching. It is often the case that once a program decides upon a treatment philosophy, alternative formulations and techniques are abandoned, rejected, or forgotten. By shutting the door on creativity and innovation, this attitude limits our ability to effectively intervene with individuals who function in a variety of different lifestyles. Uniformity beliefs and program dogmatism must consequently be challenged if research on client–treatment matching is to realize its full potential in terms of advancing our understanding of the dynamic, yet elusive, concept of change.

In an early study on client–treatment matching in a substance abusing population, Orford, Oppenheimer, and Edwards (1976) ascertained that a group of chronic (gamma) alcoholics enjoyed better 2-year outcomes if randomly assigned to treatment, whereas nongamma alcohol abusers fared better if randomly assigned to a brief advice condition. Using a somewhat larger and more recently acquired cohort of subjects sampled from this same London hospital, Edwards and Taylor (1994) failed to find evidence of a client–treatment interaction when gamma and nongamma alcohol abusers were randomly assigned to treatment and brief advice.

Classifying alcohol abusing subjects into Type A (later onset, less severe symptomatology, weak family history of substance misuse, fewer psychiatric complications) and Type B (earlier onset, more severe symptomatology, strong family history of substance misuse, more psychiatric complications), a group of investigators from the University of Connecticut School of Medicine determined that Type A patients achieved better results when randomly assigned to interactional insight-oriented therapy, whereas type B patients appeared to benefit more from cognitive–behavioral therapy (Litt, Babor, Del Boca, Kadden, & Cooney, 1992).

McLachlan (1972) predicted that alcohol abusing clients possessing low conceptual levels would respond better to structured directive interventions, while high conceptual clients would respond better to unstructured nondirective interventions. Clients properly matched (i.e., low conceptual level-structured intervention; high conceptual level-unstructured intervention) on both treatment and aftercare evidenced a 71% rate of recovery compared to 38% for clients mismatched on both treatment and aftercare.

Adding a confrontational group therapy component to a standard alcohol abuse intervention, Annis and Chan (1983) discovered that the additional intervention assisted clients with high self-esteem but detracted from the treatment experiences of low self-esteem clients. Miller, Benefield, and Tonigan (1993) determined that problem drinkers who viewed the misuse of alcohol as a "bad habit" experienced better outcomes when paired with an empathic therapist than when paired with a confrontational therapist. Problem drinkers who viewed alcohol misuse as a disease failed to demonstrate any differences in outcome in response to therapist style.

Outcomes may also vary by drug of choice or primary drug of abuse. Psychedelic drug users in one study did equally well in individual or family therapy, but fared more poorly in a confrontational milieu, whereas opiate and stimulant abusing clients profited more from the confrontational approach than from either individual or family therapy (Vaglum & Fossheim, 1980).

A group of investigators under the direction of Demaris Rohsenow studied the effects of education, anxiety, and craving on response to communication skills training and cognitive–behavioral mood management. The results of this study showed that alcohol abusing clients with less education, more anxiety, and greater craving for alcohol benefitted more from the behaviorally-oriented communication skills training, whereas clients with more education, less anxiety, and fewer urges to drink responded equally well to communication skills training and cognitive–behavioral mood management (Rohsenow et al., 1991).

McClellan, Woody, Luborsky, O'Brien, and Druley (1983) report that alcohol and drug abusing clients with less severe psychopathology responded better to outpatient therapy, while clients with more severe psychopathology profited more from inpatient therapy. In contrast, Friedman, Granick, Kreisher, and Terras (1993) found that substance abusing adolescents with severe social, occupational, and family problems achieved greater benefit from longer term outpatient counseling than from a shorter, but more intensive, course of inpatient hospitalization.

Social support correlates impressively with long-term outcome in persons released from substance abuse treatment (Booth, Russell, Soucek, & Laughlin, 1992; Higgins, Budney, Bickel, & Badger, 1994). Furthermore, the addition of a social support component to a televised smoking cessation relapse prevention program was found to significantly enhance overall program effectiveness (Gruder et al., 1993).

Longabaugh, Beattie, Noel, Stout, and Malloy (1993) appended a relationship enhancement component to a cognitive–behavioral intervention offered to alcohol abusers. A client's investment in social relations was found to moderate the strength of the relationship between posttreatment social support and alcohol involvement in a one year follow-up. Clients with high social investment did well when posttreatment social support was available and poorly when posttreatment social support was lacking, whereas clients with low social investment failed to derive any discernable benefit from posttreatment social support. Although a three-way interaction involving investment, support, and treatment failed to attain significance, an interaction did arise between support and treatment whereby clients recording high levels of posttreatment support did equally well with either a cognitive–behavioral protocol or a relationship enhancement of this protocol and clients receiving low posttreatment support benefitted more from the cognitive–behavioral program than the relationship enhanced version of this program.

Project MATCH has perhaps been the most ambitious attempt to date to seek an equitable match between alcohol abusing clients and various different interventions. Subjects were recruited from nine clinical research units affiliated with multiple treatment facilities and randomly assigned to one of three outpatient or aftercare conditions: 12 sessions of Cognitive–Behavioral Therapy (CBT), 12 sessions of Twelve-Step Facilitation (TSF), or 4 sessions of Motivational Enhancement Therapy (MET). Some of the matching variables included in this study were level of alcohol involvement, conceptual level, motivation, psychiatric severity, sociopathy, and the Type A–B typology. Although clients in all three conditions displayed significant reductions in drinking behavior over the course of treatment and at follow-up, only one matching effect surfaced: specifically, clients low in psychiatric severity demonstrated better outcomes in TSF as opposed to CBT (Project MATCH Research Group, 1997).

The Drug Cure

Medications are normally administered to persons with addictive disorders for one of four reasons. First, medications may be used to assist with the amelioration of withdrawal symptomatology. Second, they may be prescribed to reduce a person's craving for drugs. Third, they may be used to manage coexisting psychopathology. Fourth, they may be seen as a direct intervention for addictive involvement. It is to this fourth purpose that the present section speaks.

As was explained in Chapter 4, drugs that specifically block serotonin reuptake (i.e., fluoxetine, clomipramine) appear to be no more effective than placebo in the treatment of addictive behavior, with the possible exception of bulimia. Three additional chemical compounds often prescribed for addictively involved persons will be considered in this section. These chemical interventions include disulfiram for alcohol abuse, methadone for opiate abuse, and antiandrogens for sexual offending.

Disulfiram and Alcohol Abuse

Disulfiram or Antabuse is a drug that inhibits the action of aldehyde dehydrogenase and other liver enzymes. This, in turn, contributes to an accumulation of acetaldehyde in the body. As the reader may recall from discussions taking place in Chapter 3, acetaldehyde elicits facial flushing, nausea, vomiting, tachycardia, and hypotension. Physicians state that to achieve this effect in the presence of alcohol requires a standard maintenance dosage of 250 mg of disulfiram per day, although it has been documented that some individuals are still able to drink at this level (Banys, 1988). For this reason, some individuals are maintained on a daily dose of disulfiram that can be as high as 750 mg per day. Clients who are hypersensitive to the effects of disulfiram may be unable to tolerate the standard maintenance dose and may have to have their daily dosage level lowered to 125 mg.

It should be noted, although it is hardly surprising, that alcohol abusers who receive unsupervised disulfiram are generally less compliant than those who take disulfiram under supervised conditions (Brewer, 1986). In situations where supervision is unavailable or unreliable, some physicians prefer the use of subcutaneous implants of disulfiram tablets. However, this approach is of questionable utility, in part because of wide individual variations in the rate of absorption (Liskow & Goodwin, 1987).

Having a spouse or other family member supervise a client's ingestion of disulfiram is perhaps the most effective means of achieving compliance. Azrin (1976) reports that familial supervised disulfiram treatment significantly improved the efficacy of the community reinforcement approach with alcohol abusing clients. Another study chronicled a drop in absenteeism (9.8% to 1.8%) for alcohol abusing Employee Assistance Program (EAP) participants prescribed supervised disulfiram which then rose to 6.7% when the disulfiram was discontinued (Robichaud, Strickler, Bigelow, & Liebson, 1979). Furthermore, clients enrolled in outpatient alcohol abuse treatment with supervised disulfiram enjoyed better outcomes than a control group receiving supervised vitamin C (Chick et al., 1992).

Despite the positive results that have been recorded with supervised administration of disulfiram, this medication should not be viewed as a panacea. Besides the problem of compliance, disulfiram sometimes produces serious side effects, enters into interaction with other drugs, and can even promote a craving for alcohol (Liskow & Goodwin, 1987). Some of the more commonly reported side effects of disulfiram treatment include mild sedation, increased serum cholesterol, hepatotoxicity, ataxia, and depression. Disulfiram may also elicit a mild response to certain alcohol-sensitizing chemicals and drugs and therefore reduce the effectiveness of other pharmacotherapies (Banys, 1988).

Perhaps the greatest limitation of disulfiram in the treatment of alcohol abuse is a general lack of evidence for its long-term effectiveness. Sellers, Naranjo, and Peachey (1981) report that controlled trials of disulfiram show no consistent improvement in drinking status over time. The results of a study conducted in several VA medical centers suggest that disulfiram treatment, as conventionally practiced, is no more effective in the long run than drug counseling (Fuller et al., 1986).

Studies showing differential effects suggest that disulfiram is more effective with clients over the age of 40 who are socially stable, cognitively intact, not depressed, tolerant of dependency, and motivated to attend AA meetings (Banys, 1988). However, these are also characteristics that portend good future outcomes with psychotherapy and other forms of intervention. For this reason, it is uncertain whether these characteristics are specific indicators of disulfiram response or simply good general prognostic signs.

Methadone and Heroin Abuse

Methadone hydrochloride is an organic opioid compound sometimes used as a substitute for heroin. What some clinicians fail to realize is that methadone promotes an even stronger physical dependency than heroin. It is employed in the treatment of heroin abuse because it can be administered in liquid form and presumably exerts a less profound effect on a person's behavioral functions, thereby permitting more normal activity over the course of a day. Although methadone was initially introduced as a way of weaning clients off heroin, it is now more generally used as a long term maintenance strategy. It is not uncommon to find clients who have been maintained on methadone for a decade or longer.

Dosage levels are of major consequence in determining the efficacy of chemical intervention, and methadone is no exception. Heroin abusers taking less than 46 mg of methadone a day are five times more likely to use illicit opiates than heroin abusers ingesting more than 71 mg of methadone a day (Ball & Ross, 1991). This outcome finds cross-national support in a study of Australian opiate abusers in which heroin use was 2.2 times more prevalent in patients prescribed a 40 mg daily dose of methadone relative to patients receiving 80 mg of methadone daily (Caplehorn, Bell, Kleinbaum, & Gerbski, 1993). The potential hazards associated with methadone maintenance need to be more fully elaborated, however, before its ultimate utility can be determined.

Lippas, Jenner, and Vicente (1988) have reviewed the primary arguments in favor of methadone maintenance and conclude that methadone maintenance, like disulfiram treatment, suffers from several noteworthy limitations. First, these authors recount a growing number of registered heroin addicts in England despite the increased availability of methadone and a rising rate of cocaine abuse in clients attending methadone maintenance clinics for heroin abuse in the United States. As to whether methadone maintenance leads to reduced mortality, Lippas et al. call attention to a 1977 report in the *New York Times* showing a greater number of deaths attributable to methadone than to heroin in the New York metropolitan area.

Improved social adjustment and reduced crime are additional perceived benefits of methadone maintenance. However, studies continue to document high levels of social and occupational maladjustment in methadone-maintained heroin abusers (Kosten, Rounsaville, & Kleber, 1987). Also, while much of the evidence suggests that heroin abusers commit fewer crimes when on methadone (Hunt, Lipton, Goldsmith, Strug, and Spunt, 1985), the results of at least one study suggest that crime may increase during methadone maintenance if other forms of support are not also provided (Boudouris, 1976). This latter finding suggests that methadone maintenance alone may be insufficient unless accompanied by additional methods of psychosocial intervention.

Antiandrogens and Sex Offending
Antiandrogens block receptors in the brain and various target organs that appear to regulate sexual response and behavior. Two antiandrogens in particular have been used in the treatment of sex offenders: cyproterone acetate (CPA) and medroxyprogesterone acetate (MPA), better known as Depo Provera. Cooper (1981) reports that relative to a placebo, CPA reduced plasma testosterone, sexual arousal, and sex drive in nine "hypersexual" males. Bradford (1985) further notes that CPA may effectively reduce sex offender recidivism. There is also some indication that antiandrogens like

CPA reduce deviant sexual practices without effecting normative sexual behavior. In this regard, Bradford and Pawlak (1993) determined that CPA successfully reduced pedophilic sexual interest without adversely affecting arousal to adult mutually consenting heterosexual interactions.

Studies comparing paraphiliac patients who agree to take MPA with those who refuse (e.g., Meyer, Cole, & Emory, 1992) show that those who take MPA suffer a lower rate of recidivism. However, these studies typically fail to control for important group differences in motivation and length of follow-up. Cooper, Sandu, Losztyn, and Cernovsky (1992) found both CPA and MPA efficacious in reducing sexual thoughts and fantasies, early morning erections, masturbatory activities, and sexual frustration in a small group of pedophiles. An Australian study, however, failed to find MPA any more effective than imaginal desensitization in the treatment of 30 sex offenders randomly assigned to one of three conditions: Imaginal Desensitization, MPA, Imaginal Desensitization + MPA (McConaghy, Blaszczynski, & Kidson, 1988).

One of the major drawbacks to antiandrogen therapy with sexually preoccupied clients is compliance. Many clients discontinue antiandrogen treatment after experiencing its irritating and potentially harmful side effects. Reduced volume of ejaculate, weight gain, fatigue, and mild depression have been reported with short term use and gall bladder problems, diabetes, hypertension, and possible thromboembolic difficulties with long term use of the antiandrogens (Cooper et al., 1992). Whereas side effects have been documented in some research centers and not others, they are of concern to clients, and as such, limit compliance with treatment. The use of antiandrogens with sex offenders raises additional legal and ethical issues (Melella, Travin, & Cullen, 1989). Moreover, there are wide individual variations in client response to antiandrogen therapy. Just as some individuals drink while on disulfiram or inject heroin while on methadone, there are sex offenders who have relapsed while on antiandrogens.

The three medications described above may hold some potential utility in intervening with persons engaged in specific addictive behaviors. However, they should not be viewed as a "cure" for the alcohol abusing, heroin misusing, or sexual offending client. One alternative would be to eliminate terms like addiction, cure, and treatment from our vocabularies and replace them with such alternatives as lifestyle, coping, and change. Some of these issues are addressed in the next section on maintenance.

MAINTENANCE STRATEGIES

Maintenance strategies are designed to preserve changes achieved through formal intervention. It is becoming increasingly apparent that expanding the number of treatment contacts may yield few additional benefits beyond one's base intervention (Hall, 1980). As the section on intensity of intervention implies, "less" intervention is often as effective as "more" intervention. Consequently, it may make more sense to focus our attention on behavioral maintenance. The two maintenance strategies that will be described in this section are relapse prevention and self-help programming.

Of all the models reviewed in Chapters 3 through 6, the relapse prevention approach is probably the one that is least affiliated with the addiction concept, although it may place a slight emphasis on the preoccupation element. The self-help model described in this section is based on the 12 steps of Alcoholics Anonymous and Narcotics Anonymous. In contrast to the relapse prevention model, the 12-step approach is strongly allied with the addiction concept, emphasizing both the progression and loss of control elements.

Relapse Prevention

The relapse prevention model is designed to enhance the maintenance of initial treatment gains by furnishing clients with skills and cognitive strategies useful in anticipating and coping with problems that often arise during the posttreatment or follow-up period (Marlatt & Gordon, 1985). There are three primary phases of relapse prevention. The first phase requires therapists to assist clients in identifying high risk situations. The reader should note that high risk situations are those that threaten a person's sense of control, thereby increasing his or her chances of lapsing or relapsing into addictive behavior.

The second phase of the relapse prevention model entails teaching clients to anticipate and manage high risk situations via skills training, modeling, practice, feedback, and a technique known as relapse rehearsal. With relapse rehearsal the individual imagines that a slip or lapse has already occurred and goes about enacting coping behaviors designed to minimize the preliminary damage created by the relapse.

The third and final phase of relapse prevention involves developing global self-control strategies designed to promote a healthy lifestyle and aid the client in identifying and coping with the covert precipitants of relapse. The relapse prevention model uses a biopsychosocial definition of addiction (Zucker & Gomberg, 1986) in which addictive behavior is held to be a complex function of interacting biological, psychological, and sociological forces.

Research addressing the utility of the relapse prevention model in alcohol abusing populations has been generally supportive of the model's underlying assumptions and tenets. Allsop and Saunders (1989), for instance, randomly assigned alcohol abusing clients to performance-based relapse prevention, verbally-mediated relapse prevention, and a treatment-as-usual group. A six month follow-up revealed that the verbally-mediated relapse prevention and treatment-as-usual groups reported twice as many heavy drinking days as subjects in the performance-based relapse prevention group. The results of this study also demonstrate that enhancing initial commitment to change and boosting client self-efficacy can act to further reduce drinking behavior.

Relapse prevention is particularly valuable in situations where specific high risk situations can be identified. Annis (1988) classified the risk profiles of 83 alcohol abusing clients as either generalized (similar drinking risk across eight drinking risk situations) or differentiated (greater drinking risk for some situations than others) and randomly assigned subjects to either a relapse prevention program or traditional outpatient counseling. The outcome of this study revealed that while clients possessing generalized risk profiles did equally well in either relapse prevention training or traditional counseling, clients with differentiated risk profiles performed significantly better in the relapse prevention program.

Application of the relapse prevention model to substances other than alcohol has met with mixed results. Cinciripini, Lapitsky, Wallfisch, Mace, and Nezami (1994) compared a cognitive behavioral program for smoking cessation that incorporated a strong relapse prevention component and a control group that received the American Cancer Society's "I Quit Kit." Follow-up evaluations conducted 6 and 12 months after the intervention revealed abstinence rates of 53% and 41%, respectively, for subjects participating in the cognitive behavioral intervention and 6% for control subjects during both follow-ups. Stephens, Roffman, and Simpson (1994), on the other hand, failed to discern a significant difference in outcome in a controlled comparison of relapse prevention for marijuana dependence and a standard social support group intervention. Both groups nonetheless showed improvement over baseline.

Wells, Peterson, Gainey, Hawkins, and Catalano (1994) randomly assigned cocaine abusers to a relapse prevention or 12-step intervention and discovered that both groups showed similar improvement in subsequent use of cocaine but that 12-step participants demonstrated a significantly greater reduction in alcohol usage. Cocaine abusers randomly assigned to relapse prevention or general clinical management displayed comparable reductions in usage and similar improvements in personal adjustment, although the relapse prevention program was significantly more effective than general clinical management in assisting high severity cases (Carroll et al., 1994).

The relapse prevention model has also been applied to nonsubstance forms of addictive behavior. Bujold, Ladouceur, Sylvain, and Boisvert (1994) effectively used relapse prevention to intervene with three problem gamblers. A multiple baseline design revealed that by the end of treatment all three subjects had terminated their involvement with gambling and had achieved a sense of control over themselves and their gambling.

Pithers and Cumming (1989) successfully used relapse prevention principles with 167 sex offending clients (147 pedophiles, 20 rapists). Fifteen percent of the rapists enrolled in the program committed an additional sexual assault during a 6-year follow-up, as opposed to 3% of the pedophiles. These findings may reflect variations in the base rate of relapse between these two offense categories or signal that the relapse prevention model is more effective with pedophiles than rapists. Pithers and Cumming further discerned that significantly fewer of their pedophiles relapsed relative to a group of pedophiles graduating from a state hospital-based milieu therapy program (3% versus 18%). Their rapists also relapsed at a lower rate than rapists from the state hospital, but the difference failed to achieve statistical significance (15% versus 26%).

Wilson, Rossiter, Kleifield, and Lindholm (1986) found relapse prevention strategies useful in augmenting the efficacy of a group cognitive–behavioral intervention for bulimia nervosa, although it is uncertain which of the program components (cognitive–behavioral skills training, exposure to food-related cues, prevention of the vomiting response, or relapse prevention) accounted for the positive outcomes obtained in this study.

Self-Help Programming

Self-help groups provide a forum in which people struggling with a common problem share their individual perceptions and offer each other support and guidance. Alcoholics Anonymous (AA), perhaps the most famous self-help group for addictive behavior, has over 36,000 active local chapters world-wide (Alcoholics Anonymous World Services, 1987). AA is so prolific that it has given birth to a new generation of self-help groups, many of which adhere to the 12-step philosophy. The 12 steps of AA are outlined in Table 6–2. Related self-help groups, like Gamblers Anonymous, Sexaholics Anonymous, and Overeaters Anonymous, follow these same 12 steps but supplant the term alcohol with gambling, sex, and overeating, respectively.

The 12-step tradition of anonymity has complicated research on AA and other self-help groups, although isolated studies suggest that attendance and abstinence in AA (Harrison & Hoffman, 1987), and attendance and self-esteem in Narcotics Anonymous (NA) (Christo & Sutton, 1994), may be linked. It should be noted, however, that because the Christo and Sutton study was cross-sectional in nature, the results may simply reflect the fact that people with low self-esteem are more apt to drop out of NA than persons with high self-esteem. Moreover, follow-ups conducted on alcohol abusers randomly assigned to AA or a control condition revealed that subjects

TABLE 6–2   The Twelve Steps of Alcoholics Anonymous

1. We admitted we were powerless over alcohol—that our lives had become unmanageable.
2. Came to believe that a Power greater than ourselves could restore us to sanity.
3. Made a decision to turn our will and our lives over to the care of God *as we understood Him.*
4. Made a searching and fearless moral inventory of ourselves.
5. Admitted to God, to ourselves and to another human being the exact nature of our wrongs.
6. Were entirely ready to have God remove all these defects of character.
7. Humbly asked Him to remove our shortcomings.
8. Made a list of all persons we had harmed, and became willing to make amends to them all.
9. Made direct amends to such people whenever possible, except when to do so would injure them or others.
10. Continued to take personal inventory and when we were wrong promptly admitted it.
11. Sought through prayer and meditation to improve our conscious contact with God, *as we understood Him,* praying only for knowledge of His will for us and the power to carry that out.
12. Having had a spiritual awakening as the result of these steps, we tried to carry this message to alcoholics, and to practice these principles in all our affairs.

Source: The Twelve Steps are reprinted with permission of Alcoholics Anonymous World Services, Inc. Permission to reprint the Twelve Steps does not mean that A.A. has reviewed or approved the contents of this publication, nor that A.A. agrees with the views expressed herein. A.A. is a program of recovery from alcoholism *only*—use of the Twelve Steps in connection with programs and activities which are patterned after A.A., but which address other problems, or in any other non-A.A. context, does not imply otherwise.

in the AA condition participated in more binge drinking episodes at three months and were no less likely to drink than control subjects at 12 months (Brandsma, Maultsby, & Welsh, 1980). Because of a lack of controlled research on this issue it is difficult to know if 12-step programs contribute directly to recovery or whether people committed to recovery simply remain in 12-step groups longer than those with less commitment.

In that the efficacy of self-help programming for addictive behavior has yet to be established, attempts to understand the working ingredients of self-help programs may be premature. Speculation on this issue nevertheless abounds. Knight, Wollert, Levy, Frame, and Padgett (1980) distributed questionnaires to several different self-help groups (e.g., AA, OA, Parents Anonymous) and discovered that participants viewed social support as the single most important feature of these groups. A follow-up study was conducted which revealed that these self-help groups relied on supportive, expressive, and insight-oriented comments to facilitate change, while minimizing direct confrontation (Wollert, Levy, & Knight, 1982). The formation of a collective group identity (Jurik, 1987), encouragement of an external locus of control for addictive behavior (Bridgman & McQueen, 1987), deliverance from long term isolation (Khantzian & Mack, 1994), and the predictability and regularity of self-help meetings (Hopson & Beaird–Spiller, 1995) have also been cited as possible mediators of the presumed success of AA and other 12-step self-help groups.

In one of the more methodologically sound studies on change as a result of self-help participation, Snow, Prochaska, and Rossi (1994) surmised that AA members reporting positive change went through a process similar to persons who abandoned an alcohol abusing lifestyle on their own. In both cases the change process appeared to proceed through stages (i.e., precontemplation, contemplation, action, and maintenance) and encompassed many of the same strategies (i.e., stimulus control, behavioral management, helping relationships, and consciousness raising).

The 12-step model relies on a spiritual disease conceptualization of addictive behavior. As such, it has links to the medical disease model of addiction, but also has its own separate identity (see Miller & Kurtz, 1994). By virtue of its similarity to the medical disease model, the 12-step approach to addictive behavior suffers from some of the same limitations that plague the physical disease model (i.e., poor operationalization of terms, lack of empirical support). Additionally, there is evidence that 12-step self-help groups experience relatively high rates of attrition. Chappell (1993) notes that approximately half of all new members to AA drop out within the first three months, while Stewart and Brown (1988) report that nearly half of all new members to Gamblers Anonymous (GA) drop out by the third meeting.

The fact that many clients have trouble accepting the quasi-religious tenor of this approach has necessitated alternatives to the 12-step philosophy. Rational Recovery is one such alternative. The goal of Rational Recovery, a self-help program modeled after Albert Ellis' (1970) rational emotive approach to intervention, is to identify and challenge the irrational beliefs that support a person's problematic relationship with substances. Although not nearly as celebrated or visible as AA, Rational Recovery continues to attract adherents and has proven itself an effective maintenance strategy (Galanter, Egelko, & Edwards, 1993). It would seem that self-help groups are a potentially effective means of maintaining change, although they require empirical evaluation and expansion beyond the narrow boundaries of the 12-step tradition.

RESEARCH FOCUS: THERAPIST EFFECTS

Crits–Christoph, Beebe, and Connolly (1990) argue that therapists should be specified as "random" factors rather than as "fixed" factors in psychotherapy research. These authors therefore recommend that the error term for studies investigating the relative efficacy of divergent treatment modalities be based on therapists rather than clients. However, in a review of 33 articles on treatment outcome published during the mid-1970s, Martindale (1978) identified only one study that included the therapist variable as a random factor. Reviewing more recent studies on treatment outcome, Crits–Christoph and Mintz (1991) report that most investigators continue to ignore this issue. It would appear that many researchers continue to remain ignorant of the fact that therapist variation impacts strongly on treatment efficacy.

Rather than treating therapists as error variance, an even more productive strategy may be to incorporate them into the design as an independent variable. Lambert (1989) reports that certain therapist characteristics may be more strongly predictive of treatment outcome than either specific therapeutic techniques or the theoretical orientation of the therapist. This echoes the conclusions of an earlier review that uncovered wide discrepancies in outcome within as well as between therapists, and greater association between therapist qualities and outcome than between types of treatment and outcome (Luborsky et al., 1986).

Research specific to substance abuse counseling shows that individual drug abuse counselors achieve differing levels of success with clients (McLellan, Woody, Luborsky, & Goehn, 1988). Miller, Taylor, and West (1980), for instance, determined that therapist empathy accounted for over two-thirds of the variance in outcomes obtained by a group of problem drinkers, although there was no connection between the experience level of the nine paraprofessional counselors participating in this study and client response. One and two year follow-ups of these clients revealed that therapist empathy continued to explain one-half and one-quarter of the variance in client outcome respectively (Miller & Baca, 1983).

Valle (1981) randomly assigned 247 persons admitted to an inpatient alcohol treatment unit to one of eight counselors who had previously provided answers to a series of stimulus statements. The clients of counselors whose responses to the stimulus statements reflected high interpersonal functioning recorded significantly lower rates of relapse 6, 12, 18, and 24 months later. After randomly assigning 110 methadone maintained heroin abusers to 18 drug counselors and nine psychotherapists, Luborsky, McLellan, Woody, O'Brien, and Auerbach (1985) witnessed a moderate relationship between client outcome and therapist adjustment, skill, and attitude. However, the strongest predictor of outcome in this study was the quality of the client–therapist relationship. Miller, Benefield, and Tonigan (1993) report that the more a therapist confronted problem drinking clients with sarcasm, incredulity, contradictions, and head-on disputes, the more alcohol the client consumed.

The relationship between therapist characteristics and treatment outcome is vaguely reminiscent of ancient views on shamanism. Found primarily in primitive hunting and gathering societies, the shaman performs a variety of different community functions: medicine man, healer, ritualist, spiritual medium, and keeper of cultural myths (Walsh, 1989). It is speculated that psychotherapy may be a modern version of shamanism. In primitive societies, the shaman helps members of the village accept a generalized cultural mythical world-view that frames experiences and problems (Dow, 1986). The shaman intervenes by acting out culturally-prescribed mythical dramas with clients designed to facilitate the process of psychological healing (Levi–Strauss, 1967).

Some scholars presume that shamans use their status as cultural symbols to encourage a change in perspective on the part of clients (Scheff, 1979). Psychotherapists may serve a similar function by forming a shared cultural meaning with their clients. Lifestyle theory maintains that this shared meaning has a cultural mythical foundation that supplies clients with access to natural reservoirs of change. This may also explain the numerous difficulties encountered by therapists attempting to conduct cross-cultural counseling (Atkinson, Morton, & Sue, 1993). Although a mythical construction, it is essential that this phenomenon, referred to from this point forward as the *shaman effect*, be defined as precisely as possible, an issue to which the present discussion now turns.

Therapists who instill confidence in their clients may be better able to create a shaman effect than therapists who fail to inspire such confidence. Williams and Chambless (1990) note that agoraphobic clients who viewed their therapists as more self-confident, caring, and involved displayed greater improvement on a behavioral avoidance task than agoraphobic clients who rated their therapists as less self-confident, caring, and involved.

Attending to a client's frame of reference and being able to accurately predict client behavior is a second therapeutic strategy capable of promoting a shaman effect. In this regard, Alpher and Turkat (1986) determined that therapists who accurately interpreted a client's behavior were perceived by clients as more aware of their inner-world and more capable of stimulating positive therapeutic change than therapists who used reflection or posed questions.

A third factor contributing to the success of the shaman effect is the quality of the therapeutic relationship. Numerous studies indicate that the therapist–client relationship is vital to the success of psychotherapy (see Bergin & Garfield, 1994). Connors, Carroll, DiClemente, Longabaugh, and Donovan (1997) determined that a strong therapeutic alliance predicted ongoing participation and good drinking-related outcomes in several groups of outpatient clients enrolled in alcohol abuse counseling. It is proposed that the merging of these three components—confidence, internal frame of reference, and therapeutic relationship—may promote a change in client perspective that can eventually translate into a significant change in behavior.

AN ALTERNATE VIEW

The term treatment, with its medical model connotations, may be less than ideal as one searches for ways to effectively change addictive behavior. An alternative approach would be to study the natural change process and learn how it can be encouraged, sustained, and enhanced. Lifestyle theory contends that it is the nature of humankind to change but that people are unaware of a majority of the changes that occur both within and outside of themselves. In employing a lifestyle, a person learns to deny the reality of personal change through implementation of rigid and ritualistic patterns of behavior and routinized styles of thought. This is another way of saying that a lifestyle affords a person a false sense of immutability or nonchange. This, in turn, makes for poor adaptability in the face of a constantly changing environment.

Since change is a necessary precondition for adaptive living, lifestyle behavior stands in the way of effective adaptation. Lifestyle theory would argue that sensitivity to environmental information and flexibility in the face of a constantly changing environment are remedies for rigid lifestyle patterns. Such outcomes may be achieved naturally (unassisted change) or through intervention (assisted change). Commitment to change is a necessary prerequisite, however, as illustrated by the results of one study in which compliance with an assigned medication (whether lithium carbonate or placebo), along with regular attendance at AA meetings, predicted positive outcomes 18 months later (Pisani, Fawcett, Clark, & McGuire, 1993).

Lifestyle theory uses principles and techniques developed by people who have abandoned the lifestyle without formal assistance (unassisted change) to construct programs of effective assisted change. These principles have been organized into a system of formal intervention known as the Lifestyle Change Program (LCP). The LCP is broken down into three tiers or phases: a 10-week introductory class, three 20-week advanced classes designed to help participants assess their own levels of lifestyle involvement, and a 40-week relapse prevention class in which participants are instructed in how to cope with the conditions, choices, and cognitions that often lead back to a lifestyle. A 5-year follow-up of this program uncovered a robust negative correlation between program participation and the number of subsequent institutional disciplinary reports received and slightly better community adjustment on the part of program participants relative to a group of individuals scheduled to participate in the program but who had been transferred or released prior to their enrollment (Walters, in press).

One of the primary goals of lifestyle intervention, whether achieved in individual sessions or as part of a larger program, is the creation of a shaman effect. This effect is believed to foster change by impacting on a cognitive process known as the attribution triad. The attribution triad is a series of three inter-related beliefs, constructions, or expectancy-based preconditions for change (Walters, 1994c). The first component of the attribution triad is a belief in the necessity of change. Clients who have acquired a belief in the necessity of change appreciate the urgency of change and realize that it must come from within rather than from without. The second component of the attribution triad is a belief in the possibility of change. This construction accepts the theoretical possibility of change with the understanding that change is often difficult. The third and final component of the attribution triad is a belief in one's ability to effect change. This particular branch of the attribution triad encompasses both a generalized sense of confidence in one's ability to cope with life's difficulties as well as increased self-efficacy for specific high risk situations.

All three components of the attribution triad must be in place before meaningful change can occur. By demonstrating competence and furnishing the client with hope, reassurance, and direction, therapists can help create a shaman effect. The confidence engendered by the shaman effect is fertile soil for the evolution of a robust series of self-attributions capable of sustaining a client's efforts to cope with the problems and frustrations of everyday living. Furthermore, since the shaman effect is grounded in one or more cultural myths, it affords the client an opportunity to mend the severed bond between the person and society. For therapists working with problem gamblers, for instance, the mythical underpinnings of one's intervention might incorporate the cultural belief that it is unwise to expect something for nothing. Effort therefore needs to be directed at identifying and clarifying the relevant cultural myths.

We would do well to remember that, in the words of one residential program director, "the secret of being a successful alcoholism treatment center is being the place where people come when they finally decide to stop drinking" (cited in Miller, 1993, p. 1,479). Thus, instead of envisioning our clinical work with substance abusing, gambling, sexually preoccupied, and eating disordered clients as treatment of a disease over which the client has little or no control, it may be more useful to view ourselves as entering into a collaborative relationship with the client to develop attitudes and skills that will facilitate the natural change process. The overall mood of this chapter might lead one to conclude that pragmatic interpretations of addictive behavior (with the possible exception of the relapse prevention model which is only marginally tied to the addiction concept) are no more successful than their biological, psychological, or sociological counterparts. However, the seeming ineffectiveness of pragmatic interpretations of addictive behavior may have more to do with their tacit affiliation with the addiction concept than with a lack of good ideas or techniques. Consequently, before these ideas and techniques can come to fruition, the guiding models may need to abandon their addiction concept roots.

7

LOGICAL LIMITATIONS
OF THE ADDICTION CONCEPT

Logic makes use of methods and principles that help differentiate between correct and incorrect reasoning, propositions and arguments being the principle tools of the logician (Copi, 1982). A proposition is a statement that can be judged true or false, while an argument is a series of propositions. The conclusion of an argument is the proposition inferred from one or more preceding propositions known as premises. The premise of an argument, therefore, is the foundation upon which the argument's ultimate conclusion is based. Logicians inform us that while premises and conclusions are either affirmed or denied, arguments are judged on the basis of their validity.

It is customary to divide arguments into two general categories: deductive and inductive. Deductive arguments establish a conclusion that follows necessarily from one or more premises. As such, a deductive argument is either valid or invalid. Inductive arguments, on the other hand, necessitate the derivation of general principles. Consequently, while a deductive argument provides definitive grounds for a conclusion, an inductive argument accounts for only a portion of the grounds upon which a conclusion is based. Deductive logic will be emphasized in this chapter.

A *syllogism* is a deductive technique comprised of a major premise, a minor premise, and a conclusion. Consider the following syllogism:

All men are Homo sapiens.
All Homo sapiens are mammals.
Therefore, all men are mammals.

In this example "All men are Homo sapiens." serves as the major premise, "All Homo sapiens are mammals." constitutes the minor premise, and

"Therefore, all men are mammals." is the conclusion. This illustrates a valid argument predicated on two affirmed premises.

A valid argument can also be derived from a false premise, as illustrated by the following syllogism:

> *Warts are exclusive to witches.*
> *Some women have warts.*
> *Therefore, some women are witches.*

Here, the conclusion follows logically from the premises, but the conclusion is false because the major premise is untrue.

It is also possible to reach a false conclusion even though both premises are true. Take, for instance, the following syllogism:

> *All apes are hairy.*
> *Some men are hairy.*
> *Therefore, some men are apes.*

Despite the fact that both premises are true, the conclusion drawn from them is false. Owing to its inferential nature, this argument is traditionally referred to as the logical analogy.

Logical analogies are invalid because they violate a principal rule of standard form syllogisms: specifically, that the middle term of a syllogism should be distributed in at least one premise of an argument (Copi, 1982). What this means is that at least one of the two terms in the conclusion (either men or apes) must be related to the whole, rather than a part, of the middle term (hairy). The conclusion is false because the two terms in the conclusion reference different aspects, features, or qualities of the term.

The possibility that a logical analogy underlies the loss of control element of the addiction concept will be the first topic considered in this chapter. This will be followed by a review of other logical fallacies common to either the major elements of the addiction concept or working models derived from this concept. These fallacies include logically incongruent premises, *argumentum ad verecundian* (appeals to authority), *argumentum ad baculum* (appeals to force), *argumentum ad ignorantiam* (arguments from ignorance), *petitio principii* (begging the question), composition, and division. The chapter begins, however, with loss of control as a logical analogy.

THE LOGICAL ANALOGY: LOSS OF CONTROL

As previously defined, a logical analogy occurs when one assumes full distribution of a concept that is only partially distributed (Copi, 1982). The logic of the loss of control element of the addiction concept (as applied to drinking) can be summarized as follows:

Some people report losing control over their drinking.
Alcohol is known to effect perceptions of control.
Therefore, a defining characteristic of alcohol abuse is loss of control.

The premises of the above argument are true in the sense that both can be affirmed through empirical observation. First, many alcohol abusers report experiencing decreased control over their lives as a result of their drinking behavior (see Room & Leigh, 1992). Second, the profound effect alcohol is capable of exerting over a person's perceptions of control is well documented (see Nathan, 1990). The problem is that these two premises reference different distributions of the middle term (loss of control). Whereas the major premise reflects a global sense of losing control over one's life, the minor premise endorses a more circumscribed distribution in which loss of control signifies a specific disturbance in physical and mental functioning. The conclusion, on the other hand, references yet another definition of loss of control; namely, a reaction created by the ingestion of alcohol that then compels the individual to drink uncontrollably (Jellinek, 1960; Milam & Ketcham, 1983).

The logic of the loss of control argument is also undermined by its inability to explain expectancy effects, controlled drinking, and counter-regulatory behavior in clients with eating disorders.

Expectancy Effects

It is now known that alcohol in the bloodstream does not necessarily trigger uncontrollable drinking, even in persons with a history of chronic alcohol abuse. Take, for instance, research on outcome expectancies. Employing a balanced placebo design, Marlatt, Demming, and Reid (1973) randomly assigned moderate and heavy drinkers to one of four conditions:

1. administered alcohol and informed that they had, in fact, consumed alcohol
2. administered tonic water with no alcohol (placebo) and informed that they had received a placebo
3. administered alcohol and informed that they had received a placebo
4. administered a placebo and informed that they had consumed alcohol

The results of this study revealed that subjects drank more when they believed they were consuming alcohol, regardless of the drink's actual alcohol content.

Another group of investigators using this same design surmised that the responses of a group of heavy drinkers to a small priming dose of alcohol or placebo were controlled by expectancies rather than by the pharmacological properties of the priming dose (Berg, Laberg, Skutle, & Ohman, 1981). Although most studies employing the balanced placebo design note that expectancies are more important determinants of drinking behavior than alcohol (Hull & Bond, 1986), the results of at least one study suggest that the expectancy effect may be a more powerful determinant of "moderate alcohol dependence" than "severe alcohol dependence" (Stockwell, Hodgson, Rankin, & Taylor, 1982).

Controlled Drinking

Theorists who emphasize the loss of control element of the addiction concept generally believe that having a serious alcohol problem precludes the possibility of future social drinking because of the person's propensity to lose control over his or her drinking (Jellinek, 1960). Although the success of controlled drinking interventions vary widely as a function of client age (Miller, Leckman, Delaney, & Tinkcom, 1992), gender (Sanchez–Craig, Spivak, & Davila, 1991), and chronicity (Miller & Hester, 1986), there is evidence that a certain portion of the alcohol abusing population can learn to drink in a controlled manner (Heather & Robertson, 1983).

Studies comparing programs that stress abstinence versus controlled drinking have achieved mixed outcomes, with some studies favoring abstinence-based interventions (Hall, Havassy, & Wasserman, 1991) and other studies favoring the controlled drinking protocol (Alden, 1988). The majority of researchers investigating this topic, however, report that abstinence and controlled drinking programs achieve roughly equivalent results (Booth, Dale, Slade, & Dewey, 1992; Miller et al., 1992). Whereas the actual number of alcohol abusers who eventually learn to drink socially is unknown, the fact that this goal has been realized, even with a modicum of success, challenges the validity of the loss of control tenet of the addiction concept.

Counter-Regulation in Eating Disorders

Herman and Polivy (1984) have advanced a counter-regulatory model of bulimia nervosa in which dietary restraint is said to promote loss of control binging in the presence of food cues. Research conducted in both laboratory and naturalistic settings, however, has failed to generate support for this supposition (Laessle, Tuschl, Kotthaus, & Pirke, 1989; Wardle & Beales, 1988). Delving further into this issue, Dritschel, Cooper, and Charnock (1993) asked groups of high and low restraining college students to taste test biscuits after a preload of an 8 oz glass of water or a 12 oz milk shake. The results of this study refute the counter-regulatory model in the sense that there were no significant group differences in the number of biscuits consumed or in self-reported eating behavior when the sample was segregated into high and low restraining subjects and those who were and were not dieting on the day of the experiment.

Contrasting clinical samples of overweight binge eaters and normal weight bulimics with noneating disordered controls, Duchmann, Williamson, and Stricker (1989) preloaded subjects on chocolate pudding and had them taste test two flavors of ice cream with the understanding that they would not be able to leave the room until 90 minutes after completion of the taste test. The outcome of this study revealed that bulimics consumed significantly less ice cream than overweight subjects and were no more likely to overeat than control subjects, signifying that bulimics can control their consumption of high calorie snacks when opportunities for purging are blocked.

Reconceptualizing Loss of Control

As the present discussion implies, loss of control is a poorly defined construct that appears to have been applied to addictive behavior in an arbitrary and capricious manner. Perhaps the concept would be more useful if defined more precisely. Fear of losing control is prominent in the reports of people who misuse substances (Newcomb & Harlow, 1986), gamble incessantly (Hraba, Mok, & Huff, 1990), and engage in eating disordered behavior (Pyle, Neuman, Halvorson, & Mitchell, 1991). I argue that the term *craving* may better describe these concerns.

Loss of control means many things to many people. Unfortunately, so does craving. Were we to restrict our definition of craving to observable, measurable behavior, however, the concept may be more useful (Kozlowski & Wilkinson, 1987). Marlatt (1985) offers one such definition: "(craving) is a subjective state mediated by the positive incentive properties of positive outcome expectancies" (p. 138).

Another potential alternative to loss of control is the dyscontrol concept proposed by Edwards (1986). Besides amassing empirical support (Kahler, Epstein, & McCrady, 1995), the dyscontrol concept can be distributed along a continuum that varies by time, person, and situation. Our efforts might therefore be better spent identifying and establishing behavioral referents for craving and dyscontrol than stubbornly defending loss of control as a defining characteristic of addictive behavior.

LOGICALLY INCONGRUENT PREMISES: SPLIT RESPONSIBILITY

There are times when the logic of addiction becomes contradictory. A prime example of such inconsistency can be found in the first three steps of the spiritual disease model. Step one of this model requires that people concede their powerlessness over the addictive process. Step two asserts a belief in a higher power that can restore the person to sanity. Thus far, the steps are logically consistent. A logical error is encountered, however, when the first two steps are considered in conjunction with the third step in which the person is informed of the necessity of making a decision to turn his or her will and life over to a higher power. This third step is logically incongruent with the first two steps because one cannot make a decision to turn one's will over to a higher power if one is powerless and wholly dependent on this higher power for change. In a manner of speaking, one cannot surrender something one does not possess.

The illogic of the first three of the 12 steps is a result of split responsibility in which the person is held responsible for some behaviors but not others. Hopson and Beaird–Spiller (1995) acknowledge the logical inconsistency of the 12 steps and other examples of split responsibility found in the spiritual disease model, but maintain that split responsibility arguments can be helpful in establishing a paradox with the power to promote therapeutic change. The logic behind split responsibility arguments, however, is weak and weak logic makes for weak theory. Before a theoretical construct can be evaluated it must be logical. This is a standard on which 12-step programs and other models heavily invested in the addiction concept seem to fall short of the mark.

ARGUMENTUM AD VERECUNDIAN: DEIFICATION OF THE 12 STEPS

Argumentum ad verecundian, also known as appeals to authority, refers to the use of an authority to establish the credibility of an argument or position that is outside the authority's scope of expertise (Copi, 1982). Many advertisers owe their existence to the *argumentum ad verecundian* fallacy. Arranging for a retired athlete to peddle a pain reliever in a television commercial, unless that individual is a medical expert, is a prime example of *argumentum ad verecundian.*

An even greater authority has been used to market the spiritual disease model of addiction. Five of the 12 steps in the spiritual disease model make clear reference to God. Proponents of this model have allied themselves with organized religion and people's perception of God in an effort to appeal to a higher authority and establish the alleged validity of their position. Anyone who challenges the underlying tenets of the model is then branded a heretic and their ideas are subsequently dismissed.

The addiction-as-disease model also relies on the *argumentum ad verecundian* fallacy by using the prestige of the medical profession and the power of the American Medical Association to "prove" the correctness of the model. However, there is nothing to say that a physician is any more qualified to assist a problem drinker than say, a minister, a probation officer, or one's next-door neighbor. According to lifestyle theory, prior training in the medical model may actually hinder a professional's ability to foster positive change in addicted persons.

ARGUMENTUM AD BACULUM: THE CONTROLLED DRINKING CONTROVERSY

Argumentum ad baculum (appeals to force) are used to intimidate, frighten, or bully a listener into accepting the speaker's position (Copi, 1982). There was a time when force, threat, and coercion were exercised at the end of a blade or gun; now it is more likely to be exercised at the tip of a lawyer's pen. Such appeals are sometimes voiced by proponents of the addiction concept. After failing to replicate the positive results obtained by Mark and Linda Sobell (1976) in their research on controlled drinking, Pendery, Maltzman, and West (1982) accused the Sobells of misrepresenting their data. An independent blue-ribbon panel, however, failed to substantiate these claims and subsequently exonerated the Sobells of any wrongdoing (Marlatt, 1983). Unfortunately, the popular media spent significantly more time covering the initial charges than publicizing the ensuing vindication.

Even more alarming than the actual charges leveled by the Pendery group was the vigor with which they attacked the Sobells' integrity despite their own failure to conduct a proper evaluation (see Marlatt, 1983). As a case in point, Pendery et al. (1982) brought attention to the fact that four of the 20 controlled drinking subjects included in the Sobell's follow-up eventually died of alcohol-related causes. However, they failed to mention that six out of 20 control subjects receiving a standard abstinence-based intervention also died within this same time frame.

It has been suggested that instructing clients in controlled drinking may make a therapist liable for the negative consequences that befall a client who continues drinking (Nathan & McCrady, 1987). The fact that one person could be held legally responsible for the decisions of another is a sad commentary on the state of the American judicial system. Beyond this, however, the logical underpinnings of this argument are weak.

If therapists who instruct clients in controlled drinking can be held liable for the future drinking behavior of their clients, then therapists who insist on abstinence in the face of contradictory evidence (Heather & Robertson, 1983) may be guilty of violating their clients' inalienable right to the pursuit of happiness as outlined in the Declaration of Independence and reiterated in the Constitution of the United States. While, on the one hand, it may seem preposterous to hold abstinence-promoting therapists responsible for human rights violations, few people see the absurdity of holding therapists who follow a controlled drinking regimen liable for the future alcohol-related behavior of their clients. The solution is to supply clients with accurate information about the advantages and disadvantages of each approach and then allow them to select the approach they perceive as most relevant to their situation. Should the client be dissatisfied with the long term consequences of his or her decision, then the responsibility rests with him or her to make a new choice.

Before concluding this section there is one area of research that needs to be considered with reference to moderate use of alcohol and other substances. Empirical studies indicate that adults who drink moderately enjoy better psychological adjustment than heavy drinkers and those who abstain altogether (Winefield, Winefield, Tiggemann, & Smith, 1987). There is also a growing body of evidence to suggest that moderate alcohol consumption protects against coronary disease (Cowie, 1997). Likewise, a relationship has been observed between good psychological adjustment and moderate use of marijuana in adolescents and young adults (Shedler & Block, 1980). These findings suggest that moderation in the use of some substances may prove beneficial.

It is uncertain whether moderate use of alcohol in adults or moderate use of marijuana in adolescents promotes improved psychological adjustment, or if well adjusted adults and adolescents are just better able to control their ingestion of mind-altering substances. Baum–Baicker (1985) nonetheless lists five benefits that might reasonably be anticipated from moderate alcohol consumption. This list includes relief from depression, reduced levels of stress and anxiety, increased positive emotion, improved task performance, and alleviation of geropsychiatric problems. The goal of lifestyle intervention is to supply clients with skills, knowledge, and confidence designed to help them make better decisions, accept responsibility for the consequences of their decisions, and alter decisions that are no longer consistent with their goals and needs.

ARGUMENTUM AD IGNORANTIAM: ADDICTIVE LIABILITY

A discussant employs *argumentum ad ignorantiam,* arguing out of ignorance, when he or she assumes that a proposition is true simply because it has not been proven false (Copi, 1982). Several models of addiction assert that some substances and activities are inherently addictive. A 1988 conference held in Princeton, New Jersey sought answers to questions about the abuse liability of various chemical compounds. Findings from this conference indicated that while alcohol, marijuana, stimulants, and sedative or hypnotic agents possess moderate to moderately high abuse liability, host factors and the effects of setting impact heavily on the drug-liability relationship (Fischman & Mello, 1989).

The universality of abuse liability for the process or activity addictions— for example, exercise, sex, gambling, buying, or television viewing—is even less certain. Simply because it has not been conclusively demonstrated that these substances and activities are nonaddictive does not, as a matter of logic, make them addictive. The vast majority of people who ingest abusable substances or engage in activities like gambling or sex do not become preoc-cupied with these substances or activities. Adding a vulnerable host to the equation fails to explain why some previously preoccupied individuals eventually perform the behavior without incident. It would seem that to argue for universal or partial addictive liability on the basis of observations that do not categorically dismiss the possibility of such liability is to commit the logical fallacy of *argumentum ad ignorantiam.*

PETITIO PRINCIPII: THE TAUTOLOGY OF ADDICTION

A person commits the logical fallacy of *petitio principii* when the same prop-osition serves as both the premise and conclusion of his or her argument (Copi, 1982). This is most clearly represented by the tautologies found in sev-eral key addiction model assumptions and premises. Heather and Robertson (1985) contend that the traditional loss of control argument is tautological in the sense that the concept serves both a descriptive and an etiological func-tion. They state that while the concept may be useful at a descriptive level, making it both the cause and effect of addictive involvement is circular. Iron-ically, Heather and Robertson's alternative model—that problem drinking is a learned process—has been criticized on these very same grounds.

Gorman (1989) asserts that the Heather and Robertson model simply substitutes one tautology for another, in that, like the disease concept, it fails to distinguish between cause and description. The learning model, accord-ing to Gorman, eliminates nonlearning variables as potential causes of addictive involvement but retains a tautological stance by intermixing etiol-ogy and description. In establishing loss of control or learning as both the cause (etiology) and effect (description) of a particular behavior, one's theory is confirmed through tautology. Two additional tautologies—the prediction tautology and the denial tautology—are commonly encountered in addic-tive theories of behavior.

The prediction tautology arises when one offers a prediction but then modifies the premises of the prediction when the prediction fails to find support. Addiction advocates might predict that a problem gambler will never be able to gamble in a controlled manner or a sexually preoccupied individual will never recover on his or her own. If it could be demonstrated that a problem gambler was able to gamble in a controlled manner, as is suggested in several case studies (Dickerson & Weeks, 1979; Rankin, 1982), or a sexually preoccupied individual was able to reduce his or her sexual preoccupation without treatment, the tautological position would be that these individuals were never addicted in the first place or else the prediction would have been confirmed. By modifying the initial premise of one's argument the conclusion is preserved, but at the cost of making a serious error in logic.

The denial tautology is also marked by circular reasoning in that any time a client disagrees with aspects of the addictive argument this is interpreted as evidence of denial which, in turn, "proves" that the client is addicted since denial is a major symptom of addiction. Agreement with the addictive premise verifies the argument; disagreement puts one in the position of denying "reality." Either way, the addictive argument is confirmed. Tautologies establish "truths" unamenable to empirical analysis. As such, they are viewed as unhelpful in advancing our understanding of human behavior.

COMPOSITION: DICHOTOMY VERSUS CONTINUUM

Composition occurs when a discussant categorically assumes that what is true of a part must, by necessity, be true of the whole (Copi, 1982). It is possible, even defensible, to break specific behaviors down into dichotomous categories for the purpose of classification. However, in combining discrete categories of behaviors into larger patterns, the multidimensional nature of the whole frequently dictates that individual dichotomies be replaced by continua. This seems particularly true of addictive behavior where a dichotomy (addicted–nonaddicted) is assumed. Roizen, Cahalan, and Shanks (1978), for instance, determined that many problem drinkers reduce their intake of alcohol without abstaining. This and other findings run counter to the alcoholic–nonalcoholic dichotomy posed by many models allied with the addiction concept.

Widiger and Smith (1994) question the wisdom of using a substance abuse–dependence dichotomy and instead recommend a single diagnostic dimension modeled after Edwards' (1986) dyscontrol concept. A confirmatory factor analysis of drinking practices and problems unearthed little support for the abuse–dependence dichotomy and determined that a single factor model fit the drinking data significantly better than either two- or multiple-factor models (Hasin, Muthuen, Wisnicki, & Grant, 1994). Conducting a survival–hazard analysis of 369 clients sampled from eight different addiction centers, Langenbucher and Chung (1995) identified an orderly progression of symptomatology that connoted the presence of three discrete stages of alcohol involvement: alcohol abuse, dependence, and accommodation to the illness. Whereas this finding appears inconsistent with the continuum concept, the study is limited by the fact that the sample was drawn from addiction treatment centers (62% of the subjects having been sampled from an inpatient facility).

The continuum concept also appears to apply to problem gambling. Hayano (1982) has proposed that problem gambling is simply the end point of a continuum characterized by faulty betting strategies, erroneous risk appraisal, and inept money management. Ladouceur, Maynard, and Tourigny (1984) supplied high and low frequency gamblers with $100 in tokens and informed them that they would be allowed to retain 10% of the tokens that were left after several games of roulette. High frequency gamblers bet higher stakes and accepted riskier odds than low frequency gamblers, but with prolonged exposure the low frequency gamblers adopted many of these same strategies. Perceived loss of control was found to correlate with increased gambling involvement in both problem and high frequency nonproblem gamblers participating in a second study, although this perception was more indicative of the thinking of problem gambling subjects (Dickerson, 1985).

Evidence favoring a dimensional or continuum interpretation of gambling behavior can be inferred from the results of a study in which problem gamblers, high frequency gamblers, and low frequency gamblers were compared on a self-control measure (Corless & Dickerson, 1989). Like the earlier Dickerson (1985) study, however, certain findings were unique to the problem gambling group; specifically, problem gamblers were more inclined to reference mood-related ("to forget my troubles") and irrational ("chasing") reasons in describing the initiation and maintenance of their gambling behavior.

The continuum concept may also extend to sexual preoccupation. Orford (1978), for one, questions the logic of arbitrarily dividing the sexual continuum into normal and abnormal categories given the wide diversity of people labeled, the sociocultural factors that influence the practice of labeling, and the profound effect labeling can have on a person's behavior. Based on these observations, Orford recommends that "normal" and "deviant" sexual behavior be viewed as points along a continuum of sexual activity. Comparing men with DSM–III–R-defined paraphilias and men reporting nonparaphilic sexual "addictions" on multiple indices of sexual functioning, Kafka and Prentky (1992a) discerned that the paraphilic and nonparaphilic groups displayed comparable levels of sexually-related symptomatology and social impairment. However, whereas paraphilic men exhibited a nonsignificant trend toward more unconventional sexual involvement, nonparaphilic subjects displayed a nonsignificant trend toward greater involvement in conventional sexual activities.

On the basis of their results, Kafka and Prentky concluded that non-paraphilic sexual addictions represent alternative forms of sexual pathology that differ from the paraphilias only in the degree to which they deviate from established cultural norms, practices, and preferences. Instead of viewing the two groups as embodiments of related pathology, lifestyle theory adopts the position that these two behavioral patterns fall at points close to one another in the vicinity of the deviant pole of the sexual continuum.

Despite its facility in explaining substance misuse, problem gambling, and sexual preoccupation, the continuum concept may be most applicable to eating disordered behavior (Rodin, Silberstein, & Striegel–Moore, 1985). In a national survey of 628 women with eating-related concerns, Yager, Landsverk, and Edelstein (1987) discovered that these concerns fell along a continuum. Overlap between diagnostic categories (anorexia, bulimia, subclinical eating disorder) and moderate movement across categories after 20 months led Yager and his colleagues to propose a continuum of weight preoccupation with subclinical, largely culturally influenced, cases falling at the lower end of the continuum and women with greater psychological and physiological impairments falling at the upper end of the continuum. In this study, as well as in several others (see, for example, Ruderman & Besbeas, 1992), anorexia was seen as falling closer to the eating disordered pole of the continuum than bulimia.

Drewnowski, Yee, Kurth, and Krahn (1994) enlisted support for the continuum concept in a 6-month longitudinal investigation of 557 college women. Although bulimic subjects were found to score near the upper end of the continuum, there was a moderate degree of movement between adjacent categories (nondieters, casual dieters, intensive dieters, dieters at risk, and bulimics). In a related vein, studies have failed to verify the meaningfulness of the restricting–binging dichotomy proposed by DSM–IV (Steiger, Liquornik, Chapman, & Hussain, 1991). Welch, Hall, and Renner (1990) were likewise unable to identify a restricting–binging dichotomy in groups of anorexic, bulimic, and anorexic–bulimic patients.

David Garner and his colleagues argue that eating disordered behavior may conform to both a continuum and dichotomy. They ascertained that chronic dieting, weight preoccupied noneating disordered women participating in several studies formed two general clusters: one indistinguishable from a group of eating disordered women and another demonstrating equivalent concerns about weight, eating, and thinness but without the ego dysfunction commonly observed in eating disordered female patients (Garner, Olmsted, Polivy, & Garfinkel, 1984).

Laessle, Tuschl, Waadt, and Pirke (1989) uncovered additional support for Garner's "two-component" model of eating disordered behavior in a study comparing bulimics, restrained eaters, and unrestrained eaters. Whereas bulimic subjects shared a similar level of concern about dieting and physical appearance with noneating disordered restrained eaters, they scored significantly higher than restrained eaters on measures of personal ineffectiveness, distorted interoceptive awareness, and interpersonal distrust.

Another source of support for a continuity–discontinuity interpretation of eating disordered behavior can be found in the results of a study by Ruderman and Besbeas (1992). In this investigation, dieters described themselves in more socially undesirable terms than nondieters, whereas bulimics produced significantly higher scores on measures of psychopathology and self-esteem than dieters. Similar results have been recorded in studies on gambling behavior in which problem gamblers acted more on their emotions and reported less control over their behavior than high frequency nonproblem gamblers (Corless & Dickerson, 1989).

The body of evidence on the relative merits of continuity and discontinuity in conceptualizing eating disordered behavior suggests that while it may be possible to dichotomize behavior into discrete categories, these categories likely exist on a continuum. Attie and Brooks–Gunn (1992) propose three dimensions or continua related to eating disordered behavior: normal versus pathological eating; restricting versus binging; healthy versus disturbed ego functioning. Additional research is required to determine whether these dimensions are interrelated or independent, additive or multiplicative, simultaneous or sequential.

The lifestyle model proposes an interrelated, multiplicative, sequential perspective in which eating-related concerns are organized along a socioculturally informed continuum. Individuals functioning at the upper end of this continuum may eventually enter an adjacent dimension or continuum in which emotional adjustment issues take precedence. According to lifestyle theory, this transition is mediated by elements of both a physical and psychological nature. Prolonged involvement in an addictive activity may create certain physical changes that help maintain the activity. This has been documented in persons who chronically abuse alcohol (Oscar–Berman, 1990), cocaine (O'Malley & Gawin, 1990), and opiates (Woody, McLellan, & O'Brien, 1990), but also relates to the severe weight loss observed in anorexia and the electrolyte imbalances that can occur with bulimia (Mickley, 1994). Continued involvement in addictive behavior may also give rise to a lifestyle of patterned behavior. Physiological and lifestyle changes appear to maintain initial addictive involvement and may do so by encouraging a shift in continua.

DIVISION: THE UNIFORMITY MYTH

Division is the opposite of composition. Rather than generalizing from a specific instance, the discussant assumes that what is true of the whole must, by

necessity, be true of each of the individual parts (Copi, 1982). Theory building is vital to scientific advancement. However, to assume that any one theory applies to all individuals is to commit the logical fallacy of division. This
is because a part may contribute to the whole, yet not mirror the whole. As
a case in point, group statistics tend to obscure individual differences by
averaging across subjects. To assume that every subject possesses a common
or similar trait simply because the trait is observed in the group as a whole
is to fall victim to the logical error of division.

Research indicates that diversity, not uniformity, characterizes the
behavior of persons labeled alcoholic (Hasin, Grant, & Endicott, 1990), problem gambler (Dickerson, 1984), compulsive buyer (Schlosser, Black, Repertinger, & Freet, 1994), TV addict (Smith, 1986), and codependent (Mintz,
Kashubeck, & Tracy, 1995). All theories, not just those postulating the existence of addiction, are subject to divisional errors of logic. It is recommended
that theorists wishing to avoid the problem of division specify the boundaries of their theoretical views and remain true to these boundaries.

The present review demonstrates that the logic of the overall addiction
concept, along with several of its key elements (e.g., loss of control) and
some of the more popular models derived from the addiction concept (i.e.,
medical and disease models), is grounded in weak, oftentimes contradictory
premises, faulty conclusions, and essentially invalid arguments. Before a
concept can be properly evaluated and its practical merit assessed, the logic
of its assumptions must be established. This may, in fact, be what has limited
the empirical and practical utility of the addiction concept, issues covered in
the next two chapters of this text.

8

EMPIRICAL LIMITATIONS OF THE ADDICTION CONCEPT

Whereas one might use deductive logic to test the validity of arguments and decipher the truth of conclusions, inductive logic is designed to construct general principles from specific facts and findings. This chapter dissects the inductive logic of the addiction concept in a survey of contradictory empirical findings. Although a detailed and exhaustive review of the empirical literature on addictive involvement is beyond the scope of this chapter, eight topics that challenge the four key elements of the addiction concept—progression, preoccupation, loss of control, persistence—will be discussed. The chapter begins with a review of empirical findings that defy the progression element (controlled involvement, unassisted change), followed by research that challenges the preoccupation (brief, environmental, and behavioral interventions), loss of control (expectancies, attributions, volition), and persistence (sociocultural parameters, setting effects) assumptions.

CONTROLLED INVOLVEMENT

More than content and technique separate traditional and behavioral interventions for addictive behavior. There are times when the primary goal of intervention also varies. In contrast to most traditional treatment programs that set abstinence as the sole or primary objective of intervention, some behavioral therapists are willing to entertain the possibility of instructing clients in controlled involvement. Before moderation can be accepted as a viable change goal, however, the possibility of controlled involvement must be established. If controlled involvement in an "addictive" activity can be demonstrated, this would tend to cast aspersions on the progression and loss of control elements of the addiction concept.

The Possibility of Controlled Involvement

It is generally agreed that people are capable of controlled alcohol usage, gambling, and dieting, since the majority of people who engage in these activities do so without suffering major life consequences. Less acceptable, in many corners, is the prospect of people with prior problems in these areas resuming involvement without incident. However, re-interviews conducted with a group of problem drinkers 7 to 11 years after completing a traditional alcoholism treatment program found that 8% of the group were drinking in a controlled manner (Davies, 1962). The Rand Corporation conducted a comparable study in the United States and determined that 18% of their sample was engaged in a pattern of controlled drinking three years after program termination (Armor, Polich, & Stambul, 1976). These data fly in the face of the conventional wisdom promoted by an industry that would have us believe "once an alcoholic, always an alcoholic."

Similar findings have been reported for other addictive behaviors. Nearly 40% of a group of problem gamblers exposed to inpatient treatment for gambling were apparently able to gamble socially without suffering adverse consequences (Russo, Taber, McCormick, & Ramirez, 1984). In a 5-year follow-up of problem gamblers graduating from a brief behavioral program, 14.2% achieved total abstinence over the entire 5-year span, 28.6% achieved relative abstinence, and 38% reported gambling in a controlled manner (Blaszczynski, McConaghy, & Frankova, 1991). Interestingly, subjects achieving abstinence and controlled gambling outcomes were comparable in terms of social and financial functioning, psychological distress, and level of emotional disturbance. Additionally, a different study found that many successfully treated weight-recovered anorectics continue to diet and express concerns about the food they eat (Greenfeld, Anyan, Hobart, Quinlan, & Plantes, 1991).

Whereas it is assumed that many people can drink, gamble, and diet in a controlled manner, this assumption may not extend to all activities considered addictive. Drug use in the form of cigarette smoking, cocaine inhalation, and heroin consumption are among the behaviors traditionally viewed to be outside the realm of possible moderation. Perhaps this is because the number of people who engage in the controlled use of these substances is outweighed by the number who have trouble moderating their use. However, this does not preclude the possibility that some people are capable of controlling their use of tobacco, cocaine, or heroin. Research shows that this is more than just a theoretical possibility.

Noting that people who reliably ingest low levels of tobacco without suffering physiological or psychological dependence are clearly in the minority (approximately 10% of all smokers), Shiffman (1989) studied a small group of tobacco "chippers," defined as persons who smoked no more than five cigarettes a day at least four days a week. Unlike a comparison group of heavy smokers, the 18 tobacco "chippers" participating in the Shiffman study evidenced fewer signs of subjective reaction to nicotine and no signs of withdrawal when deprived of cigarettes. These individuals also displayed lower levels of stress, more effective coping strategies, and stronger networks of social support than habitual users. It would seem that these controlled users of cigarettes were somehow protected from experiencing high levels of stress and were consequently much less likely to resort to tobacco use in an effort to cope with depression or frustration.

Despite images created by the popular media that people cannot use cocaine without falling prey to its addictive influence, there is empirical evidence that a sizable proportion of the cocaine using population do not suffer long range negative consequences. In a study of 99 social–recreational users of cocaine, Siegel (1984) discovered that after nine years half the sample was still using cocaine in a social–recreational manner. Another 32% of the sample could be classified as circumstantial–situational users who ingested the drug to improve performance at work or stave off the effects of fatigue. Eight percent of the sample were heavy users and another 10% were classified as "compulsive" users of freebase cocaine.

Murphy, Reinarman, and Waldorf (1989) followed a small network of cocaine users for 11 years and at the end of the investigation ascertained that only one of the 21 members was currently involved in heavy cocaine usage. A small number of individuals in this network had stopped using cocaine entirely, but one-third continued using it in a controlled fashion. Like the social–recreational users in the Siegel study, these individuals attributed their nonproblem use of cocaine to the fact that they approached cocaine inhalation as a social event. Additional strategies employed by the members of this network that may have helped reinforce their efforts to moderate cocaine usage were the avoidance of certain routes of administration (freebasing, injection), the establishment of rules for when and where cocaine use was appropriate, the denigration of compulsive use of cocaine, and the subordination of cocaine to family and career plans.

Heroin has a reputation for leading to rapid and progressive addiction after only a few doses. However, perception and reality do not always correspond when it comes to heroin. Of servicemembers undergoing opiate detoxification in Vietnam, only 12% relapsed into heroin dependence once they returned to the United States, even though half the group subsequently used heroin (Robins, Helzer, & Davis, 1975). In another study, Zinberg (1984) identified an enclave of controlled opiate users who kept their use secret from everyone except each other and a small network of outside suppliers. The kinship that developed between members of this subculture was viewed as instrumental in preventing them from progressing into uncontrolled opiate usage. Reports from this group also suggest that they disparagingly referred to those who habitually abuse heroin as "junkies" and worked hard to avoid attracting this label themselves.

The informal social control exercised by the members of Zinberg's subculture of controlled users may have played an integral role in their success with the controlled use of heroin. It is interesting that the rituals of these controlled opiate users failed to differ meaningfully from the rituals practiced by a group of habitual users interviewed for the same study. However, the two groups differed widely in their use of structure. Whereas the controlled opiate users established definite rules for the amount of heroin to be consumed at any one time, the frequency of use, and the setting in which heroin ingestion would occur, the habitual heroin users failed to follow any such rules. The controlled opiate users participating in this study apparently employed rules and rituals to control their use of the drug, whereas the habitual opiate users devised rules and rituals that supported the unbridled misuse of heroin.

Teaching Controlled Involvement

Since the possibility of controlled involvement in an addictive behavior is reasonably well established, the next step will be to determine whether people who have experienced problems with these behaviors can be taught to control their future involvement. Lovibond and Caddy (1970) appear to have been the first investigators to formally test the feasibility of using controlled drinking strategies with alcohol abusing clients. Although the results of this investigation generally corroborated the controlled drinking hypothesis, the integrity of the research design was compromised by a lack of control and a short follow-up.

Sobell and Sobell (1976) were the next group of investigators to examine the perceived benefits of instructing alcohol abusing clients in controlled drinking. Taking 40 good prognosis clients from an alcohol inpatient unit at a state hospital, Sobell and Sobell randomly assigned half the group to a controlled drinking regimen and the other half to a traditional abstinence program. A 1-year follow-up revealed that subjects in the controlled drinking condition displayed good functioning an average of 71% of all days as compared to 35% for subjects in the control condition. After two years these figures were 85% and 42%, respectively.

Pendery, Maltzman, and West (1982) subsequently challenged the validity of the Sobells' findings after conducting retrospective interviews with the controlled drinking subjects. Although the Pendery group severely criticized the design used by the Sobells, at least two critical flaws were identified in their own study. First, follow-up data were provided for the experimental (controlled drinking) group but not for the traditional treatment group; and second, outcomes were based on subject recollections of events that had transpired 5 to 10 years earlier. In the end, the Sobells were vindicated (Marlatt, 1983).

The majority of randomized controlled studies conducted since the Sobells' pioneering work on controlled drinking show a lack of superiority for either controlled drinking or traditional abstinence treatment (Orford & Keddie, 1986). There is clear evidence, however, that some clients may benefit from training in controlled drinking. With follow-ups spanning 3.5 to 8 years, Miller, Leckman, Delaney, and Tinkcom (1992) determined that 23% of the subjects participating in a program of controlled drinking were completely abstinent, 14% were asymptomatic drinkers, 22% were improved but impaired, and 35% remained problem drinkers. In this study subjects who viewed the "alcoholic" label as descriptive of themselves and a goal of abstinence as most applicable to their ambitions tended to be abstinent at the follow-up, while subjects rejecting the "alcoholic" label and selecting a goal of moderation were more likely to be asymptomatic drinkers. Prior level of physical dependence on alcohol, however, failed to differentiate between the two groups.

The results obtained by Miller and his colleagues echo the conclusions of Orford and Keddie (1986). Orford and Keddie failed to observe any outcome-relevant interactions between treatment condition (abstinence, moderation) and a client's level of physical dependence on alcohol, but did note an outcome-relevant interaction between treatment condition and a client's belief in his or her capacity for controlled drinking. This suggests that clients confident in their ability to achieve moderation may be more suitable for enrollment in a controlled drinking program than clients who are unsettled about the prospect of moderation. The latter group of individuals might be better served by a program of total abstinence.

Alcohol use is not the only behavior for which training in controlled involvement has been devised. Frederiksen and Simon (1978) used a controlled smoking intervention to effectively reduce tobacco usage in heavy smokers. Glasgow, Kleges, Godding, and Gegelman (1983) have also successfully taught clients to control their use of cigarettes and observed changes in smoking behavior and carbon monoxide levels that persisted three to six months after treatment.

Hall, Havassy, and Wasserman (1991) report that cocaine users endorsing a goal of total abstinence were at lower risk for an initial slip than cocaine users professing less stringent goals. The limitation of this study is that it considered initial slips rather than relapse, and as evidenced by research on the Abstinence Violation Effect (see pages 156–160), a person's reaction to an initial slip may be more critical in determining his or her future risk of relapse than the presence of a slip.

Although there are no empirical data addressing the efficacy of controlled wagering interventions with problem gamblers, two case studies suggest that controlled gambling may be a realistic alternative for some clients (Dickerson & Weeks, 1979; Rankin, 1982). These procedures may also be useful in teaching controlled involvement to persons with eating disorders and sexual preoccupation. Teaching an anorectic patient to diet in a controlled manner or a sexually preoccupied client to masturbate in moderation are not only possible, but may even be advisable under some circumstances.

The reader may well question the wisdom of teaching an alcohol abuser to drink or an anorexic to diet in a controlled manner. Would not a goal of total abstinence make more sense than teaching clients to control a previously problematic behavior? The legal ramifications of teaching controlled drinking, gambling, and dieting were discussed in Chapter 7, and as was noted in that discussion, the legal points on controlled involvement are complex and contradictory. Peele (1984) writes that antagonism toward controlled drinking is grounded in a cultural attitude that treats with suspicion anything that flies in the face of the traditional disease model. Therefore, while the general public has been exposed to the controlled involvement movement through popular books like Audrey Kishline's *Moderate Drinking* (1995) in which an approach known as Moderation Management (MM) is described, a cultural attitudinal change will need to take place before controlled involvement becomes the norm rather than the exception.

Practical issues related to controlled involvement may be even less supportive of the total abstinence position. What must be kept in mind is that not all clients are willing to accept total abstinence as the goal of an intervention. From a practical standpoint, then, it may be necessary to follow a controlled involvement strategy in order to secure a client's cooperation. Success in controlled drinking may then make the client more receptive to and capable of abstinence (Heather & Robertson, 1983).

A second practical point to keep in mind is that abstinence may not be appropriate for all clients. The belief that abstinence is the universal goal of intervention is a notion promulgated by advocates of the addiction-as-disease model. By viewing problem drinking in terms of a continuum, rather than a dichotomy, and seeking to reduce the harm associated with drinking, Marlatt, Larimer, Baer, and Quigley (1993) successfully taught heavy drinking college students to moderate their use of alcohol as a way of reducing the number of drinking-related problems they were experiencing. It would seem that controlled involvement is attainable in at least some cases and that the goals of intervention (moderation versus abstinence) are best dictated by the client in consultation with an open-minded therapist after a thorough evaluation of the risks and benefits of each approach.

UNASSISTED CHANGE

Winick (1962) observed that up to two-thirds of the heroin "addicts" he studied terminated their involvement with opiates on their own. Winick labeled this process maturing out of addiction, while others consider it a manifestation of spontaneous remission. However, the change process may be neither spontaneous nor remitting in that it is often precipitated by environmental events and does not necessarily return the individual to a previous state of "health." Given the medical model connotations of an expression like spontaneous remission, alternative phrases, like natural recovery, have been offered. Lifestyle theorists, on the other hand, prefer the term unassisted change (McMurran, 1994). Change is conceptualized by lifestyle theory as an ongoing process that can be inhibited or derailed by participation in one or more lifestyles. Although lifestyles provide a person with a false sense of immutability, change cannot be deferred indefinitely. Eventually, problems arise that may encourage the person to seek change.

Exiting a lifestyle dictates that a person open him or herself up to change. This process can be initiated, encouraged, or mediated by a friend, family member, or mental health professional, but may also occur without assistance. Although unassisted change can be defined as improving without help from anyone, a more liberal definition will be employed in this section: unassisted change is defined as change accomplished without assistance from a treatment provider or formal program of intervention. Like evidence of controlled involvement, the prospect of unassisted change challenges the addiction concept's progression assumption. The first issue to be addressed in this section is the possibility of unassisted change; assuming the first issue is answered in the affirmative, this will be followed by a section on identifying the patterns and processes responsible for unassisted change.

The Possibility of Unassisted Change

Menard and Huizinga (1989) identified a nonlinear relationship between age and alcohol, marijuana, and polydrug use, with involvement peaking at age 20, in a longitudinal analysis of data gathered over a seven year period. Using a somewhat older sample and two separate cohorts, Fillmore (1987) discerned a declining rate of heavy drinking and alcohol-related problems after age 20 that was independent of various cohort effects. This same pattern has also been observed in cross-cultural studies of alcohol consumption in different age groups (Fillmore et al., 1993). A group of Swedish investigators set out to probe the relationship between alcohol use practices in adolescence (ages 14 to 16) and alcohol-related problems in young adulthood (ages 18 to 24) and found that 70%–80% of the youth acknowledging adolescent alcohol use could not be found in the official registry of alcohol-related problems for young adults (Andersson & Magnusson, 1988).

The above findings insinuate that a substantial portion of people reduce, limit, or cease their use of alcohol with age. Severe alcohol abuse may follow a similar pattern. Vaillant (1983) discerned that 49 out of 110 individuals with histories of severe alcohol abuse experienced a year or more of abstinence, often without formal intervention, in a follow-up conducted 16 to 22 years after an initial determination of alcoholism had been made. Interestingly, the severity of alcohol abuse in this particular sample predicted future success in avoiding the use of alcohol. Similar outcomes were recorded in a study by Hermos, Locastro, Glynn, Bouchard, & DeLabry (1988) where signs of severe drinking were detected in the backgrounds of abusers who successfully achieved abstinence and higher prior consumption levels were observed in abusers who successfully reduced their alcohol intake.

The results of one study denote that 90% of smokers successfully quit on their own, whereas only 80% of unsuccessful quitters tried to stop without assistance (Fiore et al., 1990). Although these percentages imply that self-quitters were twice as successful as program participants, it is important to remember that subjects were not randomly assigned to conditions (self-quitting, program). Hence, it is possible that clinics receive smokers who are more chronic or severe, or who have a history of unsuccessful attempts to stop smoking.

Schachter (1982) surmised that subjects who tried quitting on their own were two to three times more successful than subjects attending a formal cessation program and that heavy smokers and light smokers were equally successful in achieving abstinence. A large scale longitudinal investigation challenges several of Schachter's conclusions while finding support for his overall assertion that quitting is a dynamic process. Results from this study revealed that subjects smoking 20 or fewer cigarettes a day were 2.2 times more likely to quit than subjects smoking more than 20 cigarettes a day and that self-quitters were no more likely to achieve long term abstinence than those matriculating through a formal program of smoking cessation (Cohen et al., 1989). Interviewing 308 heavy smokers at three points in time, Carey, Kalra, Carey, Halperin, and Richards (1993) determined that 33% of the sample had smoked continuously in a year's time, 39% had quit for at least one day and then resumed smoking, and 15% had quit smoking entirely, a finding confirmed by biochemical testing.

Kandel and Raveis (1989) have enumerated the process of marijuana and cocaine desistance in a longitudinal investigation of young adults. Of the subjects who reported using marijuana at age 24 or 25, 34% of the men and 45% of the women were no longer using this substance four years later. The majority of these subjects terminated their involvement with marijuana decisively, 67% of the males and 77% of the females stopping after their initial attempt. Of cohort members who reported using cocaine at age 24 or 25, 49% of the men and 56% of the women were no longer using cocaine four years later. Again, the decision to stop using was definitive, with 65% of male cohort members and 88% of female cohort members remaining abstinent after their first attempt at cessation.

Subjects in the Kandel and Raveis study who terminated their use of marijuana and cocaine were less deviant, started using these drugs at a later age, and enjoyed a social support network more opposed to drug use than nonremitting subjects. In addition, one of the main reasons cited by subjects participating in this study for terminating their use of marijuana or cocaine was the assumption of adult responsibilities, such as marriage or child birth, in the four year hiatus between the two interviews. Finally, subjects who stopped using marijuana were more likely to have been using it for social reasons, whereas those who continued using often gave personal reasons ("pleasure," "to enhance sex") for smoking marijuana.

Unassisted change has also been observed in those who abuse heroin as was revealed in a study by Biernacki (1990). Biernacki interviewed 101 individuals who, after having been physically dependent on heroin for one or more years, achieved abstinence without formal intervention. The two principle challenges facing these individuals were: (1) filling the void created by their abandonment of a heroin-based lifestyle, and (2) coping with the urge to use. These individuals often overcame the first challenge by making certain activities—such as family, work, or religion—the exclusive focus of their attention. As they went along, these individuals encountered experiences in common with nonusers, which then laid the groundwork for a new social environment and identity. The second challenge, that of craving, was ordinarily handled in one of two ways: either by finding a substitute like alcohol, marijuana, or tranquilizers or by implementing cognitive coping strategies that served to reinterpret and redirect urge-promoting thoughts.

Waldorf (1983) also found evidence of unassisted change in a group of individuals previously dependent on heroin. A 24 year longitudinal investigation of habitual heroin use showed a fairly stable pattern of involvement after the late 30's, although individuals who eventually desisted without treatment were less involved in the criminal justice system, more likely to be employed, smoked fewer cigarettes, and consumed more alcohol than those who continued using heroin (Hser, Anglin, & Powers, 1993).

As remarkable as it may sound, a sizable proportion of eating disordered patients also recover without treatment. Theander (1985) interviewed 94 essentially untreated anorexics 3, 6, 12, and 24 years after the onset of symptomatology and found that slightly more than half the sample experienced good outcomes (stable body weight, normal eating, regular menstruation) after 6 years and three-quarters of the sample experienced good outcomes after 24 years. Deaths attributable to anorexia or suicide unfortunately also rose, from 4% after 3 years, to 7% after 6 years, to 16% after 24 years. Poor out-comes, on the other hand, declined from 37% after three years, to 18% after six years, to 7% after 24 years.

Whereas the Theander study was conducted in Sweden, similar results have been recorded in the United States. Questionnaires completed 20 months apart by 628 eating preoccupied women showed that 29% of the women initially satisfying criteria for anorexia symptomatology and 43% of the women initially satisfying criteria for bulimia had improved to the point that their behavior could now be classified as a subclinical eating disorder (Yager, Landsverk, & Edelstein, 1987). Of equal significance is the fact that there were no outcome differences between those who did and did not seek professional assistance during the interim.

In a study conducted on a group of London schoolgirls, Patton (1988) witnessed significant cross-over in eating-related diagnoses over a 1-year period. According to the results of this study, 21% of the schoolgirls initially classified as dieters later fulfilled criteria indicative of a full or partial eating disorder, while 41% of the girls initially classified as eating disordered were subsequently re-classified as noneating disordered dieters or nondieters. Unassisted change also appears to occur on a fairly regular basis with prob-lem gamblers (Walters, 1997).

Explaining Unassisted Change

Now that the prospect of unassisted change has been demonstrated, the next order of business is to clarify the mechanisms responsible for this phenom-enon. Klingemann (1992) interviewed 60 individuals who had recovered from either an alcohol or heroin problem without formal intervention in an effort to address this issue. The results of Klingemann's interviews favored Prochaska and DiClemente's (1992) stages of change model. This model is comprised of five stages: precontemplation, contemplation, preparation, action, and maintenance.

The initial challenge faced by the alcohol and heroin abusing subjects participating in the Klingemann study was summoning the motivation for change. This issue is addressed in the second and third of Prochaska and DiClemente's five stages, contemplation and preparation. Next, these former alcohol and heroin abusers set out to put their decision for change into effect, a process that corresponds with the fourth or action stage of the Prochaska and DiClemente model. Finally, subjects interviewed by Klingemann reported that the final phase of the change process involved negotiating a new identity or life meaning. These issues appear to fit the theme of the fifth and final stage of the Prochaska and DiClemente model, maintenance.

In further support of this model, Tucker, Vuchinich, and Gladsjo (1994) identified two sets of variables that prompted self-change in a group of former alcohol abusers, one set that initiated behavioral change and another set that maintained this change. What follows is a brief survey of how unassisted change conforms to the stages of change outlined by Prochaska and DiClemente.

The contemplation and preparation stages of the change process are evident in the results of several studies. Tuchfeld (1981) reports that a motivating force frequently mentioned by the self-remitting alcohol abusers he interviewed was the mounting negative physical and social consequences they experienced as a result of their continued misuse of alcohol. Ludwig (1985) identified a perception of having "hit bottom" as a major impetus for self-initiated change in the alcohol abusers he studied, while Simpson and Marsh (1986) chronicled similar sentiments in a group of heroin abusers who stopped using heroin without treatment.

In contrast to the avoidance-oriented incentives for self-change mentioned by subjects in the Tuchfeld and Ludwig studies, Kandel and Raveis (1989) uncovered a number of approach-oriented incentives for unassisted change in interviews with young adult marijuana and cocaine users. These included the assumption of family responsibilities and the desire to serve as positive role models. Walters (1996b) examined self-change in a group of incarcerated drug users and identified both avoidance-oriented and approach-oriented reasons for abandoning a drug lifestyle without professional assistance. Strong incentive for change, presumably encompassing both avoidance-oriented and approach-oriented motives, preceded successful desistance from cigarette smoking in another study (Marlatt, Curry, & Gordon, 1988).

The action stage of the Prochaska and DiClemente model is also represented in research on unassisted change. Various change strategies have been employed by people exiting a drug or other lifestyle without benefit of formal intervention. Strategies that increase self-efficacy and self-esteem, for instance, have been observed repeatedly in self-quitting smokers (Carey et al., 1993) and problem drinkers (Vaillant, 1983). Social support is another factor capable of transforming a desire for change into a behavioral reality (Sobell, Cunningham, Sobell, & Toneatto, 1993). Naturalistic behavior modification, in which the immediate negative consequences of one's involvement in an addictive activity are brought into focus, is also a powerful vehicle for change (Vaillant, 1983).

Lack of deviance is another key factor in the transition from desire to action. One group of investigators surmised that involvement with property crime and drug sales served to suppress the natural tendency for subjects to terminate their misuse of heroin as they grew older (Anglin, Brecht, Woodward, & Bonett, 1986). Conversely, increased involvement in conventional activities facilitated the natural change process in a group of young adult marijuana and cocaine users (Kandel & Raveis, 1989) and investment in a conventional life and identity apparently motivated self-change in a group of cocaine users, some of whom had been using cocaine for many years (Waldorf, Reinarman, & Murphy, 1991).

Tuchfeld (1981) was one of the first researchers to show that identity transformation normally accompanies natural desistance from problem drinking and that this helps maintain established changes in behavior. Biernacki (1990) recorded a similar outcome in a group of self-changing heroin "addicts." In order to maintain preliminary behavioral change, these individuals forged an identity incompatible with the continued misuse of heroin. This included reverting to an identity in place prior to the heroin-based identity and not significantly damaged by it, extending a nondrug identity that had previously coexisted with the heroin-based identity, or engaging in an emergent identity that neither preceded nor coexisted with the heroin-based identity. Biernacki's greatest contribution, however, may have been in showing that self-change is facilitated by acceptance of a view of oneself as "ordinary," because such a view permits increased identification and social interaction with nonusers.

Development of a new relationship uncontaminated by old injuries and resentments was found to be crucial in maintaining initial change in Vaillant's (1983) survey of self-remitting alcohol abusers. Tucker, Vuchinich, and Gladsjo (1994) likewise determined that a change in attributional style in the direction of increased internal control and personal responsibility was associated with maintenance in a group of self-remitting alcohol abusers.

Taken as a whole, these findings insinuate that some people cease addictive involvement in the absence of formal intervention and proceed through a series of stages characterized by increased motivation for change, implementation of change strategies, and maintenance of initial change through identity and behavioral transformation. Before concluding this section, however, it is important to understand that investigators have postulated the existence of two distinct pathways of desistance from an alcohol-centered lifestyle (Vaillant, 1983). One pathway is marked by higher levels of education and socioeconomic status, moderate alcohol usage, higher self-esteem, and a relatively strong social support system. The other pathway is characterized by lower education and socioeconomic status, more severe alcohol abuse, lower self-esteem, and fewer social supports.

Events that trigger and maintain change are believed to be different for the two pathways described above. Whereas a subjective belief in the destructiveness of the lifestyle may trigger change and social support may help maintain the change for persons taking the first pathway to desistance, concrete stressors (e.g., health problems, relationship problems, and low self-esteem) are more apt to trigger change and involvement with Alcoholics Anonymous (AA) is more likely to maintain change for persons adopting the second pathway (Humphreys, Moos, & Finney, 1995). Controlled drinking would therefore be a more realistic option for clients falling into the first of these two pathways to self-change.

BRIEF, ENVIRONMENTAL,
AND BEHAVIORAL INTERVENTIONS

Given the presumed strength of addiction to create profound preoccupation, a reasonable assumption would be that intervention must be protracted, dynamic, and complex in order to be effective. However, as the review in Chapter 6 suggests, intervention length and magnitude have little bearing on treatment outcome. This section consequently considers the value of brief, environmental, and behavioral interventions for addictive involvement as alternatives to a lifetime of treatment and how this challenges the preoccupation element of the addiction concept.

Motivational interviewing will be the brief intervention approach described in this section, followed by a review of the environmentally informed Community Reinforcement Approach (CRA) and the behaviorally oriented cue exposure model. Although all three change models were originally designed for alcohol abusing populations, each has proven itself effective with other forms of addictive involvement and may have utility in addressing a wide spectrum of life problems.

Brief Intervention: Motivational Interviewing

William Miller (1985) asserts that motivation is a dynamic process that develops between a therapist and client, rather than a static client trait. Motivational interviewing, a brief intervention comprised of several hours of assessment and a 1-hour feedback session in which the therapist sensitively and nonjudgmentally shares the results of the evaluation with the client, was introduced by Miller in an attempt to facilitate this dynamic process. Miller, Sovereign, and Krege (1988) and Miller, Benefield, and Tonigan (1993) successfully employed the motivational interviewing technique with several groups of problem drinkers.

Because the alcohol use problems of some of the subjects in the two Miller studies were relatively mild, the applicability of motivational interviewing to a more severe and chronic population of abusers has been questioned. In fact, one group of investigators argued that motivational interviewing had no appreciable effect on problem drinking in a group of chronic alcohol abusers (Kuchipudi, Hobein, Flickinger, & Iber, 1990). More recently, Bien, Miller, and Boroughs (1993) examined the utility of motivational interviewing in a group of severe alcohol dependent Veterans Administration outpatients. A 3-month follow-up revealed fewer total drinks, lower peak alcohol levels, and more days of abstinence in subjects exposed to a program in which motivational interviewing was included as a component, although these differences were no longer significant after six months, suggesting that the motivational interviewing effect may be time-limited when applied to those with more severe drinking histories.

Motivational interviewing has also been used to encourage change in persons dependent on heroin. Saunders, Wilkinson, and Phillips (1995) randomly assigned opiate abusing methadone maintenance clients to a brief (one hour) motivational interview or a 1-hour educational presentation and discussion. After six months, subjects receiving the motivational interviewing intervention displayed greater compliance with the methadone program, a more powerful commitment to change and abstinence, fewer opiate-related problems, and a less rapid return to drug use than subjects in the control condition.

Baker, Kochan, Dixon, Heather, and Wodak (1994) report that intravenous drug users randomly assigned to either a 1-session motivational interview or nonintervention control group significantly reduced injecting behaviors associated with elevated risk of HIV. The fact that the two groups failed to differ on this outcome measure was interpreted as evidence that simply directing people's attention to high risk behaviors may sometimes be sufficient to promote change. Dickerson, Hinchy, and Legg England (1990) obtained similar results in a study evaluating the usefulness of a self-help manual for problem gambling. Whether or not this manual was accompanied by a 90-minute interview, subjects receiving the manual reduced the frequency and intensity of their gambling involvement in follow-ups conducted 3 to 6 months later.

Environmental Intervention: The Community Reinforcement Approach

The Community Reinforcement Approach (CRA) employs operant learning principles and social support to aid clients interested in abandoning a lifestyle of alcohol or other drug involvement (Sisson & Azrin, 1989). One goal of CRA is to provide relationship enhancement counseling as a means of soliciting social support for clients. Teaching clients to identify and anticipate the antecedents and consequences of their behavior is another major component of the CRA paradigm. In this regard, clients are sometimes placed on disulfiram to illustrate the immediate negative consequences of alcohol ingestion. Other clients may be enrolled in a program of skills training in an effort to demonstrate the positive consequences of handling one's problems without drugs. Employment counseling is a third component of the CRA package and a fourth component is the development of new recreational interests and re-involvement in recreational activities previously abandoned.

Alcohol abusing clients offered CRA as part of a traditional residential treatment program displayed significantly greater levels of sobriety, employment, and social adjustment than alcohol abusing clients receiving only the traditional residential program (Hunt & Azrin, 1973). The CRA approach has also produced positive results when administered to alcohol abusers as an outpatient intervention (Azrin, Sisson, Meyers, & Godley, 1982).

Stephen Higgins and his colleagues at the University of Vermont have successfully implemented the CRA model with cocaine abusing outpatients. In a nonrandomized control study, Higgins et al. (1991) offered 13 cocaine abusing outpatients CRA and followed a group of 15 outpatients enrolled in a traditional 12-step counseling program. The CRA condition experienced significantly higher retention after 12 weeks of programming (85% versus 42%) and CRA participants were more likely to have achieved initial cocaine abstinence than those participating in the 12-step program.

These findings were subsequently replicated in a randomized control study of 38 outpatient cocaine abusers exposed to 24 weeks of intervention. From the results of this study, Higgins et al. (1993) determined that significantly more CRA than 12-step participants prevailed in their respective programs after 12 (84% versus 26%) and 24 (58% versus 11%) weeks. Moreover, a significantly greater proportion of CRA subjects achieved 4 (74% versus 16%), 8 (68% versus 11%), and 16 (42% versus 5%) consecutive weeks of abstinence during the treatment program. A 12-month follow-up revealed greater cocaine abstinence in the CRA group as measured by both urinalysis and self-report data, although only the urinalysis results were statistically significant (Higgins, Budney, & Bickel, 1994).

Behavioral Intervention: Cue Exposure

Cue exposure is a behavioral intervention in which clients are exposed to addiction-relevant cues designed to initially increase the urge to become involved in the addictive activity. The urge is then extinguished by continually presenting the cue without permitting the client to emit or complete the addictive response, a procedure known as response prevention. Blakey and Baker (1980) successfully used imaginal presentation of alcohol-related cues to reduce the craving for alcohol in a group of chronic alcohol abusers. Rankin, Hodgson, and Stockwell (1983) modified this procedure by administering a small priming dose of vodka to a group of inpatient alcohol abusers and then encouraged them to resist the urge to drink during a 45-minute period in which they were exposed to the sight and smell of alcohol but were prevented from consuming the beverage. Subjects completing this procedure experienced reduced craving for alcohol and increased ability to control the speed of their drinking.

Drummond and Glautier (1994) sequentially assigned alcohol abusing clients to either a cue exposure or a relaxation control group and discovered that subjects in the cue exposure condition consumed significantly less alcohol and lapsed into heavy drinking more slowly than control subjects during a 6-month period of follow-up. Studies in which cue exposure has been employed as an intervention for cocaine (O'Brien, Childress, McLellan, & Ehrman, 1990), tobacco (Raw & Russell, 1980), and heroin (Dawe et al., 1993) misuse have met with mixed reviews and indeterminate outcomes.

Cue exposure has also been used to intervene with eating disordered clients. Wilson, Rossiter, Kleifield, and Lindholm (1986) used cue exposure (consumption of a large meal) and response prevention (remaining in the room after the meal) to reduce binge eating and vomiting in a group of bulimic patients. The confirmatory results recorded in this study were interpreted by Wilson et al. as support for the view that cue exposure enhances perceptions of self-efficacy in bulimic patients by teaching them to manage uncomfortable feelings and thoughts without purging. Two of four bulimics receiving 12 sessions of therapist-aided cue exposure to food stimuli demonstrated reduced craving for food during the sessions and decreased frequency of binges and vomiting between sessions (Schmidt & Marks, 1988). A third subject displayed improvement only after the end of the intervention and a fourth subject dropped out of the program after the ninth session.

Jansen, Broekmate, and Heymans (1992) randomly assigned 12 overweight bulimics to one of two conditions: cue exposure with response prevention and self-control training with relapse prevention. Whereas both groups showed improvement over the baseline, 33% of the self control subjects were binge-free after one year as opposed to 100% of the cue exposure subjects. Cue exposure and response prevention have also been found effective in reducing heavy exercising in weight-recovered anorectics (Long & Hollin, 1995) and tension, depression, guilt, and bulimic urges in binge–purge subtype anorectics (Kennedy, Katz, Neitzer, Ralevski, & Mendlowitz, 1995).

EXPECTANCIES

Expectancies, the first of three empirical findings to challenge the loss of control assumptions of the addiction concept, can be studied using one of two basic methodologies. The first establishes an instructional set in which subjects are informed that they have just consumed alcohol or a placebo in an effort to determine the impact such "knowledge" has on a person's experiences and behavior. The second methodology involves exploring people's beliefs about the anticipated outcome of an "addictive" agent or activity and the effect these beliefs have on the person's future behavior.

The Expectancy Set

The balanced placebo design is one method used to study expectancy sets. This design requires subjects to receive either alcohol or a placebo, after which, half the members of each group are informed that they have consumed alcohol irrespective of which beverage they actually consumed, while the other half are told that they have consumed a placebo. The four cells of the balanced placebo design are:

1. consume alcohol—informed that they consumed alcohol
2. consume alcohol—informed that they consumed placebo
3. consume placebo—informed that they consumed alcohol
4. consume placebo—informed that they consumed placebo

With the balanced placebo design, Marlatt, Demming, and Reid (1973) demonstrated that the instructional set was a more powerful determinant of imbibition than the actual content of the drink. Furthermore, subsequent research has generally confirmed the power of expectancy to influence the behavior and experiences of people exposed to either alcohol or a placebo (Hull & Bond, 1986).

A study conducted recently by Sayette, Breslin, Wilson, and Rosenblum (1994) offers challenge to the integrity of the balanced placebo design for certain applications. In this study, 44% of the subjects in the anti-placebo condition (receive alcohol—informed that they consumed placebo) whose BACs were .060 or higher believed that the beverage they had consumed contained alcohol. Sayette et al. concede that lower levels of alcohol (a BAC of .035 or lower) may insure a reasonable degree of deception.

The balanced placebo design has also been used to study expectancy effects for cannabis, the results of which suggest a powerful subjective reaction in persons who believe that the cigarette they are smoking contains hashish (Camí, Guerra, Ugena, Segura, & De La Torre, 1991).

Expectancy effects can be neutralized with the aid of a procedure known as the expectancy challenge. The expectancy challenge is designed to disrupt the traditional association presumed to exist between drinking and behavior by illustrating how difficult it is to distinguish between those who have consumed small amounts of alcohol and those who have ingested a placebo. Darkes and Goldman (1993) established the practical value of the expectancy challenge in a large sample of male undergraduates. Students participating in the expectancy challenge consumed either alcohol or a placebo and then interacted with a small group of other students who had also been exposed to either alcohol or a placebo. Subjects were then questioned about what they believed was in the drink they and other group members had consumed.

Subjects participating in the Darkes and Goldman study estimated their own condition (alcohol–placebo) at a purely chance level and failed to accurately identify fellow group members who received either alcohol or an inert substance made to look and taste like alcohol. Subjects enrolled in the expectancy challenge condition eventually received a brief lecture on expectancies and the role of expectancies in promoting effects traditionally ascribed to the physiological action of alcohol. Darkes and Goldman discerned that subjects in the expectancy challenge condition subsequently reduced their consumption of alcohol relative to subjects in a traditional alcohol education program or nonintervention control. These results suggest that expectancy sets may not only play a causal role in the use and misuse of alcohol but that the expectancy challenge may be an effective intervention for high risk drinkers.

Outcome Expectancies

Outcome expectancies are the experiences people anticipate from their involvement in an addictive activity. Unlike research on expectancy sets, outcome expectancies extend to all forms of addictive involvement. With the exception of alcohol, however, there is minimal empirical information on the outcome expectancies of behavior viewed to be addictive. Like any learned behavior, outcome expectancies are formed directly—through personal experience and the development of conditioned emotional reactions—as well as indirectly—through observation and the modeling of other peoples' behavior. Alcohol expectancies have been observed in children (Miller, Smith, & Goldman, 1990) and adolescents (Christiansen & Goldman, 1983) prior to any personal experience with alcohol. Apparently, children acquire expectancies from cultural modeling (MacAndrew & Edgerton, 1969) and observational learning, particularly of their parents (Brown, Creamer, & Stetson, 1987).

Wide cultural differences have been noted in the expectancies people form for alcohol (Christiansen & Teahan, 1987) and the relationship presumed to exist between drinking and aggression (Lindman & Lang, 1994). Furthermore, there is compelling evidence that expectancies may determine, in part, when people start drinking, how much they drink, and whether or not they develop a drinking problem (Leigh, 1989). Research studies show that outcome expectancies are also capable of predicting the onset and frequency of marijuana and cocaine usage (Schafer & Brown, 1991), although these expectancies are only loosely tied to the pharmacological properties of the chemical substances imbibed (Stacy, Galaif, Sussman, & Dent, 1996). Expectancies may also be of value in explaining the binging and purging activities of bulimic patients (Elmore & de Castro, 1990).

Three principal classes of expectancy are cited in the literature: positive reinforcing expectancies, negative reinforcing expectancies, and negative consequence expectancies. Positive reinforcing expectancies portray the use of alcohol as providing outcomes that are enjoyable, conducive to good social relationships, and capable of enhancing performance. Negative reinforcing expectancies, on the other hand, view alcohol as effective in reducing uncomfortable emotions like anxiety or removing barriers to enjoyment like fear. Negative consequence expectancies are beliefs that acknowledge the adverse short and long term effects of involvement in an addictive activity.

Given that negative consequences tend to be less immediate than the reinforcing consequences of addictive involvement, this particular class of expectancies may have reduced dominion over the actions of people who habitually engage in addictive behavior. Whether this distal-over-proximal expectancy style is a cause or a consequence of addictive involvement is a question that requires further study. However, preliminary evidence suggests that this style may be both a cause and an effect of one's involvement in an addictive behavior. The results of a 3-wave longitudinal panel study, for instance, denote that a reciprocal relationship forms between outcome expectancies and behavior. In this study, adolescents who believed that alcohol would improve their social relationships consumed more alcohol, and those teens who drank more developed more positive expectancies for alcohol's capacity to facilitate these relationships (Smith, Goldman, Greenbaum, & Christiansen, 1995).

Brown, Creamer, and Stetson (1987) report that adolescent alcohol abusers anticipate greater cognitive and motor enhancement from alcohol than their nonalcohol abusing peers. When it comes to chronically involved persons, however, most studies find that positive reinforcement expectancies have little predictive value, whether the substance being studied is alcohol (Rather & Sherman, 1989) or tobacco (Wetter et al., 1994). Investigators seem divided on the issue of whether negative reinforcement expectancies, such as the belief that alcohol will reduce tension (Frone, Russell, & Cooper, 1993), or negative consequence expectancies, such as the belief that alcohol is capable of creating serious long term family difficulties (Jones & McMahon, 1994), are better at differentiating between chronic abusers and those who eventually desist or who never develop a problem in the first place. In all probability, both classes of expectancy are important.

Schafer and Fals–Stewart (1993) conducted a study on outcome expectancies for cocaine and observed that the proximal and distal positive reinforcement expectancies for cocaine failed to distinguish between users and nonusers. However, nonusers had more active negative consequence expectancies, both proximally and distally. Before outcome expectancies can be fully understood, the proximal and distal features of all three categories of

expectancy—positive reinforcing, negative reinforcing, and negative consequences—must be specified and the reciprocal relationship that forms
between outcome expectancies and behavior clarified.

ATTRIBUTIONS: THE ABSTINENCE
VIOLATION EFFECT

Attributions, like expectancies, are beliefs. However, rather than focusing on
the anticipated outcome of a particular action, attributions are inferences
drawn about the nature and causes of one's own or another's behavior.
Attribution theory asserts that the perceived causes of success or failure can
be ordered along four dimensions: internal versus external, stable versus
unstable, controllable versus uncontrollable, and global versus specific
(Weiner, 1974). Marlatt (1985) considers attributions crucial in explaining
why some people recover from an initial slip while others relapse. By rigidly
adhering to abstinence as the only way out of an addictive lifestyle and
attributing a slip to internal, stable, uncontrollable, and global causes (e.g.,
lack of willpower) one is, in effect, setting oneself up for relapse and failure
through activation of what Marlatt refers to as the Abstinence Violation
Effect (AVE).

The AVE is less likely to occur when a person attributes a lapse to external, unstable, controllable, and specific causes (e.g., lack of skill in handling
a particular situation). This individual is much less likely to relapse following a slip or lapse than someone who views abstinence as the sole criterion
for success. The AVE is therefore comprised of two interrelated processes: a
set of attributions, based in part on a person's commitment to a goal of abstinence, followed by a negative emotional reaction in the form of guilt, shame,
or depression that then increases the person's risk of relapse.

The studies listed in Table 8–1 address the AVE, although only six provide a direct test of Marlatt's (1985) AVE construct. O'Donnell (1984) witnessed dysphoric moods in outpatient alcohol abusers who eventually
relapsed following a slip, but failed to appraise the attributions of individual
clients. Inasmuch as Ruderman and McKirnan (1984) report that they witnessed outcomes inconsistent with the AVE hypothesis, they too neglected
to consider the attributions of individual subjects. Grove (1983) specifically
measured the attributional styles of individual subjects but there was no
future behavioral outcome (i.e., relapse) included in his study. Finally, Birke,
Edelmann, and Davis (1990) probed the general attributional styles of 21
illicit drug users rather than making the attributions specific to the individual's most recent lapse and then combined relapsers with one-time lapsers
(thereby mixing subjects with differing intensities of AVE).

Of the six studies listed in Table 8–1 that directly assessed the AVE, four (Curry, Marlatt, & Gordon, 1987; Grilo & Shiffman, 1994; Mooney, Burling, Hartman, & Brenner–Lis, 1992; Stephens, Curtin, Simpson, & Roffman, 1994) offer verification of Marlatt's original premise and lend additional weight to those who would challenge the loss of control element of the addiction concept. One of the direct tests that fail to corroborate the AVE formulation (Schoeneman, Hollis, Stevens, Fisher, & Cheek, 1988) notes that subjects relapsing after a slip were more apt to have relied on characterological and external attributions than those recovering from a slip. This one inconsistent study points to a key limitation of the AVE construct.

VOLITION

Volition entails self-determination and the capacity to make choices and decisions in life. The AVE considers two features of volition—locus of causality (internal–external) and controllability—and appears to make an illogical match of the two. Like addiction theories that hold people not responsible for the development of an addictive problem but responsible for its resolution, the AVE proposes that events viewed as controllable but external in origin are those least likely to result in relapse. This may, in fact, explain the conflicting results obtained by Schoeneman and his colleagues (1988) in one of the two direct tests of the AVE to have produced an unambiguous disconfirmatory finding. Similar to the smokers in the Schoeneman study, internally oriented clients that had habitually abused alcohol (Baumann, Obitz, & Reich, 1982) or heroin (Bradley, Gossop, Brewin, Phillips, & Green, 1992) experienced better outcomes than externally oriented alcohol and opiate abusers. Volition, therefore, not only entails assuming control over one's life through the decision-making process, but also requires that one assume responsibility for these decisions. Furthermore, like research on expectancies and attributes, it disputes the loss of control element of the addiction concept.

Over 25 years ago laboratory studies showed that "chronic alcoholics" were capable of exercising volition in their use of ethanol. When the cost requirements for receiving alcohol were increased after two drinks, chronic alcohol abusers participating in one of these studies increased the temporal span between drinks in an effort to minimize the amount of work required to receive beverage alcohol (Bigelow & Liebson, 1972). In this same study, near-abstinence was achieved in several of these alcohol dependent subjects when the cost requirements for alcohol were raised. Additional evidence of volitional factors in alcohol misuse is found in a study pitting heavy drinkers who voluntarily signed a pledge to abstain from drinking for one week

TABLE 8–1 Studies on the Abstinence Violation Effect

Study	Sample	AT[1]	EM[2]	BO[3]	Outcome
O'Donnell (1984)	82 outpatient alcohol abusers	No	Yes	Yes	Belief in self-fulfilling prophesy had no effect on recovery from a slip, but dysphoric mood predicted relapse
Ruderman & McKirnan (1984)	47 restrained and unrestrained drinkers	No	No	Yes	Restrained drinkers given a preload of alcohol were less likely to select alcohol over soda than restrained drinkers not administered an alcohol preload
Barrios & Niehaus (1985)	68 smokers	No	Yes	Yes	Successful quitters reported higher self-efficacy and fewer negative moods than unsuccessful quitters
Brandon, Tiffany, & Baker (1986)	82 smokers	No	Yes	Yes	No evidence that reacting to a lapse with depression or hopelessness led to a worse outcome
Curry et al. (1987)	41 smokers	Yes	Yes	Yes	Smokers who relapsed within a week of a slip reported more intense AVEs than subjects who maintained abstinence after a slip
Schoeneman et al. (1988)	32 smokers	Yes	Yes	Yes	Slip-relapsers attributed slip to behavioral shortcomings and mood as much as stop-abstainers; slip-relapsers were more likely to attribute slip to characterologic and external factors
Birke et al. (1990)	21 illicit drug users	Yes[4]	No	Yes	Combined group of lapsers and relapsers failed to differ from abstainers on attributional dimensions of internality, stability, and globality
Kales (1990)	21 normal-weight bulimics	No	No	Yes	Dichotomous attitude toward eating and specific foods correlated with an increased number of binges
Collins & Lapp (1991)	323 social drinkers	Yes[4]	No	Yes	Attributing the causes of drinking-related events to internal, stable, and global factors correlated with more drinks consumed and more drinking problems

Study	Sample	Attributions[1]	Emotions[2]	Behavioral outcome[3]	Findings
Mooney et al. (1992)	80 moderately to morbidly obese fasters	Yes	Yes	Yes	Fasters attributing their first lapse to internal, stable, and global causes lost a smaller portion of their excess weight than fasters experiencing a less intense AVE
Grove (1993)	121 smokers	Yes	Yes	No	High self-efficacy smokers experienced a less intense AVE
Grilo & Shiffman (1994)	50 normal-weight female bingers	Yes	Yes	Yes	When subjects made more internal, global, and uncontrollable attributions for a binge a second binge followed significantly sooner
Stephens et al. (1994)	75 marijuana users	Yes	Yes	Yes	Subjects returning to regular marijuana use following an initial lapse made more internal, stable, and global attributions for lapse than those not relapsing
Walton, Castro, & Barrington (1994)	97 alcohol and other drug abusers	Yes	No	Yes	Relapsers made more stable and global attributions than lapsers; no internal–external differences
Ward, Hudson, & Marshall (1994)	26 incarcerated male child molesters	No	Yes	Yes[5]	Identified an AVE at relapse (actual offense) but not at first lapse (initial sexual opportunity)
Johnson, Schlundt, Barclay, Carr-Nongle, & Engler (1995)	44 binge-eating females	No	No	Yes	Probability of binge eating episode increased with presence of earlier episode consistent with AVE
Shiffman et al. (1996)	133 smokers	Yes	Yes	Yes	Affective reactions to a lapse (e.g., guilt), self-blaming attributions for the lapse, and self-efficacy all failed to predict progression toward relapse

[1] attributions (internality, stability, controllability, and globality) measured
[2] emotions (guilt, hopelessness, and depression) measured
[3] behavioral outcome
[4] attributions measured in general rather than for a specific lapse
[5] retrospective accounts serve as outcome

against heavy drinkers who self-monitored their drinking behavior but were not asked to sign a pledge. The results indicated that subjects asked to sign the pledge achieved significantly greater levels of abstinence (46% of group) and reductions in alcohol intake (74% below baseline) relative to the control group (Sadava, 1986).

Notions of choice and subjective expected utilities have likewise been applied to gambling (Mobilia, 1993) and risky sexual activity (Pinkerton & Abramson, 1992). Consummatory behavior may also be under volitional control. Lazarick, Fishbein, Loiello, and Howard (1988) studied 17 self-identified binge eating undergraduates and discovered that the number of binge episodes could be decreased by establishing "no-binge" days and having students substitute vegetable binges for regular food binges.

The reader should not assume from this favorable review that volition is either absolute or boundless. First, volition must be viewed within the context of a person's current situation since some situations present more options than others. There are generally more options available in a disagreement with one's spouse than in interactions with a gun-wielding carjacker. Volition also has clear developmental parameters. A 4-year old child does not possess the same number and quality of options as a 14-year old adolescent. An expanding scope of experience, coupled with neurological maturation, makes for increased volitional capacity with age. Third, people do not always select the "best" option. Decisions may be made in haste, with limited information, or against one's own best interests, but this does not refute the capacity for choice.

Lifestyle theorists argue that volition need not be immutable, invariant, or impeccable to exist. This does not mean that lifestyle theorists view addictive involvement as a simple matter of willpower. It would be more accurate to say that addictive involvement is an exercise in volition, although the volition being exercised by someone preoccupied with alcohol, gambling, or sex is geared more toward immediate gratification than long term satisfaction.

THE SOCIOCULTURAL PARAMETERS OF ADDICTIVE INVOLVEMENT

There are wide cultural differences in the use and misuse of alcohol and other mind-altering substances incongruent with the persistence and loss of control elements of the addiction concept. Bennett, Janca, Grant, and Sartorius (1993) surveyed subjects from nine separate cultures and discovered that respondents from seven of the nine cultures viewed "normal drinking" as a valid cultural concept. A substantial minority of the Navajo subjects from Flagstaff, Arizona and a majority of subjects from Bangalore, India characterized "normal drinking" as largely unattainable in each of their societies, whereas respondents from Athens, Greece and Santander, Spain perceived "normal drinking" as essential to their respective cultures. Cultural differences in attitudes towards normal and heavy drinking and alcohol-related expectancies were also observed. Christiansen and Teahan (1987) note that such expectancies exert a profound effect on drinking behavior. They report that Irish youth not only acknowledged less frequent social drinking and less recurrent problem drinking than American youth, but also held more negative expectancies for the anticipated effects of alcohol.

Kitano, Chi, Rhee, Law, and Lubben (1992) detected a similar trend in a study of Japanese subjects living in Japan, Hawaii, and California. The more permissive attitudes toward male alcohol use in Japan and toward female alcohol use in the United States were reflected in the standard consumption practices of these two cultures. A review of the international literature on gender and alcohol consumption, in fact, implies that sociocultural norms, roles, and expectations play a more integral role in the drinking behavior of men and women than innate physiologically based gender differences in alcohol response (Heath, 1991).

Definitions and patterns of alcohol abuse also vary by culture. Room (1985) conceptualized loss of control as a cultural manifestation of societies that adhere to a strict Calvinistic view of control. According to Room, a key element of the addiction concept—loss of control—is nothing more than a cultural invention designed to perpetuate a mythical construction that may inhibit change in persons who do not accept the legitimacy of the construct. In their classic study on cross-cultural differences in alcohol-influenced behavior, MacAndrew and Edgerton (1969) determined that each culture establishes guidelines for the appropriate use of alcohol and one's actions while under the influence of intoxicating beverages. These investigators witnessed drunken sex orgies in several of these cultures, but were amazed to discover that participants rarely violated societal taboos (e.g., incest).

Further evidence for a sociocultural view of substance use is provided by Cinquemani (1975) who writes that the Central Mexican Indian tribes that he observed habitually consumed large amounts of alcohol but acted in a very different manner when drunk: men of the Los Pastores tribe, it seemed, became verbally and physically aggressive under the influence of alcohol, while men of the Mixtecan tribe drank heavily but avoided alcohol-related violence. Cinquemani traces these variations in drunken comportment to differences in cultural attitudes and expectancies. Whereas the Los Pastores fatalistically believe that alcohol provokes men to violence, the Mixtecans associate neither violence nor loss of control with heavy drinking. Interestingly, even the Los Pastores eschew violence during rituals and religious ceremonies.

Other forms of addictive involvement similarly reflect strong cross-cultural effects. Hayano (1989), for instance, speculates that cultural differences in gambling deportment may parallel a culture's colonial history and pattern of urbanization. Cultural variations have likewise been observed in sexual scripts (Simon & Gagnon, 1986) and love relationships (Dion & Dion, 1993). Sociocultural factors may also encourage eating disorders. Studies insinuate that bulimia and anorexia are relatively rare in developing nations (Buhrich, 1981), in non-Western cultures (Nasser, 1986), and among nonwhites living in Western societies (King, 1989). Furnham and Alibhai (1983) ascertained that Kenyans who had immigrated to Great Britain and assumed English standards of physical attractiveness found a thin body significantly more appealing than Kenyans who had not yet integrated into British society. Whitehouse and Mumford (1988), on the other hand, surmised that Asian girls living in England expressed substantially more eating-related concerns if raised in a traditional Asian family then if brought up in homes dominated by Western values.

Questions have been raised about the overall meaning of studies comparing the addictive practices of different cultures since there is a lack of controlled research on the cross-cultural correlates of eating disordered behavior. Hence, these findings may be more indicative of cultural variations in reporting practice than differences in eating behavior. Furthermore, researchers need to develop measures that are conceptually equivalent to those that have been employed with Western subjects.

A number of explanations for cross-cultural variations in addictive behavior have been offered, one of which will be described in this section. People are socialized to accept the norms, values, and beliefs of the society in which they are raised. This socialization, in turn, affects the patterns of subsequent behavior displayed by the members of that society. Perhaps this is most clearly illustrated in research on acculturation.

Caetano and Medina–Mora (1988) unearthed evidence of an acculturation effect in a study of Mexican American males who consumed significantly more alcohol five years after immigrating to the United States than a group of nonimmigrating Mexican males. An acculturation effect can also be inferred from the results of a study by Wagner–Echeagaray, Schütz, Chilcoat, and Anthony (1994). In this study, Mexican American subjects presumed to be more acculturated to American society (i.e., chose to be interviewed in English) were significantly more likely to have smoked crack than subjects selecting the Spanish interview format. The outcome of this study is open to alternate interpretations, however, since language is only one facet of acculturation. Moreover, there were no differences in crack usage between Puerto Rican subjects choosing to be interviewed in English and those choosing to be interviewed in Spanish.

Acculturation effects have also been documented for sexual experience and eating attitudes. Mexican American females demonstrating greater acculturation to American standards acknowledge an earlier age of initial intercourse (Slonin–Nevo, 1992) and more eating-related pathology (Pumar-iega, 1986) than less acculturated Mexican American females.

SETTING EFFECTS

Besides having an indirect effect on behavior, as evidenced by cross-cultural patterns of addictive involvement, environmental factors may also exert a direct effect on behavior. The setting in which an addictive activity takes place provides an example of how the environment directly affects behavior. Heavy drinkers who consumed a small amount of alcohol or an alcohol-like placebo in a simulated bar or lounge environment were more apt to report a craving for alcohol than immoderate drinkers imbibing alcohol or a placebo in a laboratory setting (McCusker & Brown, 1990). The craving for cocaine (Childress, McLellan, Ehrman, & O'Brien, 1987) and opiates (Childress, McLellan, & O'Brien, 1986) has also been attributed to environmental cues.

The euphorigenic effects of drugs have also been shown to vary as a function of the setting in which the drugs are consumed. Both alcohol (Sher, 1985) and marijuana (Carlin, Bakker, Halpern, & Post, 1972) have been found to produce greater subjective feelings of euphoria and well-being when taken in a social or natural milieu than when ingested in the barren confines of a university laboratory. Amphetamines, on the other hand, produce equivalent levels of hypermotility, elation, and gregariousness regardless of where they are consumed (Zacny, Bodker, & de Wit, 1992).

Although setting effects have been observed primarily with chemical substances, other forms of addictive involvement may also respond to direct environmental influences. This possibility, in fact, is what lead Dickerson (1993) to question the value of gambling research conducted in settings where the ambiance deviates dramatically from the stimulus conditions found in the natural gambling environment. Sexual preoccupation and eating disorders also appear to respond to setting effects. The powerful effects that both direct and indirect environmental influences have on addictive behavior certainly bring the persistence assumptions of the addiction concept into serious question and demonstrate the complexity of behavior traditionally viewed to be addictive.

The eight empirical issues described in this chapter were not randomly selected from all areas of research on addictive behavior. Nonetheless, they cover a range of topics of sufficient breadth to seriously question the validity of the four principal components of the addiction concept. First, it was demonstrated that behaviors traditionally conceptualized as addictive do not inevitably lapse into progressive deterioration without treatment and that controlled involvement in an addictive activity is possible. Second, it was shown that addictive behavior is not so preoccupying that it prevents clients from responding to brief, environmental, and behavioral interventions. Third, research on expectancies, attributions, and volition demonstrates the fallacy of the loss of control element of the addiction concept. Fourth, addictive behavior has been found to respond to both direct and indirect environmental influences and so may not be as persistent as proponents of the addiction concept have alleged. In short, solid empirical support appears to be lacking for the four key elements of the addiction concept.

9

PRACTICAL LIMITATIONS
OF THE ADDICTION CONCEPT

Besides the logical and empirical limitations described in the two preceding chapters, the addiction concept is also handicapped by certain practical considerations. Pragmatic constructions of addiction were reviewed in Chapter 6, with the results showing that these models may be no more capable of clarifying the underlying motives of drug users, problem gamblers, and bulimics than their biological, psychological, or sociological counterparts. Ironically, most pragmatic constructions are so ambiguous, contradictory, and flawed as to be largely impractical.

The present chapter explores the issue of practicality by investigating two practical problems with the general concept of addiction: first reductionism and then options and opportunities. Following a discussion of these two practical problems with the overall addiction concept, the practical limitations of each of the four key elements of the addiction concept will be considered: stages of change in the case of progression, overfocusing in the case of preoccupation, accountability in the case of loss of control, and identity in the case of persistence.

REDUCTIONISM

Reductionism involves reducing a whole or gestalt to its individual parts. Edwards (1994) states that reductionism is the sine qua non of the scientific method and that empirical understanding depends on the ability to break objects and ideas down into their constituent parts. However, as was explained in Chapter 7, this line of reasoning, taken to an extreme, can lead to an illogical conclusion—that these parts necessarily represent the whole—if one overlooks the natural limitations of the reductionistic process. Conceptualizations that neglect a behavior's situational context are doomed to misapply the reductionistic principle. Edwards (1994) asserts that "good science necessarily takes things to bits and the bad scientist then mistakes the bits for the whole" (p. 11). To borrow an oft-repeated phrase, the whole is greater than the sum of its individual parts. It may be possible, however, to break the whole down into its constituent parts and then fit the parts back together to form a more integrated whole.

Reductionism and integration, rather than being antagonistic processes, are actually capable of complementing one another. Studies denote that the richness of the language by which a culture describes a phenomenon—a possible outcome of both reductionism and integration—is directly proportional to the culture's depth of understanding and ability to effectively manage the phenomenon (Efran, Heffner, & Lukens, 1987). Interestingly, people who display a related attribute—cognitive complexity—typically cope better with depression, anxiety, and manifestations of life stress than less cognitively complex people (Dixon & Baumeister, 1991).

A second meaning for reductionism in the social sciences is a belief in the existence of a dominant theory or discipline to which all other theories and disciplines can be reduced. Again, the relevance of this interpretation to addictive forms of behavior is obvious. The belief that all theories and ideas should conform or reduce to one model, addictive or behavioral, creates a practical dilemma in that no one theory can realistically account for all aspects of phenomena as complex as drug use, gambling, and sex. Many behaviors can be reduced to biochemistry, but this does not mean that biochemical explanations supersede or negate other avenues of inquiry, explanation, and meaning (Efran & Heffner, 1991).

The principle of complementarity has been used by physicists to account for the fact that light possesses characteristics of both a wave and particle. This illustrates how a physical event might be understood from two (or more) different perspectives, neither of which is necessarily subordinate to the other. Rychlak (1993) proposes complementarity in the field of psychology using four theoretical groundings: the Physikos (physical relationships), the Bios (biological functions), the Socius (group and cultural influences), and the Logos (interpretations and beliefs). He argues that a psychological phenomenon like addictive behavior can be conceptualized using any one of these four groundings and that each grounding is not reducible to the others. The willingness of scientists to entertain multiple interpretations of a phenomenon will eventually aid them in their search for knowledge concerning the object of their inquiry.

One of the primary limitations of reductionism as practiced in the field of addictions is that it has served to block our understanding of human behavior. Neuhaus (1993) writes that addiction treatment providers continue to act as if the concepts, ideas, and metaphors they invented to facilitate communication among themselves and achieve insight into the intricacies of drug use and gambling are tangible entities. These concepts, ideas, and metaphors can be helpful, but remain just concepts, ideas, and metaphors. Failure to appreciate this fact will tend to cloud one's thinking.

It is important to understand that certain groups within a society become practiced in the art of reduction. In ancient times the storyteller and soothsayer were the practitioners of reductionism. In modern times these roles have been assumed by the media and certain political interests. The media promotes reductionism by oversimplifying complex issues and politicians frequently walk the line between reductionism and demagoguery (Camí, 1994). Camí contends that scientists have an obligation to translate their work into practical statements that neither oversimplify nor distort the meaning and nature of their work. Reductionism is a necessary step in the realization of scientific understanding, but it is not the final step. Many supporters of the addiction concept appear to be of the opinion that simplification is the goal of theorizing. Lifestyle theorists, on the other hand, contend that the goal of theorizing is to effectively and meaningfully merge the simple with the complex and account for the part while remaining cognizant of the whole.

OPTIONS AND OPPORTUNITIES

The addiction concept may not only impede our understanding of addictive behavior, but may also inhibit change. One way it can do this is by limiting a person's options and opportunities. Clients who accept that they are addicted, for instance, may be denying themselves access to certain change vehicles. Eiser, Sutton, and Wober (1978), for instance, determined that smokers who viewed themselves as addicted had a greater propensity to think that they would fail in their efforts to stop smoking and were consequently less inclined to attempt cessation than smokers who viewed themselves as something other than addicted.

In analyzing data supplied by 40 couples involved in ongoing love relationships, Nelson, Hill–Barlow, and Benedict (1994) discovered that high self-esteem, self-actualizing tendencies, and emotional maturity, all of which potentially signal an expanding array of life options, correlated with increased sexual and psychological satisfaction. Acceptance of addiction, on the other hand, may serve to narrow or limit one's perspective and future capacity for change.

Therapists adopting an addictive view of problem behavior may also be limiting their options. Neuhaus (1993) contends that by pursuing a goal of converting clients to their way of thinking—namely, that drug abuse, problem gambling, and sexual preoccupation are addictions—therapists deny themselves the opportunity to explore new and previously unforeseen possibilities with clients. Change is the mother of innovation but innovation is perceived as a threat by some proponents of the addiction model. Strict adherence to a precept of addiction may consequently thwart the natural change process by limiting alternative options and suppressing opportunities for innovation.

Whereas the addiction concept may reduce opportunities for change, it opens the door to other possibilities. Truan (1993), for one, contends that a doctrine of addiction, particularly the "addiction as disease" formulation, encourages unlimited and perpetual treatment. After all, if one has an incurable disease then treatment should be continuous. Hensen and Emerick (1985) arranged for five confederates to present ambiguous drinking concerns to six different treatment facilities. Of the 29 assessments carried out, 17 resulted in diagnoses of "alcoholism," nine of which included recommendations for inpatient hospitalization. This illustrates how a concept like addiction can create opportunities for increased treatment despite empirical evidence showing that the length and intensity of intervention are generally unrelated to outcome (see Chapters 6 and 8). The addiction concept could also open up opportunities for increased governmental intrusion into the private lives of individual citizens under the guise of "protecting" people from themselves.

THE STAGES OF CHANGE

One practical limitation of the progression element of the addiction concept is failure to consider the nature of change. James Prochaska and Carlo DiClemente (1992) propose a five-stage model of change that challenges the progression element of the addiction concept. People in the initial or precontemplation stage of this model are said to be minimally motivated for change. Persons falling into the second of Prochaska and DiClemente's five stages, the contemplation stage, show interest in change but demonstrate ambivalent commitment to the process. Commitment to change is more evident during the preparation stage, the third of Prochaska and DiClemente's five stages. This is followed by the action stage in which the individual actively modifies problematic thoughts, feelings, and behaviors. The goal of maintenance, the final stage of change proposed by Prochaska and DiClemente, is to consolidate gains realized during the action stage.

According to Prochaska and DiClemente (1992), the individual continually cycles through the five stages rather than progressing sequentially from precontemplation to contemplation, contemplation to preparation, and so on. However, if the individual does not exit the cycle (termination) he or she will likely revert back to an earlier stage. This creates a practical dilemma for the traditional addiction therapist who insists that clients continue acknowledging their "addicted" status even after they have stopped engaging in the "addictive" behavior. Murphy and Hoffman (1993) report that both the initiation and maintenance of change in a group of self-remitting former alcohol abusers conformed to the Prochaska and DiClemente model, beginning with a paradigm shift after three to six months of abstinence, followed by increased distance from alcohol-dependent behavior, and ending with normalization and identity transformation.

Prochaska and DiClemente (1992) assert that the stage of change into which clients fall can have a profound effect on their response to therapy and should be taken into account when planning an intervention. As a general rule, greater change is anticipated in persons entering therapy at the preparation stage than in persons entering therapy at the precontemplation stage. It may also be possible to use this stage concept to assign or match clients to specific interventions.

In a review of cross-sectional data it was determined that self-changing smokers functioning at the contemplation stage responded best to consciousness raising (confrontations, bibliotherapy), dramatic relief (emotional expression, psychodrama), and environmental reevaluation (documentaries, empathy training) strategies. Smokers operating at the preparation stage, on the other hand, were differentially drawn to self-reevaluation tactics (imagery, values clarification), whereas smokers in the action phase found self-liberating stratagems (empowerment, logotherapy) more appealing than alternate strategies. Finally, former smokers concerned with maintenance preferred reinforcement management (contingency control, self-reinforcement), helping relationships (social support, self-help groups), counterconditioning (substitution, relaxation), and stimulus control (cue avoidance or exposure) strategies (DiClemente et al., 1991).

A two year longitudinal study of self-changing smokers revealed static patterns for the 27 subjects who remained at the precontemplation stage. Subjects who progressed over the course of this study, however, switched change strategies as they progressed through Prochaska and DiClemente's stages of change. In this sample, self-reevaluation, consciousness raising, and dramatic relief were popular strategies during the contemplation stage but were replaced by self-liberation, stimulus control, reinforcement management, and counterconditioning strategies as the individual progressed from contemplation to action (Prochaska, Dillemente, & Norcross, 1992).

One of the principal challenges facing researchers investigating Prochaska and DiClemente's stages of change model is finding a reliable and valid measure of change readiness. Rollnick, Heather, Gold, and Hall (1992) devised a 12 item questionnaire that may eventually fit the bill. A principal components analysis of responses supplied by 141 excessive drinkers to this questionnaire, referred to as the Readiness to Change Questionnaire, revealed a three-factor solution that conformed reasonably well to the precontemplation, contemplation, and action stages of the Prochaska and DiClemente model. That the maintenance stage was not represented in the factor structure of this study may be explained by the fact that the majority of participants were recent misusers of alcohol who had not yet progressed to a maintenance stage of change.

The results of the Rollnick et al. study confirm Prochaska and DiClemente's contention that adjacent stages are more highly intercorrelated than nonadjacent stages. Questionnaire responses were also correlated with items on a screening instrument of drinking behavior. As predicted, more clients in the action stage endorsed statements suggesting that they believed they drank too much, that they were prepared to reduce alcohol intake, and that they had tried to cut down on their drinking in the recent past than clients functioning at the precontemplation or contemplation stages. Although a great deal more research is required before the Readiness to Change questionnaire can be seen as appropriate for general clinical use, it possesses many of the features of a practical, reliable, and valid psychometric instrument.

The practical limitation of the progression assumption of the addiction concept for understanding and encouraging change is three-fold. First, many advocates of the addiction concept treat change as they do addictive behavior: in other words, as an "all or nothing" phenomenon. The continuum concept, on the other hand, allows for a range of intermediate outcomes. The practical limitation of the dichotomous (relapse–recovery) perspective on change is that it neglects the dynamic features of the change process and fails to capitalize on opportunities for effective intermediate intervention.

A second practical limitation of the progression assumption of the addiction concept is that by focusing on the inevitability of deterioration without outside assistance and encouraging people to repeatedly acknowledge their lack of control over this process, the addiction concept locks clients into the relapse–recovery cycle indefinitely, thereby increasing their odds of relapse. Therapists who emphasize growth beyond the addictive behavior or self-help group, in contrast, encourage identity transformation and change maintenance. As the reports of persons who have experienced unassisted change suggest (Biernacki, 1990; Klingemann, 1992; Tuchfeld, 1981), such growth has the capacity to dislodge a person from the relapse–recovery cycle.

A final practical limitation of the progression assumption of the addiction concept for the purposes of understanding and facilitating change is that the assumption fails to take advantage of research on client–intervention matching. There seems to be a belief on the part of practitioners who follow the addiction concept, particularly those subscribing to the progression assumption, that there are only a few ways to arrest the "progressive deterioration" of addiction. This has resulted in a "one size fits all" mentality on the part of many program administrators. Consistent with the continuum concept and the notion that change is a process, however, preliminary results suggest that it may be wise to match interventions with a person's readiness for change (DiClemente et al., 1991; Prochaska et al., 1992).

OVERFOCUSING

The preoccupation element of the addiction concept appears to suffer from the practical limitation of overfocusing on the addictive agent or activity. By overfocusing, other equally, and perhaps even more important factors may be overlooked by researchers and therapists. This is most apparent with substance misuse where there is a tangible substance to which the individual is allegedly addicted. In one study, however, experienced cocaine users were unable to reliably differentiate between blindly administered doses of intravenous cocaine and dextroamphetamine despite the documented disdain many such individuals have for amphetamines and amphetamine users (Fischman et al., 1976). Furthermore, most regular users of heroin recall experiencing an unpleasant or mixed initial reaction to heroin (McAuliffe, 1975). What then, encouraged them to continue using this substance?

Evidence of controlled involvement and unassisted change, as discussed in the previous chapter, also challenge the conclusion that ingestion of the agent is the primary goal in people's continued involvement with drugs. Overfocusing on the addictive agent, in addition to restricting one's perspective, hinders change by diverting attention away from other possible "causes" of addictive behavior. Just as the drug agent is the object of overfocusing in persons who would make it the primary "cause" of drug abuse, food, roulette, and pornography are the subjects of overfocusing in persons looking for a simple "cause" for bulimia, problem gambling, and sexual preoccupation, respectively.

Whereas the lifestyle model readily acknowledges the development of tolerance and withdrawal symptomatology with continued use of alcohol and heroin, there is no reason to assume that tolerance and withdrawal are a function of the chemical properties of the imbibed substance. Siegel (1988), in introducing an opponent–process model of heroin tolerance and withdrawal, states that such a process is more behavioral than physiological. To Siegel's way of thinking, environmental cues become part of a drug–opposite conditioned response that helps counterbalance the negative and jarring physical effects of the drug on the body. As these associational bonds strengthen, larger doses of the drug are required to achieve the same subjective effect (tolerance). Unfamiliar surroundings, on the other hand, fail to provide these drug–opposite cues and so elevate the person's chances of overdosing on a regimen he or she had previously been able to tolerate (Siegel & Ellsworth, 1986). Withdrawal symptoms, alternately, surface in situations where there is no drug to counterbalance the drug–opposite effect created by the environmental cues.

Studies indicate that videotape presentations of drug cues (Sideroff & Jarvick, 1980) can prompt withdrawal symptomatology in persons currently or previously dependent on heroin. These findings support Siegel's learning theory of drug tolerance and withdrawal and suggest that environmental factors are at least as important as physiological ones in eliciting tolerance and withdrawal symptomatology.

If it is not the addictive agent that is responsible for a person's involvement in an addictive activity, then what is? A 1977 survey of 91 Canadian heroin "addicts" who travelled to England to take advantage of that country's liberal policies on heroin use may provide some answers to this question. As the reader may recall, England "legalized" maintenance doses of heroin for registered "addicts" during the 1970s. Within several years, however, the majority of these 91 individuals had returned to Canada, largely because they missed the "street life" that marked their use of heroin in Canada (Solomon, 1977). Despite the increased availability of heroin and decreased legal restraints on hand in England at the time, these individuals longed for the street hustle, the clandestine meetings, and the drug-related rituals they had grown accustomed to in Canada.

The above mentioned findings imply that there is more to drug use than the addictive agent. According to lifestyle theory, it is a panorama of drug-related motives, events, and associations that drives development and maintenance of a "dependency" on heroin or any other mind-altering substance. The same could perhaps also be said of bulimia, problem gambling, and various forms of sexual preoccupation. Overfocusing on the addictive agent or activity may lead one to neglect important situational and psychological factors that underlie, support, and propagate addictive behavior.

ACCOUNTABILITY

The loss of control element of the addiction concept lends itself to the practical limitation of reduced accountability. Fingarette (1988) reports that American society is mired in confusion over alcohol abuse because in conceptualizing problem drinking as a sickness, it has ignored the prospect of personal accountability. These sentiments are echoed by DeLeon (1989) who states that regardless of the cause of addictive involvement, recovery is the sole responsibility of the individual. Attributing drug abuse to a biological predisposition or personality characteristic may help relieve guilt, but at the cost of reducing a client's felt responsibility for change.

Bybee (1988) writes that the "addiction as disease" model of problem gambling makes society, corporations, and the government responsible for the behavior of individual citizens. According to this model, the person has many rights but few responsibilities. However, as existentialists have long recognized, freedom and responsibility go hand-in-hand. In a related vein, Wilson (1991) takes the addictive model of eating disorders to task for absolving those so classified of accountability for their actions and reinforcing the same dichotomous thinking patterns that may have given rise to the eating disorder in the first place. Lack of accountability is the progenitor of excuse making, and while excuses can serve a self-protective function, they become self-defeating if used habitually. Thus, while excuses can reduce negative feelings of guilt in the short run, they tend to undermine a client's self-esteem and sense of personal control over time by way of a process known as self-handicapping (Snyder & Higgins, 1988).

It may be helpful to consider just how the loss of control element of the addiction concept can be used to avoid accountability and justify continued addictive involvement. People often rationalize their escalating drug usage with statements like, "I can't help myself, after all, I'm addicted." Addiction, with limpid connotations of loss of control, can also be used as an excuse for self- or other-destructive behavior. The possibilities are endless and extend even to statements that excuse illegal behavior, as indicated in the following four examples: "I robbed that store because I am addicted to heroin"; "I embezzled from my employer because I am addicted to gambling"; " I raped that woman because I am addicted to sex"; and "I shoplifted from that store because I am addicted to stealing." As these statements illustrate, addiction can be used to rationalize a wide array of negative behaviors.

Assuming accountability for one's behavior, rather than blaming one's actions on a substance or activity, may facilitate the change process. Programs that strive to hold people accountable for their conduct, yet maintain allegiance to the addiction construct, may unfortunately be sending mixed messages. Twelve step programs frequently insist that members be held accountable for their actions. However, by continuing to embrace the loss of control element of the addiction concept these programs may, in point of fact, be sabotaging their own best efforts by encouraging reduced client responsibility.

IDENTITY

Identity can be construed as a unique set of characteristics through which a person comes to recognize him or herself (Walters, 1996a). Lifestyle theory argues that identity is strongly influenced by a person's social relationships, and further, that identity is comprised of several interrelated self-perceptions. It will be argued here that the persistence assumptions made by the addiction concept can impact negatively on a person's identity, either through the person's efforts to establish, maintain, or transform an identity. The three issues covered in this section consequently address the identity-seeking function of addiction, the identity-maintenance function of addiction, and the identity transformation process.

The Identity-Seeking Function of Addiction

Constructing a sense of self or identity is viewed by lifestyle theorists as a prime incentive for behavior. For some people, drug use or anorexia may fulfill this function. This is particularly likely when a person believes that an isolated behavior like drug use or food restriction can serve as a foundation for his or her sense of identity. Zimmer–Höfler and Dobler–Mikola (1992) ascertained that the majority of Swiss heroin-dependent females they interviewed recalled the presence of painful identity concerns prior to their involvement with heroin and interpreted this finding as congruent with the notion that drug use can serve a stabilizing function for someone with sex role identity concerns. Cochrane (1984) also witnessed a high degree of identity-seeking during the early stages of heroin ingestion, and from this, speculated that many of the people who initially use heroin may be searching for a socially validated identity as an "addict."

Studying a large group of seventh and eighth grade students, Mosbach and Leventhal (1988) demonstrated that the desire to identify with and be a part of two specific social groups, labeled by students the "dirts" and "hot shots," correlated with increased tobacco usage. One group of investigators noted that identity concerns, especially those centering on body image, predicted disordered eating behavior in white, female middle-school students (Attie & Brooks–Gunn, 1989), while the results of a second study showed that identity confusion and an unstable self-concept were more characteristic of bulimics than controls (Schupak–Neuberg & Nemeroff, 1993). Codependency may even serve an identity function for some people. Frank and Bland (1992) report that individuals searching for an identity are particularly vulnerable to the identity-fulfilling features of the "addict" role and may be more receptive to the codependency label than persons who have a clearly established sense of identity.

The Identity-Maintaining Function of Addiction

An identity, once established, often perpetuates itself. Identifying with the street addict role, for instance, predicted increased use of heroin and other abusable substances in a study by Stephens and McBride (1975). More recently, methadone-maintained heroin users identifying with the street addict role acknowledged greater involvement in concurrent criminal activity than users identifying with the model patient role (Spunt, 1993). A 2-year participant–observer study conducted in a university-based self-help group for people with eating disorders uncovered a possible self-labeling effect in which those group members who identified strongest with the anorexic or bulimic label appeared to experience the greatest exacerbation of eating disorder symptomatology (McLorg & Taub, 1987).

Expectancies may be particularly important in maintaining an identity. This is implied in the results of a study in which experimental induction of a "high dependence" cognitive set (e.g., "I drink to make me less inhibited") produced higher levels of alcohol consumption than induction of a "low dependence" cognitive set (e.g., "Alcohol is not necessary to get full enjoyment out of life") (Oei, Foley, & Young, 1990).

Taken as a whole, these findings suggest that the persistence element of the addiction concept serves an identity-maintaining function. One way this is accomplished is by influencing the person's outcome expectancies and associated self-statements and cognitive sets. Another way the persistence assumption of the addiction concept can maintain a person's identity as an "addict" is by affecting the roles the person assumes in life. Robinson (1972) speculates that the concept of addiction promotes acceptance of the "sick role" in which feelings of helplessness, hopelessness, and dependency prevail. In support of Robinson's views on this subject, research has established that augmented self-efficacy (the opposite of helplessness, hopelessness, and dependency) is associated with recovery from substance misuse (Reilly et al., 1995).

Exploring the identity-maintaining function of the addiction concept in sexually preoccupied clients, Speziale (1994) argues that a client's acceptance of the sick role propagated by the sex addict label may actually derail any future efforts at change. Hence, in labeling a behavior addictive, one is creating conditions conducive to helplessness, hopelessness, and futility, three of the hallmarks signs of an emerging addictive lifestyle.

Identity Transformation

When someone abandons a lifestyle, with or without assistance, identity transformation, in which the person challenges the persistence assumption of the addiction concept, is often an integral part of the process. A 10-year follow-up of 16 previously treated heroin-dependent subjects revealed that change was initially precipitated by a personal crisis but maintained by a transformation in identity (Andersson, Nilsson, & Tunving, 1993). Likewise, Winick (1990) reports favorable results from a therapeutic community program that directly addressed identity concerns by focusing on attributions, thinking, and values.

The self-reports of people who have abandoned a drug or other lifestyle without professional assistance also underscore the salience of identity transformation in the maintenance of initial change. Self-remitting alcohol abusers, for instance, attributed much of their change to the identity transformation process (Tuchfeld, 1981). Biernacki (1990) observed similar outcomes in a group of self-changing heroin users. Identity materials, defined as events and relationships that permit construction of a new identity, resurrection of an old identity, or extension of a coexisting identity, were viewed by subjects in the Biernacki study as vital to the identity transformation process. Klingemann (1992), as a matter of fact, identified a robust relationship between specific identity materials—referred to as diversion, self-monitoring, and distancing—and the ability of former alcohol and heroin abusers to avoid future involvement with these substances.

It should be noted that while identity transformation may serve as a vehicle for change, it can also reinforce and consolidate an addictive lifestyle. Turner and Saunders (1990) conducted a 12-month observational study of two Gamblers Anonymous (GA) groups and surmised that the formation of a GA identity apparently blocked additional change in those members who strongly identified with the addiction-based ideals of GA. Bewley (1993) raised similar concerns about Alcoholics Anonymous (AA), asserting that in some cases continued involvement in this program may become life-limiting rather than life-enhancing. Although these findings are only correlational in nature and require replication in a study where AA or GA participants are contrasted with a control group of individuals who have never attended a meeting of either group, they nonetheless suggest that self-help programs are not for everybody.

Most 12-step programs promote and advocate the relapse–recovery duality and attempt to instill fear of relapse in members, perhaps as a way of furthering the 12-step philosophy. The problem with this approach is that some people outgrow the 12-step model and seek fulfillment beyond AA or GA. Bewley refers to this as meta-recovery. Twelve step programs, in fact, can be viewed as substitutes for the addictive activities they address. Problems consequently arise when a person overidentifies with the program to the point that it becomes a major focus of his or her life and a fundamental component of his or her identity. This implies that 12-step programs can become lifestyles in and of themselves, with the capacity to constrain further growth. Therefore, while self-help programming can be useful, it should be considered an aid in recovery rather than the ultimate goal.

It has been determined that people who abandon a drug lifestyle often find solace in a substitute drug or activity. Hence, alcohol abusers have been known to substitute marijuana, tranquilizers, and food for alcohol (Vaillant, 1983) whereas opiate abusers sometimes substitute alcohol for heroin (Lehman, Barrett, & Simpson, 1990). It is also apparent that some individuals exchange a dependency on drugs, gambling, sex, food, or exercise for a dependency on 12-step or other self-help programs. Even clients who initially benefit from self-help programming express an interest in what Bewley (1993) calls meta-recovery, whereby they seek to move beyond the 12-step principle of dependence on a higher power. In support of the meta-recovery process, the lifestyle model strives to replace helplessness, hopelessness, and dependence with empowerment, hope, and autonomy.

10

MANAGING THE LIMITATIONS
OF THE ADDICTION CONCEPT

It is easier to criticize than to provide solutions. Hopefully, this book accomplishes both by critiquing the addiction concept and producing an alternative in the form of the lifestyle model. Although lifestyle theory was discussed in Chapter 2, it is still uncertain whether it offers an advantage over traditional models that are grounded in the addiction concept. This chapter affords the reader an opportunity to consider how the lifestyle model seeks to resolve the 22 logical, empirical, and practical limitations of the addiction concept described in the three preceding chapters.

THE LOGICAL LIMITATIONS
OF THE ADDICTION CONCEPT

The Logical Analogy

Rather than relying on poorly defined and easily confused concepts like loss of control, the lifestyle model seeks to operationalize its terminology. Take, for instance, the drug lifestyle, which is defined by four behavioral styles: irresponsibility or pseudoresponsibility, stress–coping imbalance, interpersonal triviality, and social rule breaking or bending. Irresponsibility reflects an overt lack of accountability in meeting one's obligations at school, work, or in the home, while pseudoresponsibility is a superficial attempt to appear responsible that fails to disguise the person's lack of concern for the feelings and personal needs of significant others. The second behavioral style, stress–coping imbalance, denotes weak stress management skills and a tendency to rely on short term coping strategies (i.e., drug use) in managing stress. Interpersonal triviality is characterized by superficial social relationships and a tendency to replace nondrug associations with drug-based rituals. Social rule breaking or bending encompasses direct violations of society's rules and norms (social rule breaking) as well as deceit, chicanery, and duplicity in achieving drug-related ends (social rule bending). Each of these behavioral styles is delimited by a distinct set of roles, rules, rituals, and relationships that are assessed using the Drug Lifestyle Screening Interview (DLSI), an instrument with demonstrated reliability and validity (Walters, 1994a, 1995).

Logically Incongruent Premises

Logically incongruent premises abound in many popular models of addictive behavior. As a case in point, the first three steps of the spiritual disease model's 12 steps are logically incompatible in the sense that one is asked to profess one's powerlessness over the addictive behavior, identify a higher power, and then make a decision to turn one's life over to this higher power. In order to avoid the dilemma of incongruent premises, pains were taken to insure that the defining postulates of lifestyle theory were internally consistent. A review of Table 2–1 reveals that each premise in the lifestyle model is congruent with the one before and after it, and in nearly all cases is a logical extension of the preceding premise.

Argumentum ad Verecundian

Argumentum ad Verecundian, or appeals to authority, are traps that snare many popular theories of addiction. After basic logic, there are only two authorities to which the lifestyle model adheres. One such authority is empirical research. Unlike many of the models that have evolved from the addiction concept, the lifestyle approach welcomes investigation of its postulates and methods. This is why so much time and effort was spent clarifying key terms and creating internally consistent postulates. In point of fact, the lifestyle model can be equated with the adaptive individual to the extent that it continually modifies itself in response to new information which is compared, contrasted, and then synthesized with old information. Dogmatism and deification have no place in a scientific theory of human behavior. The lifestyle approach attempts to overcome these problems by providing a working hypothesis that is amenable to empirical evaluation and can be modified with the introduction of new information.

The second authority to which the lifestyle approach submits is the individual client. An assumption made by those who subscribe to the lifestyle model of intervention is that nobody understands a person better than the person him or herself. Quite obviously, people sometimes get so mesmerized by the patterned and ritualistic behavior of a lifestyle that they wind up compromising their principles and losing sight of their goals. This does not mean, however, that the individual is incapable of rediscovering old principles, values, and perspectives, or developing new ones without assistance from a mental health professional. When conducting an intervention, the lifestyle therapist takes his or her lead from the client, rather than forcing the client into a standardized therapeutic script. The helper can reflect back thoughts and feelings, and offer interpretations or advise, but should refrain from assuming that he or she knows what is best for the client.

Argumentum ad Baculum

Argumentum ad Baculum, or appeals to force, also have no place in a scientific theory of human behavior. Lifestyle theory is viewed as an unfolding process that is never fully realized or completed. As such, efforts to force people to accept the theory or its underlying tenets make little sense since both are in a constant state of evolution. If the person does not appreciate the process of lifestyle theory, he or she may not understand lifestyle theory. In terms of applying the lifestyle model to clinical situations, the emphasis is on building a working alliance with the client and using the lifestyle model to achieve this alliance. To the extent that lifestyle theory helps foster a good working client–therapist relationship and offers concrete suggestions for intervention, it should be used. In situations where lifestyle theory does not help in the development of a therapeutic alliance or in the creation of specific therapeutic goals, it should be replaced by an alternative model.

Argumentum ad Ignorantiam

Argumentum ad ignorantiam, or arguing out of ignorance, appears to be quite prevalent in the addictions field. This is understandable in light of the many gaps that currently exist in our knowledge about the addictions. Where a serious problem arises is in assuming that until disconfirmatory evidence is brought to bear on a model or theory, the model or theory remains viable. Empirical evaluation is important, but is only one way by which a model or theory can be evaluated. Another way a model or theory is tested is through logical analysis. What the chapter on the logical limitations of the addiction concept revealed was that the overall addiction concept and many of the working models that have been derived from it do not conform to the rudimentary conventions of logic. The lifestyle approach offers an alternative more in tune with many of these logical issues and which seeks to validate or invalidate itself through empirical research.

Petitio Principii

One of the principal tautologies occurring in popular theories of addictive behavior entails failing to distinguish between description and explanation.

The lifestyle approach seeks to redress this problem by offering two separate models: a descriptive or structural model and an explanatory or functional one. While the structural model describes the lifestyle, the functional model aspires to account for the origins, development, and purpose of lifestyle behavior. The structural elements of an "addictive" lifestyle are comprised of the four behavioral styles previously described—irresponsibility or pseudoresponsibility, stress–coping imbalance, interpersonal triviality, and social rule breaking or bending. The functional elements of an "addictive" lifestyle are outlined in some of the postulates listed in Table 2–1. It is therefore possible to test the functional model using the description of a lifestyle provided by the structural model. It should be noted that one model may turn out to be valid or useful and the other one not. Under such circumstances, the useful model should be retained and the useless one discarded.

Composition

The lifestyle approach addresses the problem of composition by taking a continuous rather than dichotomous view of lifestyles. A lifestyle is not an "all or nothing" proposition, but rather, a matter of degree. Therefore, rather than existing as a disease or personality entity that people either have or don't have, a drug lifestyle pertains to everyone while being more relevant to some than others. A person's location on the drug lifestyle continuum can be judged from his or her position on four behavioral continua derived from the four behavioral styles of irresponsibility or pseudoresponsibility, stress–coping imbalance, interpersonal triviality, and social rule breaking or bending. People are viewed by lifestyle theory as moving up and down the full length of these four open behavioral continua from the lower end (highly responsible) to the upper end (highly irresponsible). In other words, most people exhibit features of all four behavioral styles, but move up and down each continua. People who are heavily involved in, committed to, and identified with a drug or other lifestyle, on the other hand, spend the majority of their time at the upper end of the four continua.

As several studies reviewed in Chapter 7 suggest, there is evidence of both a continuum and dichotomy in people's approaches to addictive behavior. Lifestyle theory proposes that with habitual involvement at the upper end of a continuum, the open continuum, where the individual moves up and down the length of the dimension, may convert into a closed continuum where the individual remains "stuck" in a particular pattern. The point at which this conversion takes place, if the conversion even does take place, is a matter of speculation, but the process is believed to signal transformation from an early stage of lifestyle development to an advanced stage. As much as possible, however, the dichotomous view must be deemphasized with clients because it encourages an "us" versus "them" mentality that then interferes with the client's ability to reintegrate back into the community or social group, the latter being one of the primary vehicles by which change is maintained upon release from a program (Booth, Russell, Soucek, & Laughlin, 1992; Higgins, Budney, Bickel, & Badger, 1994).

Division

The logical error of division is committed whenever everyone with a particular problem is viewed as coming out of the same mold. This is a fallacy adopted by several models with strong allegiance to the addiction concept. Two of the greatest violators of this logical rule are codependency advocates who believe that simply growing up in a home with an alcohol abusing parent creates a pervasive negative influence that very few people escape, and the medical model treatment approach in which a single model of intervention is seen as appropriate for a wide cross-section of substance using individuals. The lifestyle paradigm, on the other hand, celebrates diversity and rejects the assumption that simply because two people have encountered similar experiences, they are, by necessity, identical in some fundamental way or will respond analogously to the same intervention.

While there may be a tendency for people to become more similar (and less diverse) as they become increasingly more involved in, committed to, and identified with a drug, gambling, sexual, or eating disordered lifestyle, diversity and individuality are two factors that aid a person's exodus from a lifestyle pattern of behavior. One of the great ironies of addictive behavior is that it often provides people with a sense of individuality and uniqueness, when, in fact, it actually strips them of their identity. According to lifestyle theory, clients must view alternative ways of living as supplying them with individuality and uniqueness or they will find it difficult to give up the lifestyle.

THE EMPIRICAL LIMITATIONS
OF THE ADDICTION CONCEPT

Controlled Involvement

The lifestyle model has no fixed policy on controlled involvement in activities that have served as a lifestyle for clients. As was mentioned in Chapter 8, there are factors that influence the likely success of attempts to achieve controlled involvement. Younger individuals with less extensive involvement in the "addictive" activity who have had some success in controlling their involvement in the activity are better candidates for controlled involvement than older persons with a more extensive history of prior involvement who have been largely unsuccessful in their attempts to control their involvement. The lifestyle therapist shares this information with the client, discusses the various options, informs the client that there is always a risk of returning to the lifestyle with reenactment of the behavior, and then asks the client if engaging in the behavior is worth taking the risk of returning to the lifestyle. The ultimate decision is the client's, however, and the therapist must avoid the trap of assuming that he or she knows what is best for the client.

Unassisted Change

The lifestyle model has no illusions about the power of intervention programs. There has not been a program developed that can match the power of the natural environment to influence a person's behavior. In fact, the lifestyle approach to change is based on research showing that most people discontinue a drug or other lifestyle without professional assistance (Biernacki, 1990; Fiore et al., 1990; Kandel & Raveis, 1989; Vaillant, 1983; & Yager, Landsverk, & Edelstein, 1987). Whether the activity is substance abuse, gambling, or exercise, people who desist on their own cite three primary vehicles for change. The first vehicle consists of a change in involvement, whereby the individual changes what he or she does and who he or she does it with. The second vehicle concerns changes in commitments, marked by changes in goals, values, and priorities. The third vehicle involves a change in identity. These three vehicles figure prominently in the lifestyle approach to assisted change described in Chapter 11.

Brief, Environmental, and Behavioral Interventions

Rather than dismissing brief, environmental, or behavioral interventions as superficial attempts at symptom relief, the lifestyle approach welcomes procedures of demonstrated efficacy that are less intrusive and expensive than the common fare offered people seeking relief from addictive behavior. In addition, these procedures are highly congruent with the lifestyle model's overall theory of intervention and change (see Chapter 11). The second or vehicle phase of intervention is designed to educate clients about the lifestyle and help them develop skills designed to enable them to more effectively manage the problems of everyday living. Brief, education-oriented interventions can be especially helpful in teaching clients about the lifestyle and both environmental and behavioral interventions provide an avenue through which basic skills can be taught. Limited resources are probably better spent refining brief, environmental, and behavioral interventions than reinventing traditional treatment programs given the former's greater level of documented empirical efficacy.

Expectancies

Expectancies play an important role in lifestyle theory. In fact, expectancies are believed to facilitate the transition from initiation to maintenance. An adolescent may start drinking alcohol because of peer pressure or experimenting with diet pills because of thinness messages conveyed in the media. However, this initial experimentation gives way to a full blown lifestyle with the creation and expression of certain expectancies. The boy who feels powerful after consuming alcohol or the girl who is complemented after losing several pounds form expectancies for these activities that lead to further involvement and ultimately to maintenance of the behavior. The effect can be particularly pernicious if the expectancy (e.g., "gambling makes me feel like an important person") promises to settle primitive fears (e.g., "I'm afraid of being a nobody"). Educating clients about the role expectancies play in the evolution of a lifestyle can also be an important means of intervention.

Attributions

Like expectancies, attributions are concepts borrowed from social learning theory. As defined in Chapter 8, an attribution is a belief about the causes of one's own or another's behavior. Attributions, like expectancies, play an important role in the development of a person's self-image. This is particularly true of lifestyle change. As will be described in Chapter 11, most change is believed to begin with a crisis. However, because a crisis only temporarily arrests the lifestyle, the arresting process must be extended. Extending the arresting process initiated by a crisis is facilitated by three beliefs known as the attribution triad: (1) a belief in the necessity of change; (2) a belief in the possibility of change; and (3) a belief in one's ability to effect change. Consonant with lifestyle theory, these beliefs can be realized without the aid of a professional therapist. However, they can also become the focal point of one's interventions with clients in that they are capable of extending the arresting process, thereby making the client more amenable to educational and skill-based programming.

Volition

Rather than conceiving of the individual as a victim of forces over which he or she has little or no control, lifestyle theory emphasizes the volitional aspects of human deportment. Accordingly, choice and decision-making figure prominently in lifestyle interpretations of addictive behavior. Choice is conceptualized as a developmental process that unfolds with age and experience. A 2-year-old child and an adult do not have equivalent capacity for volition, although the young child does, with the development of schemas and other internalized representations of reality, possess a rudimentary sense of volition. Rudimentary volition expands with cognitive maturation and an ever-expanding sphere of experience.

Martin, who developed positive expectancies for gambling by watching his father and several uncles playing poker in the back room of a neighborhood pool parlor, saw nothing wrong with pitching pennies during recess. Over time, however, he was exposed to other information that ran counter to his father's early teachings. Although Martin may have retained the expectancies he formed from watching his father and uncles play cards, a growing array of environmental experiences and an evolving capacity to consider a number of different options and interpretations supplied Martin with the capacity for choice as he grew older.

It is not the capacity for choice that must be learned, for this already exists. What must be learned is that choice is possible. In the course of a lifestyle, people often dupe themselves into believing that they had no choice because they grew up in the ghetto, didn't get a college education, or weren't loved enough as children. This belief must be challenged and the person made to realize that choice exists for all people, even young children. Once clients accept the fact that choice is possible, the next step is to teach them how to make better choices and decisions. This can be accomplished by instructing them in ways of expanding their options through brainstorming and social skill development and improving their ability to evaluate each option through cost–benefit analysis and the clarification of values.

The Sociocultural Parameters of Addictive Involvement

The lifestyle model views the sociocultural parameters of addictive behavior as important in defining the cultural and personal myths that sometimes encourage addictive involvement. In pre-industrialized societies, myths were passed down by word of mouth through fables, legends, and stories. This method, however, proved to be impractical and cumbersome in more complex, multi-layered societies. Instead, the mass media has assumed a critical role in the circulation, recitation, and preservation of cultural myths in modern society.

The French anthropologist, Marc Augé (1986), contends that many American TV shows transmit cultural themes by furnishing a recognizable stimulus of sufficient ambiguity to allow identification and projection on the part of the viewer. Like the epic poems and folktales of ancient Greece, television shows address contemporary issues. Westerns and science fiction, therefore, speak more to current problems than to past or future events, in part because they are written, produced, and performed by people living in a contemporary sociocultural context. Augé concedes that culture cannot be reduced to a television show, but is quick to remind us that such shows provide salient clues to the contemporary cultural mythology of a society.

Joseph Campbell (1988) contends that when the "great coordinating mythologies" of a culture are construed as lies, people experience both community and self alienation. This implies that crises created by the disintegration or loss of myth can have a devastating effect on both the person and society. Myths afford people hope, inspiration, and self-direction; as such, their absence often leads to cynicism and cultural impoverishment. Felkins and Goldman (1993) documented just such an effect in evaluating myths relating to the life and times of former president John F. Kennedy.

Lifestyles may arise from poor socialization to conventional social myths (e.g., crime), strong socialization to destructive cultural myths (e.g., eating disorders), or a lack of congruence between personal and cultural mythology. Assisted change, in fact, may derive its power from the change agent's ability to negotiate a rapprochement of personal and cultural myths, a role similar to that fulfilled by shamans in pre-industrialized societies. This, then, is the rationale behind use of the term shaman effect in describing the nonspecific relationship factors that appear to guide the assisted change process.

Setting Effects

Addictive behavior may not be as persistent as supporters of the addiction concept have argued. There is ample evidence that the setting in which an addictive behavior is performed can greatly influence the outcome of one's involvement. Shepard Siegel's (1988) work on drug anticipation demonstrates that environmental cues become conditioned to the drug use experience, and that while some of these cues promote a drug-like effect, others produce a compensatory drug-opposite effect designed to counter the drug response and maintain homeostasis. Since the compensatory conditioned response grows more rapidly than the conditioned drug response, larger doses of the drug are required to achieve the desired effect with continued use (tolerance) and the compensatory conditioned response predominates in situations where the drug is no longer available (withdrawal). According to this perspective, changing environments, a tactic often maligned by proponents of the disease version of the addiction concept, can be of assistance to people genuinely interested in changing their behavior.

THE PRACTICAL LIMITATIONS
OF THE ADDICTION CONCEPT

Reductionism

As was mentioned in Chapter 9, the addiction concept and several of the working models to which it has given birth, the medical disease model in particular, take a highly reductionistic approach to human behavior. Despite the fact the lifestyle model considers existential fear the prime incentive for behavior, including the patterned behavior of a lifestyle, it avoids reductionism by making use of Allport's (1961) functional autonomy concept. Thus, while a pattern of behavior may have its roots in existential fear, this behavior becomes functionally autonomous over time to where the maintaining variables diverge from those that gave rise to the behavior initially. For this reason, it is felt that behavior cannot be reduced to its inaugural conditions.

The goal of lifestyle intervention is to address the variables that are maintaining the lifestyle rather than spending an excessive amount of time examining the variables that may have initiated the behavior. Some clients wish to understand how their lifestyle pattern began and, to the extent that this provides them with a sense of empowerment or closure, these issues can be explored. However, this is neither necessary nor advisable in a majority of cases. With Martin, the focus of intervention has been nearly exclusively on how he can change his current thoughts and actions as a way of terminating his relationship with the drug, gambling, and sexual lifestyles.

Although there are a wide variety of factors capable of maintaining a lifestyle, physiological changes and secondary gain being two of the more prominent, the maintaining variable emphasized by lifestyle theory proves to be the person's belief system because of its amenability to intervention and change. The belief system of someone heavily involved with drugs, committed to gambling, or overly identified with sex is influenced by specific thinking patterns that protect and maintain the lifestyle. These eight thinking patterns—mollification, implosion, entitlement, power orientation, sentimentality, superoptimism, cognitive indolence, and discontinuity—are defined and described below:

Mollification
Mollification manifests itself in comments that shift responsibility for one's thoughts, decisions, and actions onto other people and sundry environmental events. Mollification is used to excuse one's behavior by blaming the negative consequences of one's actions on factors external to oneself. Lack of responsibility, in turn, impedes change by neutralizing corrective feedback. A bulimic college student might use mollification to justify her binging and purging behavior with such statements as "it's no big deal, everyone does it."

Implosion
This thinking pattern, also known as the cutoff, surfaces whenever a person rapidly eliminates deterrents to irresponsible behavior. A simple but frequently employed cutoff is the two word phrase "fuck it." Other forms of implosion include musical themes, visual images, and drug use. A high school student who consumes a large quantity of liquor prior to making a series of obscene phone calls to female classmates is using alcohol to implode fears, anxieties, and other deterrents that would ordinarily prevent him from making the calls.

Entitlement

Entitlement involves granting oneself permission to engage in a particular lifestyle behavior. A man who uses entitlement to grant himself permission to park himself in front of the television set all weekend reasons: "I deserve a break, after all, I've worked hard this week and must put up with a nagging wife and demanding boss." The concept of addiction may contribute to the formation of an attitude of entitlement in that various behaviors are justified on the basis of an addiction over which the person feels powerless.

Power Orientation

The power orientation is driven by the desire to achieve control over other people or one's own physical state. The former is typified by the gambler who "lives" to defeat and humiliate his opponents or the exhibitionist who gets a "rush" from exposing herself and watching other people's reactions. The latter is exemplified by the drug user who ingests barbiturates as a way of manipulating his mood or the anorexic who restricts her diet in an effort to experience a sense of control over her eating behavior. Like all eight of the thinking styles described in this section, denial plays a leading role in the power orientation. Denial in the lifestyle model is identified by the thinking pattern to which it is attached.

Sentimentality

Yochelson and Samenow (1976) coined the term sentimentality to describe the propensity of habitual offenders to perceive themselves as kind and beneficent despite their continuing involvement in crime. This practice can also be observed in people who engage in behaviors traditionally conceptualized as addictive, whether this entails drug use, masturbation, or binge eating. The problem gambler who purchases a gift for his wife after losing his paycheck in Atlantic City is using sentimentality to relieve the guilt he now experiences for having broken the promise he made to his wife never to gamble again. Sentimentality inhibits change by allowing the person to disregard or minimize the negative impact of his or her irresponsible behavior on others.

Superoptimism

Superoptimism projects a sense of unfounded confidence in one's ability to avoid the negative long term consequences of continued involvement in an "addictive" lifestyle. Like sentimentality, this concept was originally defined by Yochelson and Samenow (1976). A woman who spends an exorbitant amount of time and money in shopping malls may use superoptimism to protect her evolving shopping lifestyle: "I'm not like Betty or Sally, I can stop anytime I want; I just don't want to stop."

Cognitive Indolence

The lazy thinking that constitutes cognitive indolence protects the lifestyle by interfering with a person's ability to anticipate the long term consequences of his or her actions. This thinking style is marked by impulsive behavior and shortcut decision making. The escapism modeled by a woman who smokes large quantities of marijuana rather than deal with her problems reflects cognitive indolence.

Discontinuity

Discontinuity is predicated on a person's failure to follow through on initially good intentions and a proclivity to be sidetracked by environmental events and distractions. This thinking style serves a lifestyle-promoting function by fragmenting perception and interfering with a person's ability to comprehend the ramifications of his or her actions. People who become so engrossed in exercise that they lose sight of other important life goals or who provide self-definitions that vary with their involvement in a particular activity—"I'm a good person when I work out, but I'm lazy and no good if I miss even a day of exercise"—are displaying discontinuity.

Options and Opportunities

Rather than restricting client options and therapist opportunities, lifestyle theory attempts to expand options and foster opportunities. The purpose of providing clients with education and skills training is to increase their options. The person who understands his or her behavior and has good social and coping skills has more options than the person who lacks insight into his or her behavior and is largely unskilled in dealing with people and coping with stress. By the same token, the lifestyle approach attempts to increase opportunities for clinicians to approach clients as individuals rather than as diagnoses, with the understanding that no two people are the same and that a different approach will be required with each client. The lifestyle approach supplies the therapist with a general framework, but avoids the dictates and dogma of models that affiliate strongly with the addiction concept. No one, client or therapist, should become a slave to a technique or philosophy.

The Stages of Change

In contrast to the assumption of progression made by many models derived from the addiction concept, the lifestyle model views change as an ongoing process. Motivation for change is not constant, nor is it a characteristic of the client. Taking its lead from Miller (1985), the lifestyle model considers motivation a function of the relationship that forms between the client and helper. Accordingly, two major goals of lifestyle intervention are the development of rapport with the client and use of the therapeutic relationship to explore the client's past and present aspirations and behavior, pointing out discrepancies but allowing the client to decide what to do about these discrepancies.

Congruent with views expressed by Prochaska and DiClemente (1992), the lifestyle approach to intervention identifies the stage at which the client is currently functioning (precontemplation, contemplation, preparation, action, or maintenance) and tailors itself to the needs of the client. It also views movement between stages as variable rather than fixed. Interventions emanating out of lifestyle theory are therefore neither standard nor forced, for they take into account the necessity of creating a strong therapeutic alliance with the client and placing the needs of the client above the needs of the therapist, program, or treatment philosophy.

Overfocusing

The lifestyle concept is designed to shift the focus away from the chosen behavior, whether drug use, gambling, sex, or restrictive eating, to the lifestyle that evolves in support of the behavior. There is more to a drug lifestyle than the use of drugs, as attested to by the study that Solomon (1977) did on Canadian heroin users who emigrated to England and then returned several years later. There is more to a gambling lifestyle than putting money down on a football game and there is more to a sexual lifestyle than having an orgasm. We must also consider how others react to the person's behavior, how the behavior helps the person structure his or her time, and how the person views him or herself when engaged in the behavior. Eating, shopping, exercise, and television viewing all follow a similar pattern. The lifestyle approach strives to compensate for the limitations created by the preoccupation element's tendency to overfocus on the addictive activity by highlighting the panorama of internal and external events that help maintain the addictive pattern.

Accountability

The loss of control element of the addiction concept can become an excuse for continued involvement in addictive behavior. The lifestyle model consequently rejects the loss of control notion in favor of an emphasis on responsibility. In fact, several of the thinking styles that support a lifestyle—for example, mollification, entitlement, and sentimentality—are ways people avoid being held accountable for their own behavior. Insisting that clients accept responsibility for the consequences of their actions is one of the few hard and fast rules of lifestyle intervention. Anything less would put the therapist in the position of enabling the client in the continuation of a self-destructive pattern of behavior.

Identity

Lifestyle theory takes exception to the AA and NA practice of labeling others or oneself an "alcoholic" or "addict." Such labels tend to restrict a person's options and have a negative effect on a person's identity. Keeping in mind that the lifestyle concept, like the addiction concept, is a prototype or caricature, lifestyle therapists help clients gauge their distance from the prototype, but never equate the person with the caricature. To do so would be to sacrifice the individual's humanity, for no human being can be adequately characterized with reference to a single set of descriptors. Clients are therefore encouraged to view themselves as people who have had problems with alcohol, gambling, or sex in the past, but who are not "alcoholics," "degenerate gamblers," or "sex addicts."

Some readers may argue that the addiction concept is a fanciful caricature dreamed up by the author with no real basis in reality. While it is true that no single working model of addictive behavior fully embraces all four elements of the addiction concept, it is important to remember that these four elements were drawn from the DSM–IV criteria for substance dependence and pathological gambling and Goodman's (1993) criteria for sexual addiction. Therefore, even though the addiction concept may be a prototype, important features of this prototype have been integrated into major working models of addictive behavior. The problem is that proposing one or more of these elements as explanations for addictive behavior is an invitation to conceptual disaster since neither the general concept nor any of the individual elements stands up to logical, empirical, or practical scrutiny.

11

FACILITATING CHANGE

Change, whether assisted or unassisted, normally begins with a crisis. Broadly defined, a crisis is the realization of certain negative long term consequences stemming from one's involvement in an addictive lifestyle. External events, such as an ultimatum from one's spouse or employer, confinement in jail or prison, or development of a serious medical condition, may precipitate a crisis, but so may internal processes. The desire to pursue goals incompatible with one's continued involvement in an addictive activity or a growing sense of disgust with the negative consequences of one's lifestyle can be just as important in stimulating a crisis as a spousal ultimatum or a jail term. The crises identified by Martin were the embarrassment his mother experiences each time she visits him in prison and the desire to serve as a good role model for his children.

Experience suggests that crises come and go, often without effecting meaningful change in a person's long term goals and actions. Thus, while experiencing a crisis may be a necessary initial step in the change process, three additional conditions must be satisfied before a crisis can be transformed into purposeful long term behavioral change. These three conditions are referred to as phases of change within the lifestyle model. The first phase, the foundation, is characterized by important changes in the person's attributions for him or herself. The second phase, vehicles, is where the person gains knowledge and skills designed to facilitate abandonment of the lifestyle. The third and final phase of the change process is resocialization whereby the person finds an alternative way of life in an effort to avoid reverting back to the lifestyle.

THE FOUNDATIONAL PHASE

Beliefs are capable of both arresting a lifestyle and extending the initial arresting process beyond the crisis. These beliefs, referred to as the attribution

193

triad, foster responsibility, hope, and empowerment as part of an active shaman effect. As the reader may recall, the shaman effect is an interpersonal process of cultural mythical proportions that promotes change by helping clients establish a belief in the necessity, possibility, and surety of change. The shaman effect frequently achieves its goals through imagery and metaphor. Kirmayer (1993), for instance, has observed that clients frequently couch their concerns and personal difficulties in the language of metaphor. Examples include the problem gambler who visualizes his betting behavior as a bottomless pit or the anorexic client who metaphorically symbolizes her lack of social involvement as a slowly engulfing sense of invisibility.

Analyzing tapes from the Vanderbilt Psychotherapy Project, McMullen (1989) discovered that successful psychotherapy frequently contains a central metaphor or theme that is elaborated upon, developed, and altered by the therapist. Using interpretation and instruction, the therapist guides the client on a journey in which the client is reconciled with the major "coordinating" myths of his or her culture. This provides the client with increased self-confidence, a key goal of lifestyle intervention. The three beliefs that help guide this journey, and upon which the shaman effect is based, are a belief in the necessity of change, a belief in the possibility of change, and a belief in one's ability to effect change.

Belief in the Necessity of Change

Belief in the necessity of change entails acknowledging that a problem exists and that resolution of the problem will likely require hard work, commitment, and a change in identity. The personal responsibility encompassed by a belief in the necessity of change relates closely to the concept of locus of control. Empirical studies show that locus of control, defined as a person's generalized expectancies concerning the causes of his or her behavior (Rotter, 1966), is more external than internal in addictively involved persons. Contrasting 25 substance abusing clients with three control groups, Haines and Ayliffe (1991) surmised that the substance abusing group achieved significantly higher external locus of control scores than subjects in either of the three control groups. An external locus of control has also been observed in male horse race enthusiasts (Kusyszyn & Rubenstein, 1985) and in both male and female lottery players (Hong & Chiu, 1988). Eating disorders may also be characterized by an external locus of control. However, even though an external locus of control has been observed in bulimic patients (Shisslak, Pazda, & Crago, 1990), research on the relationship between locus of control and anorexia is more equivocal (see, for example, Harding & Lachenmeyer, 1986; Hood, Moore, & Garner, 1982).

It has been observed that people who abuse either alcohol (Rohsenow & O'Leary, 1978) or cocaine (Oswald, Walker, Krajewski, & Reilly, 1994) become increasingly more internally-oriented over the course of therapy. Initial outcome is less favorable (Canton et al., 1988), attrition more common (Walker, van Ryn, Frederic, Reynolds, & O'Leary, 1980), and relapse more likely (Johnson, Nora, Tan, & Bustos, 1991) in externally-oriented clients. Striving to capitalize on the apparent relapse-retarding properties of internality, Figurelli, Hartman, and Kowalski (1994) administered a cognitively oriented pre-intervention to substance abusing adolescents. Whereas the pre-intervention promoted a belief in internal control and participating subjects were less likely to produce a urine sample positive for illegal substances (i.e., 25% versus 46%), the latter finding failed to achieve statistical significance. Male child molesters exhibiting an internal locus of control (assumed personal responsibility for their sexually aberrant behavior) were more apt to benefit from a multimodal cognitive–behavioral intervention than male child molesters who showed signs of an external locus of control (failed to accept responsibility for their sexually deviant behavior).

The results of the previously reviewed studies insinuate that externality correlates reasonably well with substance misuse and other forms of addictive involvement and may respond favorably to intervention. This could be interpreted as proof that externality has a causative effect on substance misuse and other forms of addictive involvement. However, it could just as easily be argued that addictive involvement causes externality. Gustafson and Källmén (1989), for example, observed an upward shift in external orientation when moderate social drinking women consumed 1.0 ml of pure alcohol per kg of body weight. This implies that externality and substance use, if not other forms of addictive involvement, enter into a reciprocal relationship.

Whereas research fairly convincingly demonstrates that externality is associated with addictive involvement, social learning theory holds that the relationship should increase in magnitude when the internal–external measure is made more situationally specific. Koski–Jännes (1994) administered a drinking-specific internal–external scale to alcohol abusing clients just prior to their release from an inpatient treatment program. Follow-ups conducted 6 and 12 months later revealed that internal subjects started drinking later, consumed less alcohol on the first drinking occasion, and continued drinking for fewer days than external subjects. Furthermore, an internal orientation was more common in abstinent subjects, while an external orientation was more customary of unimproved subjects. Oswald, Walker, Krajewski, & Reilly (1994) administered both general and specific locus of control measures to a group of cocaine abusers and discovered that both indices discriminated between active and former users. However, only the specific measure remained significant after controlling for initial group differences in age.

Belief in the Possibility of Change

The client may believe that change is necessary yet still not view it as realistically attainable. Such lack of faith in the prospect of change quite obviously stands in the way of a person's ability to abandon lifestyle behavior. Encouraging hope by instilling a belief in the possibility of change is therefore a second major objective of the foundation phase of lifestyle intervention. Hobbs, Birtchnell, Harte, and Lacey (1989) interviewed five female bulimic patients and their two therapists after completion of a 10-week group therapy intervention. Both "specific" (self-understanding, and self-disclosure) and "nonspecific" (instillation of hope, universality) factors were cited by therapists and clients as helpful in facilitating change, but clients believed that "nonspecific" factors were far more important. Adkins, Taber, and Russo (1985) sought to instill hope and an attitude of universality in problem gamblers through a group intervention in which members constructed personal autobiographies that were then shared with the rest of the group.

Another way to demonstrate the possibility of change is through existential dream analysis in which the ongoing dialectics between the personal myths represented in the client's dreams are exposed, analyzed, and synthesized (Krippner, 1986). Arranging for clients to meet with those who have exited an addictive lifestyle, with or without assistance, or running clients through a rational–behavioral exercise designed to demonstrate how a change in thinking can lead to emotional and behavioral change (see Walters, 1996d), are two additional ways of promoting a belief in the possibility of change.

Hope can also be realized through social support and commitment. Social support not only improves the outcome of an intervention, it also helps prevent relapse. This has been documented with clients exiting an alcohol (Booth, Russell, Soucek, & Laughlin, 1992), cocaine (Higgins, Budney, Bickel, & Badger, 1994), tobacco (Cohen & Lichtenstein, 1990), or gambling (Stein, 1993) lifestyle. Alcohol abusers who perceive their AA sponsors as supportive are more willing to complete aftercare substance abuse counseling than problem drinkers who describe their AA sponsors as unsupportive (Huselid, Self, & Gutierres, 1991). The results of one recent study suggest that social support may facilitate change in addictively involved persons by insulating them from stress, elevating their self-confidence, and bolstering their belief in the possibility of change (McCartney, 1995).

Personal commitment to change may also bode well for future success in achieving change, perhaps by raising hope. Commitment to aftercare, for instance, predicted favorable outcomes in a group of alcohol abusers followed over a nine month period (Walker, Donovan, Kivlahan, & O'Leary, 1983). Likewise, persons committed to a methadone maintenance program, as represented by an express desire for help, were significantly more likely to remain in the program than persons lacking such commitment (Simpson & Joe, 1993).

It is speculated that hope achieved through an interaction of social support and personal commitment may be a particularly salient motive for change. The results of a study by Tice (1992) show that commitments made before an audience of strangers lead to greater self-concept change than commitments made anonymously. Establishing a commitment in front of family members or one's support system may be an even more important source of hope and inspiration.

Belief in One's Ability to Effect Change

Belief in the ability to effect change relates to the social learning concept of self-efficacy, which is defined as an appraisal of one's ability to follow a particular course of action and deal effectively with impending high risk situations (Bandura, 1986). As opposed to a general sense of confidence, self-efficacy is a situationally-specific expectancy. A problem drinker's estimated ability to refrain from using alcohol following an argument with his wife or a bulimic's appraisal of her chances of avoiding the impulse to purge after a large meal are two examples of efficacy expectancies. Ellickson and Hays (1990–1991) note that low resistance self-efficacy in eighth-graders naive to drugs correlated with anticipated future drug involvement at the time of assessment and predicted actual drug usage nine months later.

Aas, Klepp, Laberg, and Aarø (1995) measured alcohol-specific self-efficacy in Norwegian adolescents and discerned that subjects with prior drinking experience scored significantly lower on this measure than persons with no drinking background and that low alcohol-related self-efficacy predicted intentions to drink, independent of drinking experience. Allen, Leadbeater, and Aber (1990) identified low self-efficacy in juveniles reporting "hard" drug usage and regular participation in unprotected sexual activity. Although Epstein, Botvin, Diaz, Toth, and Schinke (1995) failed to uncover a relationship between self-efficacy and marijuana usage in a large group of African American and Latino American seventh-graders, they employed a general estimate of efficacy rather than a measure specific to drug use.

Low self-efficacy may also be a robust predictor of relapse. Rychtarik, Prue, Rapp, and King (1992) relate that low intake self-efficacy alcohol abusing clients released from a VA inpatient program were at increased risk for future relapse, although discharge self-efficacy scores had no bearing on outcome. These authors speculate that the discharge measure may have failed to predict relapse because of a ceiling effect. Conversely, Sitharthan and Kavanagh (1990) assessed self-efficacy for drinking situations at discharge and determined that self-efficacy predicted consumption levels six months later. Resistance self-efficacy for cigarettes, food, and purging, moreover, correlate negatively with later tobacco usage (Sperry & Nicki, 1991), excessive eating (Weinberg, Hughes, Critelli, England, & Jackson, 1984), and self-induced vomiting (Schneider, O'Leary, & Agras, 1987), respectively.

Like internality, self-efficacy tends to rise as a result of involvement in an intervention (Solomon & Annis, 1990). Furthermore, larger gains in self-efficacy often portend more favorable outcomes than smaller gains (Burling, Reilly, Moltzen, & Ziff, 1989).

Results incompatible with the self-efficacy model were recorded in a study conducted at Maudsley Hospital in London. Opiate users reporting high self-efficacy just prior to release from a detoxification program were using more heroin six months later than opiate abusers reporting low self-efficacy (Powell et al., 1993). One possible explanation for this outcome is that low self-efficacy subjects were more cautious in their early interactions with the environment, and were thus in a better position to avoid relapse-promoting high risk situations.

Self-efficacy appears to be a rather complex phenomenon. In separate studies, bulimic conduct in the general population of a midwestern high school (Bennett, Spoth, & Borgen, 1991) and binging and purging episodes in clinically identified bulimics (Love, Ollendick, Johnson, & Schlesinger, 1985) correlated with both general and specific measures of self-efficacy. However, in both cases the specific indices were superior to the global ones. As these results imply, self-efficacy is probably best construed as a situation-ally specific construct. To complicate matters even further, research has shown that the predictive value of self-efficacy may be limited by time.

Patrick Reilly and a group of investigators from the University of California, San Francisco followed 74 opiate dependent subjects during three phases of a 180-day methadone maintenance detoxification program. They determined that self-efficacy increased after methadone treatment was initiated, stabilized during the methadone administration phase, and declined during the detoxification or tapering phase. Self-efficacy measures taken at the beginning of each phase predicted opiate usage during that phase, but failed to correspond with outcomes obtained in later phases. Thus, when a person has had little experience with a phase of intervention, self-efficacy ratings may be reasonably accurate predictors of behavior since they reflect a person's appraisal of his or her ability to avoid the situation. However, once experience is gained, behavior becomes more a matter of current drug usage than anticipated self-efficacy (Reilly et al., 1995).

Self-efficacy is a situationally-specific, time-limited concept that reflects a person's confidence in his or her ability to effect change, deal with temptation, and prevent relapse in specific situations, although the point at which self-efficacy measures are most predictive of behavior remains to be determined. Research depicting the time-limited nature of the self-efficacy concept indicates that the effect is probably short-lived, although it may have long-ranging repercussions if innervated during a "critical" period in the change process. Investigators might therefore wish to consider the possibility that "critical" periods or points demarcate the stages of change proposed by Prochaska and DiClemente (1992) and others. Such a possibility may also help explain some of the conflicting results obtained in research on self-efficacy as a predictor of relapse.

It should be noted that overconfidence or superoptimism may confound the results of research on self-efficacy and should be assessed and controlled in more rigorously designed studies on the relationship between self-efficacy and relapse. For the time being, clinicians interested in promoting self-efficacy and a more general sense of confidence and self-esteem can do so by encouraging clients to identify areas of personal strength, develop adaptive skills, form new self- and world-views (Gutierrez, 1990), and accentuate the positive (McGuire & McGuire, 1996). The mythic content of the imagery one uses to cope with problems is probably also important since powerful images and symbols tend to foster a stronger sense of self-efficacy and better outcomes than more permeable and nebulous symbols (Krippner, 1987).

THE VEHICLE PHASE

Lifestyle theory divides constructional thinking into four levels or categories. The first and most primitive level is that of myth, those prescientific constructions based in emotion, intuition, and faith that are also capable of creating a sense of empowerment. Empirical constructions, at the second level of constructional thought, focus on the establishment, evaluation, and modification of hypotheses. The third level of constructional thought involves teleological constructions that provide purpose, goals, and a historiocultural context to one's investigation. Epistemological constructs are situated at the fourth level of constructional thought. In contrast to empirical and teleological constructions that form the basis of the scientific method, epistemological constructions are considered postscientific to the extent that they explore the nature, origins, and limits of science and a person's investigative efforts.

The attitudinal forerunners of change, as manifested in the attribution triad and personified in the shamanistic features of psychotherapeutic intervention, function at the level of myth or belief. Lifestyle change, however, requires that empirical, teleological, and epistemological constructions be considered also. It is not the predominance of any one category of construction that is sought, but the integration and balancing of all four categories. Interventions that neglect the mythic features of change often degenerate into a mindless succession of recapitulated techniques. Ignoring the empirical, teleological, or epistemological, however, can be just as destructive, since these particular constructional styles often provide the change process with direction.

All four categories of construction are necessary, and in combination, buttress the vitality of assisted change programs. Reviews and meta-analyses of the intervention literature in the areas of substance abuse (Najavits & Weiss, 1994), problem gambling (Rugle & Rosenthal, 1994), and eating disorders (Hartmann, Herzog, & Drinkmann, 1992) indicate that the wide discrepancies noted in client outcome can be traced to the therapist's level of interpersonal skill and the quality of the client–therapist relationship. The attribution triad derives strength from these relationship factors but provides only general guidelines for intervention. The empirical and teleological perspectives, in contrast, may provide greater structure and specificity.

It is apparent that skill building can aid in the development of a shaman effect. Possessing certain skills not only enhances competence (ability to effect change), but also instills in clients a sense of hope (possibility of change) and personal responsibility (necessity of change). Three general skill areas are typically addressed with clients as part of the skill development phase of intervention: condition-based skills, choice-based skills, and cognition-based skills. These three general areas are then broken down into more specific skills. Lifestyle-supporting conditions like stress, cues, availability, and interpersonal pressure, for instance, can be managed through programs of assisted change in which stress management, cue exposure, access reduction, and assertiveness training are emphasized.

A choice, once made, cannot be rescinded, but people can learn to make better choices by increasing their options and efficiently evaluating the options available in a particular situation. Social and life skills training can be used to expand a client's range of options, while cost–benefit analysis, values clarification, and goal-setting can be used to teach clients how to more effectively evaluate their options in life. Cognitively, the eight thinking patterns that protect and maintain the lifestyle (see Chapter 10) must be identified, challenged, and eliminated before the client is in a position to move beyond the confines of a drug, gambling, sexual, or eating disordered lifestyle. Educating clients about the lifestyle can also serve an important function during the vehicle phase of intervention.

THE RESOCIALIZATION PHASE

Lifestyles are learned primarily through socialization whereby the person becomes increasingly more involved in, committed to, and identified with a particular lifestyle. Desistance from a lifestyle consequently requires involvement in, commitment to, and identification with ideas, goals, and activities incompatible with the old lifestyle. Proponents of the lifestyle approach refer to this as resocialization. Initially, the individual may pursue a replacement activity or substitute lifestyle. Methadone maintenance may serve the first purpose, 12 step programs the second. However, some individuals eventually outgrow the substitute and seek increased autonomy through adaptability. Bewley (1993) refers to this as meta-recovery. In addition to altering a client's involvements, resocialization requires a change in associates, goals, and identity.

Although the three phases of change may occur without assistance, they are the cornerstone of the lifestyle program of assisted change. Moving from the attribution triad, to skill development and resocialization, and back again, we can see how the attribution triad, as manifest in the shaman effect, can provide the impetus for later skill development and resocialization, yet depends on the specificity and guidance of skill development and resocialization to achieve it ends. The necessity, possibility, and surety of change dictate the enactment of specific behavioral strategies that then support responsibility, establish hope, and create a sense of empowerment, all within the context of a growing interpersonal relationship that reconciles the client with the mythology of his or her culture. This implies that the three phases of lifestyle intervention frequently blend into one another.

THE LIFESTYLE CHANGE PROGRAM

The Lifestyle Change Program (LCP) is a three phase program developed in a medium security federal prison to facilitate change in persons interested in abandoning a criminal, drug, and/or gambling lifestyle. The first phase of the LCP is a 10-week class in which participants receive basic information including the behavioral styles that define a lifestyle, the thinking styles that support a lifestyle, developmental parameters, and the process by which people abandon a lifestyle. The second phase of the program consists of three 20-week advanced groups that address the three lifestyles most commonly observed in inmate populations (criminal, drug, and gambling). The goal of these advanced groups is to teach participants how to apply the lifestyle concept to themselves so that they can understand its impact on their lives. The third phase of the LCP involves a 40-week relapse prevention group that emphasizes skill development (condition-based skills, choice-based skills, and cognition-based skills) and resocialization.

A 5-year follow-up of all participants who had enrolled in the LCP was recently conducted (Walters, in press). The results of this follow-up showed that participants had accumulated one-third the number of disciplinary reports acquired by a group of control subjects who had signed up for the program but were transferred or released prior to their matriculation into the program. Release outcome was also assessed, and while the results favored the LCP group, these findings failed to achieve statistical significance due, in part, to the small number of LCP graduates and control subjects who had been released at the time of follow-up. Consistent with other program research done on criminal offenders (Andrews, et al., 1990), high risk individuals (one or more prior disciplinary reports; three or more prior arrests) were found to benefit more from the program than low risk individuals (no prior disciplinary reports; two or fewer prior arrests).

LIFESTYLE INTERVENTIONS WITH MARTIN

Martin selected the metaphor of a car stuck in the mud as a means of describing his life. He indicated that pressing down on the accelerator (i.e., past efforts at change) only served to land him even deeper in the mud (i.e., the dissatisfaction he had with his life). Adding to his metaphor, I gradually introduced wooden planks that could be placed under his tires for traction (knowledge), chains that could be attached to his bumper for propulsion (skills), and a truck filled with people who could help free him from the mud (social support). Martin participated in all three phases of the LCP as well as periodic individual sessions, and his metaphor of a car stuck in the mud slowly being freed through knowledge, skill, and social support served as the integrating point for all interventions. This metaphor also helped Martin form a belief in the necessity, possibility, and surety of change.

Martin received a great deal of instruction in a number of skill areas. He was introduced to the lifestyle concept in a 10-week introductory class and then completed 20-week classes on the criminal, drug, and gambling lifestyles, three lifestyles that have served as major sources of involvement, commitment, and identity for him. He also received individual attention in terms of his preoccupation with sex. However, his involvement in a 40-week relapse prevention group that focused on skill development may have exerted the greatest impact on his ability to transcend his current situation and learn to deal with the problems of everyday living. Through his involvement in the relapse prevention group, Martin began to take control of his life—in turn, lessening his fear of powerlessness. Martin commenced his personal program of change by terminating his use of cigarettes. Over a period of one month he gradually reduced his cigarette intake from two packs a day to total abstinence.

Martin states that he has not smoked a single cigarette in over two years and that this experience gave him the confidence to start working on problems in others areas of his life. When he first arrived in prison, Martin would regularly bet on football games or play cards for money. However, in response to successfully discontinuing his use of tobacco, he decided to terminate his relationship with gambling as well. Martin maintains that the last time he placed a bet for money was two Super Bowls ago. With his release date approaching, Martin has taken his newfound self-efficacy and begun applying it to all aspects of his life. In resocializing himself to another way of life incompatible with continued involvement in crime, drug abuse, gambling, and sexual promiscuity, Martin has been in contact with both a cousin who seems interested in hiring him and with his children. Martin's efforts are currently directed toward the development of a new way of life. Whether he is able to maintain this change will depend largely on how satisfying he finds this new life and his ability to balance various goals and priorities.

This book construes addiction as a myth. This is not an entirely negative characterization, however, since mythology facilitates production of the shaman effect. The problem with the addiction concept as an agent of change is that by ignoring empirical, teleological, and epistemological constructions, it limits the power and scope of the shaman effect. Belief may be sufficient in a pre-industrial village, but not in a complex, multi-layered, mechanized society. Additionally, the addiction concept may be inadequate even as a mythical construct.

The first leg of the attribution triad (belief in the necessity of change) highlights the need for clients to assume responsibility for their actions. To the extent that the addiction construct encourages, if not forces, people into accepting the sick role (Acker, 1993), it violates the internalization and personal responsibility assumptions of the attribution triad, thereby weakening the shaman effect. The second leg of the attribution triad entails a belief in the possibility of change. Several versions of the addiction concept seek to inculcate hope, but then sabotage their own best efforts by conceptualizing "addiction" as an "incurable" life-long process.

The two above mentioned limitations notwithstanding, the addiction concept's greatest weakness as a mythical construct may be its failure to promote client confidence in his or her ability to effect change, the final leg of the attribution triad. Any model that emphasizes loss of control and powerlessness will have little success instilling a sense of personal empowerment in clients. The addiction concept thus appears to be a mythical construction that fails to capitalize on the power of myth because of its handling of the three legs of the attribution triad.

12

ADDICTION DENIED

In evaluating the usefulness of the addiction concept, it is imperative that the reader appreciate the diverse nature of addiction models. The addiction concept is a prototype comprised of four elements: progression, preoccupation, perceived loss of control, and pervasiveness. Each of the addiction models reviewed in this text, regardless of which element is emphasized, suffers from a range of logical, empirical, and practical problems. As Heisenberg noted in his work with subatomic particles, the mere act of observing and measuring a phenomenon may irrevocably alter its activity to the point where absolute prediction is impossible. The fact that a flawless model is unattainable should not deter us from looking for a better model. One goal of this book was to determine whether the flaws introduced by the addiction concept are of sufficient magnitude to preclude it from serving as a good working hypothesis. Before any final conclusions can be offered in this regard, however, the nature, purpose, and features of a good working hypothesis will be reviewed.

ATTRIBUTES OF A GOOD WORKING HYPOTHESIS

A hypothesis is a testable statement accounting for certain observations and findings. A working hypothesis is a testable statement or set of statements that can be altered or modified as contradictory or disconfirmatory evidence is brought to bear on a subject. A good working hypothesis is a testable and alterable statement or set of statements that possess the following five characteristics: precision, parsimony, coherence, fruitfulness, and balance.

Precision

Precision is a function of the operationality and clarity of one's concepts and axioms. Operationality entails concretizing the hypothesis with specific behavioral referents. The assertions, assumptions, and premises that comprise a good working hypothesis must also be clearly articulated so as to avoid ambiguity, confusion, and equivocacy. Poor precision, as exemplified by weak operationality and a general lack of clarity, makes for an untestable hypothesis which, in turn, reduces the usefulness of one's theory. Imprecise hypotheses are inadequate because they interfere with the researcher's ability to authenticate major elements of the hypothesis.

Parsimony

Simplicity, or parsimony, is a second criterion against which a working hypothesis can be evaluated. Assuming that two models achieve roughly equivalent explanatory power, the simpler of the two models would be more parsimonious. Hypotheses that make fewer assumptions are superior to hypotheses that make more assumptions, provided, of course, that the two hypotheses account for roughly the same amount of information. When it comes to highly complex phenomena like human behavior, however, it is often the case that simple models fail to achieve an acceptable level of explanatory power.

Coherence

The coherence of a working hypothesis is the degree to which its statements are logically and conceptually congruent. Internal contradictions create serious problems for both researchers and clinicians. Lack of coherence in a working hypothesis makes the derivation of specific predictions virtually impossible. It also prevents clinicians from applying principles from the model to situations not directly covered by the working hypothesis. Although it is unrealistic to expect a working hypothesis to address all relevant aspects of a phenomenon, a more defensible extrapolation of the concept is possible if the contributing models' premises are internally consistent.

Fruitfulness

A working hypothesis is fruitful if it generates discussion, controversy, and research, even if the outcome is unfavorable to the hypothesis. Rather than being a matter of empirical validity, fruitfulness is the degree to which a working hypothesis stimulates continued investigative effort and creative theorizing. Without fruitful ideas upon which to build, a working hypothesis will lose its vitality and ability to impact on the field. As such, unfruitful working hypotheses should be considered inadequate regardless of their level of precision, parsimony, and coherence.

Balance

Balance refers to the fact that all four constructional styles—mythical, empirical, teleological, and epistemological—are represented in the working hypothesis. First, the working hypothesis must be capable of stimulating faith and belief, for without face validity a hypothesis is often unacceptable to the very people it is designed to help. Second, the hypothesis must not only be fruitful, but empirically valid as well. Third, a good working hypothesis is organized around a larger theme, plan, or purpose. Finally, a good working hypothesis should take into account its own limitations. The balance of these four constructional styles permits the fluid adjustment of premises and subhypotheses as new information is gathered, additional analyses conducted, and corrections made.

EVALUATION OF THE ADDICTION
AND LIFESTYLE PARADIGMS

The five criteria highlight the shortcomings of the addiction concept. As studies reviewed in this book clearly demonstrate, most applications of the addiction concept suffer from poor precision. Terms like loss of control, progression, and preoccupation are too vague and nonspecific to be of much use in coordinating research. The parsimony of the addiction concept may be one of its primary strengths, but simplicity can be a double-edged sword. The addiction concept contains fewer postulates than the average psychological or sociological theorem. However, it may also possess significantly less explanatory power than these alternative models. Simply stated, the parsimony of the addiction concept may actually handicap its ability to explain complex human behavior.

The addiction concept also appears to lack cohesion. As indicated in Chapter 7, many of the tenets and postulates generated by models based on the addiction concept are incongruous, illogical, and contradictory. Equally problematic is the fact that many of these models have become less fruitful as their adherents have become more entrenched and doctrinaire. For this reason, many models affiliated with the addiction concept fail to generate the level of discussion, research, and inquiry required of a robust working hypothesis (see Chiauzzi & Liljegren, 1993). Finally, many applications of the addiction concept demonstrate poor balance in that mythical constructions predominate over other avenues of understanding. What is more, empirical, teleological, and epistemological constructs are sometimes depreciated, denigrated, or ignored by proponents of these models.

As the title of this book suggests, my principal objective has been to determine whether the addiction concept is more properly classified as a working hypothesis or self-fulfilling prophesy. A self-fulfilling prophesy is defined as fulfillment realized through prediction, expectancy, or application of a label. In school settings this is sometimes referred to as the Pygmalion effect. Research indicates that a teacher's expectancies concerning a child's ability, whether or not based on accurate information, can exert a profound effect on the child's future academic performance. The expectancy in the present case is addiction and the fulfillment is a lifestyle over which the person feels powerless.

Many of the models based on the addiction concept are predicated on informing the client that he or she suffers from an addiction that can only be controlled by accepting the "fact" that he or she is an addict. Unfortunately, labels narrow people's options by restricting their potential. The fact that expectancies, whether outcome or efficacy, can both facilitate addictive involvement and promote positive change was explored in Chapters 8, 10, and 11 of this text. However, before new expectancies can be defined, alternatives to the addiction concept must be identified. This book has introduced one such alternative, that which views addictive behavior as a lifestyle.

The lifestyle model can be evaluated against the same five criteria as the addiction concept. The descriptive model of lifestyle theory seems more precise than the addiction concept, although there are aspects of the functional model (e.g., existential fear) that require additional operationalization. While the lifestyle model may not be as parsimonious as the addiction concept, it seems that the lifestyle approach may account for more information than the addiction model. Lifestyle theory may also possess greater coherence than the addiction concept, an offshoot of the attention paid to internal consistency in the derivation of the former's tenets, postulates, and hypotheses.

In light of the relative youthfulness of the lifestyle model, its fruitfulness remains to be determined. However, it does appear to provide a novel perspective on addictive behavior. Balance, the fifth criterion, may be the lifestyle model's strongest feature. Unlike the addiction concept, lifestyle theory goes beyond mythology and belief. Unlike the behavioral model, lifestyle theory is willing to entertain mythical forms of understanding. The balancing of the four constructional styles is a fundamental tenet of lifestyle theory. This optimistic assessment notwithstanding, there are only a handful of studies directly assessing the practical utility of the lifestyle model, most of which have been cited at various points in this book.

BARRIERS TO A NEW PARADIGM

It is unclear whether the lifestyle paradigm has the capacity to propel the addictions field into what Kuhn (1962) calls "normal science." There is little question, however, that the addiction concept is woefully inadequate in this regard. Imprecision, oversimplicity, incoherence, dogmatism, and imbalance prevent the addiction concept from moving the addictions field beyond its current preparadigmal state. One might well ask why, in the face of such glaring logical, empirical, and practical defects, do so many people in the field continue to abide by the addiction concept? It is certainly not because of the absence of viable alternatives. Despite its own limitations, the behavioral model enjoys numerous empirical and practical advantages over the addiction paradigm. No, the addiction concept does not retain its current state of popularity for lack of a reasonable alternative, but owes its ongoing prosperity to the fact that certain groups have a vested interest in its continuance. These groups, discussed next, serve as barriers to a new paradigm.

The Medical Profession

Regardless of whether the American Medical Association was initially motivated by financial self-interest to recognize alcohol abuse as a medical disease, there is little doubt that it is now one of the chief beneficiaries of the disease and addiction concepts. Heather and Robertson (1985) contend that the medical community accrues power, influence, and fiscal security from its support of the disease concept of addiction. This is because disease has traditionally been considered the exclusive province of the medical profession. It could be argued, however, that physicians, precisely because of their medical training, are ill-equipped to handle the subtle manipulations of the addictively involved individual. Thomas Szasz (1971) is so unenthralled with the medical disease application of the addiction concept that he has called for a medical reformation, similar to the Protestant Reformation, in which addiction is demystified and the physician removed as the intermediary between the person and his or her body. However, physicians, like other professional groups with vested interest in the addiction concept, are not about to voluntarily loosen their grip on the golden goose of addiction.

The Addiction Treatment Industry

An entire industry has sprung up around the addiction concept. It began with alcohol abuse treatment in the 1970s and has expanded to include other drugs and a variety of nondrug activities, from gambling to sex. In his book, *Diseasing of America: Addiction Treatment Out of Control*, Stanton Peele (1989) explains how the addiction as disease concept has given rise to a proliferation of for-profit treatment organizations and centers. By viewing addictive behavior as an incurable disease, the disease concept of addiction provides opportunities for unlimited and never-ending treatment. In Europe, where a large profit-making treatment industry has not taken root, the addiction as disease model is much less influential than it is here (Miller, 1986). The addiction treatment industry has as much to gain from the addiction concept as the medical profession, and like the medical profession, it does not want to see the addiction concept replaced by a less lucrative alternative.

Clients and Former Clients

Clients and former clients form another group that frequently stands behind the addiction concept. This may be because the disease model and other versions of the addiction concept correspond reasonably well to their subjective experience. For many of those who participate regularly in an addictive activity, the authority such involvement seemingly commands over their behavior is best captured by a concept that accentuates preoccupation, progression, loss of control, and persistence. The addiction concept also encourages assumption of the "sick role," which can be highly reinforcing to clients because of its ability to relieve them of their daily responsibilities (Acker, 1993). Given the power of myth, it seems likely that a belief in the addiction concept may facilitate change in a certain portion of persons exposed to treatment or self-help programming. However, not everyone is willing to buy into the mythology of traditional addiction-based treatment. Alternatives are consequently required, one of which (the lifestyle model) strives to address mythology and belief during the early stages of the assisted change process.

Economic Interests

Yet another financial reason that the addiction concept continues to attract adherents despite its obvious flaws is that the concept has been a boom for business. According to figures for the early 1990s, the American public spends somewhere in the neighborhood of $96 billion a year on alcohol ("Spending on alcoholic beverages," 1993), $50 billion a year on tobacco (Bureau of Economic Analysis, 1995), and $33 billion a year on weight loss products and services (Garner, 1993). In 1994 legalized gambling operations grossed $450 billion, netted $40 billion in revenue, and provided jobs for over one million people (Shapiro, 1996).

A host-centered view of addiction is in the best interests of the alcohol, tobacco, weight loss, and gambling industries because it assumes that aside from the relatively small percentage of people who become "addicted" to these substances and activities, people can drink, smoke, diet, and gamble without suffering any ill effects. Viewing addictive behavior along a continuum, however, leads to a very different conclusion—everyone has the potential to become preoccupied with these substances and activities, although some people are more vulnerable than others, and the level of involvement is more important than a trait-like propensity to become addicted in pinpointing a person's position on the continuum.

The Media

Reporters working for William Randolph Hearst in the early 1900s characterized illegal drugs and the people who used them as beasts in an effort to entice readers to purchase their newspapers. Even today, sensationalized accounts of drug use and abuse, as well as other forms of addictive involvement, clutter the print and telecommunication medias. Newspaper headlines, magazine covers, radio talk shows, and feature films all provide electrifying accounts of persons who have fallen victim to one or more "addictions." The payoff is increased circulation and advertising profits, but at the cost of perpetuating a view of addictive behavior that is neither accurate nor particularly helpful.

Supporters of the addiction concept often dictate how addictive behavior is portrayed in the media. Marty Mann and her colleagues at the National Council on Alcoholism (NCA) made sure that some of the older Hollywood productions featuring alcohol misuse, such as *The Lost Weekend* (1945) and *The Days of Wine and Roses* (1962), embodied the philosophy of NCA, which was, in effect, the philosophy of addiction (Peele, 1989). It would seem, then, that even the media caters to the addiction concept, partly because it sells news time and partly because of the zealotry of some of the more vocal proponents of the addiction concept.

Politicians

In an attempt to generate simplistic answers to complex and difficult questions, politicians may look to the addiction concept as an explanation for behavior. Simplicity, however, is not the only aspect of the addiction concept that appeals to politicians. Many politicians are adept at modifying their positions in order to win votes. A majority of these individuals, in reinventing the abolitionist position and the days of "demon rum," take an agent-centered view of illegal drug use (i.e., drugs turn people into monsters) that helps divert attention away from more pressing foreign and domestic issues, but then turn around and espouse a host-centered view of alcohol and legalized gambling (most people can drink and gamble without suffering serious problems) in deference to the special interests of contributing industrialists, tax-paying casinos, and state lotteries.

Whereas many in the business community view addiction as a money-maker, politicians perceive it as a vote-getter. In fact, once elected, some politicians use the addiction concept to further their political careers. Rothman (1980), for instance, writes that by attaching the deviance label to drug use, excessive sexuality, and frequent gambling, the state opens the door to increased governmental control and intrusion into the private lives of its citizens. Powerful people are generally motivated to expand their base of power and one way this can be accomplished is by promoting a concept like addiction whereby the person is viewed as powerless and in need of help from others.

The Legal Profession

Since many politicians were trained as lawyers, it is not surprising that a commonality of motives unite these two groups in their support for the addiction concept. Nonetheless, there are aspects of the addiction concept that are particularly attractive to legal practitioners. Addiction, for instance, has been successfully employed as a defense in certain criminal cases. Defendants have been acquitted of murder on the basis of a perceived addiction to illegal drugs, prescription medications, and various foods.

The reader may recall the case of Dan White, confessed killer of San Francisco mayor George Moscone and city councilman Harvey Milk, who claimed that his murderous behavior stemmed from an "addiction" to sugar-based junk food. Deliberating what would soon become known as the "Twinkie defense," the jury, instead of convicting White of first degree murder, found him guilty of the lesser charge of diminished capacity manslaughter.

Convincing a jury of a client's innocence is one of the defense attorney's principal functions. In cases where there is little doubt about a defendant's guilt, pleas for leniency are often based on a defendant's state of mind at the time of the offense. Addiction, with its emphasis on loss of control, is a ready-made argument for such a defense. Accordingly, defense attorneys are no less eager to covet the golden goose of addiction than physicians, reporters, and treatment professionals.

The General Public

Like politicians and media representatives, the general public is looking for simple solutions to complex problems. The addiction concept appears to supply people with pat answers to difficult questions, thereby sating their appetite for explanations that make intuitive sense (Mulford, 1994). While it is recommended that theorists package their ideas in ways that make them more accessible to others, overly simplistic models, like those that have been derived from the addiction concept, have trouble accounting for a significant portion of the variance in addictive behavior. Such models also frequently fail to consider the value and attitudinal changes that must occur if one is to outgrow the destructive habits that have been relabeled addictions in our society (Peele, 1991).

Frustration, disillusionment, and acrimony build as people come to realize that a popular explanation is incomplete, faulty, or altogether false. Unfortunately, the anger generated by this process is occasionally directed at addictively involved persons, as if they were somehow responsible for the failings of the concept. What starts out as a noble effort to minimize guilt and blame may wind up precipitating a backlash of animosity toward the very people the concept is designed to help. The solution is to educate the general public on addictive behavior rather than inventing fictions designed to frighten, stupefy, or confuse them.

Chapin (1994) proposes the existence of a game-like conflict between the alcohol production and alcohol treatment industries. He states that such conflict promotes a homeostatic balance between these two seemingly antagonistic systems. An alternative view is that these two industries are, at least to a certain extent, dependent on one another. The alcohol production industry creates jobs for those working in the alcohol treatment industry, whereas the treatment industry, particularly that segment that holds to a host-centered view of behavior classified as addictive, legitimizes the use of alcohol for everyone except "alcoholics."

In reality, all eight of the systems described may be engaged in an unwitting conspiracy of convenience whereby mutual self-interest is realized at the expense of a more balanced dialogue on human behavior. Thus, whereas melodramatic media portrayals of cocaine "addiction" increase sales, ratings, and profits, they also aid other systems in their efforts to exploit the addiction concept, from the medical profession (medical doctors are portrayed as the only professionals equipped to "treat" addiction), to the legal profession (addiction is so powerful that it can override personal controls), to the political profession (addicts must be protected from themselves through legislative decree). The moral of this story is that the barriers erected through this conspiracy of convenience must be removed before an organizing paradigm can be identified for the addictions field.

CLOSING COMMENT

Each and every day, friends, family, employers, clergypeople, and clinicians try to convince someone that it would be in their best interests to give up an addictive behavior. Ironically, before this can be accomplished, it may be necessary to abandon the concept of addiction and remove the attitudinal barriers that stand in the way of a new paradigm. For the logical, empirical, and practical reasons described in this text, the time has come to reject the addiction concept. Alternatives exist, the behavioral and lifestyle models being but two examples, although more research is required before it can be concluded that conceptualizing drug use, problem gambling, sexual preoccupation, and eating disorders as behavioral habits or lifestyles proves any more fruitful than conceptualizing them as addictions.

The need for an alternative paradigm for the addictions field is apparent. What is less apparent is the form such an alternative should take. At the very least, this new paradigm should be able to integrate the four constructional levels (mythology, empiricism, teleology, and epistemology) since mythology provides the belief, empiricism the facts, teleology the direction, and epistemology the humility that go into a person's self- and world-views. The addiction concept fails to accomplish this, for besides serving as a self-fulfilling prophesy, it possesses many of the characteristics of a lifestyle (i.e., rigid, defensive, and mythically dominant). Given the zeal with which some people continue to defend the addiction concept, efforts at change will require faith, courage, and perseverance. Scholars and clinicians often advise people wishing to abandon an addictive lifestyle to pursue these same goals. Should they demand anything less of themselves?

REFERENCES

Aas, H., Klepp, K. I., Laberg, J. C., & Aarø, L. E. (1995). Predicting adolescent's intentions to drink alcohol: Outcome expectancies and self-efficacy. *Journal of Studies on Alcohol, 56,* 293–299.

Abel, G. G., Barlow, D. H., Blanchard, E. B., & Guild, D. (1977). The components of rapists' sexual arousal. *Archives of General Psychiatry, 34,* 895–903.

Abel, G. G., & Osborn, C. (1992). The paraphilias: The extent and nature of sexually deviant and criminal behavior. *Psychiatric Clinics of North America, 15,* 675–687.

Abramson, E. E., & Lucido, G. M. (1991). Childhood sexual experience and bulimia. *Addictive Behaviors, 16,* 529–532.

Acker, C. J. (1993). Stigma or legitimation? A historical examination of the social potentials of addiction disease models. *Journal of Psychoactive Drugs, 25,* 193–205.

Ackerman, J. M., Womble, M. D., & Moises, H. C. (1994). Multiple effects of long-term morphine treatment on postsynaptic ß-adrenergic receptor function in hippocampus: An intracellular analysis. *Brain Research, 656,* 309–318.

Adkins, B. J., Taber, J. I., & Russo, A. M. (1985). The spoken autobiography: A powerful tool in group psychotherapy. *Social Work, 30,* 435–439.

Ainsworth, M. D. S. (1979). Infant–mother attachment. *American Psychologist, 24,* 932–937.

Alcoholics Anonymous World Services. (1987). *Alcoholics Anonymous.* New York: Author.

Alden, L. (1988). Behavioral self-management controlled-drinking strategies in a context of secondary prevention. *Journal of Consulting and Clinical Psychology, 56,* 280–286.

Alexander, B. K., & Dibbs, G. S. (1977). Interpersonal perception in addict families. *Family Process, 16,* 17–38.

Allen, J. P., Leadbeater, B. J., & Aber, J. L. (1990). The relationship of adolescent's expectations and values to delinquency, hard drug use, and unprotected sexual intercourse. *Development and Psychopathology, 2,* 85–98.

Allport, G. (1961). *Pattern and growth in personality.* New York: Holt, Rinehart, & Winston.

Allsop, S., & Saunders, B. (1989). Relapse and alcohol problems. In M. Gossop (Ed.), *Relapse and addictive behavior* (pp. 11–40). London: Tavistock/ Routledge.

Alpher, V. S., & Turkat, I. D. (1986). Prediction versus reflection in therapist demonstrations of understanding: A replication with clinical cases. *British Journal of Medical Psychology, 59,* 235–236.

Alterman, A. I., Searles, J. S., & Hall, J. G. (1989). Failure to find differences in drinking behavior as a function of familial risk for alcoholism: A replication. *Journal of Abnormal Psychology, 98,* 50–53.

Amadéo, S., Abbar, M., Fourcade, M. L., Waksman, G., Leroux, M. G., Mader, A., Selin, M., Champiant, J. C., Brethome, A., Leclaire, Y., Castelnau, D., Venisse, J. L., & Mallet, J. (1993). D$_2$ dopamine receptor gene and alcoholism. *Journal of Psychosomatic Research, 27,* 173–179.

American Psychiatric Association. (1952). *Diagnostic and statistical manual of mental disorders* (1st ed.). Washington, DC: Author.

American Psychiatric Association. (1968). *Diagnostic and statistical manual of mental disorders* (2nd ed.). Washington, DC: Author.

American Psychiatric Association. (1980). *Diagnostic and statistical manual of mental disorders* (3rd ed.). Washington, DC: Author.

American Psychiatric Association. (1994). *Diagnostic and statistical manual of mental disorders* (4th ed.). Washington, DC: Author.

Anderson, A. E., & DiDomenico, L. (1992). Diet vs. shape content of popular male and female magazines: A dose-response relationship to the incidence of eating disorders? *International Journal of Eating Disorders, 11,* 283–287.

Anderson, G., & Brown, F. (1984). Real and laboratory gambling, sensation seeking and arousal: Towards a Pavlovian component in general theories of gambling and gambling addictions. *British Journal of Psychiatry, 75,* 401–411.

Andersson, B., Nilsson, K., & Tunving, K. (1993). Drug careers in perspective. *Acta Psychiatrica Scandinavica, 67,* 249–257.

Andersson, T., & Magnusson, D. (1988). Drinking habits and alcohol abuse among young men: A prospective longitudinal study. *Journal of Studies on Alcohol, 49,* 245–252.

Andrews, D. A., Zinger, I., Hoge, R. D., Bonta, J., Gendreau, P., & Cullen, F. T. (1990). Does correctional treatment work? A clinically relevant and psychologically informed meta-analysis. *Criminology, 28,* 369–404.

Anglin, M. D., Brecht, M. L., Woodward, J. A., & Bonett, D. G. (1986). An empirical study of maturing out: Conditional factors. *International Journal of the Addictions, 21,* 233–246.

Annis, H. M. (1988). Patient–treatment matching in the management of alcoholism. *NIDA Research Monograph Series, 90,* 152–161.

Annis, H. M., & Chan, D. (1983). The differential treatment model: Empirical evidence from a personality typology of adult offenders. *Criminal Justice and Behavior, 10,* 159–173.

Arinami, T., Itokawa, M., Komiyama, T., Mitshushio, H., Mori, H., Mifune, H., Hamaguchi, H., & Toru, M. (1993). Association between severity of alcoholism and the A1 allele of the dopamine D$_2$ receptor gene TaqI A RFLP in Japanese. *Biological Psychiatry, 33,* 108–114.

Armor, D. J., Polich, J. M., & Stambul, H. B. (1976). *Alcoholism and treatment.* Santa Monica, CA: Rand Corporation.

Armstrong, J., & Roth, D. M. (1989). Attachment and separation difficulties in eating disorders: A preliminary investigation. *International Journal of Eating Disorders, 8,* 141–155.

Asher, R., & Brissett, D. (1988). Codependency: A view from women married to alcoholics. *International Journal of the Addictions, 23,* 331–350.

Atkinson, D. R., Morton, G., & Sue, D. W. (1993). *Counseling American minorities: A cross-cultural perspective* (4th ed.). Madison, WI: Brown & Benchmark.

Attie, I., & Brooks–Gunn, J. (1989). Development of eating problems in adolescent girls: A longitudinal study. *Developmental Psychology, 25,* 70–79.

Attie, I., & Brooks–Gunn, J. (1992). Developmental issues in the study of eating problems and disorders. In J. H. Crowther, D. L. Tennenbaum, S. E. Hobfoll, & M. A. P. Stephens (Eds.), *The etiology of bulimia nervosa: The individual and familial context* (pp. 35–58). Washington, DC: Hemisphere.

Augé, M. (1986). Teleculture heroes: Or, a night at the embassy. *Current Anthropology, 27,* 184–188.

Azrin, N. H. (1976). Improvements in the community-reinforcement approach to alcoholism. *Behaviour Research and Therapy, 14,* 330–348.

Azrin, N. H., Sisson, R. W., Meyers, R. W., & Godley, M. (1982). Alcoholism treatment by disulfiram and community reinforcement therapy. *Journal of Behaviour Therapy and Experimental Psychiatry, 13,* 105–112.

Baer, J. S., Marlatt, G. A., Kivlahan, D. R., Fromme, K., Larimer, M. E., & Williams, E. (1992). An experimental test of three methods of alcohol risk reduction with young adults. *Journal of Consulting and Clinical Psychology, 60,* 974–979.

Baily, C. A., & Gibbons, S. J. (1989). Physical victimization and bulimic-like symptoms: Is there a relationship? *Deviant Behavior, 10,* 335–352.

Baker, A., Kochan, N., Dixon, J., Heather, N., & Wodak, A. (1994). Controlled evaluation of a brief intervention for HIV prevention among injecting drug users not in treatment. *AIDS Care, 6,* 559–570.

Ball, J. C., & Ross, A. (1991). *The effectiveness of methadone maintenance treatment.* New York: Springer–Verlag.

Bandura, A. (1986). *Social foundations of thought and action.* Englewood Cliffs, NJ: Prentice–Hall.

Banys, P. (1988). The clinical use of disulfiram (antabuse®): A review. *Journal of Psychoactive Drugs, 20,* 243–260.

Barnes, G. M., Farrell, M. P., & Cairns, A. (1986). Parental socialization factors and adolescent drinking behaviors. *Journal of Marriage and the Family, 48,* 27–36.

Baron, M. (1993). The D_2 dopamine receptor gene and alcoholism: A tempest in a wine cup? *Biological Psychiatry, 34,* 821–823.

Barrios, F. X., & Niehaus, J. C. (1985). The influence of smoker status, smoking history, sex, and situational variables on smokers' self-efficacy. *Addictive Behaviors, 10,* 425–429.

Barth, R. J., & Kinder, B. N. (1987). The mislabeling of sexual impulsivity. *Journal of Sex and Marital Therapy, 13,* 15–23.

Bauman, K. E., & Ennett, S. T. (1994). Peer influence on adolescent drug use. *American Psychologist, 49,* 820–822.

Baumann, D. J., Obitz, F., & Reich, J. W. (1982). Attribution theory: A fit with problems of substance abuse. *International Journal of the Addictions, 17,* 295–303.

Baum–Baicker, C. (1985). The psychological benefits of moderate alcohol consumption: A review of the literature. *Drug and Alcohol Dependence, 15,* 305–322.

Beattie, M. (1987). *Codependent no more: How to stop controlling others and start caring for yourself.* New York: Harper/ Hazelden.

Beckman, K. A., & Burns, G. L. (1990). Relation of sexual abuse and bulimia in college women. *International Journal of Eating Disorders, 9,* 487–492.

Begleiter, H., Porjesz, B., Bihari, B., & Kissin, B. (1984). Event-related brain potentials in boys at risk for alcoholism. *Science, 225,* 1493–1496.

Bellodi, L., Pasquali, L., Diaferia, G., Sciuto, G., Bernardesch, L., & Cocchi, S. (1992). Do eating, mood and obsessive compulsive patients share a common personality profile? *New Trends in Experimental and Clinical Psychiatry, 8,* 87–94.

Bem, D. J. (1977). Predicting more of the people more of the time: Some thoughts on the Allen–Potkay studies of intraindividual variability. *Journal of Personality, 45,* 327–333.

Bennett, L. A., Janca, A., Grant, B. F., & Sartorius, N. (1993). Boundaries between normal and pathological drinking: A cross-cultural comparison. *Alcohol Health and Research World, 17,* 190–195.

Bennett, L. A., Wolin, S. J., & Reiss, D. (1988). Cognitive, behavioral, and emotional problems among school-age children of alcoholic parents. *American Journal of Psychiatry, 145,* 185–190.

Bennett, L. A., Wolin, S. J., Reiss, D., & Teitelbaum, M. A. (1987). Couples at risk for transmission of alcoholism: Protective influences. *Family Process, 26,* 111–129.

Bennett, N. A. M., Spoth, R. L., & Borgen, F. H. (1991). Bulimic symptoms in high school females: Prevalence and relationship with multiple measures of psychological health. *Journal of Community Psychology, 19,* 13–28.

Bensley, L. S., & Spieker, S. (1992, July). *Parenting behavior of adolescent children of alcoholics.* Paper presented at the National Conference on Research in Women's Health and Perinatal Nursing, Seattle, WA.

Berg, G., Laberg, J. C., Skutle, A., & Ohman, A. (1981). Instructed versus pharmacological effects of alcohol in alcoholics and social drinkers. *Behaviour Research and Therapy, 19,* 55–66.

Bergin, A. E., & Garfield, S. L. (1994). *Handbook of psychotherapy and behavior change* (4th ed.). New York: Wiley.

Berkowitz, A., & Perkins, H. W. (1988). Personality characteristics of children of alcoholics. *Journal of Consulting and Clinical Psychology, 56,* 206–209.

Berman, S. M., Whipple, S. C., Fitch, R. J., & Noble, E. P. (1993). P3 in young boys as a predictor of adolescent substance use. *Alcohol, 10,* 69–76.

Bewley, A. R. (1993). Addiction and meta-recovery: Wellness beyond the limits of Alcoholics Anonymous. *Alcohol Treatment Quarterly, 10,* 1–22.

Bibb, J., & Chambliss, D. L. (1986). Alcohol use and abuse among diagnosed agoraphobics. *Behaviour Research and Therapy, 24,* 49–58.

Bien, T. H., Miller, W. R., & Boroughs, J. M. (1993). Motivational interviewing with alcohol outpatients. *Behavioural and Cognitive Psychotherapy, 21,* 347–356.

Biernacki, P. (1990). Recovery from opiate addiction without treatment. A summary. *NIDA Research Monograph Series, 98,* 113–119.

Bigelow, G. E., Griffiths, R. R., & Liebson, I. A. (1977). Pharmacological influences upon ethanol self-administration. In M. M. Gross (Ed.), *Alcohol intoxication and withdrawal* (Vol. 3B, pp. 523–538). New York: Plenum.

Bigelow, G. E., & Liebson, I. A. (1972). Cost factors controlling alcoholic drinking. *Psychological Record, 22,* 305–314.

Binion, V. J. (1979). A descriptive comparison of families of origin of women heroin users and nonusers. In *Addicted women: Family dynamics, self perceptions, and support systems.* Washington, DC: U.S. Government Printing Office.

Birke, S. A., Edelmann, R. J., & Davis, P. E. (1990). An analysis of the abstinence violation effect in a sample of illicit drug users. *British Journal of Addiction, 85,* 1299–1307.

Black, C. (1981). *It will never happen to me.* Denver, CO: Medical Administration Company.

Black, C., Bucky, S., & Wilder–Padilla, S. (1986). The interpersonal and emotional consequences of being an adult child of an alcoholic. *International Journal of the Addictions, 21,* 213–231.

Black, D. W., Goldstein, R. B., Noyes, R., & Blum, N. (1994). Compulsive behaviors and obsessive–compulsive disorder (OCD): Lack of a relationship between OCD, eating disorders, and gambling. *Comprehensive Psychiatry, 35,* 145–148.

Black, D. W., Noyes, R., Goldstein, R. B., & Blum, N. (1992). A family study of obsessive–compulsive disorder. *Archives of General Psychiatry, 49,* 362–368.

Blakey, R., & Baker, R. (1980). An exposure approach to alcohol abuse. *Behaviour Research and Therapy, 18,* 319–325.

Blanco, C. (1996). Pathological gambling and platelet MAO activity: A psychobiological study. *American Journal of Psychiatry, 153,* 119–121.

Blaszczynski, A. P., Buhrich, N., & McConaghy, N. (1985). Pathological gamblers, heroin addicts and controls compared on the E.P.Q. 'Addiction Scale.' *British Journal of Addiction, 80,* 315–319.

Blaszczynski, A. P., & McConaghy, N. (1989). Anxiety and/or depression in the pathogenesis of addictive gambling. *International Journal of the Addictions, 24,* 337–350.

Blaszczynski, A. P., McConaghy, N., & Frankova, A. (1991). Control versus abstinence in the treatment of pathological gambling: A two to nine year follow-up. *British Journal of Addiction, 86,* 299–306.

Blaszczynski, A. P., Wilson, A. C., & McConaghy, N. (1986). Sensation seeking and pathological gambling. *British Journal of Addiction, 81,* 113–117.

Blaszczynski, A. P., Winter, S. W., & McConaghy, N. (1986). Plasma endorphin levels in pathological gamblers. *Journal of Gambling Behavior, 2,* 3–15.

Blum, K., Nobel, E. P., Sheridan, P. J., Finley, O., Montgomery, A., Ritchie, T., Ozkaragoz, T., Fitch, R. J., Sadlack, F., Sheffield, D., Dahlmann, T., Halbandier, S., & Nogami, H. (1991). Association of the A1 allele of the D_2 dopamine receptor gene with severe alcoholism. *Alcohol, 8,* 409–416.

Blum, K., Nobel, E. P., Sheridan, P. J., Montgomery, A., Ritchie, T., Jagadreswaron, P., Nogami, H., Briggs, A. H., & Cohn, J. B. (1990). Allelic association of human dopamine D_2 receptor gene in alcoholism. *Journal of the American Medical Association, 263,* 2055–2060.

Bohman, M., Sigvardsson, S., & Cloninger, C. R. (1981). Maternal inheritance of alcohol abuse: Crossfostering analysis of adopted women. *Archives of General Psychiatry, 38,* 965–969.

Bolos, A. M., Dean, M., Lucas–Derse, S., Ramsburg, M., Brown, G. L., & Goldman, D. (1990). Population and pedigree studies reveal a lack of association between the dopamine D_2 receptor gene and alcoholism. *Journal of the American Medical Association, 264,* 3156–3160.

Booth, B. M., Russell, D. W., Soucek, S., & Laughlin, P. R. (1992). Social support and outcome of alcoholism treatment: An exploratory analysis. *American Journal of Drug and Alcohol Abuse, 18,* 87–101.

Booth, P. G., Dale, B., Slade, P. D., & Dewey, M. E. (1992). A follow-up study of problem drinkers offered a goal choice option. *Journal of Studies on Alcohol, 53,* 594–600.

Borrell, F. (1988). *Manual de Entrevista Clínica.* Barcelona: Ed. DOYMA, S.A.

Bosron, W. F., & Li, T.-K. (1987). Catalytic properties of human liver alcohol dehydrogenase isoenzymes. *Enzyme, 37,* 19–28.

Botvin, G. J., Baker, E., Dusenbury, L., Tortu, S., & Botvin, E. M. (1990). Preventing adolescent drug abuse through a multimodal cognitive–behavioral approach: Results of a 3-year study. *Journal of Consulting and Clinical Psychology, 58,* 437–446.

Boudouris, J. (1976). Criminality and addiction. *International Journal of the Addictions, 11,* 951–966.

Bradford, J. M. W. (1985). Organic treatments for the male sexual offender. *Behavioral Sciences and the Law, 3,* 355–375.

Bradford, J. M. W., Boulet, J., & Pawlak, A. (1992). The paraphilias: A multiplicity of deviant behavior. *Canadian Journal of Psychiatry, 37,* 104–108.

Bradford, J. M. W., & Pawlak, A. (1993). Double-blind placebo crossover study of cyproterone acetate in the treatment of the paraphilias. *Archives of Sexual Behavior, 22,* 383–402.

Bradley, B. P., Gossop, M., Brewin, C. R., Phillips, G., & Green, L. (1992). Attribution and relapse in opiate addicts. *Journal of Consulting and Clinical Psychology, 60,* 470–472.

Branchey, M. H., Buydens–Branchey, L., & Horvath, T. B. (1993). Event-related potentials in substance abusing individuals after long-term abstinence. *American Journal on Addictions, 2,* 141–148.

Brandon, T. H., Tiffany, S. T., & Baker, T. B. (1986). The process of smoking relapse. *NIDA Research Monograph Series, 72,* 104–117.

Brandsma, J. M., Maultsby, M. C., & Welsh, R. J. (1980). *The outpatient treatment of alcoholism: A review and comparative study.* Baltimore: University Park.

Brecher, E. M. (Ed.). (1972). *Licit and illicit drugs.* Boston: Little, Brown.

Brewer, C. (1986). Patterns of compliance and evasion in treatment programs which include supervised disulfiram. *Alcohol, 21,* 385–388.

Bridgman, L. P., & McQueen, W. M. (1987). The success of Alcoholics Anonymous: Locus of control and God's general revelation. *Journal of Psychology and Theology, 15,* 124–131.

Brook, J. S., Brook, D. W., Gordon, A. S., Whiteman, M., & Cohen, P. (1990). The psychosocial etiology of adolescent drug use: A family interactional approach. *Genetic, Social, and General Psychology Monographs, 116,* 2.

Brown, S. A., Creamer, V. A., & Stetson, B. A. (1987). Adolescent alcohol expectancies in relation to personal and parental drinking patterns. *Journal of Abnormal Psychology, 96,* 117–121.

Browne, B. A., & Brown, D. J. (1994). Predictors of lottery gambling among American college students. *Journal of Social Psychology, 134,* 339–347.

Bruch, H. (1973). *Eating disorders: Obesity, anorexia nervosa and the person within.* New York: Basic Books.

Brumberg, J. J. (1988). *Fasting girls: The emergence of anorexia nervosa as a modern disease.* Cambridge, MA: Harvard University Press.

Buhrich, N. (1981). Frequency and presentation of anorexia nervosa in Malaysia. *Australian and New Zealand Journal of Psychiatry, 15,* 153–155.

Bujold, A., Ladouceur, R., Sylvain, C., & Boisvert, J. M. (1994). Treatment of pathological gamblers: An experimental study. *Journal of Behaviour Therapy and Experimental Psychiatry, 25,* 275–282.

Bulik, C. M. (1987). Drug and alcohol abuse by bulimic women and their families. *American Journal of Psychiatry, 144,* 1604–1606.

Bulik, C. M. (1992). Abuse of drugs associated with eating disorders. *Journal of Substance Abuse, 4,* 69–70.

Bulik, C. M., Beidel, D. C., Duchmann, E., Weltzin, T. E., & Kaye, W. H. (1991). An analysis of social anxiety in anorexic, bulimic, social phobic, and control women. *Journal of Psychopathology and Behavioral Assessment, 13,* 199–211.

Bulik, C. M., & Sullivan, P. F. (1993). Comorbidity of bulimia and substance abuse: Perceptions of family of origin. *International Journal of Eating Disorders, 13,* 49–56.

Bulik, C. M., Sullivan, P. F., & Rorty, M. (1989). Childhood sexual abuse in women with bulimia. *Journal of Clinical Psychiatry, 50,* 460–464.

Bureau of Economic Analysis. (1995). *Selected personal consumption expenditures in the U.S. (1990–1993).* Washington, DC: U.S. Department of Commerce.

Burk, J. P., & Sher, K. J. (1990). Labeling the child of an alcoholic: Negative stereotyping by mental health professionals and peers. *Journal of Studies on Alcohol, 51,* 156–163.

Burling, T. A., Reilly, P. M., Moltzen, J. O., & Ziff, D. C. (1989). Self-efficacy and relapse among inpatient drug and alcohol abusers: A predictor of outcome. *Journal of Studies on Alcohol, 50,* 354–360.

Bybee, S. (1988). Problem gambling: One view from the gaming industry side. *Journal of Gambling Behavior, 4,* 301–308.

Cadoret, R. J., O'Gorman, T. W., Troughton, E., & Heywood, E. (1985). Alcoholism and antisocial personality: Interrelationships, genetic and environmental factors. *Archives of General Psychiatry, 42,* 161–167.

Cadoret, R. J., Troughton, E., O'Gorman, T. W., & Heywood, E. (1986). An adoption study of genetic and environmental factors in drug abuse. *Archives of General Psychiatry, 43,* 1131–1136.

Caetano, R., & Medina–Mora, M. E. (1988). Acculturation and drinking among people of Mexican descent in Mexico and the United States. *Journal of Studies on Alcohol, 49,* 462–471.

Calam, R. M., & Slade, P. D. (1989). Sexual experiences and eating problems in female undergraduates. *International Journal of Eating Disorders, 8,* 391–397.

Camí, J. (1994). The need for instruments both fantastic and mythical. *Addiction, 89,* 9–12.

Camí, J., Guerra, D., Ugena, B., Segura, J., & De La Torre, R. (1991). Effect of subject expectancy on the THC intoxication and disposition from smoked hashish cigarettes. *Pharmacology Biochemistry and Behavior, 40,* 115–119.

Campbell, J. (1988). *The power of myth* (with Bill Moyers). New York: Doubleday.

Canton, G., Giannini, L., Magni, G., Bertinario, A., Cibin, M., & Gallimberti, L. (1988). Locus of control, life events and treatment outcome in alcohol dependent patients. *Acta Psychiatrica Scandinavica, 78,* 18–23.

Caplehorn, J. R. M., Bell, J., Kleinbaum, D. G., & Gerbski, V. J. (1993). Methadone dose and heroin use during maintenance treatment. *Addiction, 88,* 119–124.

Carey, M. P., Kalra, D. L., Carey, K. B., Haperin, S., & Richards, S. (1993). Stress and unaided smoking cessation: A prospective investigation. *Journal of Consulting and Clinical Psychology, 61,* 831–838.

Carlin, A. S., Bakker, C. B., Halpern, L., & Post, R. D. (1972). Social facilitation of marijuana intoxication: Impact of social set and pharmacological activity. *Journal of Abnormal Psychology, 80,* 132–140.

Carlson, N. R. (1994). *Physiology of behavior* (5th ed.) Boston: Allyn & Bacon.

Carmelli, D., Swan, G. E., Robinette, D., & Fabsitz, R. (1992). Genetic influence on smoking—A study of male twins. *New England Journal of Medicine, 327,* 829–833.

Carnes, P. (1992). *Out of the shadows: Understanding sexual addiction* (2nd ed.). Center City, MN: Hazelden.

Carroll, K. M., Rounsaville, B. J., Gordon, L. T., Nich, C., Jatlow, P., Bisighini, R. M., & Gawin, F. H. (1994). Psychotherapy and pharmacotherapy for ambulatory cocaine abusers. *Archives of General Psychiatry, 51,* 177–187.

Castaneda, R., Galanter, M., & Franco, H. (1989). Self-medication among addicts with primary psychiatric disorders. *Comprehensive Psychiatry, 30,* 80–83.

Castaneda, R., Lifshutz, H., Galanter, M., & Franco, H. (1994). Empirical assessment of the self-medication hypothesis among dually diagnosed inpatients. *Comprehensive Psychiatry, 35,* 180–184.

Cermack, T. L. (1984). Children of alcoholics and the case for a new diagnostic category of codependency.

Alcohol Health and Research World, 3, 38–42.

Chambless, D. L., Cherney, J., Caputao, G. C., & Rheinstein, B. J. G. (1987). Anxiety disorders and alcoholism: A study with inpatient alcoholics. *Journal of Anxiety Disorders, 1,* 29–40.

Chapin M. (1994). Functional conflict theory, the alcohol beverage industry, and the alcoholism treatment industry. *Journal of Applied Social Sciences, 18,* 169–182.

Chapman, P. L. H., & Huygens, I. (1988). An evaluation of three treatment programmes for alcoholism: An experimental study with 6- and 18-month follow-ups. *British Journal of Addiction, 83,* 67–81.

Chappell, J. N. (1993). Working a program of recovery in Alcoholics Anonymous. *Journal of Substance Abuse Treatment, 11,* 99–104.

Chassin, L., Pillow, D. R., Curran, P. J., Molina, B. S. G., & Barrera, M. (1993). Relation of parental alcoholism to early adolescent substance use: A test of three mediating mechanisms. *Journal of Abnormal Psychology, 102,* 3–19.

Cheung, Y. W. (1993). Beyond liver and culture: A review of theories and research in drinking among Chinese in North America. *International Journal of the Addictions, 28,* 1497–1513.

Chiauzzi, E. J., & Liljegren, S. (1993). Taboo topics in addiction treatment: An empirical review of clinical folklore. *Journal of Substance Abuse Treatment, 10,* 303–316.

Chick, J., Gough, K., Falkowski, W., Kershaw, P., Hore, B., Mehta, B., Ritson, B., Ropner, R., & Torely, D. (1992). Disulfiram treatment of alcoholism. *British Journal of Psychiatry, 161,* 84–89.

Chick, J., Ritson, B., Connaughton, J., Stewart, A., & Chick, J. (1988). Advice versus extended treatment for alcoholism: A controlled study. *British Journal of Addiction, 83*, 159–170.

Childress, A. R., Ehrman, R., McLellan, A. T., MacRae, J., Natale, M., & O'Brien, C. P. (1994). Can induced moods trigger drug-related responses in opiate abuse patients? *Journal of Substance Abuse Treatment, 11*, 17–23.

Childress, A. R., McLellan, A. T., Ehrman, R., & O'Brien, C. P. (1987). Extinction of conditioned responses in abstinent cocaine or opioid users. *NIDA Research Monograph Series, 76*, 189–195.

Childress, A. R., McLellan, A. T., & O'Brien, C. P. (1986). Conditioned responses in a methadone population: A comparison of laboratory, clinical, and natural setting. *Journal of Substance Abuse Treatment, 3*, 173–179.

Chiordo, J., & Latimer, P. R. (1983). Vomiting as a learned weight-control technique in bulimia. *Journal of Behaviour Therapy and Experimental Psychiatry, 14*, 131–135.

Christiansen, B. A., & Goldman, M. S. (1983). Alcohol-related expectancies versus demographic/background variables in the prediction of adolescent drinking. *Journal of Consulting and Clinical Psychology, 51*, 249–257.

Christiansen, B. A., & Teahan, J. E. (1987). Cross-cultural comparisons of Irish and American adolescent drinking practices and beliefs. *Journal of Studies on Alcohol, 48*, 558–562.

Christo, G., & Sutton, S. (1994). Anxiety and self-esteem as a function of abstinence time among recovering addicts attending Narcotics Anonymous. *British Journal of Clinical Psychology, 33*, 198–200.

Cinciripini, P. M., Lapitsky, L. G., Wallfisch, A., Mace, R., & Nezami, E. (1994). An evaluation of a multicomponent treatment program involving scheduled smoking and relapse prevention procedures: Initial findings. *Addictive Behaviors, 19*, 13–22.

Cinquemani, D. K. (1975). *Drinking and violence among Middle American Indians*. Unpublished doctoral dissertation, Columbia University, New York.

Clair, D., & Genest, M. (1987). Variables associated with the adjustment of offspring of alcoholic fathers. *Journal of Studies on Alcohol, 48*, 345–355.

Clark, D. B., & Sayette, M. A. (1993). Anxiety and the development of alcoholism: Clinical and scientific issues. *American Journal on Addictions, 2*, 59–76.

Clark, J., & Stoffel, V. C. (1992). Assessment of codependency behavior in two health student groups. *American Journal of Occupational Therapy, 46*, 821–828.

Clark, N. H. (1976). *Deliver us from evil: An interpretation of American prohibition*. New York: Norton.

Cloninger, C. R. (1987). Neurogenetic adaptive mechanisms in alcoholism. *Science, 236*, 410–416.

Cloninger, C. R. (1991). D_2 dopamine receptor gene is associated but not linked with alcoholism. *Journal of the American Medical Association, 266*, 1833–1834.

Cloninger, C. R., Bohman, M., & Sigvardsson, S. (1981). Inheritance of alcohol abuse: Cross-fostering analysis of adopted men. *Archives of General Psychiatry, 38*, 861–868.

Cochrane, R. (1984). Social aspects of illegal drug use. In D. J. Sanger & D. E. Blackman (Eds.), *Aspects of psychopharmacology* (pp. 110–139). London: Methuen.

Cohen, S., & Lichtenstein, E. (1990). Partner behaviors that support quitting smoking. *Journal of Consulting and Clinical Psychology, 58*, 304–309.

Cohen, S., Lichtenstein, E., Prochaska, J. O., Rossi, J. S., Gritz, E. R., Carr,

C. R., Orleans, C. T., Schoenbach, V. J., Biener, L., Abrams, D., DiClemente, C., Curry, S., Marlatt, G. A., Cummings, K. M., Emont, S. L., Giovino, G., & Ossip–Klein, D. (1989). Debunking myths about self-quitting: Evidence from 10 prospective studies of persons who attempt to quit smoking themselves. *American Psychologist, 44,* 1355–1365.

Coleman, E. (1991). Compulsive sexual behavior: New concepts and treatments. *Journal of Psychology and Human Sexuality, 4,* 37–52.

Collins, R. L., & Lapp, W. M. (1991). Restraint and attributions: Evidence of the abstinence violation effect in alcohol consumption. *Cognitive Therapy and Research, 15,* 69–84.

Comings, D. E., Comings, B. G., Muhleman, D., Dietz, G., Shahbahrami, B., Tast, D., Knell, E., Kocsis, P., Baumgarten, R., Kovacs, B., Levy, D. L., Smith, M., Borison, R. L., Evans, D. D., Klein, D. N., MacMurray, J., Tosk, J. M., Sverd, J., Gysin, R., & Flanagan, S. D. (1991). The dopamine D_2 receptor locus as a modifying gene in neuropsychiatric disorders. *Journal of the American Medical Association, 256,* 1793–1800.

Comstock, G. A. (1980). *Television in America.* Beverly Hills, CA: Sage.

Connors, G. J., Carroll, K. M., DiClemente, C. C., Longabaugh, R., & Donovan, D. M. (1997). The therapeutic alliance and its relationship to alcoholism treatment participation and outcome. *Journal of Consulting and Clinical Psychology, 65,* 588–598.

Connors, M. E., & Morse, W. (1993). Sexual abuse and eating disorders: A review. *International Journal of Eating Disorders, 13,* 1–11.

Cook, B. L., Wang, Z. W., Crowe, R. R., Hauser, R., & Freimer, M. (1992). Alcoholism and the D_2 receptor gene. *Alcoholism: Clinical and Experimental Research, 4,* 806–809.

Coombs, R. H., & Paulson, M. J. (1988). Contrasting family patterns of adolescent drug users and nonusers. *Journal of Chemical Dependency Treatment, 1,* 59–72.

Coombs, R. H., Paulson, M. J., & Richardson, M. A. (1991). Peer vs. parental influence in substance use among Hispanic and Anglo children and adolescents. *Journal of Youth and Adolescence, 20,* 73–88.

Cooper, A. J. (1981). A placebo controlled trial of the antiandrogen cyproterone acetate in deviant hypersexuality. *Comprehensive Psychiatry, 22,* 458–464.

Cooper, A. J., Sandu, S., Losztyn, S., & Cernovsky, Z. (1992). A double-blind placebo controlled trial of medroxyprogesterone acetate and cyproterone acetate with seven pedophiles. *Canadian Journal of Psychiatry, 37,* 687–693.

Cooper, J. R., Bloom, F. E., & Roth, R. H. (1987). *The biochemical basis of neuropharmacology* (5th ed.). New York: Oxford University Press.

Cooper, P. J., & Fairburn, C. G. (1986). The depressive symptoms of bulimia nervosa. *British Journal of Psychiatry, 148,* 268–274.

Copi, I. M. (1982). *Introduction to logic* (6th ed.). New York: Macmillan.

Corless, T., & Dickerson, M. (1989). Gamblers' self-perceptions of the determinants of impaired control. *British Journal of Addiction, 84,* 1527–1537.

Coryell, W., & Noyes, R. (1988). Placebo response in panic disorder. *American Journal of Psychiatry, 145,* 1138–1140.

Cotton, N. S. (1979). The familial incidence of alcoholism: A review. *Journal of Studies on Alcohol, 40,* 89–116.

Coventry, K. R., & Brown, I. F. (1993). Sensation seeking in gamblers and non-gamblers and its relation to preference for gambling activities, chasing, arousal and loss of control in regular gamblers. In W. R. Eadington & J. A. Cornelius (Eds.), *Gambling behavior and problem gambling* (pp. 25–49). Reno, NV: University of Nevada.

Covi, L., Hess, J. M., Kreiter, N. A., & Jaffee, J. H. (1993). Fluoxetine and counseling for PCP abuse. *NIDA Research Monograph Series, 132*, 321.

Cowie, M. R. (1997). Alcohol and the heart. *British Journal of Hospital Medicine, 57*, 457–460.

Cox, W. M. (1985). Personality correlates of substance abuse. In M. Galizio & S. A. Maisto (Eds.), *Determinants of substance abuse: Biological, psychological, and environmental factors* (pp. 209–246). New York: Plenum.

Crabb, D. W., Edenberg, H. J., Bosron, W. F., & Li, T.-K. (1989). Genotypes for aldehyde dehydrogenase deficiency and alcohol sensitivity: The inactive ALDH2^2 allele is dominant. *Journal of Clinical Investigation, 83*, 314–316.

Crandall, C. S. (1988). Social contagion of binge eating. *Journal of Personality and Social Psychology, 55*, 588–598.

Crisp, A. H. (1984). The psychopathology of anorexia nervosa: Getting the "heat" out of the system. In A. J. Stunkard & E. Stellar (Eds.), *Eating and its disorders* (pp. 209–234). New York: Raven.

Crits–Christoph, P., Beebe, K. L., & Connolly, M. B. (1990). Therapist effects in the treatment of drug dependence: Implications for conducting comparative treatment studies. *NIDA Research Monograph Series, 104*, 39–49.

Crits–Christoph, P., & Mintz, J. (1991). Implications of therapist effects for the design and analysis of comparative studies of psychotherapies. *Journal of Consulting and Clinical Psychology, 59*, 20–26.

Curran, P. J., Stice, E., & Chassin, L. (1997). The relation between adolescent alcohol use and peer alcohol use: A longitudinal random coefficients model. *Journal of Consulting and Clinical Psychology, 65*, 130–140.

Currier, K. D., & Aponte, J. F. (1991). Sexual dysfunction in female adult children of alcoholics. *International Journal of the Addictions, 26*, 195–201.

Curry, S., Marlatt, G. A., & Gordon, J. R. (1987). Abstinence violation effect: Validation of an attributional construct with smoking cessation. *Journal of Consulting and Clinical Psychology, 55*, 145–149.

Custer, R. L. (1982). An overview of compulsive gambling. In P. A. Carone, S. F. Yoles, S. N. Kiefer, & L. Krinsky (Eds.), *Addictive disorders update: Alcoholism, drug abuse, gambling* (pp. 107–124). New York: Human Services.

Cutrona, C. E., Cadoret, R. J., Suhr, J. A., Richards, C. C., Troughton, E., Schutte, K., & Woodworth, G. (1994). Interpersonal variables in the prediction of alcoholism among adoptees: Evidence for gene-environment interaction. *Comprehensive Psychiatry, 35*, 171–179.

Dalack, G. W., Glassman, A. H., Rivelli, S., Covey, L., & Stetner, F. (1995). Mood, major depression, and fluoxetine response in cigarette smokers. *American Journal of Psychiatry, 152*, 398–403.

Dalgard, O. S., & Kringlen, E. (1976). A Norwegian twin study of criminality. *British Journal of Psychiatry, 16*, 213–232.

Darkes, J., & Goldman, M. S. (1993). Expectancy challenge and drinking reduction: Experimental evidence for a mediational process. *Journal of Consulting and Clinical Psychology, 61*, 344–353.

Davidson, K. M., & Ritson, E. B. (1993). The relationship between alcohol dependence and depression. *Alcohol and Alcoholism, 28,* 147–155.

Davies, D. L. (1962). Normal drinking in recovered alcoholic addicts. *Quarterly Journal of Studies on Alcohol, 23,* 94–104.

Davis, C. (1990). Weight and diet preoccupation and addictiveness: The role of exercise. *Personality and Individual Differences, 11,* 823–827.

Davis, C., Brewer, H., & Ratusny, D. (1993). Behavioral frequency and psychological commitment: Necessary concepts in the study of excessive exercising. *Journal of Behavioral Medicine, 16,* 611–628.

Davis, C. M., & Bauserman, R. (1993). Exposure to sexually explicit materials: An attitude change perspective. *Annual Review of Sex Research, 4,* 121–209.

Dawe, S., Powell, J., Richards, D., Gossop, M., Marks, I., Strang, J., & Gray, J. A. (1993). Does post-withdrawal cue exposure improve outcome in opiate addiction? A controlled trial. *Addiction, 88,* 1233–1245.

DeLeon, G. (1989). Alcohol: The hidden drug among substance abusers. *British Journal of Addiction, 84,* 837–840.

DeSilva, P., & Eysenck, S. B. G. (1987). Personality and addictiveness in anorexic and bulimic patients. *Personality and Individual Differences, 8,* 749–751.

de Wit, H. (1991). Preference procedures for testing the abuse liability of drugs in humans. *British Journal of Addiction, 86,* 1579–1586.

de Wit, H., Uhlenhuth, E. H., Hedeker, D., McCracken, S., & Johanson, C. E. (1986). Lack of preference for diazepam in anxious volunteers. *Archives of General Psychiatry, 43,* 533–541.

de Wit, H., Uhlenhuth, E. H., Pierri, J., & Johanson, C. E. (1987). Individual differences in behavioral and subjec-

tive response to alcohol. *Alcoholism, 11,* 52–59.

Dickerson, M. G. (1984). *Compulsive gamblers.* London: Longman.

Dickerson, M. G. (1985). The characteristics of the compulsive gambler: A rejection of a typology. In G. Caldwell, B. Haig, M. G. Dickerson, & L. Sylvan (Eds.), *Gambling in Australia.* Sydney: Croom-Helm.

Dickerson, M. G. (1993). Internal and external determinants of persistent gambling: Problems in generalizing from one form of gambling to another. In W. R. Eadington & J. A. Cornelius (Eds.), *Gambling behavior and problem gambling* (pp. 3–24). Reno, NV: University of Nevada.

Dickerson, M. G., Cunningham, R., Legg England, S. L., & Hinchy, J. (1991). On the determinants of persistent gambling. III. Personality, prior mood, and poker machine play. *International Journal of the Addictions, 26,* 531–548.

Dickerson, M. G., Hinchy, J., & Legg England, S. (1990). Minimal treatments and problem gamblers: A preliminary investigation. *Journal of Gambling Studies, 6,* 87–102.

Dickerson, M. G., & Weeks, D. (1979). Controlled gambling as a therapeutic technique for compulsive gamblers. *Journal of Behaviour Therapy and Experimental Psychiatry, 10,* 139–141.

DiClemente, C. C., Prochaska, J. O., Fairhurst, S. K., Velicer, W. F., Velasquez, M. M., & Rossi, J. S. (1991). The process of smoking cessation: An analysis of precontemplation, contemplation, and preparation stages of change. *Journal of Consulting and Clinical Psychology, 59,* 295–304.

Dielman, T. E., Butchart, A. T., & Shope, J. T. (1993). Structural equation model tests of patterns of family interaction, peer alcohol use, and intrapersonal predictors of adolescent alcohol use and misuse. *Journal of Drug Education, 23,* 273–316.

Dijkstra, A., DeVries, H., & Bakker, M. (1996). Pros and cons of quitting, self-efficacy, and the stages of change in smoking cessation. *Journal of Consulting and Clinical Psychology, 64,* 758–763.

Dimitriou, E. C., Lavrenthiadis, G., & Dimitriou, C. E. (1993). Obsessive–compulsive disorder and alcohol use. *European Journal of Psychiatry, 7,* 244–248.

Diner, B., Holcomb, P., & Dykman, R. (1985). P300 in major depression disorders. *Psychiatry Research, 15,* 175–184.

Dion, K. L., & Dion, K. K. (1993). Gender and ethnocultural comparisons in styles of love. *Psychology of Women Quarterly, 17,* 463–473.

Dixon, T. M., & Baumeister, R. F. (1991). Escaping the self: The moderating effect of self-complexity. *Personality and Social Psychology Bulletin, 17,* 363–368.

Donchin, E., Karis, D., Bashore, T. R., Coles, M. G. H., & Gratton, G. (1986). Cognitive psychophysiology and human information processing. In M. G. H. Coles, E. Donchin, & S. W. Porges (Eds.), *Psychophysiology: Systems, processes, and applications* (pp. 244–267). New York: Guilford.

Dow, J. (1986). Universal aspects of symbolic healing: A theoretical synthesis. *American Anthropologist, 88,* 56–69.

Downs, W. R. (1987). A panel study of normative structure, adolescent alcohol use and peer alcohol use. *Journal of Studies on Alcohol, 48,* 167–175.

Drewnowski, A., Yee, D. K., Kurth, C. L., & Krahn, D. D. (1994). Eating pathology and DSM–III–R bulimia nervosa: A continuum of behavior.

American Journal of Psychiatry, 151, 1217–1219.

Dritschel B., Cooper, P. J., & Charnock, D. (1993). A problematic counter-regulation experiment: Implications for the link between dietary restraint and overeating. *International Journal of Eating Disorders, 13,* 297–304.

Drozd, L. M., & Dalenberg, C. J. (1994). The self as mediator in the psychopathology of female children of alcoholics, *International Journal of the Addictions, 29,* 1787–1800.

Drummond, D. C., & Glautier, S. (1994). A controlled trial of cue exposure treatment in alcohol dependence. *Journal of Consulting and Clinical Psychology, 62,* 809–817.

Duchmann, E. G., Williamson, D. A., & Stricker, P. M. (1989). Bulimia, dietary restraint, and concern for dieting. *Journal of Psychopathology and Behavioral Assessment, 11,* 1–13.

Edwards, G. (1986). The alcohol dependence syndrome: A concept as stimulus to enquiry. *British Journal of Addiction, 81,* 171–183.

Edwards, G. (1994). Addiction, reductionism and Aaron's rod. *Addiction, 89,* 9–12.

Edwards, G., & Guthrie, S. (1966). A comparison of inpatient and outpatient treatment of alcohol dependence. *Lancet, 1,* 467–477.

Edwards, G., Orford, J., Egert, S., Guthrie, S., Hawker, A., Hensman, C., Mitcheson, M., Oppenheimer, E., & Taylor, C. (1977). Alcoholism: A controlled trial of "treatment" and "advice." *Journal of Studies on Alcohol, 38,* 1004–1031.

Edwards, G., & Taylor, C. (1994). A test of the matching hypothesis: Alcohol dependence, intensity of treatment, and 12-month outcome. *Addiction, 89,* 553–561.

Edwards, P. Harvey, C., & Whitehead, P. C. (1973). Wives of alcoholics: A critical review and analysis. *Quarterly Journal of Studies on Alcohol, 34*, 112–132.

Efran, J. S., & Heffner, K. P. (1991). Change the name and you change the game. *Journal of Strategic and Systemic Therapies, 10*, 50–65.

Efran, J. S., Heffner, K. P., & Lukens, R. J. (1987). Alcoholism as an opinion: Structure determinism applied to problem drinking. *Alcohol Treatment Quarterly, 4*, 67–85.

Eiseman, R. (1993). Belief that drug usage in the United States is increasing when it is really decreasing: An example of the availability heuristic. *Bulletin of the Psychonomic Society, 31*, 249–252.

Eisen, J. L., & Rasmussen, S. A. (1989). Coexisting obsessive compulsive disorder and alcoholism. *Journal of Clinical Psychiatry, 50*, 96–98.

Eiser, J. R., Sutton, S. R., & Wober, M. (1978). "Consonant" and "dissonant" smokers and the self-attribution of addiction. *Addictive Behaviors, 3*, 99–106.

Elder, J. P., Stern, R. A., Anderson, M., Hovell, M. F., Molgaard, C. A., & Seidman, R. L. (1987). Contingency-based strategies for preventing alcohol, drug, and tobacco use: Missing or unwanted components of adolescent health promotion? *Education and Treatment of Children, 10*, 33–47.

Elia, C., & Jacobs, D. F. (1993). The incidence of pathological gambling among native Americans treated for alcohol dependence. *International Journal of the Addictions, 28*, 659–666.

Ellickson, P. L., & Hays, R. D. (1990–1991). Beliefs about resistance self-efficacy and drug prevalence: Do they really affect drug use? *International Journal of the Addictions, 25*, 1353–1378.

Elliott, D. S., Huzinga, D., & Ageton, S. S. (1985). *Explaining delinquency and drug use.* Beverly Hills, CA: Sage.

Ellis, A. (1970). *The essence of rational psychotherapy: A comprehensive approach to treatment.* New York: Institute of Rational Living.

Elmasian, R., Neville, H., Woods, D., Schuckit, M., & Bloom, F. E. (1982). Event-related brain potentials are different in individuals at high and low risk for developing alcoholism. *Proceedings of the National Academy of Science, 79*, 7900–7903.

Elmore, D. K., & de Castro, J. M. (1990). Self-rated moods and hunger in relation to spontaneous eating behavior in bulimics, recovered bulimics, and normals. *International Journal of Eating Disorders, 9*, 179–190.

Emmelkamp, P. M. G., & Heeres, H. (1988). Drug addiction and parental rearing style: A controlled study. *International Journal of the Addictions, 23*, 207–216.

Ennett, S. T., & Bauman, K. E. (1993). Peer group structure and adolescent cigarette smoking: A social network analysis. *Journal of Health and Social Behavior, 34*, 226–236.

Enomoto, N., Takase, S., Yasuhara, M., & Takada, A. (1991). Acetaldehyde in different aldehyde dehydrogenase 2 genotypes. *Alcoholism: Clinical and Experimental Research, 15*, 141–144.

Epstein, J. A., Botvin, G. J., Diaz, T., Toth, V., & Schinke, S. P. (1995). Social and personal factors in marijuana use and intentions to use drugs among inner city minority youth. *Developmental and Behavioral Pediatrics, 16*, 14–20.

Epstein, S. (1977). Traits are alive and well. In D. Magnusson & N. W. Endler (Eds.), *Personality at the crossroads: Current issues in interactional psychology* (pp. 83–98). Hillsdale, NJ: Erlbaum.

Epstein, S., & O'Brien, E. J. (1985). The person–situation debate in historical and current perspective. *Psychological Bulletin, 98,* 513–537.

Esparon, J., & Yellowlees, A. (1992). Perceived parental rearing practices and eating disorders. *British Review of Bulimia and Anorexia Nervosa, 6,* 39–44.

Eysenck, H. J., & Eysenck, S. B. (1975). *Manual for the Eysenck Personality Questionnaire.* London: Hodder & Stoughton.

Fahy, T. A. (1990). Obsessive–compulsive symptoms in eating disorders. *Behaviour Research and Therapy, 29,* 113–116.

Fahy, T. A., Oscar, A., & Marks, I. (1993). History of eating disorders in female patients with obsessive–compulsive disorder. *International Journal of Eating Disorders, 14,* 439–443.

Fals–Stewart, W., & Angarano, K. (1994). Obsessive–compulsive disorder among patients entering substance abuse treatment: Prevalence and accuracy of diagnosis. *Journal of Nervous and Mental Disease, 182,* 715–719.

Fals–Stewart, W., & Schafer, J. (1992). The treatment of substance abusers with obsessive–compulsive disorder: An outcome study. *Journal of Substance Abuse Treatment, 9,* 365–370.

Farrell, A. D., & Danish, S. J. (1993). Peer drug associations and emotional restraint: Causes or consequences of adolescents's drug use? *Journal of Consulting and Clinical Psychology, 61,* 327–334.

Farrell, A. D., Danish, S. J., & Howard, C. W. (1992). Relationship between drug use and other problem behaviors in urban adolescents. *Journal of Consulting and Clinical Psychology, 60,* 705–712.

Fava, M., Copeland, P. M., Schweiger, U., & Herzog, D. B. (1989). Neurochemical abnormalities of anorexia nervosa and bulimia nervosa. *American Journal of Psychiatry, 146,* 963–971.

Felkins, P. K., & Goldman, I. (1993). Political myth as subjective narrative: Some interpretations and understandings of John F. Kennedy. *Political Psychology, 14,* 447–467.

Fichter, M. M., & Noegel, R. (1990). Concordance for bulimia nervosa in twins. *International Journal of Eating Disorders, 9,* 255–263.

Fiese, B. H., & Scaturo, D. J. (1995). The use of self-help terminology in focus-group discussions with adult children of alcoholics: Implications for research and clinical practice. *Family Therapy, 22,* 1–8.

Figurelli, G. A., Hartman, B. W., & Kowalski, F. X. (1994). Assessment of change in scores on personal control orientation and use of drugs and alcohol of adolescents who participate in a cognitively oriented pretreatment intervention. *Psychological Reports, 75,* 939–944.

Fillmore, K. M. (1987). Prevalence, incidence and chronicity of drinking patterns and problems among men as a function of age: A longitudinal and cohort analysis. *British Journal of Addiction, 82,* 77–83.

Fillmore, K. M., Golding, J. M., Leino, E. V., Motoyoshi, M., Shoemaker, C., Terry, H., Ager, C. R., & Ferier, H. P. (1993). Cross-national comparisons of drinking behavior as determined from the collaborative alcohol-related longitudinal project. *Alcohol Health and Research World, 17,* 198–204.

Fingarette, H. (1988). *Heavy drinking: The myth of alcoholism as a disease.* Berkeley, CA: University of California Press.

Finkelhor, D. (1979). *Sexually victimized children.* New York: Free Press.

Finn, S. E., Hartman, M., Leon, G. R., & Lawson, L. (1986). Eating disorders and sexual abuse: Lack of confirmation for a clinical hypothesis. *International Journal of Eating Disorders, 5,* 1051–1060.

Fiore, M. C., Novotny, T. E., Pierce, J. P., Giovino, G. A., Hatziandreu, E. J., Newcomb, P. A., Surawicz, T. S., & Davis, R. M. (1990). Methods used to quit smoking in the United States: Do cessation programs help? *Journal of the American Medical Association, 263,* 2760–2765.

Fischer, J. L., & Crawford, D. W. (1992). Codependency and parenting styles. *Journal of Adolescent Research, 7,* 352–363.

Fischman, M. W., & Mello, N. K. (Eds.). (1989). Testing for abuse liability of drugs in humans. *NIDA Research Monograph Series, 92.*

Fischman, M. W., & Rachlinski, J. J. (1989). *Cocaine self-administration in humans: A laboratory analysis.* Unpublished manuscript, John Hopkins University School of Medicine.

Fischman, M. W., & Schuster, C. R. (1982). Cocaine self-administration in humans. *Federal Proceedings, 41,* 241–246.

Fischman, M. W., Schuster, C. R., Resnekov, L., Schick, J. F. E., Krasnegor, N. A., Fennell, W., & Freedman, D. X. (1976). Cardiovascular and subjective effects of intravenous cocaine administration in humans. *Archives of General Psychiatry, 33,* 983–989.

Fisher, G. L., Jenkins, S. J., Harrison, T. C., & Jesch, K. (1993). Personality characteristics of adult children of alcoholics, other adults from dysfunctional families, and adults from nondysfunctional families. *International Journal of the Addictions, 28,* 477–485.

Fisher, L. A., & Bauman, K. E. (1988). Influence and selection in the friend–adolescent relationship: Findings from studies of adolescent smoking and drinking. *Journal of Applied Social Psychology, 18,* 289–314.

Fluoxetine Bulimia Nervosa Collaborative Study Group. (1992). Fluoxetine in the treatment of bulimia nervosa: A multicenter, placebo-controlled, double-blind trial. *Archives of General Psychiatry, 49,* 139–147.

Folsom, V., Krahn, D., Nairn, K., Gold, L., Demitrack, M. A., & Silk, K. R. (1993). The impact of sexual and physical abuse on eating disordered and psychiatric symptoms: A comparison of eating disordered and psychiatric inpatients. *International Journal of Eating Disorders, 13,* 249–257.

Frank, L., & Bland, C. (1992). What's in a name? Considering the co-dependent label. *Journal of Strategic and Systemic Therapies, 11,* 1–14.

Frederiksen, L. W., & Simon, S. J. (1978). Modifying how people smoke: Instructional control and generalization. *Journal of Applied Behavior Analysis, 11,* 431–432.

French, D. J., Nicki, R. M., & Cane, D. B. (1993). Bulimia nervosa: An examination of the anxiety-inhibiting properties of the prospect of vomiting. *Behavioural Psychotherapy, 21,* 97–106.

Freund, B., & Steketee, G. (1989). Sexual history, attitude and functioning of obsessive–compulsive patients. *Journal of Sex and Marital Therapy, 15,* 31–41.

Friedman, A. S., Granick, S., Kreisher, C., & Terras, A. (1993). Matching adolescents who abuse drugs to treatment. *American Journal on Addictions, 2,* 232–237.

Frone, M. R., Russell, M., & Cooper, M. L. (1993). Relationship of work–family conflict, gender, and alcohol expectancies to alcohol use/abuse. *Journal of Organizational Behavior, 14,* 545–558.

Fuller, R. K., Branchey, L., Brightwell, D. R., Derman, R. M., Emrick, C. D., Iber, F. L., James, K. E., Lacoursiere, R. B., Lee, K. K., Lowenstam, I., Maany, I., Neiderhiser, D., Nocks, J. J., & Shaw, S. (1986). Disulfiram treatment of alcoholism: A Veterans Administration cooperative study. *Journal of the American Medical Association, 256,* 1449–1455.

Furnham, A., & Alibhai, N. (1983). Crosscultural differences in the perception of female body shape. *Psychological Medicine, 13,* 829–837.

Gaboury, A., & Ladouceur, R. (1993). Evaluation of a prevention program for pathological gambling among adolescents. *Journal of Primary Prevention, 14,* 21–28.

Gaines, L. S., & Connors, G. J. (1982). Drinking and personality: Present knowledge and future trends. In *Alcohol concepts and related problems* (pp. 331–346). Washington, DC: National Institute on Alcohol Abuse and Alcoholism.

Galanter, M., Egelko, S., & Edwards, H. (1993). Rational recovery: Alternative to AA for addiction? *American Journal of Drug and Alcohol Abuse, 19,* 499–510.

Gamblers Anonymous. (1989). *Gamblers Anonymous.* Los Angeles, CA: Author.

Garfinkel, P. E., & Garner, D. M. (1982). *Anorexia nervosa: A multidimensional perspective.* New York: Brunner/ Mazel.

Garmezy, N. (1985). Stress-resistant children: The search for protective factors. In J. E. Stevenson (Ed.), *Recent research in developmental psychopathology* (pp. 213–233). Oxford: Pergamon.

Garner, D. M. (1985). Iatrogenesis in anorexia nervosa and bulimia nervosa. *International Journal of Eating Disorders, 4,* 701–726.

Garner, D. M. (1993). Alternatives to dieting for obese women. *Women's Psychiatric Health, 2,* 3–8.

Garner, D. M., Garfinkel, P. E., Schwartz, D., & Thompson, M. (1980). Cultural expectations of thinness in women. *Psychological Reports, 47,* 483–491.

Garner, D. M., Olmsted, M. P., Bohr, Y., & Garfinkel, P. E. (1982). The Eating Attitudes Test: Psychometric features and clinical correlates. *Psychological Medicine, 12,* 871–878.

Garner, D. M., Olmsted, M. P., & Polivy, J. (1983). Development and validation of a multidimensional eating disorder inventory for anorexia nervosa and bulimia. *Internatinal Journal of Eating Disorders, 2,* 15–34.

Garner, D. M., Olmsted, M. P., Polivy, J., & Garfinkel, P. E. (1984). Comparison between weight-preoccupied women and anorexia nervosa. *Psychosomatic Medicine, 46,* 255–266.

Gawin, F. H., & Ellinwood, E. H. (1988). Abstinence symptomatology and psychiatric diagnosis in cocaine abusers. *Archives of General Psychiatry, 43,* 107–113.

Geijer, T., Neiman, J., Rydberg, U., Gyllander, A., Jönsson, E., Sedvail, G., Valverius, P., & Terenius, L. (1994). Dopamine D_2-receptor gene polymorphisms in Scandinavian chronic alcoholics. *European Archives of Psychiatry and Clinical Neuroscience, 244,* 26–32.

Gelernter, J., Goldman, D., & Risch, N. (1993). The A1 allele at the D_2 dopamine receptor gene and alcoholism: A reappraisal. *Journal of the American Medical Association, 269,* 1673–1677.

Gelernter, J., O'Malley, S., Risch, K., Kranzler, H. R., Krystal, J., Merikangas, K., Kennedy, J. L., & Kidd, K. K. (1991). No association between an allele at the D_2 dopamine receptor gene (DRD2) and alcoholism. *Journal of the American Medical Association, 256,* 1801–1807.

Gendreau, P., & Gendreau, L. P. (1970). The "addiction-prone" personality: A study of Canadian heroin addicts. *Canadian Journal of Behavioral Science, 2,* 18–25.

Gersick, K. E., Grady, K., & Snow, D. L. (1988). Social–cognitive skill development with sixth graders and its initial impact on substance use. *Journal of Drug Education, 18,* 55–70.

Gibbs, R. E. (1986). Social factors in exaggerated eating behavior among high school students. *International Journal of Eating Disorders, 5,* 1103–1107.

Gierymski, T., & Williams, T. (1986). Codependency. *Journal of Psychoactive Drugs, 18,* 7–13.

Gilligan, C. (1982). *In a different voice: Psychological theory and women's development.* Cambridge, MA: Harvard University Press.

Giunta, C. T., & Compas, B. E. (1994). Adult daughters of alcoholics: Are they unique? *Journal of Studies on Alcohol, 55,* 600–606.

Glasgow, R. E., Kleges, R. C., Godding, P. R., & Gegelman, R. (1983). Controlled smoking, with or without carbon monoxide feedback, as an alternative for chronic smokers. *Behavior Therapy, 14,* 386–397.

Gleick, J. (1987). *Chaos: Making of a science.* New York: Viking.

Glueck, S., & Glueck, E. (1968). *Delinquents and non-delinquents in perspective.* Cambridge, MA: Harvard University Press.

Glynn, T. J. (1984). Adolescent drug use and the family environment: A review. Journal of Drug Issues, 14, 271–295.

Goehl, L., Nunes, E., Quitkin, F., & Hilton, I. (1993). Social networks and methadone treatment outcome: The costs and benefits of social ties. *American Journal of Drug and Alcohol Abuse, 19,* 251–262.

Goldbloom, D. S., & Garfinkel, P. E. (1990). The serotonin hypothesis of bulimia nervosa: Theory and evidence. *Canadian Journal of Psychiatry, 35,* 741–744.

Goldbloom, D. S., Garfinkel, P. E., & Shaw, B. F. (1991). Biochemical aspects of bulimia nervosa. *Journal of Psychosomatic Research, 35,* 11–22.

Goldman, D., Brown, G. L., Albaugh, B., Robin, R., Goodson, S., Trunzo, M., Akhtar, L., Lucas–Derse, S., Long, J., Linnoila, M., & Dean, M. (1993). DRD2 dopamine receptor genotype, linkage disequilibrium, and alcoholism in American Indians and other populations. *Alcoholism: Clinical and Experimental Research, 17,* 199–204.

Goldman, D., Dean, M., Brown, G. L., Bolos, A. M., Tokola, R., Virkkunen, M., & Linnoila, M. (1992). D_2 dopamine receptor genotype and cerebrospinal fluid homovanillic acid, 5-hydroxindoleacetic acid and 3-methoxy-4-hydroxyphenylglycol in Finnish and American alcoholics. *Acta Psychiatrica Scandinavica, 86,* 351–357.

Gomberg, E. S. L. (1989). On terms used and abused: The concept of "codependency." *Drugs and Society, 3,* 113–132.

Goodman, A. (1993). Diagnosis and treatment of sexual addiction. *Journal of Sex and Marital Therapy, 19,* 225–251.

Goodstadt, M. S. (1984). Drug education: A turn on or a turn off? In S. Eiseman, J. Wingard, & G. Huba (Eds.), *Drug abuse: Foundations for a psychosocial approach* (pp. 70–80). Farmingdale, NY: Baywood.

Goodwin, D. W., Schulsinger, F., Hermansen, L., Guze, S. B., & Winokur, G. (1973). Alcohol problems in adoptees raised apart from their alcoholic biological parents. *Archives of General Psychiatry, 28,* 238–242.

Goodwin, D. W., Schulsinger, F., Knop, J., Mednick, S., & Guze, S. B. (1977). Alcoholism and depression in adopted-out daughters of alcoholics. *Archives of General Psychiatry, 34,* 751–755.

Gorman, D. M. (1989). Is the 'new' problem drinking concept of Heather and Robertson more useful in advancing our scientific knowledge than the 'old' disease concept. *British Journal of Addiction, 84,* 843–845.

Gossop, M., Johns, A., & Green, L. (1986). Opiate withdrawal: Inpatient versus outpatient programmes and preferred versus random assignment to treatment. *British Medical Journal, 293,* 103–104.

Grabowski, J., Rhodes, H., Elk, R., Schmitz, J., Davis, C., Creson, D., & Kirby, K. (1995). Fluoxetine is ineffective for treatment of cocaine dependence or concurrent opiate and cocaine dependence: Two placebo controlled double-blind trials. *Journal of Clinical Psychopharmacology, 15,* 163–174.

Graham, J. R., & Strenger, V. E. (1988). MMPI characteristics of alcoholics: A review. *Journal of Consulting and Clinical Psychology, 56,* 197–205.

Grandy, D. K., Litt, N., Allen, L., Bunzow, J. R., Marchionni, M., Makam, H., Reed, L., Magenis, E., & Civelli, O. (1989). The human dopamine D$_2$ receptor gene is located on chromosome 11 at q22–q23 and identifies at TaqI RFLP. *American Journal of Human Genetics, 45,* 778–785.

Greene, R. L., Adyanthaya, A. E., Morse, R. M., & Davis, L. J. (1993). Personality variables in cocaine- and marijuana-dependent patients. *Journal of Personality Assessment, 61,* 224–230.

Greenfeld, D. G., Anyan, W. R., Hobart, M., Quilan, D. W., & Plantes, A. (1991). Insight into illness and outcome in anorexia nervosa. *International Journal of Eating Disorders, 10,* 101–109.

Griffiths, R. R., Bigelow, G. E., & Liebson, I. A. (1976). Human sedative self-administration: Effects of interingestion interval and dose. *Journal of Pharmacology and Experimental Therapeutics, 197,* 488–494.

Grilo, C. M., & Shiffman, S. (1994). Longitudinal investigation of the abstinence violation effect in binge eaters. *Journal of Consulting and Clinical Psychology, 62,* 611–619.

Grove, J. R. (1983). Attributional correlates of cessation self-efficacy among smokers. *Addictive Behaviors, 18,* 311–320.

Gruder, C. L., Marmelstein, R. J., Kirkendol, S., Hedeker, D., Wong, S. C., Schreckengost, J., Warnecke, R. B., Burzette, R., & Miller, T. Q. (1993). Effects of social support and relapse prevention training as adjuncts to a televised smoking-cessation intervention. *Journal of Consulting and Clinical Psychology, 61,* 113–120.

Gurling, H. M. D., Murray, R. M., & Clifford, C. A. (1981). Investigations into the genetics of alcohol dependence and into its effects on brain function. In L. Gedda, P. Parsis, & W. E. Nance (Eds.), *Twin research 3: Epidemiology and clinical studies* (pp. 77–87). New York: Alan R. Liss.

Gustafson, R., & Källmén, H. (1989). Alcohol effects on cognitive and personality style in women with special reference to primary and secondary process. *Alcoholism: Clinical and Experimental Research, 13,* 644–648.

Gutierrez, L. M. (1990). Working with women of color: An empowerment perspective. *Social Work, 35,* 149–153.

Haines, P., & Ayliffe, G. (1991). Locus of control of behaviour: Is high externality associated with substance misuse? *British Journal of Addiction, 86,* 1111–1117.

Hall, A., & Crisp, A. H. (1987). Brief psychotherapy in the treatment of anorexia nervosa: Outcome at one year. *British Journal of Psychiatry, 151,* 185–191.

Hall, R. C. W., Tice, L., Beresford, T. P., Wooley, B., & Hall, A. K. (1989). Sexual abuse in patients with anorexia nervosa and bulimia. *Psychosomatics, 30,* 73–79.

Hall, S. (1980). Self-management and therapeutic maintenance: Theory and research. In P. Karoly & J. J. Steffen (Eds.), *Toward a psychology of therapeutic maintenance: Widening perspectives.* New York: Gardner.

Hall, S. M., Havassy, B. E., & Wasserman, D. A. (1991). Effects of commitment to abstinence, positive moods, stress, and coping on relapse to cocaine use. *Journal of Consulting and Clinical Psychology, 59,* 526–532.

Halmi, K. A., Eckert, E., Marchi, P., Sampugnaro, V., Apple, R., & Cohen, J. (1991). Comorbidity of psychiatric diagnoses in anorexia nervosa. *Archives of General Psychiatry, 48,* 712–718.

Hamilton, K., & Waller, G. (1993). Media influences on body shape estimation in anorexia and bulimia: An empirical study. *British Journal of Psychiatry, 162,* 837–840.

Hanson, D. J. (1982). The effectiveness of alcohol and drug education. *Journal of Alcohol and Drug Education, 27,* 1–13.

Harada, S., Agarwal, D. P., Goedde, H. W., & Ishikawa, B. (1983). Aldehyde dehydrogenase isozyme variation and alcoholism in Japan. *Pharmacology Biochemistry and Behavior, 18* (Suppl. 1), 151–153.

Harburg, E., DiFranceisco, W., Webster, D. L., Gleiberman, L., & Schork, A. (1990). Familial transmission of alcohol use: II. Imitation of and aversion to parent drinking (1960) by adult offspring (1977)—Tecumseh Michigan. *Journal of Studies on Alcohol, 51,* 245–256.

Harden, P. W., & Pihl, R. O. (1995). Cognitive function, cardiovascular reactivity, and behavior in boys at high risk for alcoholism. *Journal of Abnormal Psychology, 104,* 94–103.

Harding, T. P., & Lachenmeyer, J. R. (1986). Family interaction patterns and locus of control as predictors of the presence and severity of anorexia nervosa. *Journal of Clinical Psychology, 42,* 440–448.

Harrison, P. A., & Hoffman, N. G. (1987). *CATOR 1987 report/Adolescent residential treatment: Intake and followup findings.* St. Paul, MN: Ramsey Clinic.

Hartmann, A., Herzog, T., & Drinkmann, A. (1992). Psychotherapy of bulimia nervosa: What is effective? A meta-analysis. *Journal of Psychosomatic Research, 36,* 159–167.

Hartshorne, H., & May, M. A. (1928). *Studies in the nature of character: Vol. 1. Studies in deceit.* New York: Macmillan.

Harvey, J. M., & Dodd, D. K. (1993). Variables associated with alcohol abuse among self-identified collegiate COAs and their peers. *Addictive Behaviors, 18,* 567–575.

Hasin, D. S., & Grant, B. (1987). Psychiatric diagnosis of patients with substance abuse problems: A comparison of two procedures, the DIS and the SADS-L. *Journal of Psychiatric Research, 21,* 7–22.

Hasin, D. S., Grant, B., & Endicott, J. (1990). Natural history of alcohol abuse: Implications for definitions of alcohol use disorders. *American Journal of Psychiatry, 147,* 1537–1541.

Hasin, D. S., Muthuen, B., Wisnicki, K. S., & Grant, B. (1994). Validity of the bi-axil dependence concept: A test in the US general population. *Addiction, 89,* 573–579.

Hastings, T., & Kern, J. M. (1994). Relationships between bulimia, childhood sexual abuse, and family environment. *International Journal of Eating Disorders, 15,* 103–111.

Havey, J. M., Boswell, D. L., & Romans, J. S. C. (1995). The relationship of self-perception and stress in adult children of alcoholics and their peers. *Journal of Drug Education, 25,* 23–29.

Hayano, D. M. (1982). *Poker faces: The life and work of professional card players.* Berkeley, CA: University of California Press.

Hayano, D. M. (1989). Like eating money: Card gambling in a Papua New Guinea highlands village. *Journal of Gambling Behavior, 5,* 231–245.

Hays, R. D., & Ellickson, P. L. (1990). How generalizable are adolescents' beliefs about pro-drug pressures and resistance self-efficacy. *Journal of Applied Social Psychology, 20,* 321–340.

Heath, D. B. (1991). Women and alcohol: Cross-cultural perspectives. *Journal of Substance Abuse, 3,* 175–185.

Heather, N., & Robertson, I. (1983). *Controlled drinking* (rev. ed.). London: Methuen.

Heather, N., & Robertson, I. (1985). *Problem drinking: The new approach.* Harmondsworth, England: Penguin.

Heesacker, R. S., & Neimeyer, G. J. (1990). Assessing object relations and social cognitive correlates of eating disorders. *Journal of Counseling Psychology, 37,* 419–426.

Helzer, J. E., Burnam, A., & McEvoy, L. T. (1991). Alcohol abuse and dependence. In L. N. Robins & D. A. Regier (Eds.), *Psychiatric disorders in America* (pp. 81–115). New York: Free Press.

Henderson, M., & Freeman, C. P. L. (1987)., A self-rating scale for bulimia: The "BITE." *British Journal of Psychiatry, 150,* 18–24.

Henningfield, J. E., Chait, L. D., & Griffiths, R. R. (1983). Cigarette smoking and subject responses in alcoholics: Effects of pentobarbital. *Clinical Pharmacology and Therapeutics, 33,* 806–812.

Henningfield, J. E., & Griffiths, R. R. (1980). Effects of ventilated cigarette holders on cigarette smoking by humans. *Psychopharmacology, 68,* 115–119.

Hensen, J., & Emerick, C. D. (1985). Who are we calling an 'alcoholic'? *Bulletin of the Society of Psychologists in Addictive Behaviors, 2,* 164–178.

Herman, C. P., & Polivy, J. (1984). A boundary model for the regulation of eating. In A. J. Stunkard & E. Steller (Eds.), *Eating and its disorders* (pp. 141–156). New York: Raven.

Hermos, J. A., Locastro, J. S., Glynn, R. J., Bouchard, G. R., & De Labry, L. O. (1988). Predictors of reduction and cessation of drinking in community-dwelling men: Results from the normative aging study. *Journal of Studies on Alcohol, 49,* 363–368.

Hester, R. K., & Miller, W. R. (1988). Empirical guidelines for optimal client-treatment matching. *NIDA Research Monograph Series, 77,* 27–38.

Higgins, S. T., Budney, A. J., & Bickel, W. K. (1994). Applying behavioral concepts and principles to the treatment of cocaine dependence. *Drug and Alcohol Dependence, 34,* 87–97.

Higgins, S. T., Budney, A. J., Bickel, W. K., & Badger, G. J. (1994). Participation of significant others in outpatient behavioral treatment predicts greater cocaine abstinence. *American Journal of Drug and Alcohol Abuse, 20,* 47–56.

Higgins, S. T., Budney, A. J., Bickel, W. K., Hughes, J. R., Foerg, F., & Badger, G. J. (1993). Achieving cocaine abstinence with a behavioral approach. *American Journal of Psychiatry, 150,* 763–769.

Higgins, S. T., Delaney, D. D., Budney, A. J., Bickel, W. K., Hughes, J. R., Foerg, F., & Fenwick, J. W. (1991). A behavioral approach to achieving initial cocaine abstinence. *American Journal of Psychiatry, 148,* 1218–1224.

Higuchi, S., Parrish, K. M., Dufour, M. C., Towle, L. H., & Harford, T. C. (1992). The relationship between three subtypes of the flushing response and DSM–III alcohol abuse in Japanese. *Journal of Studies on Alcohol, 53,* 553–560.

Hill, S. Y., & Steinhauer, S. R. (1993). Event-related potentials in women at risk for alcoholism. *Alcohol, 10,* 349–354.

Hinson, R. C., Becker, L. S., Handal, P. J., & Katz, B. M. (1993). The heterogeneity of children of alcoholics: Emotional needs and help-seeking propensity. *Journal of College Student Development, 34,* 47–52.

Hinz, L. D., & Williamson, D. A. (1987). Bulimia and depression: A review of the affective variant hypothesis. *Psychological Bulletin, 102,* 150–158.

Hobbs, M., Birtchnell, S., Harte, A., & Lacey, H. (1989). Therapeutic factors in short-term group therapy for women with bulimia. *International Journal of Eating Disorders, 8,* 623–633.

Holcomb, P., Ackerman, P., & Dykman, R. (1985). Cognitive event-related brain potentials in children with attention and reading deficits. *Psychophysiology, 22,* 656–667.

Holland, A. J., Sicotte, N., & Treasure, J. (1988). Anorexia nervosa: Evidence for a genetic basis. *Journal of Psychosomatic Research, 32,* 561–571.

Hollander, E. (1991). Serotonergic drugs and the treatment of disorders related to obsessive–compulsive disorder. In M. Pato & J. Zohar (Eds.), *Current treatments of obsessive–compulsive disorder* (pp. 173–192). Washington, DC: American Psychiatric Press.

Hollander, E., Frenkel, M., DeCaria, C., Trungold, S., & Stein, D. J. (1992). Treatment of pathological gambling with clomipramine. *American Journal of Psychiatry, 149,* 710–711.

Hong, Y.-Y., & Chiu, C. Y. (1988). Sex, locus of control, and illusion of control in Hong Kong as correlates of gambling involvement. *Journal of Social Psychology, 128,* 667–673.

Hood, J., Moore, T. E., & Garner, D. M. (1982). Locus of control as a measure of ineffectiveness in anorexia nervosa. *Journal of Consulting and Clinical Psychology, 50,* 3–13.

Hopson, R. E., & Beaird–Spiller, B. (1995). Why AA works: A psychological analysis of the addictive experience and the efficacy of Alcoholics Anonymous. *Alcohol Treatment Quarterly, 12,* 1–17.

Horgan, J. (1993, June). Eugenics revisited: Trends in behavioral genetics. *Scientific American, 268,* 122–131.

Hraba, J., Mok, W. P., & Huff, D. (1990). Lottery play and problem gambling. *Journal of Gambling Studies, 6,* 355–377.

Hrubec, Z., & Omenn, G. S. (1981). Evidence of genetic predisposition to alcoholic cirrhosis and psychosis: Twin concordances for alcoholism and its biological end points by zygosity among male veterans. *Alcoholism: Clinical and Experimental Research, 5,* 207–215.

Hser, Y.-I., Anglin, M. D., & Powers, K. (1993). A 24-year follow-up of California narcotics addicts. *Archives of General Psychiatry, 50,* 577–584.

Hsu, L. K. G., Chesler, B. E., & Santhouse, R. (1990). Bulimia nervosa in eleven sets of twins: A clinical report. *International Journal of Eating Disorders, 9,* 275–282.

Hsu, L. K. G., Kaye, W., & Weltzin, T. (1993). Are eating disorders related to obsessive compulsive disorder? *International Journal of Eating Disorders, 14,* 305–318.

Hull, J. G., & Bond, C. F. (1986). Social and behavioral consequences of alcohol consumption and expectancy: A meta-analysis. *Psychological Bulletin, 99,* 347–360.

Humphrey, L. L. (1989). Observed family interactions among subtypes of eating disorders using structural analysis of social behaviors. *Journal of Consulting and Clinical Psychology, 57,* 206–214.

Humphreys, K., Moos, R. H., & Finney, J. W. (1995). Two pathways out of drinking problems without professional treatment. *Addictive Behaviors, 20,* 427–441.

Hunt, D. E., Lipton, D. S., Goldsmith, D. S., Strug, D. L., & Spunt, B. (1985). It takes your heart: The image of methadone maintenance in the addict world and its effect on recruitment into treatment. *International Journal of the Addictions, 20,* 1751–1771.

Hunt, G. M., & Azrin, N. H. (1973). A community-reinforcement approach to alcoholism. *Behaviour Research and Therapy, 11,* 91–104.

Huselid, R. F., Self, E. A., & Gutierres, S. E. (1991). Predictors of successful completion of a halfway-house program for chemically-dependent women. *American Journal of Drug and Alcohol Abuse, 17,* 89–101.

Jackson, J. G. (1985). The personality characteristics of adult daughters of alcoholic fathers as compared with adult daughters of non-alcoholic fathers (Doctoral dissertation, United States International University, 1984). *Dissertation Abstracts International, 46,* 338B.

Jacob, T., & Leonard, K. (1986). Psychosocial functioning in children of alcoholic fathers, depressed fathers and control fathers. *Journal of Studies on Alcohol, 47,* 373–380.

Jacobs, D. F. (1986). A general theory of addictions: A new theoretical model. *Journal of Gambling Behavior, 2,* 15–31.

Janata, J. W., Klonoff, E. A., & Ginsberg, A. J. (1985, November). *Psychophysiological arousal and urges to binge and purge in adolescent bulimics monitored in vivo.* Paper presented at the annual convention of the Association for the Advancement of Behavior Therapy, Houston, TX.

Jansen, A., Broekmate, J., & Heymans, M. (1992). Cue-exposure vs self-control in the treatment of binge eating: A pilot study. *Behaviour Research and Therapy, 30,* 235–241.

Jarmas, A. L., & Kazak, A. E. (1992). Young adult children of alcoholic fathers: Depressive experiences, coping styles, and family systems. *Journal of Consulting and Clinical Psychology, 60,* 244–251.

Jellinek, E. M. (1960). *The disease concept of alcoholism.* New Brunswick, NJ: Hillhouse.

Jenkins, S. J., Fisher, G. L., & Harrison, T. C. (1993). Adult children of dysfunctional families: Childhood roles. *Journal of Mental Health Counseling, 15,* 310–319.

Jenkins–Hall, K. (1994). Outpatient treatment of child molesters: Motivational factors and outcome. *Journal of Offender Rehabilitation, 21,* 139–150.

Jessor, R., & Jessor, S. L. (1977). *Problem behavior and psychosocial development.* San Diego, CA: Academic Press.

Johnson, C. A., Pentz, M. A., Weber, M. D., Dwyer, J. H., Baer, N., Mackinnon, D. P., Hansen, W. B., & Flay, B. R. (1990). Relative effectiveness of comprehensive community programming for drug abuse prevention with high-risk and low-risk adolescents. *Journal of Consulting and Clinical Psychology, 58,* 447–456.

Johnson, E. E., Nora, R. M., Tan, B., & Bustos, N. (1991). Comparison of two locus of control scales in predicting relapse in an alcoholic population. *Perceptual and Motor Skills, 72,* 43–50.

Johnson, H. L., Glassman, M. B., Fiks, K. B., & Rosen, T. S. (1990). Resilient children: Individual differences in developmental outcome of children born to drug abusers. *Journal of Genetic Psychology, 151,* 523–539.

Johnson, R. E., Marcos, A. C., & Bahr, S. J. (1987). The role of peers in the complex etiology of adolescent drug use. *Criminology, 25,* 323–340.

Johnson, R. S., Tobin, J. W., & Cellucci, T. (1992). Personality characteristics of cocaine and alcohol abusers: More alike than different. *Addictive Behaviors, 17,* 159–166.

Johnson, W. G., Schlundt, D. G., Barclay, D. R., Carr–Nongle, R. E., & Engler, L. B. (1995). A naturalistic functional analysis of binge eating. *Behavior Therapy, 26,* 101–118.

Jones, B. E., & Prada, J. A. (1975). Drug-seeking behavior during methadone maintenance. *Psychopharmacologia, 41,* 7–10.

Jones, B. T., & McMahon, J. (1994). Negative alcohol expectancy predicts post-treatment abstinence survivorship: The whether, when, and why of relapse to a first drink. *Addiction, 89,* 1653–1665.

Jones, D. C., & Houts, R. (1992). Parental drinking, parent–child communication, and social skills in young adults. *Journal of Studies on Alcohol, 53,* 48–56.

Jones, J. P., & Kinnick, B. C. (1995). Adult children of alcoholics: Characteris-

tics of students in a university setting. *Journal of Alcohol and Drug Education, 40,* 58–70.

Jonsson, E., & Nilsson, T. (1968). Alcoholism in monozygotic and dizygotic twins. *Nordsk Hygienisk Tidskrift, 49,* 21–25.

Jurik, N. C. (1987). Persuasion in a self-help group: Process and consequences. *Small Group Behavior, 18,* 368–397.

Kafka, M. P., & Prentky, R. A. (1992a). A comparative study of nonparaphilic sexual addictions and paraphilias in men. *Journal of Clinical Psychiatry, 53,* 345–350.

Kafka, M. P., & Prentky, R. A. (1992b). Fluoxetine treatment of nonparaphilic sexual addictions and paraphilias in men. *Journal of Clinical Psychiatry, 53,* 351–358.

Kafka, M. P., & Prentky, R. A. (1994). Preliminary observations of DSM–III–R Axis I comorbidity in men with paraphilias and paraphilia-related disorders. *Journal of Clinical Psychiatry, 55,* 481–487.

Kagan, D. M. (1987). Additive personality factors. *Journal of Psychology, 12,* 533–538.

Kahler, C. W., Epstein, E. E., & McCrady, B. S. (1995). Loss of control and inability to abstain: The measurement of and the relationship between two constructs in male alcoholics. *Addiction, 90,* 1025–1036.

Kaij, L. (1960). *Alcoholism in twins.* Stockholm, Sweden: Almqvist & Wiksell.

Kales, E. F. (1990). Macronutrient analysis of binge eating in bulimia. *Physiology and Behavior, 48,* 837–840.

Kaminer, W. (1992). *I'm dysfunctional, you're dysfunctional.* Reading, MA: Addison–Wesley.

Kandel, D. B., & Davies, M. (1992). Progression to regular marijuana involvement: Phenomenology and risk factors for near-daily use. In M. Glantz & R. Pickens (Eds.), *Vulnerability to drug abuse* (pp. 211–253). Washington, DC: American Psychological Association.

Kandel, D. B., Kessler, R. C., & Margulies, R. Z. (1978). Antecedents of adolescent initiation into stages of drug use: A developmental analysis. *Journal of Youth and Adolescence, 7,* 13–40.

Kandel, D. B., & Raveis, V. H. (1989). Cessation of illicit drug use in young adulthood. *Archives of General Psychiatry, 46,* 109–116.

Kaprio, J., Koskenvuo, M., Langinvainio, H., Romanov, K., Sarna, S., & Rose, R. J. (1987). Genetic influences on use and abuse of alcohol: A study of 5638 adult Finnish twin brothers. *Alcoholism: Clinical and Experimental Research, 11,* 349–356.

Kasvikis, Y. G., Tsakiris, F., Marks, I. M., Basoglu, M., & Noshirvani, H. F. (1986). Past history of anorexia nervosa in women with obsessive–compulsive disorder. *International Journal of Eating Disorders, 5,* 1069–1075.

Kaufman, E. (1981). Family structures of narcotic addicts. *International Journal of the Addictions, 16,* 273–282.

Kaye, W. H., Ballenger, J. C., Lydiard, R. B., Stuart, G. W., Laraia, M. T., O'Neil, P., Fossey, M. D., Stevens, V., Lesser, S., & Hsu, G. (1990). CSF monoamine levels in normal-weight bulimia: Evidence for abnormal noradrenergic activity. *American Journal of Psychiatry, 147,* 225–229.

Kaye, W. H., Ebert, M. H., Gwirtsman, H. E., & Weiss, S. R. (1984). Differences between serotonergic metabolism between nonbulimic and bulimic patients with anorexia nervosa. *American Journal of Psychiatry, 141,* 1598–1601.

Keck, P. E., Pope, H. G., Hudson, J. L., McElroy, S. L., Yurgelun–Todd, D., &

Hundert, E. M. (1990). A controlled study of phenomenology and family history in outpatients with bulimia nervosa. *Comprehensive Psychiatry, 31,* 275–283.

Keller, M. (1972). On the loss-of-control phenomenon in alcoholism. *Journal of Studies on Alcohol, 67,* 153–166.

Kelly, G. A. (1954). *The psychology of personal constructs.* New York: Norton.

Kendler, K. S., MacLean, C., Neale, M., Kessler, R., Heath, A., & Eaves, L. (1991). The genetic epidemiology of bulimia nervosa. *American Journal of Psychiatry, 148,* 1627–1637.

Kendler, K. S., Neale, M. C., Heath, A. C., Kessler, R. C., & Eaves, L. J. (1994). A twin-family study of alcoholism in women. *American Journal of Psychiatry, 151,* 707–715.

Kennedy, S. H., Katz, R., Neitzert, C. S., Ralevski, E., & Mendlowitz, S. (1995). Exposure with response prevention treatment of anorexia nervosa–bulimia subtypes and bulimia nervosa. *Behaviour Research and Therapy, 33,* 685–689.

Kenny, M. E., & Hart, K. (1992). Relationship between parental attachment and eating disorders in an inpatient and a college sample. *Journal of Counseling Psychology, 39,* 521–526.

Kerr, A. S., & Hill, E. W. (1992). An exploratory study comparing ACoAs to non-ACoAs on current family relationships. *Alcohol Treatment Quarterly, 9,* 23–38.

Kessler, R. C., Price, R. H., & Wortman, C. B. (1985). Social factors in psychopathology: Stress, social support, and coping processes. *Annual Review of Psychology, 36,* 531–572.

Khantzian, E. J. (1985). The self-medication hypothesis of addictive disorders: Focus on heroin and cocaine dependence. *American Journal of Psychiatry, 142,* 1259–1264.

Khantzian, E. J., & Mack, J. E. (1994). How AA works and why it's important for clinicians to understand. *Journal of Substance Abuse Treatment, 11*, 77–92.

Kidogami, Y., Yoneda, H., Asaba, H., & Sakai, T. (1992). P300 in first-degree relatives of schizophrenics. *Schizophrenia Research, 6*, 9–13.

Killen, J. D., Taylor, C. B., Hammer, L. D., Litt, I., Wilson, D. M., Rich, T., Hayward, C., Simmonds, B., Kraemer, H., & Varady, A. (1993). Attempt to modify unhealthful eating attitudes and weight regulation practices of young adolescent girls. *International Journal of Eating Disorders, 13*, 360–384.

Killen, J. D., Taylor, C. B., Telch, M. J., Saylor, K. E., Maron, D. J., & Robinson, T. N. (1987). Evidence for an alcohol-stress link among normal weight adolescents reporting purging behavior. *International Journal of Eating Disorders, 6*, 349–356.

King, M. B. (1989). Eating disorders in a general practice population: Prevalence, characteristics and follow-up at 12 to 18 months. *Psychological Medicine, 14*, 1–34.

Kinzl, J. F., Traweger, C., Guenther, V., & Biebl, W. (1994). Family background and sexual abuse associated with eating disorders. *American Journal of Psychiatry, 151*, 1127–1131.

Kirmayer, L. J. (1993). Healing and invention of metaphor: The effectiveness of symbols revisited. *Culture, Medicine and Psychiatry, 17*, 161–195.

Kishline, A. (1995). *Moderate drinking: The Moderation Management guide for people who want to reduce their drinking.* New York: Crown.

Kitano, H. H. L., Chi, I., Rhee, S., Law, C. K., & Lubben, J. E. (1992). Norms and alcohol consumption: Japanese in Japan, Hawaii and California. *Journal of Studies on Alcohol, 53*, 33–39.

Klingemann, H. K.-H. (1992). Coping and maintenance strategies of spontaneous remitters from problem use of alcohol and heroin in Switzerland. *International Journal of the Addictions, 27*, 1359–1388.

Knight, B., Wollert, R. W., Levy, L. H., Frame, C. L., & Padgett, V. P. (1980). Self-help groups: The members' perspectives. *American Journal of Community Psychology, 8*, 53–65.

Kog, E., & Vandereycken, W. (1985). Family characteristics of anorexia nervosa and bulimia: A review of the research literature. *Clinical Psychology Review, 5*, 159–180.

Kokkevi, A., & Stefanis, C. (1988). Parental rearing patterns and drug abuse: Preliminary report. *Acta Psychiatrica Scandinavica, 78* (Suppl. 344), 151–157.

Kolb, D. E., Gunderson, K. E., & Nail, R. L. (1974). Pre-service drug abuse: Family and social history characteristics. *Journal of Community Psychology, 2*, 278–282.

Koski–Jännes, A. (1994). Drinking-related locus of control as a predictor of drinking after treatment. *Addictive Behaviors, 19*, 491–495.

Kosten, T. R., Rounsaville, B. J., & Kleber, H. D. (1987). A 2.5 year follow-up of abstinence and relapse to cocaine abuse in opioid addicts. *NIDA Research Monograph Series, 81*, 231–236.

Kozlowski, L. T., & Harford, M. R. (1976). On the significance of never using a drug: An example from cigarette smoking. *Journal of Abnormal Psychology, 85*, 433–434.

Kozlowski, L. T., & Wilkinson, D. A. (1987). Use and misuse of the concept of craving by alcohol, tobacco, and drug researchers. *British Journal of Addiction, 82,* 31–36.

Kranzler, H. R., Burleson, J. A., Korner, P., Del Boca, F. K., Bohn, M. J., Brown, J., & Liebowitz, N. (1995). Placebo-controlled trial of fluoxetine as an adjunct to relapse prevention in alcoholics. *American Journal of Psychiatry, 152,* 391–397.

Krippner, S. (1986). Dreams and the development of a personal mythology. *Journal of Mind and Behavior, 7,* 449–461.

Krippner, S. (1987). Shamanism, personal mythology, and behavior change. *International Journal of Psychosomatics, 34,* 22–27.

Kruesi, M. J. P., Fine, S., Valladares, L., Phillips, R. A., & Rapoport, J. L. (1992). Paraphilias: A double-blind crossover comparison of clomipramine versus desipramine. *Archives of Sexual Behavior, 21,* 587–593.

Kuchipudi, V., Hobein, K., Flickinger, A., & Iber, F. L. (1990). Failure of a 2-hour motivational intervention to alter recurrent drinking behavior in alcoholics with gastrointestinal disease. *Journal of Studies on Alcohol, 51,* 356–360.

Kuhn, T. S. (1962). *The structure of scientific revolutions.* Chicago, IL: University of Chicago Press.

Kusyszyn, I., & Rubenstein, L. (1985). Locus of control and race track betting behaviors: A preliminary investigation. *Journal of Gambling Behavior, 1,* 106–110.

Kusyszyn, I., & Rutter, R. (1985). Personality characteristics of male heavy gamblers, light gamblers, nongamblers, and lottery players. *Journal of Gambling Behavior, 1,* 59–63.

Labouvie, E. W., & McGee, C. R. (1986). Relation of personality to alcohol and drug use in adolescence. *Journal of Consulting and Clinical Psychology, 54,* 289–293.

Lacey, J. H., & Crisp, A. H. (1980). Hunger, food intake and weight: The impact of clomipramine on a refeeding anorexia nervosa population. *Postgraduate Medical Journal, 56,* 79–85.

Ladouceur, R., Dubé, D., & Bujold, A. (1994). Prevalence of pathological gambling and related problems among college students in the Quebec metropolitan area. *Canadian Journal of Psychiatry, 39,* 289–293.

Ladouceur, R., Maynard, M., & Tourigny, Y. (1984). *Risk taking behavior in gamblers and nongamblers during prolonged exposure.* Paper presented at the Sixth National Conference on Gambling and Risk Taking, Atlantic City, NJ.

Laessle, R. G., Tuschl, R. J., Kotthaus, B. C., & Pirke, K. M. (1989). Behavioural and biological correlates of dietary restraint in normal life. *Appetite, 12,* 83–94.

Laessle, R. G., Tuschl, R. J.,Waadt, S., & Pirke, K. M. (1989). The specific psychopathology of bulimia nervosa: A comparison with restrained and unrestrained (normal) eaters. *Journal of Consulting and Clinical Psychology, 57,* 772–775.

Lambert, M. J. (1989). The individual therapist's contribution to psychotherapy process and outcome. *Clinical Psychology Review, 9,* 469–485.

Landis, C. (1945). Theories of the alcoholic personality. *In Alcohol, science and society* (pp. 129–142). New Haven, CT: Quarterly Journal of Studies on Alcohol.

Lang, R. A., Langevin, R., Checkley, K. L., & Pugh, G. (1987). Genital exhibitionism: Courtship disorder or narcissism? *Canadian Journal of Behavioral Science, 19,* 216–232.

Langenbucher, J. W., & Chung, T. (1995). Onset and staging of DSM–IV alcohol dependence using mean age and survival-hazard methods. *Journal of Abnormal Psychology, 104,* 346–354.

Lavelle, T. L., Hammersley, T., & Forsyth, A. (1991). Personality as an explanation of drug use. *Journal of Drug Issues, 21,* 593–604.

Lazarick, D. L., Fishbein, S. S., Loiello, M. A., & Howard, G. S. (1988). Practical investigations of volition. *Journal of Counseling Psychology, 35,* 15–26.

Lehman, W. E. K., Barrett, M. E., & Simpson, D. D. (1990). Alcohol use by heroin addicts 12 years after drug abuse treatment. *Journal of Studies on Alcohol, 51,* 233–244.

Leigh, B. C. (1989). In search of the seven dwarves: Issues of measurement and meaning in alcohol expectancy research. *Psychological Bulletin, 105,* 361–373.

Leitenberg, H., Gross, H., Peterson, H., & Rosen, J. (1984). Analysis of an anxiety model in the process of change during exposure plus response prevention treatment of bulimia nervosa. *Behavior Therapy, 15,* 3–20.

LeMarquand, D., Pihl, R. O., & Benkelfat, C. (1994). Serotonin and alcohol intake, abuse, and dependence: Clinical evidence. *Biological Psychiatry, 36,* 326–337.

Lemere, F., & Smith, J. W. (1990). Hypomanic personality trait in cocaine addiction. *British Journal of Addiction, 85,* 575–576.

Leon, G. R., Fulkerson, J. A., Perry, C. L., & Early–Zald, M. B. (1995). Prospective analysis of personality and behavioral vulnerabilities and gender influences in the later development of disordered eating. *Journal of Abnormal Psychology, 104,* 140–149.

Lerner, R. M., & Spanier, G. B. (1978). A dynamic interactional view of child and family development. In R. M. Lerner & G. B. Spanier (Eds.), *Child influences on marital and family interaction: A life-span perspective* (pp. 1–22). San Francisco: Academic Press.

Leiseur, H. R., & Blume, S. B. (1987). The South Oaks Gambling Screen (The SOGS): A new instrument for the identification of pathological gamblers. *American Journal of Psychiatry, 144,* 1184–1188.

Lesieur, H. R., & Blume, S. B. (1990). Characteristics of pathological gamblers identified among patients on a psychiatric admissions service. *Hospital and Community Psychiatry, 41,* 1009–1012.

Lesieur, H. R., & Blume, S. B. (1993). Pathological gambling, eating disorders, and the psychoactive substance use disorders. *Journal of Addictive Diseases, 12,* 89–102.

Lesieur, H. R., Blume, S. B., & Zoppa, R. M. (1986). Alcoholism, drug abuse, and gambling. *Alcoholism: Clinical and Experimental Research, 10,* 33–38.

Lesieur, H. R., Cross, J., Frank, M., Welch, M., White, C. M., Rubenstein, G., Moseley, K., & Mark, M. (1991). Gambling and pathological gambling among university students. *Addictive Behaviors, 16,* 517–527.

Lesieur, H. R., & Heineman, M. (1988). Pathological gambling among youthful multiple substance abusers. *British Journal of Addiction, 83,* 765–771.

Lester, D. (1988). Genetic theory: An assessment of the heritability of alcoholism. In C. D. Chaudron & D. A. Wilkinson (Eds.), *Theories on alcoholism* (pp. 1–28). Toronto: Addiction Research Foundation.

Levant, M. D., & Bass, B. A. (1991). Parental identification of rapists and pedophiles. *Psychological Reports, 69,* 463–466.

Levine, M. P., Smolak, L., & Hayden, H. (1994). The relation of sociocultural factors to eating attitudes and behaviors among middle school girls. *Journal of Early Adolescence, 14,* 471–490.

Lévi–Strauss, C. (1967). *Structural anthropology.* New York: Doubleday.

Liakos, A. (1967). Familial transvestism. *British Journal of Psychiatry, 113,* 49–51.

Linden, R. D., Pope, H. G., & Jonas, J. M. (1986). Pathological gambling and major affective disorder: Preliminary findings. *Journal of Clinical Psychology, 47,* 201–203.

Lindman, R. E., & Lang, A. R. (1994). The alcohol-aggression stereotype: A cross-cultural comparison of beliefs. *International Journal of the Addictions, 29,* 1–13.

Linz, D., Donnerstein, E., & Penrod, S. (1988). The effects of long-term exposure to violent and sexually degrading depictions of women. *Journal of Personality and Social Psychology, 55,* 758–768.

Lippas, J. A., Jenner, F. A., & Vicente, B. (1988). Literature on methadone maintenance clinics. *International Journal of the Addictions, 23,* 927–940.

Liskow, B. I., & Goodwin, D. W. (1987). Pharmacological treatment of alcohol intoxication, withdrawal and dependence: A critical review. *Journal of Studies on Alcohol, 48,* 356–370.

Litt, M. D., Babor, T. F., Del Boca, F. K., Kadden, R. M., & Cooney, N. L. (1992). Types of alcoholics: II. Application of an empirically derived typology to treatment matching. *Archives of General Psychiatry, 49,* 609–614.

Littrell, J. (1988). The Swedish studies of the adopted children of alcoholics. *Journal of Studies on Alcohol, 49,* 491–499.

Logue, M. B., Sher, K. J., & Frensch, P. A. (1992). Purported characteristics of adult children of alcoholics: A possi-

ble "Barnum effect." *Professional Psychology: Research and Practice, 23,* 226–232.

London, E. D., Broussolle, E. P M., Links, J. M., Wong, D. F., Cascella, N. G., Dannals, R. F., Sano, M., Herning, R., Snyder, F. R., Rippetoe, L. R., Toung, T. J K., Jaffe, J. H., & Wagner, H. N. (1990). Morphine-induced metabolic changes in human brain. *Archives of General Psychiatry, 47,* 73–81.

London, E. D., Cascella, N. G., Wong, D. F., Phillips, R. L., Dannals, R. F. Links, J. M., Herning, R., Grayson, R., Jaffe, J. H., & Wagner, H. N. (1990). Cocaine-induced reduction of glucose utilization in human brain. *Archives of General Psychiatry, 47,* 567–574.

Long, C. G., & Hollin, C. R. (1995). Assessment and management of eating disordered patients who over-exercise: A four-year follow-up of six single case studies. *Journal of Mental Health, 4,* 309–316.

Longabaugh, R., Beattie, M., Noel, N., Stout, R., & Malloy, P. (1993). The effect of social investment on treatment outcome. *Journal of Studies on Alcohol, 54,* 465–478.

Longabaugh, R., McCrady, B., Fink, E., Stout, R., McAuley, T., Doyle, C., & McNeil, D. (1983). Cost effectiveness of alcoholism treatment in partial vs. inpatient settings: Six-month outcomes. *Journal of Studies on Alcohol, 44,* 1049–1071.

Loper, R. G., Kammier, M. L., & Hoffmann, H. (1973). MMPI characteristics of college freshman males who later became alcoholics. *Journal of Abnormal Psychology, 82,* 159–162.

Love, S. Q., Ollendick, T. H., Johnson, C., & Schlesinger, S. E. (1985). A preliminary report of the prediction of bulimic behaviors: A social learning analysis. *Bulletin of the Society of*

Psychologists in Addictive Behaviors, 4, 93–100.

Lovibond, S. H., & Caddy, G. (1970). Discriminative aversive control in the moderation of alcoholics' drinking behavior. *Behavior Therapy, 1,* 437–444.

Luborsky, L., Crits–Christoph, P., McLellan, T., Woody, G. E., Piper, W., Liberman, B., Imber, S., & Pilkonis, P. (1986). Do therapists vary much in their success? Findings from four outcome studies. *American Journal of Orthopsychiatry, 56,* 501–512.

Luborsky, L., McLellan, T., Woody, G. E., O'Brien, C. P., & Auerbach, A. (1985). Therapist success and its determinants. *Archives of General Psychiatry, 42,* 602–611.

Ludwig, A. M. (1985). Cognitive processes with "spontaneous" recovery from alcoholism. *Journal of Studies on Alcohol, 46,* 53–58.

Lyon, D., & Greenberg, J. (1991). Evidence of codependency in women with an alcoholic parent: Helping out Mr. Wrong. *Journal of Personality and Social Psychology, 61,* 435–439.

Lyon, M. A., & Seefeldt, R. W. (1995). Failure to validate personality characteristics of adult children of alcoholics: A replication and extension. *Alcohol Treatment Quarterly, 12,* 69–85.

MacAndrew, C., & Edgerton, R. B. (1969). *Drunken comportment: A social explanation.* New York: Aldine.

Malamuth, N. M., & Check, J. (1983). Sexual arousal to rape depictions: Individual differences. *Journal of Abnormal Psychology, 92,* 55–67.

Malamuth, N. M., Heim, M., & Feshbach, S. (1980). Sexual responsiveness of college students to rape depictions: Inhibitory and disinhibitory effects. *Journal of Personality and Social Psychology, 38,* 399–408.

Malcolm, R., Anton, R. F., Randall, C. L., Johnston, A., Brady, K., & Thevos, A.

(1992). A placebo-controlled trial of busipirone in anxious inpatient alcoholics. *Alcoholism: Clinical and Experimental Research, 16,* 1007–1013.

Mallinckrodt, B., McCreary, B. A., & Robertson, A. K. (1995). Co-occurrence of eating disorders and incest: The role of attachment, family environment, and social competencies. *Journal of Counseling Psychology, 42,* 178–186.

Maltzman, I. (1994). Why alcoholism is a disease. *Journal of Psychoactive Drugs, 26,* 13–31.

Marlatt, G. A. (1983). The controlled-drinking controversy: A commentary. *American Psychologist, 39,* 1097–1110.

Marlatt, G. A. (1985). Cognitive factors in the relapse process. In G. A. Marlatt & J. R. Gordon (Eds.), *Relapse prevention: Maintenance strategies in the treatment of addictive behaviors* (pp. 128–200). New York: Guilford.

Marlatt, G. A., Curry, S., & Gordon, J. R. (1988). A longitudinal analysis of unaided smoking cessation. *Journal of Consulting and Clinical Psychology, 56,* 715–720.

Marlatt, G. A., Demming, B., & Reid, J. B. (1973). Loss of control drinking in alcoholics: An experimental analogue. *Journal of Abnormal Psychology, 81,* 233–241.

Marlatt, G. A., & Gordon, J. R. (Eds.). (1985). *Relapse prevention: Maintenance strategies in the treatment of addictive behaviors.* New York: Guilford.

Marlatt, G. A., Larimer, M. E., Baer, J. S., & Quigley, L. A. (1993). Harm reduction for alcohol problems: Moving beyond the controlled drinking controversy. *Behavior Therapy, 24,* 461–504.

Martindale, C. (1978). The therapist-as-fixed-effect fallacy in psychotherapy research. *Journal of Consulting and Clinical Psychology, 46,* 1526–1530.

Mattick, R. P., & Jarvis, T. (1994). Inpatient setting and long duration for the treatment of alcohol dependence?: Out-patient care is as good. *Drug and Alcohol Review, 13,* 127–135.

Mayfield, D. (1985). Substance abuse in the affective disorders. In A. I. Alterman (Ed.), *Substance abuse and psychopathology* (pp. 69–136). New York: Plenum.

McAuliffe, W. E. (1975). A second look at first effects: The subjective effects of opiates on non-addicts. *Journal of Drug Issues, 5,* 369–399.

McCargar, L. J., Clandinin, M. T., Fawcett, D. M., & Johnson, J. L. (1988). Short-term changes in energy intake and serum insulin, neutral amino acids, and urinary catecholamine excretion in women. *American Journal of Clinical Nutrition, 47,* 937–941.

McCartney, J. (1995). Addictive behaviors: Relationship factors and their perceived influence on change. *Genetic, Social, and General Psychology Monographs, 121,* 41–64.

McClellan, A. T., Woody, G. E., Luborsky, L., O'Brien, C. P., & Druley, L. A. (1983). Increased effectiveness of substance abuse treatment: A prospective study of patient-treatment "matching." *Journal of Nervous and Mental Disease, 171,* 597–605.

McConaghy, N., Blaszczynski, A., & Kidson, W. (1988). Treatment of sex offenders with imaginal desensitization and/or medroxyprogesterone. *Acta Psychiatrica Scandinavica, 77,* 199–206.

McCord, J. (1988). Identifying developmental paradigms as leading to alcoholism. *Journal of Studies on Alcohol, 49,* 357–362.

McCord, W., & McCord, J. (1960). *Origins of alcoholism.* Stanford, CA: Stanford University Press.

McCormick, R. A., Russo, A. M., Ramirez, L. F., & Taber, J. I. (1984). Affective-disorders among pathological gam-

blers seeking treatment. *American Journal of Psychiatry, 141,* 215–218.

McCusker, C. G., & Brown, K. (1990). Alcohol-predictive cues enhance tolerance to and precipitate "craving" for alcohol in social drinkers. *Journal of Studies on Alcohol, 51,* 494–499.

McElroy, S. L., Keck, P. E., Pope, H. G., Smith, J. M. R., & Strakowski, S. M. (1994). Compulsive buying: A report of 20 cases. *Journal of Clinical Psychiatry, 55,* 242–248.

McGee, L., & Newcomb, M. D. (1992). General deviance syndrome: Expanded hierarchical evaluations at four ages from early adolescence to adulthood. *Journal of Consulting and Clinical Psychology, 60,* 766–776.

McGuire, W. J., & McGuire, C. V. (1996). Enhancing self-esteem by direct-thinking tasks: Cognitive and affective positivity asymmetries. *Journal of Personality and Social Psychology, 70,* 1117–1125.

McIlwraith, R., Jacobvitz, R. S., Kubey, R., & Alexander, A. (1991). Television addiction: Theories and data behind the ubiquitous metaphor. *American Behavioral Scientist, 35,* 104–121.

McLachlan, J. F. C. (1972). Benefit from group therapy as a function of patient–therapist match on conceptual level. *Psychotherapy: Research and Practice, 9,* 317–323.

McLachlan, J. F. C., & Stein, R. L. (1982). Evaluation of a day clinic for alcoholics. *Journal of Studies on Alcohol, 43,* 261–272.

McLellan, A. T., Woody, G. E., Luborsky, L., & Goehn, L. (1988). Is the counselor an "active ingredient" in substance abuse rehabilitation? An examination of treatment success among four counselors. *Journal of Nervous and Mental Disease, 176,* 423–430.

McLeod, D. R., & Griffiths, R. R. (1983). Human progressive-ratio performance:

Maintenance of pentobarbital. *Psychopharmacology, 79,* 4–9.

McLorg, P. A., & Taub, D. E. (1987). Anorexia nervosa and bulimia: The development of deviant identities. *Deviant Behavior, 8,* 177–189.

McMullen, L. M. (1989). Use of figurative language in successful and unsuccessful cases of psychotherapy: Three comparisons. *Metaphor and Symbolic Activity, 4,* 203–226.

McMurran, M. (1994). *The psychology of addiction.* Washington, DC: Taylor & Francis.

Mednick, M. (1989). On the politics of psychological constructs: Stop the bandwagon, I want to get off. *American Psychologist, 44,* 1118–1123.

Melella, J. T., Travin, S., & Cullen, K. (1989). Legal and ethical issues in the use of antiandrogens in treating sex offenders. *Bulletin of the American Academy of Psychiatry and the Law, 17,* 223–232.

Menard, S., & Huizinga, D. (1989). Age, period, and cohort size effects on self-reported alcohol, marijuana, and polydrug use: Results from the National Youth Survey. *Social Science Research, 18,* 174–194.

Mendelson, J. H., & Mello, N. K. (1984). Reinforcing properties of oral Δ^9-tetrahydrocannabinol, smoked marijuana, and nabilone: Influence of previous marijuana use. *Psychopharmacology, 83,* 351–356.

Metzler, C. W., Noell, J., Biglan, A., Ary, D., & Smolkowski, K. (1994). The social context for risky sexual behavior among adolescents. *Journal of Behavioral Medicine, 17,* 419–438.

Meyer, W. J., Cole, C., & Emory, E. (1992). Depo provera treatment for sex offending behavior: An evaluation of outcome. *Bulletin of the American Academy of Psychiatry and the Law, 20,* 249–259.

Mickley, D. W. (1994). Medical aspects of anorexia and bulimia. In B. P. Kiney (Ed.), *Eating disorders: New directions in treatment and recovery* (pp. 7–14). New York: Columbia University Press.

Milam, J. R., & Ketcham, K. (1983). *Under the influence.* New York: Bantam.

Miller, D. A F., McCluskey–Fawcett, K., & Irving, L. M. (1993). The relationship between childhood sexual abuse and subsequent onset of bulimia nervosa. *Child Abuse and Neglect, 17,* 305–314.

Miller, N. S., & Gold, M. S. (1990). The disease and adaptive models of addiction: A re-evaluation. *Journal of Drug Issues, 20,* 29–35.

Miller, P., Plant, M., Plant, M., & Duffy, J. (1995). Alcohol, tobacco, illicit drugs, and sex: An analysis of risky behaviors among young adults. *International Journal of the Addictions, 30,* 239–258.

Miller, P. M., Smith, G. T., & Goldman, M. S. (1990). Emergence of alcohol expectancies in childhood: A possible critical period. *Journal of Studies on Alcohol, 51,* 343–349.

Miller, W. R. (1985). Motivation for treatment: A review with special emphasis on alcoholism. *Psychological Bulletin, 98,* 84–107.

Miller, W. R. (1986). Haunted by the zeitgeist: Reflections on contrasting treatment goals and concepts of alcoholism in Europe and the United States. *Annals of the New York Academy of Science, 472,* 110–129.

Miller, W. R. (1993). What really drives change? *Addiction, 88,* 1479–1480.

Miller, W. R., & Baca, L. M. (1983). Two-year follow-up of bibliotherapy and therapist-directed controlled drinking training for problem drinkers. *Behavior Therapy, 14,* 441–448.

Miller, W. R., Benefield, R. G., & Tonigan, J. S. (1993). Enhancing motivation for change in problem drinking: A controlled comparison of two therapist styles. *Journal of Consulting and Clinical Psychology, 61,* 455–461.

Miller, W. R., Gribskov, C. J., & Mortell, R. L. (1981). Effectiveness of a self-control manual for problem drinkers with and without therapist contact. *International Journal of the Addictions, 16,* 827–837.

Miller, W. R., & Hester, R. K. (1986). The effectiveness of alcoholism treatment methods: What research reveals. In W. R. Miller & N. Heather (Eds.), *Treating addictive behaviors: Processes of change* (pp. 121–174). New York: Plenum.

Miller, W. R., & Kurtz, E. (1994). Models of alcoholism used in treatment: Contrasting AA and other perspectives with which it is often confused. *Journal of Studies on Alcohol, 55,* 159–166.

Miller, W. R., Leckman, A. L., Delaney, H. D., & Tinkcom, M. (1992). Long-term follow-up of behavioral self-control training. *Journal of Studies on Alcohol, 53,* 249–261.

Miller, W. R., Sovereign, R. G., & Krege, B. (1988). Motivational interviewing with problem drinkers: II. The drinker's check-up as a preventive intervention. *Behavioural Psychotherapy, 16,* 251–268.

Miller, W. R., Taylor, C. A., & West, J. C. (1980). Focused versus broad-spectrum behavior therapy for problem drinkers. *Journal of Consulting and Clinical Psychology, 48,* 590–601.

Mintz, L. B., Kashubeck, S., & Tracy, L. S. (1995). Relations among parental alcoholism, eating disorders, and substance abuse in nonclinical college women: Additional evidence against the uniformity myth. *Journal of Counseling Psychology, 42,* 65–70.

Mischel, W. (1968). *Personality and assessment.* New York: Wiley.

Mischel, W., & Peake, P. K. (1982). Beyond déjà vu in the search for cross-situational consistency. *Psychological Review, 89,* 730–755.

Mitchell, J. E., Hatsukami, D., Pyle, R. L., & Eckert, E. D. (1986). The bulimia syndrome: Course of illness and associated problems. *Comprehensive Psychiatry, 27,* 165–179.

Mizoi, Y., Tatsuno, Y., Adachi, J., Kogame, M., Fukunaga, T., Fujiwara, S., Hishida, S., & Ijiri, I. (1983). Alcohol sensitivity related to polymorphism of alcohol-metabolizing enzymes in Japanese. *Pharmacology Biochemistry and Behavior, 181,* 127–133.

Mobilia, P. (1993). Gambling as a rational addiction. *Journal of Gambling Studies, 9,* 121–151.

Monteiro, E., Alves, M. P., & Santos, M. L. (1988). Histocompatibility antigens: Markers of susceptibility to and protection from alcoholic liver disease in a Portuguese population. *Hepatology, 8,* 455–458.

Monteiro, W. O., Noshirvani, H. F., Marks, I. M., & Lelliott, P. T. (1987). Anorgasmia for clomipramine in obsessive–compulsive disorder: A controlled trial. *British Journal of Psychiatry, 151,* 107–112.

Montgomery, S. A. (1993). Obsessive compulsive disorder is not an anxiety disorder. *International Clinical Psychopharmacology, 8*(Suppl. 1), 57–62.

Mooney, J. P., Burling, T. A., Hartman, W. M., & Brenner-Lis, D. (1992). The abstinence violation effect and very low calorie diet success. *Addictive Behaviors, 17,* 319–324.

Moos, R. H., Finney, J. W., & Cronkite, R. C. (1990). *Alcoholism treatment: Process and outcome.* New York: Oxford University Press.

Moreno, I., Saiz–Ruiz, J., & Lopez–Ibor, J. J. (1991). Serotonin and gambling dependence. *Human Psychopharmacology, 6,* S9–S12.

Mosbach, P., & Leventhal, H. (1988). Peer group identification and smoking: Implications for intervention. *Journal of Abnormal Psychology, 97,* 238–245.

Mosher, V., Davis, J., Mulligan, D., & Iber, F. L. (1975). Comparison of outcome in a 9-day and 30-day alcoholism treatment program. *Journal of Studies on Alcohol, 36,* 1277–1281.

Moskalenko, V. D., Vanyukov, M. M., Solovyova, Z. V., Rakhmanova, T. V., & Vladimirsky, M. M. (1992). A genetic study of alcoholism in the Moscow population: Preliminary findings. *Journal of Studies on Alcohol, 53,* 218–224.

Mulford, H. A. (1994). What if alcoholism had not been invented? The dynamics of American alcohol mythology. *Addiction, 89,* 517–520.

Murphy, R. T., O'Farrell, T. J., Floyd, F. J., & Connors, G. S. (1991). School adjustment of children of alcoholic fathers: Comparison to normal controls. *Addictive Behaviors, 16,* 275–287.

Murphy, S. A., & Hoffman, A. L. (1993). An empirical description of phases of maintenance following treatment for alcohol dependence. *Journal of Substance Abuse, 5,* 131–143.

Murphy, S. B., Reinarman, C., & Waldorf, D. (1989). An 11-year follow-up of a network of cocaine users. *British Journal of Addiction, 84,* 427–436.

Murray, R. M., Clifford, C. A., & Gurling, H. M. D. (1983). Twin and adoption studies: How good is the evidence for a genetic role? In M. Galanter (Ed.), *Recent developments in alcoholism* (pp. 25–48). New York: Plenum.

Murray, S., Touyz, S., & Beumont, P. (1990). Knowledge about eating disorders in the community. *International Journal of Eating Disorders, 9,* 87–93.

Myer, R. A., Peterson, S. E., & Stoffel-Rosales, M. (1991). Co-dependency: An examination of underlying assumptions. *Journal of Mental Health Counseling, 13,* 449–458.

Nagoshi, C. T., & Wilson, J. R. (1987). Influence of family alcoholism history on alcohol metabolism, sensitivity, and tolerance. *Alcoholism: Clinical and Experimental Research, 11,* 392–398.

Najavits, L. M., & Weiss, R. D. (1994). Variations in therapist effectiveness in the treatment of substance use disorders: An empirical review. *Addiction, 89,* 679–688.

Nakken, C. (1988). *The addictive personality: Roots, rituals, and recovery.* Center City, MN: Hazelden.

Napier, T. L., Goe, R., & Bachtel, D. C. (1984). An assessment of the influence of peer association and identification on drug use among rural high school students. *Journal of Drug Education, 14,* 227–247.

Nasser, M. (1986). Comparative study of the prevalence of abnormal eating attitudes among Arab female students of both London and Cairo University. *Psychological Medicine, 16,* 621–625.

Nathan, P. E. (1988). The addictive personality is the behavior of the addict. *Journal of Consulting and Clinical Psychology, 56,* 183–188.

Nathan, P. E. (1990). Residual effects of alcohol. *NIDA Research Monograph Series, 101,* 112–123.

Nathan, P. E., & McCrady, B. S. (1987). Bases for use of abstinence as a goal in the behavioral treatment of alcohol abusers. *Drugs and Society, 1,* 109–131.

Needle, R., Lavee, Y., Su, S., Brown, P., & Doherty, W. (1988). Familial, interpersonal, and intrapersonal correlates of drug use: A longitudinal comparison of adolescents in treatment, drug-using adolescents not in treatment, and non-drug-using adolescents. *International Journal of the Addictions, 23,* 1211–1240.

Neff, J. A. (1994). Adult children of alcoholic or mentally ill parents: Alcohol consumption and psychological distress in a tri-ethnic community study. *Addictive Behaviors, 19,* 185–197.

Nelson, E. S., Hill–Barlow, D., & Benedict, J. O. (1994). Addiction versus intimacy as related to sexual involvement in a relationship. *Journal of Sex and Marital Therapy, 20,* 35–45.

Neuhaus, C. (1993). The disease controversy revisited: An ontologic perspective. *Journal of Drug Issues, 23,* 463–478.

Newcomb, M. D. (1994). Drug use and intimate relationships among women and men: Separating specific from general effects in prospective data using structural equation models. *Journal of Consulting and Clinical Psychology, 62,* 463–476.

Newcomb, M. D., & Harlow, L. L. (1986). Life events and substance use among adolescents: Mediating effects of perceived locus of control and meaningless in life. *Journal of Personality and Social Psychology, 51,* 564–577.

Nichter, M., & Nichter, M. (1991). Hype and weight. *Medical Anthropology, 13,* 249–284.

Noble, E. P. (1993). The D_2 dopamine receptor gene: A review of association studies in alcoholism. *Behavior Genetics, 23,* 119–129.

Noble, E. P., Blum, K., Khalsa, M. E., Ritchie, T., Montgomery, A., Wood, R. C., Fitch, R. J., Ozkaragoz, T., Sheridan, P. J., Anglin, M. D., Paredes, A., Treiman, L. J., & Sparkes, R. S. (1993). Allelic association of the D_2 dopamine receptor gene with cocaine dependence. *Drug and Alcohol Dependence, 33,* 271–285.

Noden, M. (1994, August 8). Dying to win. *Sports Illustrated, 81,* 52–60.

O'Brien, C. P., Childress, A. R., McLellan, T., & Ehrman, R. (1990). Integrating systematic cue exposures with standard treatment in recovering drug dependent patients. *Addictive Behaviors, 15,* 355–365.

O'Brien, P. E., & Gaborit, M. (1992). Codependency: A disorder separate from chemical dependency. *Journal of Clinical Psychology, 48,* 129–136.

O'Connor, L. E., Berry, J. W., Morrison, A., & Brown, S. (1992). Retrospective reports of psychiatric symptoms before, during, and after drug use in a recovering population. *Journal of Psychoactive Drugs, 24,* 65–68.

O'Donnell, P. J. (1984). The abstinence violation effect and circumstances surrounding relapse as predictors of outcome states in male alcoholic outpatients. *Journal of Psychology, 117,* 257–262.

Oei, T. P. S., Foley, J., & Young, R. M. (1990). The in vivo manipulation of alcohol-related beliefs in male social drinkers in a naturalistic setting. *British Journal of Medical Psychology, 63,* 279–286.

Oetting, E. R., & Beauvais, F. (1987). Common elements in youth drug abuse: Peer clusters and other psychosocial factors. *Journal of Drug Issues, 17,* 133–151.

Oetting, E. R., Swaim, R. C., Edwards, R. W., & Beauvais, F. (1989). Indian and Anglo adolescent alcohol use and emotional distress. Path models. *American Journal of Drug and Alcohol Abuse, 15,* 153–172.

O'Guinn, T. C., & Faber, R. J. (1989). Compulsive buying: A phenomenological exploration. *Journal of Consumer Research, 16,* 147–157.

O'Malley, S. S., & Gawin, F. H. (1990). Abstinence symptomatology and neuropsychological impairment in chronic cocaine abuse. *NIDA Research Monograph Series, 101,* 179–190.

Orcutt, J. D. (1987). Differential association and marijuana use: A closer look at Sutherland (with a little help from Becker). *Criminology, 25,* 341–358.

Orford, J. (1978). Hypersexuality: Implications for a theory of dependence. *British Journal of Addiction, 73,* 299–310.

Orford, J., & Keddie, A. (1986). Abstinence or controlled drinking in clinical practice: A test of the dependence and persuasion hypotheses. *British Journal of Addiction, 81,* 495–504.

Orford, J., Oppenheimer, E., & Edwards, G. (1976). Abstinence control: The outcome for excessive drinkers two years after consultation. *Behaviour Research and Therapy, 14,* 409–418.

Oscar–Berman, M. (1990). Learning and memory deficits in detoxified alcoholics. *NIDA Research Monograph Series, 101,* 136–155.

Oswald, L. M., Walker, G. C., Krajewski, K. J., & Reilly, E. L. (1994). General and specific locus of control in cocaine abusers. *Journal of Substance Abuse, 6,* 179–190.

Page, R. D., & Schaub, L. H. (1979). Efficacy of a three-versus five-week alcohol treatment program. *International Journal of the Addictions, 14,* 697–714.

Palmer, R. L., & Oppenheimer, R. (1992). Childhood sexual experiences with adults: A comparison of women with eating disorders and those with other diagnoses. *International Journal of Eating Disorders, 12,* 359–364.

Park, J. Y., Huang, Y.-H., Nagoshi, C. T., Yuen, S., Johnson, R. C., Ching, C. A., & Bowman, K. S. (1984). The flushing response to alcohol use among Koreans and Taiwanese. *Journal of Studies on Alcohol, 45,* 481–485.

Parsian, A., Todd, R. D., Devor, E. J., O'Malley, K. L., Suarez, B. K., Reich, T., & Cloninger, C. R. (1991). Alcoholism and alleles of the human D_2 dopamine receptor locus: Studies of association and linkage. *Archives of General Psychiatry, 48,* 655–663.

Partanen, J., Bruun, K., & Markkanen, T. (1966). *Inheritance of drinking behavior.* Helsinki: Finnish Foundation for Alcohol Studies.

Patton, G. C. (1988). The spectrum of eating disorder in adolescence. *Journal of Psychosomatic Research, 32,* 579–584.

Paunonen, S. V., Jackson, D. N., Trzebinski, J., & Forsterling, F. (1992). Personality structure across culture: A multimethod evaluation. *Journal of Personality and Social Psychology, 62,* 447–456.

Paxton, S. J., Wertheim, E. H., Gibbons, K., Szmukler, G. I., Hillier, L., & Petrovich, J. L. (1991). Body image satisfaction, dieting beliefs, and weight loss behaviors in adolescent girls and boys. *Journal of Youth and Adolescence, 20,* 361–379.

Pedersen, N. (1981). Twin similarity for usage of common drugs. In L. Gedda, P. Parsis, & W. E. Nance (Eds.), *Twin research 3: Epidemiology and clinical studies* (pp. 53–59). New York: Alan R. Liss.

Peele, S. (1984). The cultural context of psychological approaches to alcoholism: Can we control the effects of alcohol? *American Psychologist, 39,* 1337–1351.

Peele, S. (1989). *Diseasing of America: Addiction treatment out of control.* Lexington, MA: Lexington Books.

Peele, S. (1991). *The truth about addiction and recovery: The life process program for outgrowing destructive habits.* New York: Simon & Schuster.

Pendery, M. L., Maltzman, I. M., & West, L. J. (1982). Controlled drinking by alcoholics? New findings and a reevaluation of a major affirmative study. *Science, 217,* 169–174.

Penick, E. C., Powell, B. J., Bingham, S. F., Liskow, B. I., Miller, N. S., & Read, M. R. (1987). A comparative study of familial alcoholism. *Journal of Studies on Alcohol, 48,* 136–146.

Perilstein, R. D., Lipper, S., & Friedman, L. J. (1991). Three cases of paraphilias responsive to fluoxetine treatment. *Journal of Clinical Psychiatry, 52,* 169–170.

Perris, C., Jacobsson, L., Lindstrom, H., Von Knorring, L., & Perris, H. (1980). Development of a new inventory for assessing memories of parental rearing behavior. *Acta Psychiatrica Scandinavica, 61,* 265–274.

Pfefferbaum, A., Horvath, T. B., Roth, W. T., & Koppell, B. (1979). Event-related potential changes in chronic alcoholics. *Electroencephalography and Clinical Neurophysiology, 46,* 637–647.

Pickens, R. W., & Svikis, D. S. (1988). The twin method in the study of vulnerability to drug abuse. *NIDA Research Monograph Series, 89,* 41–51.

Pickens, R. W., Svikis, D. S., McGue, M., Lykken, D. T., Heston, L. L., & Clayton, P. J. (1991). Heterogeneity in the inheritance of alcoholism: A study of male and female twins. *Archives of General Psychiatry, 48,* 19–28.

Piercy, F. P., Volk, R. J., Trepper, T., Sprenkle, D. H., & Lewis, R. (1991). The relationship of family factors to patterns of adolescent substance abuse. *Family Dynamics Addiction Quarterly, 1,* 41–54.

Pike, K. M., & Rodin, J. (1991). Mothers, daughters, and disordered eating. *Journal of Abnormal Psychology, 100,* 198–204.

Pina, A. M., Guirao, J. L., Vallverdú, R. F., Planas, X. S., Mateo, M. M., & Aguado, V. M. (1991). The Catalonia survey: Personality and intelligence structure in a sample of compulsive gamblers. *Journal of Gambling Studies, 7,* 275–300.

Pinkerton, S. D., & Abramson, P. R. (1992). Is risky sex rational? *Journal of Sex Research, 29,* 561–568.

Pirke, K. M., Vandereycken, W., & Ploog, D. (1988). *The psychobiology of bulimia nervosa.* Berlin: Springer Verlag.

Pisani, V. D., Fawcett, J., Clark, D. C., & McGuire, M. (1993). The relative contributions of medication adherence and AA meeting attendance to abstinent outcome for chronic alcoholics. *Journal of Studies on Alcohol, 54,* 115–119.

Pithers, W. D., & Cumming, G. F. (1989). Can relapses be prevented? Initial outcome data from the Vermont Treatment Program for Sexual Aggressors. In D. R. Laws (Ed.), *Relapse prevention with sex offenders* (pp. 313–325). New York: Guilford.

Pittman, D. J., & Tate, R. L. (1969). A comparison of two treatment programs for alcoholics. *Journal of Studies on Alcohol, 30,* 888–899.

Polich, J., & Bloom, F. E. (1988). Event-related brain potentials in individuals at high and low risk for developing alcoholism: Failure to replicate. *Alcoholism: Clinical and Experimental Research, 12,* 368–373.

Polich, J., Pollock, V. E., & Bloom, F. E. (1993). Meta-analysis of P300 amplitude from males at risk for alcoholism. *Psychological Bulletin, 115,* 55–73.

Pols, R. G. (1984). The addictive personality: A myth. Australian *Alcohol/Drug Review 3,* 45–47.

Pope, H. G., Mangweth, B., Negrao, A. B., Hudson, J. I., & Cordas, T. A. (1994). Childhood sexual abuse and bulimia nervosa: A comparison of American, Austrian, and Brazilian women. *American Journal of Psychiatry, 151,* 732–737.

Porjesz, B., & Begleiter, H. (1981). Human evoked potentials and alcohol. *Alcoholism: Clinical and Experimental Research, 5,* 304–317.

Porjesz, B., Begleiter, H., & Garozzo, R. (1987). The N2 component of the event-related brain potential in abstinent alcoholics. *Electroencephalography and Clinical Neurophysiology, 66,* 121–131.

Post, R. M., Kotin, J., & Goodwin, F. R. (1974). The effect of cocaine on depressed patients. *American Journal of Psychiatry, 131,* 511–517.

Potamianos, G., Meade, T. W., North, W. R. S., Townsed, J., & Peters, T. J. (1986). Randomized trial of community-based centre versus conventional hospital management in treatment of alcoholism. *Lancet, 2,* 797–799.

Powell, J., Dawe, S., Richards, D., Gossop, M., Marks, I., Strang, J., & Gray, J. (1993). Can opiate addicts tell us about their relapse risk? Subjective predictors of clinical prognosis. *Addictive Behaviors, 18,* 473–490.

Pritchard, W. S. (1986). Cognitive event-related potential correlates of schizophrenia. *Psychological Bulletin, 100,* 43–66.

Prochaska, J. O., & DiClemente, C. C. (1992). Stages of change in the modification of problem behaviors. In M. Hersen, R. M. Eisler, & P. M. Miller (Eds.), *Progress in behavior modification* (pp. 184–214). Sycamore, IL: Sycamore.

Prochaska, J. O., DiClemente, C. C., & Norcross, J. C. (1992). In search of how people change: Applications to addictive behavior. *American Psychologist, 47,* 1102–1114.

Project MATCH Research Group. (1997). Matching alcoholism treatment to client heterogeneity: Project MATCH posttreatment drinking outcomes. *Journal of Studies on Alcohol, 58,* 7–29.

Pumariega, A. J. (1986). Acculturation and eating attitudes in adolescent girls: A comparative and correlational study. *Journal of the American Academy of Child Psychiatry, 25,* 276–279.

Pyle, R. L., Mitchell, J. E., Eckert, E., Halvorson, P., Neuman, P., & Goff, G. (1983). The incidence of bulimia in freshman college students. *International Journal of Eating Disorders, 2,* 75–85.

Pyle, R. L., Neuman, P. A., Halvorson, P. A., & Mitchell, J. E. (1991). An ongoing cross-sectional study of the prevalence of eating disorders in freshman college students. *International Journal of Eating Disorders, 10,* 667–677.

Quadland, M. C. (1985). Compulsive sexual behavior: Definition of a problem and an approach to treatment. *Journal of Sex and Marital Therapy, 11,* 121–132.

Rankin, H. (1982). Control rather than abstinence as a goal in the treatment of excessive gambling. *Behaviour Research and Therapy, 20,* 185–187.

Rankin, H., Hodgson, R., & Stockwell, T. (1983). Cue exposure and response prevention with alcoholics. *Behaviour Research and Therapy, 21,* 435–446.

Rasmussen, S. A., & Eisen, J. L. (1989). Clinical features and phenomenology of obsessive compulsive disorder. *Psychiatric Annals, 19,* 67–73.

Rather, B. C., & Sherman, M. F. (1989). Relationship between alcohol expectancies and length of abstinence amongst Alcoholics Anonymous members. *Addictive Behaviors, 14,* 531–536.

Rathus, S., & Nevid, J. (1991). *Abnormal psychology.* Englewood Cliffs, NJ: Prentice–Hall.

Raviv, M. (1993). Personality characteristics of sexual addicts and pathological gamblers. *Journal of Gambling Studies, 9,* 17–30.

Raw, M., & Russell, M. A. H. (1980). Rapid smoking, cue exposure and support in modification of smoking. *Behaviour Research and Therapy, 18,* 363–372.

Reed, T. E., Kalant, H., Gibbons, R. J., Kapur, B. M., & Rankin, J. G. (1976). Alcohol and acetaldehyde metabolism in Caucasians, Chinese, and Amerinds. *Canadian Medical Association Journal, 115,* 851–855.

Reilly, P. M., Sees, K. L., Shopshire, M. S., Hall, S. M., Delucchi, K. L., Tusel, D. J., Banys, P., Clark, H. W., & Piotrowski, N. A. (1995). Self-efficacy and illicit opiate use in a 180-day methadone detoxification treatment. *Journal of Consulting and Clinical Psychology, 63,* 158–162.

Rhodes, B., & Kroger, J. (1992). Parental bonding and separation-individuation difficulties among late adolescent eating disordered women. *Child Psychiatry and Human Development, 22,* 249–263.

Rhodes, J. E., & Jason, L. A. (1990). A social stress model of substance abuse. *Journal of Consulting and Clinical Psychology, 58,* 395–401.

Rieman, B. C., McNally, R. J., & Cox, W. M. (1992). The comorbidity of obsessive–compulsive disorder and alcoholism. *Journal of Anxiety Disorders, 6,* 105–110.

Roache, J. D., & Griffiths, R. R. (1987). Interactions of diazepam and caffeine: Behavioral and subjective dose effects in humans. *Pharmacology Biochemistry and Behavior, 26,* 801–812.

Robertson, I. A., Heather, N., Dzialdowski, A., Crawford, J., & Winton, M. (1986). A comparison of minimal versus intensive controlled drinking treatment interventions for problem drinkers. *British Journal of Clinical Psychology, 25,* 185–194.

Robichaud, C., Strickler, D., Bigelow, G., & Liebson, I. (1979). Disulfiram maintenance employee alcoholism treatment: A three-phase evaluation. *Behaviour Research and Therapy, 14,* 618–621.

Robins, L. N., Helzer, J. E., & Davis, D. H. (1975). Narcotic use in southeast Asia and afterward. *Archives of General Psychiatry, 32,* 955–961.

Robins, L. N., Helzer, J. E., Weissman, M. M., Orvaschel, H., Gruenberg, E., Burke, J. D., & Regier, D. A. (1984). Lifetime prevalence of specific psychiatric disorders in three sites. *Archives of General Psychiatry, 41,* 949–958.

Robinson, D. (1972). The alcohologist's addiction: Some implication of having lost control over the disease concept of addiction. *Quarterly Journal of Studies on Alcohol, 33,* 1028–1042.

Rodin, J. Silberstein, L. R., & Striegel–Moore, R. H. (1985). Women and weight: A normative discontent. In T. B. Sanderegger (Ed.), *Nebraska symposium on motivation: Vol. 32. Psychology and gender* (pp. 267–307). Lincoln, NE: University of Nebraska Press.

Rohsenow, D. J., Monti, P. M., Bindoff, J. A., Leipman, M. R., Nirenberg, T. D., & Abrams, D. B. (1991). Patient–treatment matching for alcoholic men in communication skills versus cognitive-behavioral mood management training. *Addictive Behaviors, 16,* 63–69.

Rohsenow, D. J., & O'Leary, M. R. (1978). Locus of control research on alcoholic patients: A review. I. Development, scales and treatment. *International Journal of the Addictions, 13,* 55–78.

Roizen, R., Cahalan, D., & Shanks, P. (1978). 'Spontaneous remission' among untreated problem drinkers. In D. B. Kandel (Ed.), *Longitudinal research on drug use* (pp. 197–221). Washington, DC: Hemisphere.

Rollnick, S., Heather, N., Gold, R., & Hall, W. (1992). Development of a short 'readiness to change' questionnaire for use in brief, opportunistic interventions among excessive drinkers. *British Journal of Addiction, 87*, 743–754.

Room, R. (1985). Dependence and society. *British Journal of Addiction, 80*, 133–139.

Room, R., & Leigh, B. C. (1992). Self-control concerns and drinking loss of control in general and clinical populations. *Journal of Studies on Alcohol, 53*, 590–593.

Rosecrance, J. (1985). Compulsive gambling and the medicalization of deviance. *Social Problems, 32*, 275–284.

Rosen, J. C., & Leitenberg, J. (1982). Bulimia nervosa: Treatment with exposure and response prevention. *Behavior Therapy, 13*, 117–124.

Rothenberg, A. (1990). Adolescence and eating disorder: The obsessive–compulsive syndrome. *Adolescence: Psychopathology, Normality, and Creativity, 13*, 469–488.

Rothman, D. J. (1980). *Conscience and convenience.* Boston: Little, Brown.

Rotter, J. B. (1966). Generalized expectancies for internal versus external control of reinforcement. *Psychological Monographs, 80*(1, Whole No. 609).

Rounsaville, B. J., Glazer, W., Wilbur, C. H., Weissman, M. M., & Kleber, H. D. (1983). Short-term interpersonal psychotherapy in methadone-maintained opiate addicts. *Archives of General Psychiatry, 40*, 630–636.

Rounsaville, B. J., Kosten, T. R., & Kleber, H. D. (1986). Long-term changes in current psychiatric diagnoses of treated opiate addicts. *Comprehensive Psychiatry, 27*, 480–498.

Rowe, D. C. (1983). Biometrical genetic models of self-reported delinquent behavior: A twin study. *Behavior Genetics, 13*, 473–489.

Roy, A., Adinoff, B., Roehrich, L., Lamparski, D., Custer, R., Lorenz, V., Barbaccia, M., Guidotti, A., Costa, E., & Linnoila, M. (1988). Pathological gambling: A psychobiological study. *Archives of General Psychiatry, 45*, 369–373.

Roy, A., Berrettini, W., Adinoff, B., & Linnoila, M. (1990). CSF galanin in alcoholics, pathological gamblers, and normal controls: A negative report. *Biological Psychiatry, 27*, 923–926.

Roy, A. Custer, R., Lorenz, V., & Linnoila, M. (1988). Depressed pathological gamblers. *Acta Psychiatrica Scandinavica, 77*, 163–165.

Roy, A., Custer, R., Lorenz, V., & Linnoila, M. (1989). Personality factors and pathological gambling. *Acta Psychiatrica Scandinavica, 80*, 37–39.

Roy, A., De Jong, J., Ferraro, T., Adinoff, B., Gold, P., Robinow, D., & Linnoila, M. (1989). CSF GABA and neuropeptides in pathological gamblers and normal controls. *Psychiatry Research, 30*, 137–144.

Roy, A., De Jong, J., & Linnoila, M. (1989). Extraversion in pathological gamblers: Correlates with indexes of noradrenergic function. *Archives of General Psychiatry, 46*, 679–681.

Rozin, P., & Stoess, C. (1993). Is there a general tendency to become addicted? *Addictive Behaviors, 18*, 81–87.

Rubenstein, C. S., Pigott, T. A., L'Heureux, F., Hill, J. L., & Murphy, D. L. (1992). A preliminary investigation of the lifetime prevalence of anorexia and bulimia nervosa in patients with obsessive compulsive disorder. *Journal of Clinical Psychiatry, 53*, 309–314.

Rubey, R., Brady, K. T., & Norris, G. T. (1993). Clomipramine treatment of sexual preoccupation. *Journal of Clinical Psychopharmacology, 13,* 158–159.

Ruderman, A. J. (1985). Restraint, obesity and bulimia. *Behaviour Research and Therapy, 23,* 151–156.

Ruderman, A. J., & Besbeas, M. (1992). Psychological characteristics of dieters and bulimics. *Journal of Abnormal Psychology, 101,* 383–390.

Ruderman, A. J., & McKirnan, D. J. (1984). The development of a restrained drinking scale: A test of the abstinence violation effect among alcohol users. *Addictive Behaviors, 9,* 365–371.

Rugle, L. J., & Rosenthal, R. J. (1994). Transference and countertransference reactions in the psychotherapy of pathological gamblers. *Journal of Gambling Studies, 10,* 43–65.

Russell, D. (1986). *The secret trauma: Incest in the lives of girls and women.* New York: Basic Books.

Russo, A. M., Taber, J. I., McCormick, R. A., & Ramirez, L. (1984). An outcome study of an inpatient treatment program for pathological gamblers. *Hospital and Community Psychiatry, 35,* 823–827.

Rychlak, J. F. (1993). A suggested principle of complementarity for psychology: In theory, not method. *American Psychologist, 48,* 933–942.

Rychtarik, R. G., Prue, D. M., Rapp, S. R., & King, A. C. (1992). Self-efficacy, after care and relapse in a treatment program for alcoholics. *Journal of Studies on Alcohol, 53,* 435–440.

Sadava, S. W. (1986). Voluntary abstinence from alcohol: A psychosocial study. *Bulletin of the Society of Psychologists in Addictive Behaviors, 5,* 37–47.

Sanchez–Craig, M., Spivak, K., & Davila, R. (1991). Superior outcome of females over males after brief treatment for the reduction of heavy drinking: Replication and report of therapist effects. *British Journal of Addiction, 86,* 867–876.

Sander, T., Harms, H., Podschus, J., Finck, U., Nickel, B., Rolfs, A., Rommelspacher, H., & Schmidt, L. G. (1995). Dopamine D_1, D_2 and D_3 receptor genes in alcohol dependence. *Psychiatric Genetics, 5,* 171–176.

Saunders, B., Wilkinson, C., & Phillips, M. (1995). The impact of a brief motivational intervention with opiate users attending a methadone programme. *Addiction, 90,* 415–424.

Sayette, M. A., Breslin, F. C., Wilson, G. T., & Rosenblum, G. D. (1994). An evaluation of the balanced placebo design in alcohol administration research. *Addictive Behaviors, 19,* 333–342.

Schachter, S. (1982). Recidivism and self-care of smoking and obesity. *American Psychologist, 37,* 436–444.

Schaef, A. W. (1986). *Co-dependence: Misunderstood, mistreated.* Minneapolis, MN: Winston.

Schafer, J., & Brown, S. A. (1991). Marijuana and cocaine effect expectancies and drug use patterns. *Journal of Consulting and Clinical Psychology, 59,* 558–565.

Schafer, J., & Fals–Stewart, W. (1993). Effect expectancies for cocaine intoxication: Initial vs. descendent phases. *Addictive Behaviors, 18,* 171–177.

Scheff, T. J. (1979). *Catharsis in healing, ritual, and drama.* Berkeley: University of California Press.

Schinka, J. A., Curtiss, G., & Mulloy, J. M. (1994). Personality variables and self-medication in substance abuse. *Journal of Personality Assessment, 63,* 413–422.

Schissel, B. (1993). Coping with adversity: Testing the origins of resiliency in mental health. *International Journal of Social Psychiatry, 39,* 34–46.

Schlosser, S., Black, D. W., Repertinger, S., & Freet, D. (1994). Compulsive buying: Demography, phenomenology, and comorbidity in 46 subjects. *General Hospital Psychiatry, 16,* 205–212.

Schmidt, U., & Marks, I. (1988). Cue exposure to food plus response prevention of binges for bulimia: A pilot study. *International Journal of Eating Disorders, 7,* 663–672.

Schneider, J. A., O'Leary, A., & Agras, W. S. (1987). The role of perceived self-efficacy in recovery from bulimia: A preliminary examination. *Behaviour Research and Therapy, 25,* 429–432.

Schoeneman, T. J., Hollis, J. F., Stevens, V. J., Fischer, K., & Cheek, P. R. (1988). Recovering stride versus letting it slide: Attributions for "slips" following smoking cessation treatment. *Psychology and Health, 2,* 335–347.

Schutte, K. K., Moos, R. H., & Brennan, P. L. (1995). Depression and drinking behavior among women and men: A three-wave longitudinal study of older adults. *Journal of Consulting and Clinical Psychology, 63,* 810–822.

Schuckit, M. A. (1979). Alcoholism and affective disorder: Diagnostic confusion. In D. W. Goodwin & C. K. Erickson (Eds.), *Alcoholism and affective disorders* (pp. 9–19). New York: SP Medical Scientific Books.

Schuckit, M. A. (1983). Extraversion and neuroticism in young men at higher or lower risk for alcoholism. *American Journal of Psychiatry, 140,* 1223–1224.

Schuckit, M. A. (1985). Studies of populations at high risk for alcoholism. *Psychiatric Developments, 3,* 31–63.

Schuckit, M. A., Klein, J., Twitchell, G., & Smith, T. (1994). Personality test scores as predictors of alcoholism almost a decade later. *American Journal of Psychiatry, 151,* 1038–1042.

Schuckit, M. A., & Rayses, V. (1979). Ethanol ingestion: Differences in blood acetaldehyde concentrations in relatives of alcoholics and controls. *Science, 203,* 54–55.

Schupak–Neuberg, E., & Nemeroff, C. J. (1993). Disturbances in identity and self regulation in bulimia nervosa: Implications for a metaphorical perspective of "body as self." *International Journal of Eating Disorders, 13,* 335–347.

Schwab, S., Soyka, M., Niederecker, M., Ackenheil, M., Scherer, J., & Wildenauer, D. B. (1991). Allelic association of human D_2-receptor DNA polymorphism ruled out in 45 alcoholics. *American Journal of Human Genetics, 49,* 203.

Schwitters, S. Y., Johnson, R. C., McLearn, G. E., & Wilson, J. R. (1982). Alcohol use and the flushing response in different racial–ethnic groups. *Journal of Studies on Alcohol, 43,* 1259–1262.

Searight, H. R., Manley, C. M., Binder, A. F., Krohn, E., Rogers, B. J., & Russo, J. R. (1991). The families of origin of adolescent drug abusers: Perceived autonomy and intimacy. *Contemporary Family Therapy, 13,* 71–81.

Searles, J. S. (1988). The role of genetics in the pathogenesis of alcoholism. *Journal of Abnormal Psychology, 97,* 153–167.

Searles, J. S. (1991). The genetics of alcoholism: Impact on family and sociological models of addiction. *Family Dynamics Addiction Quarterly, 1,* 8–21.

Seefeldt, R. W., & Lyon, M. A. (1992). Personality characteristics of adult children of alcoholics. *Journal of Counseling and Development, 70,* 588–593.

Sellers, E. M., Naranjo, C. A., & Peachey, J. E. (1981). Drugs to decrease alcohol consumption. *New England Journal of Medicine, 305,* 1255–1262.

Shapiro, J. P. (1996, January 15). America's gambling fever. *U.S. News and World Report,* 53–61.

Shedler, J., & Block, J. (1990). Adolescent drug use and psychological health: A longitudinal inquiry. *American Psychologist, 45,* 612–630.

Sher, K. (1985). Subjective effects of alcohol: The influence of setting and individual differences in alcohol expectancies. *Journal of Studies on Alcohol, 46,* 137–146.

Sher, K. J., Walitzer, K. S., Wood, P. K., & Brent, E. W. (1991). Characteristics of children of alcoholics: Putative risk factors, substance use and abuse, and psychopathology. *Journal of Abnormal Psychology, 100,* 427–448.

Shiffman, S. (1989). Tobacco "chippers"— Individual differences in tobacco dependence. *Psychopharmacology, 97,* 539–547.

Shiffman, S., Hickcox, M., Paty, J. A., Gnys, M., Kassell, J. D., & Richards, T. J. (1996). Progression from a smoking lapse to relapes: Prediction from abstinence violation effects, nicotine dependence, and lapse characteristics. *Journal of Consulting and Clinical Psychology, 64,* 993–1002.

Shisslak, C. M., Pazda, S. L., & Crago, M. (1990). Body weight and bulimics as discriminators of psychological characteristics among anorexic, bulimic, and obese women. *Journal of Abnormal Psychology, 99,* 380–384.

Shisslak, C. M., Schnaps, L. S., & Crago, M. (1989). Eating disorders and substance abuse in women: A comparative study of MMPI patterns. *Journal of Substance Abuse, 1,* 209–219.

Shope, J. T., Dielman, T. E., Butchart, A. T., Campanelli, P. C., & Kloska, D. D. (1992). An elementary school-based alcohol misuse prevention program: A follow-up evaluation. *Journal of Studies on Alcohol, 53,* 106–121.

Sideroff, S. I., & Jarvick, M. E. (1980). Conditioned responses to video tape showing heroin related stimuli. *International Journal of the Addictions, 15,* 529–536.

Siegel, R. K. (1984). Changing patterns of cocaine use: Longitudinal observations, consequences, and treatment. *NIDA Research Monograph Series, 50,* 92–110.

Siegel, S. (1988). Drug anticipation and the treatment of dependence. *NIDA Research Monograph Series, 84,* 1–24.

Siegel, S., & Ellsworth, D. (1986). Pavlovian conditioning and death from apparent overdose of medically prescribed morphine: A case report. *Bulletin of the Psychonomic Society, 24,* 278–280.

Silverstein, B., Perdue, L., Peterson, B., & Kelly, E. (1986). The role of the mass media in promoting a thin standard of bodily attractiveness for women. *Sex Roles, 14,* 519–532.

Simon, W., & Gagnon, J. H. (1986). Sexual scripts: Permanence and change. *Archives of Sexual Behavior, 15,* 97–120.

Simons, R. L., & Robertson, J. F. (1989). The importance of parenting factors, deviant peers, and coping styles in the etiology of adolescent substance use. *Family Relations, 38,* 273–281.

Simons, R. L., Whitbeck, L. B., Conger, R. D., & Melby, J. N. (1991). The effect of social skills, values, peers, and depression on adolescent substance use. *Journal of Early Adolescence, 11,* 466–481.

Simpson, D. D., & Joe, G. W. (1993). Motivation as a predictor of early dropout from drug abuse treatment. *Psychotherapy, 30,* 357–368.

Simpson, D. D., & Marsh, K. L. (1986). Relapse and recovery among opioid addicts 12 years after treatment. *NIDA Research Monograph Series, 72,* 86–103.

Sisson, R. W., & Azrin, N. H. (1989). The community reinforcement approach. In R. K. Hester & W. R. Miller (Eds.), *Handbook of alcoholism treatment approaches: Effective alternatives* (pp. 242–258). New York: Pergamon.

Sitharthan, T., & Kavanagh, D. J. (1990). Role of self-efficacy in predicting outcomes from a programme for controlled drinking. *Drug and Alcohol Dependence, 27,* 87–94.

Slonin–Nevo, V. (1992). First premarital intercourse among Mexican-American and Anglo-American adolescent women: Interpreting ethnic differences. *Journal of Adolescent Research, 7,* 332–351.

Smart, R. G., Finley, J., & Funston, R. (1977). The effectiveness of post-detoxication referrals: Effects on later detoxication admissions, drunkenness and criminality. *Drug and Alcohol Dependence, 2,* 149–155.

Smart, R. G., & Gray, G. (1978). Minimal, moderate and long-term treatment for alcoholism. *British Journal of Addiction, 73,* 35–38.

Smith, G. T., Goldman, M. S., Greenbaum, P. E., & Christiansen, B. A. (1995). Expectancy for social facilitation from drinking: The divergent path of high-expectancy and low-expectancy adolescents. *Journal of Abnormal Psychology, 104,* 32–40.

Smith, M., & Thelan, M. (1984). Development and validation of a test for bulimia. *Journal of Consulting and Clinical Psychology, 52,* 863–872.

Smith, R. (1986). Television addiction. In J. Bryant & D. Anderson (Eds.), *Perspectives on media effects* (pp. 109–128). Hillsdale, NJ: Erlbaum.

Smith, S. S., O'Hara, B. F., Persico, A. M., Gorelick, D. A., Newlin, D. B., Vlahov, D., Solomon, L., Pickens, R., & Uhl, G. R. (1992). Genetic vulnerability to drug abuse: The dopamine D_2 receptor TaqIB RFLP is more frequent in polysubstance abuse. *Archives of General Psychiatry, 49,* 723–727.

Smolak, L., Levin, M., & Sullins, E. (1990). Are child sexual experiences related to eating-disordered attitudes and behaviors in a college sample? *International Journal of Eating Disorders, 9,* 167–178.

Snow, M. G., Prochaska, J. O., & Rossi, J. S. (1994). Processes of change in Alcoholics Anonymous: Maintenance factors in long-term sobriety. *Journal of Studies on Alcohol, 55,* 362–371.

Snyder, C. R., & Higgins, R. L. (1988). Excuses: Their effective role in the negotiation of reality. *Psychological Bulletin, 104,* 23–35.

Sobell, L. C., Cunningham, J. A., Sobell, M. B., & Toneatto, T. (1993). A lifespan perspective on natural recovery (self-change) from alcohol problems. In J. S. Baer, G. A. Marlatt, & R. J. McMahon (Eds.), *Addictive behaviors across the life span: Prevention, treatment, and policy issues* (pp. 34–66). Newbury Park, CA: Sage.

Sobell, M. B., & Sobell, L. C. (1976). Second-year treatment outcome of alcoholics treated by individualized behavior therapy: Results. *Behaviour Research and Therapy, 14,* 195–215.

Solomon, K. E., & Annis, H. M. (1990). Outcome and efficacy expectancy in the prediction of post-treatment drinking behavior. *British Journal of Addiction, 85,* 659–665.

Solomon, R. (1977). The evolution of nonmedical opiate use in Canada. *Drug Forum—The Journal of Human Issues, 6,* 1–26.

Solyom, L. S., Freeman, R. J., & Miles, J. E. (1982). A comparative psychometric study of anorexia nervosa and obsessive neurosis. *Canadian Journal of Psychiatry, 27,* 282–286.

"Spending on alcoholic beverages increasing in 1992." (1993, April). *The Bottom Line, 14,* 5–28.

Sperry, J. M., & Nicki, R. M. (1991). Cognitive appraisal, self-efficacy, and cigarette smoking behavior. *Addictive Behaviors, 16,* 381–388.

Speziale, B. A. (1994). Marital conflict versus sex and love addiction. Families in Society: *The Journal of Contemporary Human Services, 75,* 509–512.

Spitzer, R. L., & Williams, J. B. W. (1983). *Structured clinical interview for DSM–III.* New York: New York State Psychiatric Institute.

Spunt, B. J. (1993). The link between identity and crime for the heroin addict in methadone treatment. *International Journal of the Addictions, 28,* 813–825.

Stacy, A. W., Galaif, E. R., Sussman, S., & Dent, C. W. (1996). Self-generated drug outcomes in high-risk adolescents. *Psychology of Addictive Behaviors, 10,* 18–27.

Stattin, H., Gustafson, S. B., & Magnusson, D. (1989). Peer influences on adolescent drinking: A social transition perspective. *Journal of Early Adolescence, 9,* 227–246.

Steiger, H., Liquornik, K., Chapman, J., & Hussain, N. (1991). Personality and family disturbance in eating-disorder patients: Comparison of "restricters" and "bingers" to normal controls. *International Journal of Eating Disorders, 10,* 501–512.

Steiger, L., & Zanko, M. (1990). Sexual traumata among eating-disordered, psychiatric, and normal female groups. *Journal of Interpersonal Violence, 5,* 74–86.

Stein, D. J., Hollander, E., Anthony, D. T., Schneier, F. R., Fallon, B. A., Liebowitz, M. R., & Klein, D. F. (1992). Serotonergic medication for sexual obsessions, sexual addictions, and paraphilias. *Journal of Clinical Psychiatry, 53,* 267–271.

Stein, J. A., Newcomb, M. D., & Bentler, P. M. (1987). Personality and drug use: Reciprocal effects across four years. *Personality and Individual Differences, 8,* 419–430.

Stein, L. I., Newton, J. R., & Bowman, R. S. (1975). Duration of hospitalization for alcoholism. *Archives of General Psychiatry, 32,* 247–252.

Stein, S. A. (1993). The role of support in recovery from compulsive gambling. In W. R. Eadington & J. A. Cornelius (Eds.), *Gambling behavior and problem gambling* (pp. 627–640). Reno, NV: University of Nevada Press.

Steinglass, P. (1987). *The alcoholic family.* New York: Basic Books.

Stephens, R. C., & McBride, D. (1975). Becoming a street addict. *Human Organization, 35,* 78–94.

Stephens, R. S., Curtin, L., Simpson, E. E., & Roffman, R. A. (1994). Testing the abstinence violation effect construct with marijuana cessation. *Addictive Behaviors, 19,* 23–32.

Stephens, R. S., Roffman, R. A., & Simpson, E. E. (1994). Treating adult marijuana dependence: A test of the relapse prevention model. *Journal of Consulting and Clinical Psychology, 62,* 92–99.

Stern, S. L., Dixon, K. N., Nemzee, E., Lake, M. D., Sansone, R. A., Smeltzer, D. J., Lantz, S., & Schrier, S. (1984). Affective disorder in the families of women with normal weight bulimia. *American Journal of Psychiatry, 141,* 1224–1227.

Stewart, R. M., & Brown, R. I. F. (1988). An outcome study of Gamblers Anonymous. *British Journal of Psychiatry, 152,* 284–288.

Stice, E. (1994). Review of the evidence for a sociocultural model of bulimia nervosa and an explanation of the mechanisms of action. *Clinical Psychology Review, 14,* 633–661.

Stice, E., & Barrera, M. (1995). A longitudinal examination of the reciprocal relations between perceived parenting and adolescents' substance use and externalizing behaviors. *Developmental Psychology, 31,* 322–334.

Stice, E., Schupak–Neuberg, E., Shaw, H. E., & Stein, R. I. (1994). Relation of media exposure to eating disorder symptomatology: An examination of mediating mechanisms. *Journal of Abnormal Psychology, 103,* 836–840.

Stice, E., & Shaw, H. E. (1994). Adverse effects of the media portrayed thin-ideal on women and linkages to bulimic symptomatology. *Journal of Social and Clinical Psychology, 13,* 288–308.

Stockwell, T. R., Hodgson, R., Rankin, H., & Taylor, C. (1982). Alcohol dependence, beliefs and the priming effect. *Behaviour Research and Therapy, 20,* 513–522.

Strober, M., Morrell, W., Burroughs, J., Salkin, B., & Jacobs, C. (1985). A controlled family study of anorexia nervosa. *Journal of Psychiatric Research, 19,* 239–246.

Stuart, G. W., Laraia, M. T., Ballenger, J. C., & Lydiard, R. B. (1990). Early family experiences of women with bulimia and depression. *Archives of Psychiatric Nursing, 4,* 43–52.

Swadi, H. S. (1988). Adolescent drug taking: Role of family and peers. *Drug and Alcohol Dependence, 21,* 157–160.

Swaim, R. C., Oetting, E. R., Edwards, R. W., & Beauvais, F. (1989). Links from emotional distress to adolescent drug use: A path model. *Journal of Consulting and Clinical Psychology, 57,* 227–231.

Swann, W. B., Stein–Seroussi, A., & Giesler, R. B. (1992). Why people self-verify. *Journal of Personality and Social Psychology, 62,* 392–401.

Szasz, T. S. (1971). The ethics of addiction. *American Journal of Psychiatry, 128,* 541–546.

Szmukler, G., McCance, C., McCrone, L., & Hunter, D. (1986). Anorexia nervosa: A psychiatric case register study from Aberdeen. *Psychological Medicine, 16,* 49–58.

Talbott, G. D. (1986). Alcoholism and other drug addictions: A primary disease entity. *Journal of the Medical Association of Georgia, 75,* 490–494.

Tamerin, J. S., & Mendelson, J. H. (1969). The psychodynamics of chronic inebriation: Observations of alcoholics during the process of drinking in an experimental group setting. *American Journal of Psychiatry, 125,* 886–899.

Temple, M., & Ladouceur, P. (1986). The alcohol–crime relationship as an age-specific phenomenon: A longitudinal study. *Contemporary Drug Problems, 15,* 89–115.

Theander, S. (1985). Outcome and prognosis in anorexia nervosa and bulimia: Some results of previous investigations, compared with those of a Swedish long-term study. *Journal of Psychiatric Research, 19,* 493–508.

Thiel, A., Broocks, A., Ohlmeier, M., Jacoby, G. E., & Schübler, G. (1995). Obsessive–compulsive disorder among patients with anorexia nervosa and bulimia nervosa. *American Journal of Psychiatry, 152,* 72–75.

Thomasson, H. R., Crabb, D. W., Edenberg, H. J., & Li, T.-K. (1993). Alcohol and aldehyde dehydrogenase polymorphisms. *Behavior Genetics, 23,* 131–136.

Tice, D. M. (1992). Self-concept change and self-presentation: The looking glass self is also a magnifying glass. *Journal of Personality and Social Psychology, 63,* 435–451.

Timko, C., Moos, R. H., Finney, J. W., & Moos, B. S. (1994). Outcomes of treatment for alcohol abuse and involvement in Alcoholics Anonymous among previously untreated problem drinkers. *Journal of Mental Health Administration, 21,* 145–160.

Toner, B. B., Garfinkel, P. E., & Garner, D. M. (1986). Long-term follow up of anorexia nervosa. *Psychosomatic Medicine, 48,* 520–529.

Tonnesen, H. (1992). Influence of alcohol on several physiological functions and its reversibility: A surgical view. *Alcohol, 86,* 67–71.

Troise, F. P. (1992). An examination of Cermack's conceptualization of codependency as personality disorder. *Alcoholism Treatment Quarterly, 12,* 1–15.

Truan, F. (1993). Addiction as a social construction: A postempirical view. *Journal of Psychology, 127,* 489–499.

Tuchfeld, B. S. (1981). Spontaneous remission in alcoholics: Empirical observations and theoretical implications. *Journal of Studies on Alcohol, 42,* 626–641.

Tuchfeld, B. S., Clayton, R., & Logan, J. (1982). Alcohol, drug use and delinquent and criminal behavior among male adolescents and young adults. *Journal of Drug Issues, 12,* 185–198.

Tucker, J. A., Vuchinich, R. E., & Gladsjo, J. A. (1994). Environmental events surrounding natural recovery from alcohol-related problems. *Journal of Studies on Alcohol, 55,* 401–411.

Turner, D. N., & Saunders, D. (1990). Medical relabeling in Gamblers Anonymous: The construction of an ideal member. *Small Group Research, 21,* 59–78.

Turner, E., Ewing, J., Shilling, P., Smith, T. L., Irwin, M., Schuckit, M., & Kelsoe, J. R. (1992). Lack of association between an RFLP near the D_2 dopamine receptor gene and severe alcoholism. *Biological Psychiatry, 31,* 285–290.

Turner, M. S., & Shapiro, C. M. (1992). The biochemistry of anorexia ner-

vosa. *International Journal of Eating Disorders, 12,* 179–193.

Udel, M. M. (1984). Chemical abuse dependence: Physician's occupational hazard. *Journal of the Medical Association of Georgia, 73,* 775–778.

Uhl, G. R., Persico, A. M., & Smith, S. S. (1992). Current excitement with D_2 receptor gene alleles in substance abuse. *Archives of General Psychiatry, 49,* 157–160.

Ullman, A. D., & Orenstein, A. (1994). Why some children of alcoholics become alcoholics: Emulation of the drinker. *Adolescence, 29,* 1–11.

Vaglum, P., & Fossheim, I. (1980). Differential treatment of young abusers: A quasi-experimental study of a "therapeutic community" in a psychiatric hospital. *Journal of Drug Issues, 10,* 505–516.

Vaillant, G. E. (1983). *The natural history of alcoholism.* Cambridge, MA: Harvard University Press.

Vaillant, G. E. (1990). We should retain the disease concept of alcoholism. *Harvard Medical School Mental Health Letter, 6,* 4–6.

Valentine, L., & Feinauer, L. L. (1993). Resilience factors associated with female survivors of childhood sexual abuse. *American Journal of Family Therapy, 21,* 216–224.

Valle, S. K. (1981). Interpersonal functioning of alcoholism counselors and treatment outcome. *Journal of Studies on Alcohol, 42,* 783–790.

Velleman, R., & Orford, J. (1990). Young adult offspring of parents with drinking problems: Recollections of parents' drinking and its immediate effects. *British Journal of Clinical Psychology, 29,* 297–317.

Vitousek, K., & Manke, F. (1994). Personality variables and disorders in anorexia nervosa and bulimia nervosa. *Journal of Abnormal Psychology, 103,* 137–147.

Volberg, R. A. (1993). Estimating the prevalence of pathological gambling in the United States. In W. A. Eadington & J. A. Cornelius (Eds.), *Gambling behavior and problem gambling* (pp. 365–384). Reno, NV: Univeristy of Nevada, Reno.

Wagner–Echeagaray, F. A., Schütz, C. G., Chilcoat, H. D., & Anthony, J. C. (1994). Degree of acculturation and the risk of crack cocaine smoking among Hispanic Americans. *American Journal of Public Health, 84*, 1825–1827.

Waldorf, D. (1983). Natural recovery from opiate addiction: Some social-psychological processes of untreated recovery. *Journal of Drug Issues, 13*, 237–280.

Waldorf, D., Reinarman, C., & Murphy, S. (1991). *Cocaine changes: The experience of using and quitting*. Philadelphia: Temple University Press.

Walker, M. B. (1992). *The psychology of gambling*. New York: Pergamon.

Walker, R. D., Donovan, D. M., Kivlahan, D. R., & O'Leary, M. R. (1983). Length of stay, neuropsychological performance, and aftercare: Influences on alcohol treatment outcome. *Journal of Consulting and Clinical Psychology, 51*, 900–911.

Walker, R. D., van Ryn, F., Frederic, B., Reynolds, D., & O'Leary, M. R. (1980). Drinking-related locus of control as a predictor of attrition in alcoholism treatment program. *Psychological Reports, 47*, 871–877.

Wallace, J. (1993). Modern disease models of alcoholism and other chemical dependencies: The new biopsychosocial models. *Drugs and Society, 8*, 69–87.

Walsh, D. C., Hingson, R. W., Merrigan, D. M., Levenson, S. M., Cupples, L. A., Heeren, T., Coffman, G. A.,

Becker, C. A., Barker, T. A., Hamilton, S. K., McGuire, T. G., & Kelly, C. A. (1991). A randomized trial of treatment options for alcohol-abusing workers. *New England Journal of Medicine, 325*, 775–782.

Walsh, R. (1989). What is a shaman? Definition, origin, and distribution. *Journal of Transpersonal Psychology, 21*, 1–11.

Walters, C., Smolak, L., & Sullins, E. (1987, April). *Parent–child interactions and severity of child sexual abuse*. Paper presented to the annual convention of the Society for Research in Child Development, Baltimore, Maryland.

Walters, E. E., & Kendler, K. S. (1995). Anorexia nervosa and anorexic-like syndromes in a population-based female twin sample. *American Journal of Psychiatry, 152*, 64–71.

Walters, G. D. (1994a). Discriminating between high and low volume substance abusers by means of the Drug Lifestyle Screening Interview. *American Journal of Drug and Alcohol Abuse, 20*, 19–33.

Walters, G. D. (1994b). The drug lifestyle: One pattern or several? *Psychology of Addictive Behaviors, 8*, 8–13.

Walters, G. D. (1994c). *Escaping the journey to nowhere: The psychology of alcohol and other drug abuse*. Washington, DC: Taylor & Francis.

Walters, G. D. (1994d). The gambling lifestyle: I. Theory. *Journal of Gambling Studies, 10*, 159–182.

Walters, G. D. (1995). Predictive validity of the Drug Lifestyle Screening Interview: A two-year follow-up. *American Journal of Drug and Alcohol Abuse, 21*, 187–194.

Walters, G. D. (1996a). Addiction and identity: Exploring the possibility of a relationship. *Psychology of Addictive Behaviors, 10*, 9–17.

Walters, G. D. (1996b). The natural history of substance misuse in an incarcerated criminal population. *Journal of Drug Issues, 26,* 943–959.

Walters, G. D. (1996c). Sexual preoccupation as a lifestyle. *Sexual and Marital Therapy, 11,* 373–382.

Walters, G. D. (1996d). *Substance misuse and the new road to recovery: A practitioner's guide.* Washington, DC: Taylor & Francis.

Walters, G. D. (1997). Problem gambling in a federal prison population. *Journal of Gambling Studies, 13,* 7–24.

Walters, G. D. (in press). Short-term outcome of inmates participating in the Lifestyle Change Program. *Criminal Justice and Behavior.*

Walton, M. A., Castro, F. G., & Barrington, E. H. (1994). The role of attributions in abstinence, lapse, and relapse following substance abuse treatment. *Addictive Behaviors, 19,* 319–331.

Ward, T., Hudson, S. M., & Marshall, W. L. (1994). The abstinence violation effect in child molesters. *Behaviour Research and Therapy, 32,* 431–437.

Wardle, J., & Beales, S. (1988). Control and loss of control over eating: An experimental investigation. *Journal of Abnormal Psychology, 97,* 35–40.

Waters, B. G. H., Beumont, P. J. V., Touyz, S., & Kennedy, M. (1990). Behavioral differences between twin and nontwin female sibling pairs discordant for anorexia nervosa. *International Journal of Eating Disorders, 9,* 265–273.

Watson, L. (1991). Paradigms of recovery: Theoretical implications for relapse prevention in alcoholism. *Journal of Drug Issues, 24,* 839–858.

Watts, W. D., & Wright, L. S. (1990). The relationship of alcohol, tobacco, marijuana, and other illegal drug use

to delinquency among Mexican-American, black, and white adolescent males. *Adolescence, 25,* 171–181.

Wegscheider, S. (1981). *Another chance: Hope and health for the alcoholic family.* Palo Alto, CA: Science and Behavior Books.

Wegscheider–Cruse, S. (1985). *Choice-making for co-dependents, adult children, and spirituality seekers.* Pompano Beach, FL: Health Communications.

Weinberg, R. S., Hughes, H. H., Critelli, J. W., England, R., & Jackson, A. (1984). Effects of preexisting and manipulated self-efficacy on weight loss in a self-control program. *Journal of Research on Personality, 18,* 352–358.

Weiner, B. (1974). *Achievement motivation and attribution theory.* Morristown, NJ: General Learning Press.

Weiss, K. J., & Rosenberg, D. J. (1985). Prevalence of anxiety disorder among alcoholics. *Journal of Clinical Psychiatry, 46,* 3–5.

Weiss, R. D., Griffin, M. L., & Mirin, S. M. (1992). Drug abuse as self-medication for depression: An empirical study. *American Journal of Drug and Alcohol Abuse, 18,* 121–129.

Weiss, R. D., Mirin, S. M., Griffin, M. L., & Michael, M. L. (1988). Psychopathology in cocaine abusers: Changing trends. *Journal of Nervous and Mental Disease, 176,* 719–725.

Weissman, A. D., Dam, M., & London, E. D. (1987). Alterations in local cerebral glucose utilization induced by phencyclidine. *Brain Research, 435,* 29–40.

Welch, G., Hall, A., & Renner, R. (1990). Patient subgrouping in anorexia nervosa using psychologically-based classification. *International Journal of Eating Disorders, 9,* 311–322.

Welch, S. L., & Fairburn, C. G. (1994). Sexual abuse and bulimia nervosa:

Three integrated case control comparisons. *American Journal of Psychiatry, 151*, 402–407.

Wells, E. A., Peterson, P. L., Gainey, R. R., Hawkins, J. D., & Catalano, R. F. (1994). Outpatient treatment for cocaine abuse: A controlled comparison of relapse prevention and twelve-step approaches. *American Journal of Drug and Alcohol Abuse, 20*, 1–17.

Werner, E. E. (1986). Resilient offspring of alcoholics: A longitudinal study from birth to age 18. *Journal of Studies on Alcohol, 47*, 34–40.

Wetter, D. W., Smith, S. S., Kenford, S. L., Jorenby, D. E., Fiore, M. C., Hurt, R. D., Offord, K. P., & Baker, T. B. (1994). Smoking outcome expectancies: Factor structure, predictive validity, and discriminative validity. *Journal of Abnormal Psychology, 103*, 801–811.

Whitaker, L. C. (1989). Myths and heroes: Visions of the future. *Journal of College Student Psychotherapy, 4*, 13–33.

Whitbeck, L. S., Conger, R. D., & Kao, M.-Y. (1993). The influence of parental support, depressed affect, and peers on the sexual behaviors of adolescent girls. *Journal of Family Issues, 14*, 261–278.

White, F. J. (1996). Synaptic regulation of mesocorticolimbic dopamine neurons. *Annual Review of Neuroscience, 19*, 405–436.

Whitehouse, A. M., & Mumford, D. B. (1988). Increased prevalence of bulimia nervosa amongst Asian schoolgirls. *British Medical Journal, 297*, 718.

Widiger, T. A., & Smith, G. T. (1994). Substance use disorder: Abuse, dependence, and dyscontrol. *Addiction, 89*, 267–282.

Wilbanks, W. L. (1989). Drug addiction should be treated as a lack of self-discipline. In B. Leone (Ed.), *Chemical dependency: Opposing viewpoints.* San Diego, CA: Greenhaven.

Wilhelmsen, B. V., Laberg, J. C., & Klepp, K.-N. (1994). Evaluation of two student and teacher involved alcohol prevention programmes. *Addiction, 89*, 1157–1165.

Willems, P. J. A., Letemendia, F. J. J., & Arroyave, F. (1973). A two-year follow-up study comparing short with long stay inpatient treatment of alcoholics. *British Journal of Psychiatry, 122*, 637–648.

Williams, K. E., & Chambless, D. L. (1990). The relationship between therapist characteristics and outcome of in vivo exposure treatment with agoraphobia. *Behavior Therapy, 21*, 111–116.

Williamson, D. A., Goreczny, A. J., Davis, C. J., Ruggiero, L., & McKenzie, S. J. (1988). Psychophysiological analysis of the anxiety model of bulimia nervosa. *Behavior Therapy, 19*, 1–9.

Wilson, A., White, J., & Lange, D. E. (1978). Outcome evaluation of a hospital-based alcoholism treatment programme. *British Journal of Addiction, 73*, 39–45.

Wilson, G. T. (1991). The addiction model of eating disorders: A critical analysis. *Advances in Behavioral Research and Therapy, 13*, 27–72.

Wilson, G. T., Rossiter, E. M., Kleifield, E. I., & Lindholm, L. (1986). Cognitive–behavioral treatment of bulimia nervosa: A controlled evaluation. *Behaviour Research and Therapy, 24*, 277–288.

Winefield, H. R., Winefield, A. H., Tiggemann, M., & Smith, S. (1987). Unemployment, drug use, and health in late adolescence. *Psychotherapeutics and Psychosomatics, 47*, 204–210.

Winick, C. (1962). Maturing out of narcotic addiction. *Bulletin on Narcotics, 14,* 1–7.

Winick, C. (1990). Retention and outcome at ACI, a unique therapeutic community. *International Journal of the Addictions, 25,* 1–26.

Winters, K., & Rich, T. (1996, September). *Twin study of gambling behavior.* Paper presented at the Tenth National Conference on Gambling Behavior, Chicago.

Wiseman, J. P. (1975). An alternative role of the wife of an alcoholic in Finland. *Journal of Marriage and the Family, 10,* 172–179.

Woititz, J. G. (1983). *Adult children of alcoholics.* Hollywood, FL: Heath Communications.

Wolff, P. H. (1973). Vasomotor sensitivity to alcohol in diverse mongoloid populations. *American Journal of Human Genetics, 25,* 193–199.

Wollert, R. W., Levy, L. H., & Knight, B. G. (1982). Help-giving in behavioral control and stress coping self-help groups. *Small Group Behavior, 13,* 204–218.

Wonderlich, S., Ukestad, L., & Perzacki, R. (1994). Perceptions of nonshared childhood environment in bulimia nervosa. *Journal of the American Academy of Child and Adolescent Psychiatry, 33,* 740–747.

Woody, G. E., Luborsky, L., McLellan, A. T., O'Brien, C. P., Beck, A. T., Blaine, J., Herman, I., & Hole, A. (1983). Psychotherapy for opiate addicts: Does it help? *Archives of General Psychiatry, 40,* 639–645.

Woody, G. E., McLellan, A. T., & O'Brien, C. P. (1990). Clinical–behavioral observations of the long-term effects of drug abuse. *NIDA Research Monograph Series, 101,* 71–85.

Woody, G. E., O'Brien, C. P., & Rickels, K. (1975). Depression and anxiety in heroin addicts. *American Journal of Psychiatry, 32,* 411–414.

Wright, D. M., & Heppner, P. P. (1993). Examining the well-being of nonclinical college students: Is it useful to know about the presence of parental alcoholism? *Journal of Counseling Psychology, 40,* 324–334.

Wurmser, L. (1974). Psychoanalytic consideration of the etiology of compulsive drug use. *Journal of the American Psychoanalytic Association, 22,* 820–843.

Yager, J., Landsverk, J., & Edelstein, C. K. (1987). A 20-month follow-up study of 628 women with eating disorders, I: Course and severity. *American Journal of Psychiatry, 144,* 1172–1177.

Yochelson, S., & Samenow, S. E. (1976). *The criminal personality, Vol. I: A profile for change.* New York: Jason Aronson.

Zacny, J. P., Bodker, B. K., & de Wit, H. (1992). Effects of setting on the subjective and behavioral effects of d-Amphetamine in humans. *Addictive Behaviors, 17,* 27–33.

Zillman, D., & Bryant, J. (1982). Pornography, sexual callousness, and the trivialization of rape. *Journal of Communication, 32,* 10–21.

Zimmer–Höfler, D., & Dobler–Mikola, A. (1992). Swiss heroin-addicted females: Career and social adjustment. *Journal of Substance Abuse Treatment, 9,* 159–170.

Zinberg, N. E. (1984). *Drug, set, and setting: The basis for controlled intoxicant use.* New Haven, CN: Yale University Press.

Zohar, J., Kaplan, Z., & Benjamin, J. (1994). Compulsive exhibitionism successfully treated with fluvoxamine: A controlled case study. *Journal of Clinical Psychiatry, 55,* 86–88.

Zucker, R. A., & Gomberg, E. S. L. (1986). Etiology of alcoholism reconsidered: The case for a biopsychosocial process. *American Psychologist, 41,* 783–793.

Zweben, A., Pearlman, S., & Li, S. (1988). A comparison of brief advice and conjoint therapy in the treatment of alcohol abuse: The results of the Marital Systems Study. *British Journal of Addiction, 83,* 899–916.

INDEX